THE
LOST WORLD
OF THE
OLD ONES

ALSO BY DAVID ROBERTS

Alone on the Ice: The Greatest Survival Story in the History of Exploration

The Mountain: My Time on Everest (with Ed Viesturs)

The Will to Climb: Obsession and Commitment and the Quest to Climb Annapurna (with Ed Viesturs)

Finding Everett Ruess: The Life and Unsolved Disappearance of a Legendary Wilderness Explorer

K2: Life and Death on the World's Most Dangerous Mountain (with Ed Viesturs)

The Last of His Kind: The Life and Adventures of Bradford Washburn, America's Boldest Mountaineer

Devil's Gate: Brigham Young and the Great Mormon Handcart Tragedy

No Shortcuts to the Top: Climbing the World's 14 Highest Peaks (with Ed Viesturs)

Sandstone Spine: Seeking the Anasazi on the First Traverse of the Comb Ridge

On the Ridge Between Life and Death: A Climbing Life Reexamined

The Pueblo Revolt: The Secret Rebellion That Drove the Spaniards Out of the Southwest

Four Against the Arctic: Shipwrecked for Six Years at the Top of the World

Escape from Lucania: An Epic Story of Survival

True Summit: What Really Happened on the Legendary Ascent of Annapurna

A Newer World: Kit Carson, John C. Frémont, and the Claiming of the American West

The Lost Explorer: Finding Mallory on Mount Everest (with Conrad Anker)

Escape Routes

In Search of the Old Ones: Exploring the Anasazi World of the Southwest

Once They Moved Like the Wind: Cochise, Geronimo, and the Apache Wars

Mount McKinley: The Conquest of Denali (with Bradford Washburn)

Iceland: Land of the Sagas (with Jon Krakauer)

Jean Stafford: A Biography

Great Exploration Hoaxes

Moments of Doubt

Deborah: A Wilderness Narrative

The Mountain of My Fear

THE
LOST WORLD
OF THE
OLD ONES

Discoveries in the Ancient Southwest

David Roberts

W. W. NORTON & COMPANY   New York • London

Title page: photograph © Stephanie Scott
Prologue, Chapter One, Chapter Three: photographs © Greg Child
Chapter Two: photograph © USU Eastern Prehistoric Museum
Chapter Four: photograph © Bill Hatcher
Chapter Five: photograph © Dawn Kish
Chapter Six: photograph © David Roberts
Chapter Seven, Chapter Nine, Epilogue: photographs © Matt Hale
Chapter Eight: photograph © Macduff Everton

For information about permission to reproduce selections from this book,
write to Permissions, W. W. Norton & Company, Inc.,
500 Fifth Avenue, New York, NY 10110

For information about special discounts for bulk purchases, please contact
W. W. Norton Special Sales at specialsales@wwnorton.com or 800-233-4830

Manufacturing by Courier Westford
Book design by Chris Welch Design
Production manager: Julia Druskin

ISBN 978-0-393-24162-4

W. W. Norton & Company, Inc.
500 Fifth Avenue, New York, N.Y. 10110
www.wwnorton.com

W. W. Norton & Company Ltd.
Castle House, 75/76 Wells Street, London W1T 3QT

1 2 3 4 5 6 7 8 9 0

For

Fred Blackburn

Vaughn Hadenfeldt

Matt Hale

Greg Child

Stalwart and savvy companions on many of my best adventures in the Southwest.

Contents

Prologue   WALDO'S CATWALK | 1

One   THE COWBOY'S INDIANS | 25

Two   THINGS | 57

Three   CEDAR MESA REVISITED | 91

Four   CHACO MERIDIAN | 123

Five   WANDERING THE REZ | 153

Six   LAND OF ENCHANTMENT–I | 187

Seven   LAND OF ENCHANTMENT–II | 205

Eight   EXPLORING THE FIFTY | 237

Nine   DESO DAYS | 261

Epilogue   RETURN TO THE BASKET | 287

Acknowledgments | 303
Bibliography | 309
Index | 315

Telluride

FREMONT

UNITED
STATES

ANASAZI

HOHOKAM

MOGOLLON

Paquimé,
Chihuahua, Mexico

MEXICO

Mesa
Verde

Chimney
Rock

COLORADO

Aztec Ruins

NEW MEXICO

Puyé
Ruins

Pueblo Bonito

Chaco
Canyon

Jemez
Pueblo

Santa Fe Canyon

Santa Fe

Upper Rio Grande

River

Albuquerque

WALDO'S CATWALK

For more than an hour, the three of us climbed the steep, trail-less canyon wall, pushing through scratchy thickets of scrub oak and across exposed sandstone slabs. We had long since lost sight of the curious speck in the middle of the overhanging cliff that we had scoped with binoculars from the dirt road beside Range Creek a thousand feet below us. That speck had been pointed out to us by Waldo Wilcox, the seventy-five-year-old rancher who had spent his whole adult life on the twelve-mile-long family spread in Range Creek, a tributary of the Green River in east-central Utah that carves a majestic chasm through the lofty Tavaputs Plateau.

After years of exploring the backcountry of the Southwest in search of prehistoric ruins and rock art, Greg Child and I were used to this sort of scrambling, so we chose the approach route, keeping the location of the cliff toward which we were headed tucked in the backs of our minds. For archaeologist Renee Barlow, such an adventure was relatively new, so she went along with our pathfinding with only a modicum of second-guessing.

It was a warm day in May 2005. Hiking in shorts and T-shirts, we were soaked in sweat.

Fifty-four years earlier, in 1951, only months after Waldo's parents had bought the ranch, his father Ray (known as "Budge"), his brother Don, and twenty-one-year-old Waldo had stood on the same dirt road and argued about that speck in the distant cliff.

"There's somethin' there, right in the middle of it," Waldo had said. "Some Indian thing."

"Nah," countered Don, five years older. "It's natural. Just rocks." Budge agreed: "Yep. Rocks or ledges or somethin'."

The next year, in 1952, the army drafted Waldo and shipped him to Japan. During his two-year stint in the forces, he used field glasses for the first time. The tantalizing "Indian thing" on the high cliff was often on his mind, so he bought a cheap pair of Japanese binoculars and mailed them home. Back in Range Creek in 1954, he trained the instrument on the distant apparition.

"They wasn't that good of field glasses," Waldo told me in 2005, "but I could see everything that was there. Sure enough, it was a big old granary halfway up this sheer cliff."

One day Waldo tackled the arduous scramble to the foot of the cliff, following much the same route the three of us would pursue half a century later. Arriving at the base of the precipice, he was stunned at what lay before him. He could see the "big old granary" well, sixty-five feet above him, but could not imagine how to get to it. After a good long look at this prodigy of prehistoric architecture, he descended the thousand feet to the valley. Over the years thereafter, he kept his silence about what he had found. Budge and Don, less curious than Waldo about "Indian things," never bothered to undertake the tricky bushwhack up the canyon slope to check out the granary for themselves.

After the Wilcoxes had bought the Range Creek ranch in 1951, they built sturdy gates on the old dirt road at either end of their property to keep out trespassers. Waldo's parents and his brother Don soon moved on to other ranches in the Tavaputs, while Waldo, his wife, Julie, and eventually their four kids stayed on in Range Creek. For schooling, from September to May, the kids and Julie moved into the family's snug house in Green River, thirty-five miles away, while Waldo lingered on with his cows, the lonely lord of his outback estate.

A thousand years and more ago, Range Creek had teemed with part-time hunter-gatherers who also raised corn, beans, and squash. These ancients are known to science as the Fremont people, northern neighbors of the Anasazi, or Ancestral Puebloans. Still poorly understood—we have no idea, for instance, what became of the Fremont after they vanished entirely from the archaeological record around A.D. 1500—the Fremont pose one prehistoric conundrum after another.

For fifty years, everywhere Waldo wandered in Range Creek, chasing stray cows or hunting bears and mountain lions, he stumbled upon "Indian stuff"—potsherds, chert flakes left by arrowhead makers, manos and metates for grinding corn, rings of stones outlining the shallow pithouses in which the Fremont lived, dizzy granaries on cliff ledges where they stored their precious grain, and even the graves of the long-dead. Unlike so many ranchers in the West, for whom collecting and hoarding artifacts is a time-honored tradition, Waldo left virtually everything he found in place and undisturbed. "It's the way I was brought up," Waldo said to me in 2005. "Mom and Dad always told me that just 'cause we owned the land didn't mean the Indian stuff belonged to us. They wouldn't go to the cemetery and dig folks up just for the gold in their teeth."

In 2001, with a heavy heart, Waldo succumbed at last to the limitations of old age and sold his ranch to the Trust for Public Lands and the state of Utah. Eventually the property landed under the aegis of the state's Division of Wildlife Resources (DWR), some of whose functionaries cherished visions of turning Range Creek into a prime bighorn sheep hunting reserve, with a "blue-ribbon" trout stream running through its heart—even if that might have required cutting down all the piñon and juniper trees in the canyon to "improve" the habitat. In the meantime, however, archaeologists got a look at Range Creek. Uniformly astounded, the experts agreed that Range Creek had the potential to tell us more about the Fremont than had the combined efforts of the seventy previous years of research since the culture had been identified.

Keeping Range Creek a secret for three years, an archaeology team out of the Utah Museum of Natural History (UMNH) started to make a systematic survey of the canyon's glories. But a local newspaper leaked the story in the summer of 2004, touching off a wildfire of national media coverage—and a furor among Native Americans from New Mexico to Nevada, who were royally pissed off to have been kept in the dark about a hidden valley that, some of them insisted, might have been part of their own ancestral heartland.

Mesmerized by the news about Range Creek, I got magazine assignments from *National Geographic* and *National Geographic Adventure*. Afire with a passion to explore this unknown wilderness, I made a phone call to Greg Child that put the match to his kindred ambitions. In Price, we met Renee Barlow, co-leader of the UMNH team, who at once welcomed us to join her on her prowls through Range Creek. As climbers, Greg and I could get Renee to places none of the UMNH team could reach on their own. On our first visit to the remote valley, Greg and I recognized that while the creek bottom abounded in sites and artifacts, all the most spectacular ruins lay in high eyries that would be extremely hard to get to. Oddly enough, Renee was the only member of the team who shared Greg's and my ambition to explore those inaccessible sites.

None of them exerted a more powerful allure than the speck in the overhanging cliff a thousand feet up the west side of the canyon that Waldo had spotted in 1951 and scrambled up to three years later. In the fifty-one years since his jaunt, no one else had visited the "big old granary" Waldo had discovered.

That May morning, at last we reached the ledge on the same level as the base of the overhanging cliff. We traversed to the right around a corner. Greg stopped in his tracks, stared up, and said softly, "My mind is blown."

As Waldo had reported, a twenty-five-foot-long trunk of dead Douglas fir leaned against the cliff, directly below the granary. It was apparently a Fremont ladder, still in place at least 650 years after it had been placed there. Breaching an otherwise featureless cliff inclined only a shade less than vertical, the trunk looked far too spindly to climb. Even more daunting, the "big old granary"—actually a pair of granaries sharing a common wall—hovered a good forty feet above the tip of the fir tree, and those forty feet were relentlessly overhanging.

And above the double granary, the cliff soared for another ninety feet at an even steeper overhanging angle. The lip of the cliff, 150 feet up, loomed dizzyingly in space as we craned our necks to study the Fremont wonder. Above the tip of the Douglas fir, a thin crack split a pair of arching overhangs. That crack had evidently been the ascent line of the daredevil who had pioneered the route, for halfway between the treetop and the granary, a hefty stick had been jammed endwise into the fissure, like a huge wooden piton. The stick might have been the key to reaching the hand- and footholds on the cliff above.

The double granary, whose main storage bin stood a good four to five feet tall, was perched on the skimpiest of ledges. Fifteen feet to the right, lower on the slanting ledge, its base secured by rocks mudded in place, an improbable triangular cantilever of heavy logs extended into empty air.

"That crack's gotta be 5.11, on crumbly rock," Greg murmured, eyeing the route as he graded it at a rating that only top climbers today could accomplish. Greg, who has reached the summits of K2 and Everest, put up new routes on El Capitan, and pioneered fierce new lines on desert towers, is one of the best climbers of his generation worldwide. But he could not imagine tackling the route in front of us, even with the nylon ropes and cams and nuts we had hauled up to the cliff.

Renee was as dumbfounded as we were, blurting out "Wow!" and "Oh, my gosh!" every few seconds. I contributed my own exclamations of astonishment. All of us were thinking the same thing. It was mind-boggling enough to imagine the best Fremont climber of his era soloing the route to the ledge. But once there, how had he and his cronies hauled up stones and mud and timbers, built the double granary, then figured out a way to hoist, store, and later retrieve the precious grains the storage bins must have held?

And why? Why so incredibly difficult and dangerous a place to hide your food?

On the spot, Renee named the double granary "Waldo's Catwalk." Our only hope of getting to it was to circle left, scramble to the top of the cliff, and try to rappel down to the site. An hour later, Greg tied our ropes to a pair of piñon pines and threw the ends off the precipice. Then, one by one, we rappelled the 150-foot cliff. Beyond the lip, however, we dangled in space, spinning like spiders from their silken threads.

When I reached a point in midair just above the pair of granaries, I got a great view of the site. The doors of the storage bins—flat slabs of sandstone shaped to fit—lay intact, closing the rooftop orifices that were the only entrances to the granaries. But I hung now far out from the cliff face, a good twenty feet beyond even the protruding cantilever of logs. Suspended in the air on a rope, a climber has no way to generate the momentum to swing in toward the cliff. All I could do was stare at Waldo's Catwalk.

As I slid on toward the ground, I was reconciled to defeat. We would not be able to reach the astounding prehistoric ruin. But Greg was of another mind. He urged us to leave our climbing gear on the ledge and come back for another try two days later. He still had a trick or two up his sleeve.

In 1996, I published a book called *In Search of the Old Ones*. It was the fruit of more than seven years of exploring the canyons and mesas of the Southwest, centered on the Colorado Plateau, a vast and beautiful region that encompasses southern Utah, northern Arizona, southwestern Colorado, and western New Mexico. National parks such as Mesa Verde, devoted to the dwellings of the ancients, had left me cold—even such lordly villages as Cliff Palace seemed embalmed as Park Service dioramas. Instead, I set out, both solo and with a handful of like-minded aficionados, to find my own ruins and rock art in obscure corners of the backcountry.

At the same time, I interviewed as many of the leading Southwestern archaeologists as I could, hoping to leaven the romance of my vagabondage with the solid analyses of the experts who studied the Native Americans who had left behind the abandoned dwellings and the enigmatic pictograph and petroglyph panels that abound all over the Southwest.

The book seemed to fill a niche, somewhere between such rigorous academic surveys as Linda Cordell's *Prehistory of the Southwest* and lyrical evocations of the landscape such as Edward Abbey's *Desert Solitaire*. One of my chapters was titled "In Praise of Cedar Mesa," my own paean to the glories of the four-hundred-square-mile rectangle of Bureau of Land Management (BLM) terrain in southeastern Utah that enfolds the richest array of unrestored ruins and rock art in all the Southwest.

I opened the book with an account of a four-day backpack I had undertaken alone in late October 1993 into one of the canyons on Cedar Mesa, during which I saw not another soul. On the third day of that outing, I scrambled up a devious route to the north rim of the canyon, then circled east to explore a modest five-room complex that was hidden from almost every vantage point except the opposite south rim, from which I had spotted it the day before. From above, it wasn't easy to find that ruin, tucked as it was under a series of protruding cliffs, but at last I did so. I spent more than an hour there, marveling at the canny architecture—shaped sandstone blocks mortared together with mud in which I could see the fingerprints of the builders—as well as fondling potsherds and chert flakes that lay scattered on the ground in front of the site.

Before heading back to camp, I walked the ledge on which the ruin lay to see if there were any other artifacts or structures left behind by the Old Ones. The ledge dwindled toward a dead-end seam. I was about to turn back when I suddenly saw, below me on the left, a large, intact ceramic pot, decorated in the style called "corrugated." The pot had been nestled inside a recessed stratum of marly rock, a natural hiding place. Its owner, I mused, had placed it there sometime in the thirteenth century A.D., intending to come back and retrieve it. But she never did. Was I the first person to find the vessel in more than seven hundred years?

I had found a few intact pots in remote canyons before, but never one so perfect as this. In my book, I evoked the emotions that my discovery had sent tingling from my shoulders down my spine. And in the photo insert, I included a picture of the pot in situ.

In Search of the Old Ones is still in print, nineteen years after it first appeared. The book has sold well, and I'm told that it seems to have acquired the status of a minor cult classic. Strangers have come up to me in Bluff, Utah, or Page, Arizona, and thrust well-thumbed copies of the book into my hands, asking me to autograph them.

Yet the book also provoked a backlash. In my prologue, I did not name the canyon in which I had found the pot, or give any hints (so I thought) to the location of the nearby five-room ruin. The last thing I imagined was that readers would turn *In Search of the Old Ones* into a treasure map. But that's what happened. Folks started showing up at the Kane Gulch ranger station on Cedar Mesa, my book opened to the photo of the corrugated vessel, demanding, "How do I get to Roberts's pot?"

Quite aside from the fact that BLM policy forbids them to direct hikers to prehistoric sites on Cedar Mesa, the Kane Gulch rangers were flabbergasted and annoyed by these new demands. Not surprisingly, they blamed the messenger—me. One evening, my good friend and companion on many a Cedar Mesa prowl, Vaughn Hadenfeldt, was debating the merits of *Old Ones* with one of the longtime Kane Gulch rangers. That fellow summed up his viewpoint in a pithy formula: "Tell Roberts to shut the fuck up."

Other connoisseurs of Cedar Mesa, less naïve than the ones who waved my book in the face of the rangers, took my photo and the vague description of the canyon as a personal challenge. With sleuthing skills akin to those of Sherlock Holmes, some of them found their way to the ruin—and to the pot. They told their friends how to get there, who told their friends . . . Today, I'm informed, a beaten trail leads to the ledge on which the priceless vessel was stashed seven centuries ago. The great fear, of course, is that someone will pry it loose and take it home to display on his mantel.

Meanwhile, in the same month that my book was published, *National Geographic* came out with my article "The Old Ones of the Southwest." Included were four Ira Block photos of Grand Gulch shot during an eight-day llama trek we took together from the Government Trail to Kane Gulch. The next time I applied for a permit to camp in Grand Gulch—a routine formality in the past—I was turned down. I traveled to Monticello to argue with the BLM official who had banned me from the finest of all the Cedar Mesa canyons. His argument was that by publishing an article in a national magazine, and getting paid to do so, I was practicing as a "commercial operator" without a license.

I countered, "So are you banning every photographer who's published a photo of Grand Gulch? David Muench? Tom Till? Bruce Hucko?"

"We're in the process of doing so," the man claimed. "We're starting with you."

In the end, I had to appeal the BLM fiat all the way to the Department of the Interior to get it overturned. In the meantime, I realized that the reaction of the rangers stemmed from a deeply felt but (in my view) poorly reasoned ambivalence that I had run across countless times in the Southwest: the sense that a magical place one has recently discovered should stay as it is, a secret shared only with one's fellow cognoscenti. In 1995 I had tackled this conundrum in an article called "The Moab Treehouse." Hanging out in that appealing Utah town on the Colorado River, I had plunged into the endless debate over the resort's growing popularity. The old-timers who had lived in Moab through the uranium boom and bust of the 1950s were all for growth: as one of them told me, "I'm just glad I don't have to drive a hundred miles to Grand Junction anymore to buy a two-by-four." The environmentalist newcomers, on the other hand, decried Moab's slide toward, in their words, "another Aspen or Santa Fe." I borrowed my title from the sardonic metaphor of one of the old-timers: "Some folks have found our treehouse. Now they want to pull the rope up."

When I told my editor at *National Geographic* about the BLM fuss over Grand Gulch, she uttered a pronouncement that I have ever since clung to as a personal manifesto. "This is nonsense," she said. "If a thing is worth doing, it's worth writing about."

Yet a genuine dilemma lies at the heart of this controversy. I am as dismayed as anyone when I go back to a splendid ruin that I discovered on my own, by accident, twenty years ago, when it was known to a small coterie of desert enthusiasts, only to find it swarmed over with chattering hikers who've been lured to the place by directions in a published guidebook or by GPS coordinates posted on an Internet site.

Yet I had to realize that I was as much to blame as anyone for the burgeoning popularity of Cedar Mesa. I had observed the code of the day among explorers of the prehistoric Southwest: if you commit your discoveries to print, be as vague as possible about their location, and emphasize again and again the conduct necessary to keep those sites pristine. Take home nothing, not even the tiniest flake or potsherd; don't stand or lean on ruin walls; don't touch the rock art (for the oils from human skin degrade both pigment and patina).

It was not a code that had always held sway. Photos from earlier in the twentieth century show visitors, including professional archaeologists, clambering all over the dwellings, even crawling across rooftops; chalking the petroglyphs to make the figures stand out for the camera; sawing off the ends of roof beams to get tree-ring dates; and even taking metal axes to ancient hand-and-toe trails to enlarge the holds so that modern inquisitors could climb safely to high granaries.

It was inevitable, I realized over the years, that a younger generation than mine would feel no qualms about giving precise hiking directions to the ruins and panels they had found, or posting photos on the Internet complete with GPS coordinates. And I would discover in the years after 1996 that some members of that younger generation filled their pockets with potsherds and arrowheads, while others didn't hesitate to yank on fragile dwelling doorways as they lurched their way into dwellings, or allowed their dogs to romp inside ruins as if they were backyard playpens.

The impact of my book is attested to in a quirky novel by Robert Gay called *The Marauders*, published in 2009. The heroes of this futuristic tale are a sextet of eco-terrorists bent on sabotaging a National Park Service project to pave a road to and build a visitor center around a new national monument celebrating—but keeping everyone at a distance from—Moon House, one of the finest of all the ruins on Cedar

Mesa. Two of the self-styled marauders, Hayden and Rob, groan as they read the posts about Moon House on the Internet. Says Hayden, "Most all of these guys talk about how David Roberts' book inspired them to try and find it, too."

According to Gay, *In Search of the Old Ones*

> somehow or another had managed to become the most popu-
> lar 'pop' book on the Anasazi. Devotees of the ancient pueblo
> dwellers read it like the bible, hanging on to every word. In it he
> described things that people today can no longer see . . . Thou-
> sands of hikers every year tuck the book into their packs when
> they head Out There, reading passages from it by moonlight or
> headlamp. From Page to Panguitch to Pagosa Springs, where he
> went talking about his book, people filled up the provided audi-
> toriums. Knowingly or not (a subject of some debate among his
> followers), Roberts appeared to be styling himself as the Ana-
> sazi's Ed Abbey.

Rob demurs, "I like that book." But Hayden answers, "So do I, but I think it's become too well known. It's accelerating the destruction of its subject matter. I got my copy at Mesa Verde, for god's sake. It's pervasive across the Southwest."

When I first read that passage, I was bemused. I thought briefly of writing a note to Robert Gay, described in the author bio as "a guide, a wildlife biologist, and a paleontologist . . . [who] has lived in and explored the Southwest and the Colorado Plateau for over a decade," protesting that I've never spoken in Panguitch or Pagosa Springs, and that the Mesa Verde visitor center has never carried my book, appar-ently because of the potshots I took in my opening chapter about the way the National Park Service administers its archaeological wonders. But I thought better of it. *The Marauders*, after all, is fiction.

Was it true, however, that, as Hayden claimed, *In Search of the Old Ones* was "accelerating the destruction of its subject matter"? If so, should I in the future, as Vaughn's ranger friend advised, "shut the fuck up"?

My answer, embodied in this book, a sequel to *In Search of the Old Ones*, is no.

When I research a book, I spend as much as three years immersing myself in the subject. It becomes an obsessive quest, as I ransack, for instance, the archives of the Arizona Historical Society to find the 1915 interview with Tom Jeffords, the only white man who ever befriended Cochise, or hike into Davis Gulch to search for an inscription that the lost vagabond Everett Ruess might have carved in 1934. The tiniest detail takes on supreme importance. But once the book is published, I usually set that subject aside and move on to my next project. After *Devil's Gate*, I had no desire to squint at more microfilm in the LDS Archives in Salt Lake City or to hike farther along the Mormon Trail in western Wyoming. After *Four Against the Arctic*, I was only too glad that I would never again have to prosecute a search through piles of old, unsorted documents in a dusty Russian library or trudge through a Svalbard whiteout spooked by invisible polar bears.

With *In Search of the Old Ones*, it was different. The prehistory of the Southwest had gotten under my skin, and I couldn't let go of its mysteries and delights. Virtually every spring and fall since 1996, and several summers and winters, I have returned to the Colorado Plateau and the wilderness surrounding it on all sides to hike and backpack into canyons where yet another mud-and-stone refuge or visionary pictograph panel might lurk unknown. I've cornered the next generation of archaeologists and begged them to explain their research, and I've gone to conferences where they unveil their findings via posters and PowerPoint. I've coaxed several of these experts into the field so that we could retrace their theories under our boot soles. I continue to comb what scholars call the "gray literature," and a paper titled "One Pot-Pithouses and Fremont Paradoxes" or "The Kivas of Tsama" still enthralls me. Since 1996, I've written some two dozen articles mixing cutting-edge archaeology with my own backcountry adventures for magazines ranging from *National Geographic* and *Smithsonian* to *Arizona Highways* and *El Palacio*.

It's gratifying that *In Search of the Old Ones* is still in print, and rewarding to hear the accolades of many of its readers, including a number of Native Americans, who I thought would be my most critical audience. But in some senses, the book is out of date. The last twenty years of archaeological research have refuted some of the theories that were widely accepted in 1996, while inserting startling new ideas into the conversation. My own forays into the prehistoric Southwest have made me far more sophisticated about what I see than I was when I first hiked Grand Gulch. I've gone much farther afield than I did for *Old Ones*, which was centered on the realm of the Anasazi. Since then, I've headed into central and northern Utah to make my acquaintance with the Fremont, as far south as Chihuahua in Mexico to rub shoulders with the Mogollon, and east to the edge of the New Mexico plains to witness the achievements of the Comanche. And the Southwestern scene itself, with its attendant ethics and politics, has changed dramatically since 1996, as Hayden and Rob lament in *The Marauders*.

Speaking of Anasazi: the subtitle of my book was "Exploring the Anasazi World of the Southwest." Even by 1996, a group of politically correct younger archaeologists, joined by Puebloan activists, was clamoring to expunge the term. "Anasazi" is a Navajo word that means something like "enemy ancestors" or "ancestors of our enemies." Since 1936, when it was proposed by the pioneering Southwestern scholar Alfred V. Kidder, Anasazi had been the term in univeral use for the prehistoric inhabitants of the vast region stretching from Las Vegas, Nevada, to Las Vegas, New Mexico, and from Moab, Utah, to Gallup, New Mexico. It served its purpose in distinguishing those Old Ones from their contemporaries, the Mogollon to the south, the Hohokam to the southwest, the Fremont to the north, and the isolated Arizona cultures of the Sinagua and the Salado, even while scholars wrangled

re to draw the boundaries and whether the distinctions were
of.

me Hopi, who claim descent from the Anasazi, the Navajo
s offensive. They suggested substituting "Hisatsinom," their
n for their ancestors who came from the north. But other
modern-day pueblos ranging from Zuni to Taos also claim kinship
with the ancients who abandoned the Colorado Plateau just before A.D.
1300, and they have their own names for those ancestors. Meanwhile,
the politically correct scholars began using "Ancestral Puebloans"
as a substitute for "Anasazi." From the first time I heard the term, it
stuck in my craw—an unwieldy mouthful at best, and arguably just as
offensive, since "pueblo" is a Spanish word (meaning simply "town")
that the conquistadors slapped on the villages from Hopi to Taos, to
distinguish the relatively civilized *indios pueblo* (who were still in
need of brutal subjugation and salvation by Catholic baptism) from
the nomadic savages they called *indios bárbaros* (Navajo, Apache, Ute,
Comanche, and the like), who were beyond redemption.

At the beginning of *In Search of the Old Ones* I inserted an author's
note to explain why I was stubbornly hanging onto the term "Anasazi." My motives were not merely curmudgeonly. I grew up calling
the Arctic natives who built igloos and hunted whales from skin kayaks "Eskimos." (Though the derivation is disputed, "Eskimo" may be
an Algonquian term for "eaters of raw meat.") But I didn't blink when
revisionists urged the word's replacement by "Inuit," the people's own
term for "human beings."

Throughout the world, tribes tend to get named by their neighbors
or enemies. "Navajo," in fact, is a Tewa Puebloan word, which means
approximately "people who cultivate great fields"—a curious appel-
lation, since when the Navajo first appeared in the Southwest they
were thoroughly nomadic. The Navajo call themselves "Diné," or "the
People." Yet Navajos today happily use the Tewa name, and at present
there is no p. c. movement abroad to substitute "Diné" for "Navajo."

"Ancestral Puebloans," however, seems to have won the day. At the

Pecos Conference every August, nary an archaeologist utters the word "Anasazi," even when referring strictly to the prehistoric denizens of the Colorado Plateau. As I've gone on using the supposedly offensive term, I'm regularly scolded in letters to the editor from readers who seem to think I just don't know any better. The height of p. c. absurdity, in my view, came a few years ago when the National Park Service announced it was banning from its gift shops all books with "Anasazi" in the title or subtitle—even ones published long before the nomenclature squabble, including such classics as Frank McNitt's biography *Richard Wetherill: Anasazi* or Earl Morris's *Anasazi Basketry*.

I'd be wholeheartedly in favor of renaming the Anasazi with their own word for "the People." But we not only have no idea what that term might have been (almost certainly not "Hisatsinom"), we do not even know what language or languages the so-called Ancestral Puebloans spoke.

In this book, then, I will grudgingly succumb to the orthodoxy of "Ancestral Puebloans." What I'd really like to do is adopt the clever term coined by my buddy Vaughn Hadenfeldt, who sidesteps the controversy by referring to the Old Ones as the "Snazi." To my mind, it's a brilliant circumlocution, retaining a strong echo of the term we've used for decades while importing our admiration for the achievements of the ancients in its evocation of their "snazzy" ruins and rock art. Vaughn uses his term only casually and among fellow devotees. At book length, however, "Snazi" might grate on readers' nerves even more vexsomely than my heretofore obstinate insistence on "Anasazi."

What I hope to do in *The Lost World of the Old Ones* is to make accessible to lay readers the best and most provocative research conducted in the last twenty years by Southwestern archaeologists, and to step back and see how that adjusts the picture of the past in what I believe to be the most fascinating region in the United States. The book will be structured around the journeys and discoveries I've made since 1996. I hope to take readers along on the giddiest rides through the Southwest that I've managed to complete in recent years.

Some of those trips were solo outings, on each of which I reveled in the trance that prolonged silence and solitude induce. On others I was joined by friends who shared my passion for the canyon country. For years, the most frequent and percipient of those colleagues were Vaughn Hadenfeldt and Greg Child. We've shared many a lark and many a grueling push since 1996, the most ambitious of which was the first complete traverse of the Comb Ridge, starting just east of Kayenta, Arizona, and ending northwest of Blanding, Utah. It was an eighteen-day, 125-mile backpack, in nearly continual ninety-degree September heat—the longest backpack of my life. I recounted that adventure in a short book called *Sandstone Spine*, published in 2006, so I won't repeat that chronicle here.

If Vaughn and Greg have been my most faithful companions, many another friend has helped me make discoveries and have a fine old time in the backcountry of the Southwest. In the same breath with which I voice my gratitude for their company, I hope to bring them to life as people, and to see the Old Ones through their eyes. At the end of all of our ventures, the mood infusing our tired bodies has been awe and astonishment. Long before Europeans reached North America, the Snazi and their brethren—I mean the Ancestral Puebloans and their neighbors—wrought miracles as they fitted their lives perfectly to a landscape that can be as treacherous and unforgiving as any in North America. And despite how much we've learned since Anglo-Americans first explored what they called the cliff dwellings in the 1870s, the central puzzles about the Old Ones remain unsolved.

In the meantime, I stand by my personal touchstone. If a thing is worth doing, it's worth writing about.

Once the news about Range Creek got out in the summer of 2004, the Division of Wildlife Resources opened the Wilcox spread to the public, but only in a severely restricted way. Journalists were trundled en masse in half-day outings along the creek-bottom dirt road while the archaeologists paused to point out a pithouse here, a faint rock art panel there. Expecting cliff dwellings along the lines of Mesa Verde, more than one scribe or shutterbug uttered a cry of disappointment: "So this is all there is? What's the big deal?"

As Greg and I had seen at once on our first visit, the archaeological treasures of this sanctuary lay not so much in those roadside oddities as in a prodigal abundance of granaries and redoubts perched on wildly exposed ledges and butte tops ranging from a hundred to more than a thousand feet above the valley floor. We were not allowed, of course, just to head off on our own. DWR had mandated that with every step we took as we rambled through the valley, we had to be accompanied and surveilled by a UMNH archaeologist, lest we filch the Indian stuff that Waldo Wilcox had left in place.

In befriending Renee Barlow, teaching her how to climb and rappel, and extending to the UMNH team the promise of articles in national magazines, Greg and I won the privilege of trying to get to the sites that had set our hearts soaring when we peered at them through binoculars. Later Renee would hire Greg as a climbing guide to get her to still more places she could not have reached on her own.

In other parts of the Southwest (particularly on Cedar Mesa), the use of climbing ropes to access ruins is forbidden by the BLM or the NPS. No such prohibition obtained in Range Creek. In fact, the DWR had explicitly approved ropework to enhance the archaeologists' study of the canyon full of Fremont wonders. Once our names were affixed to Renee's permit, we were good to go after Waldo's Catwalk.

Two days after we rappelled off the cliff from the rim above the double granary only to dangle in space twenty feet out from the site, the three of us repeated the arduous approach through scrub oak and across tilting slabs to reach the ledge a thousand feet above the valley bottom. Gathering up the ropes and hardware we had left there, we scrambled again to the top of the cliff.

Once more, Greg set up a rappel. This time he tied into trees some twenty feet to the right of our first attempt, where a thin crack split the overhang. As he slid down the rope over the lip, Greg inserted a cam into the crack. Lowering himself some more, he sprang away from the cliff with a thrust of his toes, then, as he swung back into the cliff, he deftly slammed another cam into the crack. And again. In this fashion, Greg stitched a pseudo-rappel tight to the cliff, at an angle thirty degrees beyond the vertical.

When he was even with the Catwalk, but twenty feet right of it, he started to pendulum, skittering back and forth across the cliff face, traveling farther with each swing. At last he pendulumed near the Catwalk ledge, where he slotted home one more cam to stabilize himself. He had reached the double granary, almost certainly the first person to do so in at least seven hundred years. One thing he knew, however: the technique he had used had not been available to the Fremont.

Now it was a simple matter, as Renee rappelled on a separate rope off our original line, for Greg to reel her in like a fish. Breathless with excitement, belayed carefully by Greg, she tiptoed up to the structures, then, with infinite care, lifted the doorlid on each. Out of sheer wonderment, she narrated out loud: "Ready? Wow, it's heavy . . . It looks like they used an adobe seal to close the doors. But the seals are broken."

To Renee's disappointment and shock, both granaries were two-thirds full not with corn, but with rodent excrement—perhaps the scat of deer mice, which, if ingested, can cause the deadly hantavirus. With a tentative scoop of a trowel, she dislodged some of the stuff to see if the grain still lay beneath it, but soon gave up. Staring into the bins, Renee exclaimed, "It's incredible. They put all their corn here. But then they must have come back and got it, and took it away. They had to break the seals to get it."

While she lingered on the precarious ledge, Renee used a tape measure to record the dimensions of the double granary. Later she calculated that the bins could have held the unfathomable total of fifty-seven bushels of corn, weighing a ton and a half. One of the hardest places to get to that the Old Ones ever reached in the Southwest had evidently served as a major storage facility for the life-sustaining grain that was the staple of the Fremont diet.

Then, involuntarily, Renee whooped out loud. "This is the coolest archaeology I've ever done! This is the thrill of my life!"

Later all three of us sat on the ledge at the foot of the cliff and stared up at Waldo's Catwalk. The same two questions that had swirled in our minds since we first arrived there two days earlier now surfaced again: *How?* And, *Why?*

If, as Greg had gauged, the climb up the crack above the tip of the Douglas fir was 5.11 on crumbly rock, we could barely imagine an ancient gymnast, probably climbing barefoot, pulling off that ascent without falling to his death. For years, Greg and I had nursed a friendly disagreement as to whether the Old Ones—Ancestral Puebloans above all, but now the Fremont as well—had made and used ropes. Greg firmly believed they had, while I was the skeptic. All over the Southwest, excavations have yielded prehistoric cordage, made out of twisted and braided fibers made of yucca, dogbane, and even human hair. Ancestral Puebloans clearly used the stuff as string, to make snares to catch rabbits and other small game, and perhaps as tump lines and handles for carrying baskets and pots. But the digs have uncovered few pieces of cordage long enough and thick enough to serve effectively as climbing ropes, or even for hauling heavy objects such as building stones and roof beams.

My conviction that climbing ropes were not part of the Ancestral Puebloan arsenal was fortified by a month-long trip I had taken to Mali in West Africa in 1988, also on assignment for *National Geographic*. The quest of our four-man team was to try to climb and rappel into the caves that another prehistoric people, the Tellem, had used for granaries and to bury their dead. The Tellem, who first appeared around A.D. 1100, only to vanish completely by 1500, were virtuoso climbers who somehow put up routes on the vertical and overhanging sandstone cliffs of the Bandiagara escarpment to reach their prized alcoves.

It was obvious from our first day in the Bandiagara that the Tellem had used ropes. Everywhere we climbed, we found long pieces of cordage made out of baobab bark, typically a full inch in diameter. And the *boulins*—hardwood sticks that the Tellem left wedged in the alcoves, where they were used as anchors and as hauling pulleys— were deeply scored with rope grooves.

If the Ancestral Puebloans, or the Fremont, had used rope with anything like the facility of the Tellem, why didn't archaeologists find pieces of rope in their digs? Greg's answer was that perhaps rope was too valuable a stuff to leave behind. "Look," he pointed out, "we find arrowheads everywhere. But why don't we find more bows and arrows?" I granted his logic. In the thirteenth century A.D., no belonging would have been guarded more fiercely than a hunter's bow and arrow. Perhaps a rope, requiring weeks of hard work to craft, was just as precious.

Greg advanced another argument. "Okay, so maybe some genius Fremont climber got up the route to the ledge. But he sure as hell didn't haul those heavy beams and the stones and water and mud for the granary on his back. Those guys had to use ropes."

In 2004, for another short article for *National Geographic*, I had queried a dozen Southwestern archaeologists, asking them if they had ever seen specimens of true prehistoric rope. The best example any of them could cite was a coiled-up rope that the Wetherill brothers, ranchers based in Mancos, Colorado, had dug out of a shallow alcove in Butler Wash in southeast Utah in the 1890s. Curated at the American Museum of Natural History, the rope was briefly lent to the Edge of the Cedars museum in Blanding, Utah, for a special exhibition. I never saw this artifact, but Vaughn Hadenfeldt, as well as his friend Winston Hurst, a Blanding-based archaeologist, had actually handled it. According to Hurst, the rope, made out of two twisted strands of yucca fiber, was about a hundred feet long and half an inch in diameter—strong enough, no doubt, to hold a heavy timber or an even heavier climber.

To test that hypothesis, we had hired Eric Blinman, an archaeologist based in Santa Fe, to manufacture two thirty-foot lengths of yucca rope using the same clever but tedious process the Ancestral Puebloans had followed. The thicker of the two cords was three-eighths of an inch in diameter. Then Blinman sent the ropes to the outdoor-gear retailer REI in Washington state, where an engineer strained them to their breaking points. The thicker segment broke at 456 pounds.

We concluded that if the ancients had used ropes to safeguard a leader's ascent, as climbers do today, they would have taken huge risks. A mere twenty-foot fall on the three-eighths-inch yucca rope would have broken it. But using such ropes to haul building materials, or even to belay a person from above, might well have been practical. Now, at Waldo's Catwalk, we were perhaps seeing for the first time the prodigy of vertical engineering that had made such inaccessible granaries possible.

As he hung on our own nylon rope, photographing Renee while she poked about the double granary, Greg had carefully studied the ascent route below it. The wooden "piton" was not just jammed into the crack—it was reinforced with stones and dried adobe. And directly beneath the cantilever triangle, Greg spotted an unmistakable vertical groove in the cliff.

"I think the cantilever," he told me when we had reached the base of the cliff, "was the key to the whole building process. It was the platform by which they hauled everything up to the ledge. With ropes. That groove was made by a rope. And I think there could have been other sticks wedged into the crack and cemented with stones and mud, to be used like rungs. What they created was not exactly a scaffold, but it may have been a series of ramps by which they zigzagged their way up." Greg had also seen that a long pole stretched diagonally from the cantilever to the roof of the bigger granary. "I'm pretty sure that was a handrail," he argued. "And the stones of the two granaries were offset beautifully to create good footholds to use when you got there."

The more I pondered it, the more Greg's theory made sense. My own belief that some acrobat had soloed the 5.11 route created further difficulties. Without ropes, indeed, how could the Fremont have hauled so much heavy material up to the ledge to build their double storage bin? And how, without ropes or a zigzag ramp system, had they repeatedly gained the ledge, gotten corn up to it, retrieved the corn, and gotten down? As Greg and I knew, climbing up a 5.11 pitch is hard enough. Climbing down it is substantially more difficult.

We agreed that in all likelihood, the Fremont had not used ropes as modern climbers do, to rappel down cliffs or to climb cracks, placing devices for protection so that a leader fall would prove less than fatal. But the wooden "piton," Greg convinced me, was not a piece of "protection," but rather a ladder rung. It was part of that crazy pseudo-scaffold, crowned by the cantilever triangle. Most of that structure, Greg posited, had disintegrated or disappeared over the centuries.

No matter what, Waldo's Catwalk was a true prehistoric marvel.

As for the "why" of the inaccessible double granary, I thought I had a plausible answer. Farther south, all across the Ancestral Puebloan world, the most radically defensive dwellings and granaries date from the thirteenth century, just before the people abandoned the whole of the Four Corners area for good. The going theory today is that famine, drought, deforestation, and the extinction of big game animals drove the people to the very edge. They began to raid one another's villages, stealing the vital corn, and in response the dwellers built granaries and houses in harder and harder places to get to.

The same environmental disaster engulfed the Fremont world. All but the very northeastern fringe of the people's domain was abandoned by A.D. 1350. So, I concluded, facing desperate times just like their neighbors to the south, the Fremont had hidden their corn in the most difficult places they could possibly stash it, Waldo's Catwalk being an extreme example. Then they had come back, having failed to weather the catastrophe that had befallen them, and retrieved every last morsel of it before moving on, abandoning their homeland for good.

In general, I thought, the wildly defensive granaries that proliferated all over Range Creek bespoke some ultimate crisis that had triggered the abandonment. This was not only my assumption: the UMNH archaeologists had come to the same conclusion. The Catwalk, then, must date from the late thirteenth or early fourteenth century.

But Renee had retrieved a single short log from the cantilever platform. Weeks later, she got a truly puzzling result from a radiocarbon test. The log dated from around A.D. 1000—not only three centuries before the abandonment, but at the very peak (so archaeologists had deduced) of Fremont affluence all over their extensive domain.

What in God's name, then, was going on in Range Creek? We were back at square one of our ignorance.

One

THE COWBOY'S INDIANS

W ho were the Fremont?

Before my first visit to Range Creek in the summer of
2004, despite all the wandering I had done in the Southwest,
I had never searched for sites in the former heartland of these northern
neighbors of the Ancestral Puebloans. Now, even while Greg and I were
exploring Range Creek, I undertook a crash course in all things Fremont.

Long before Alfred Kidder proposed the term "Anasazi" to refer to the builders of Cliff Palace, Keet Seel, Moon House, and tens of thousands of other villages on and around the Colorado Plateau, the experts assumed that virtually all the prehistoric ruins and rock art in the Southwest were the work of a single culture. At the first Pecos Conference in 1927, convened by Kidder, the leading archaeologists of the day devised the chronological classification—ranging from Archaic through Basketmaker II and III to Pueblo I, II, III, and IV—that is still widely in use today. (The hypothesized Basketmaker I period became a lacuna that was never filled.) This, despite the fact that before the invention of tree-ring dating, the scholars could only guess at the dates of the various periods.

Hohokam, as a separate culture centered around the Tucson Basin, southwest of the Anasazi, was not proposed until 1936; Mogollon, for the culture directly south of the Anasazi, only in 1933. Excavations of some sites north of the Colorado River had been undertaken before the 1930s, particularly in a far-ranging survey led by Neil Judd, whose reports appeared between 1916 and 1926. But in Kidder's magisterial 1924 synthesis, *An Introduction to the Study of Southwestern Archaeology*, all those sites were lumped together under the rubric of the "northern peripheral area of the Southwest." "Northern Periphery" came to be a somewhat dismissive label. As David B. Madsen and Steven R. Simms would write in 1998, the prehistoric northerners we now call the Fremont "became firmly fixed as a sort of poor man's Anasazi: people who grew maize, beans, and squash, made pottery, and lived in pit house villages, but who, as the country bumpkin cousins of the Anasazi, were too backward to live in multi-story masonry dwellings."

It was Noel Morss who first defined the Fremont culture, after participating in an ambitious Harvard-sponsored series of digs all over east-central Utah. In sites along the Fremont and Muddy Rivers, Morss made discoveries that struck him as different enough from Anasazi productions to warrant defining a separate ancient culture.

In his landmark 1931 paper "The Ancient Culture of the Fremont River in Utah," Morss itemized the differences as follows:

> This culture was characterized by cave sites with a slab cist architecture similar to that of the Basket-maker and Pueblo I periods; by a distinctive unpainted black or gray pottery; by the exclusive use of a unique type of moccasin; by a cult of unbaked clay figurines obviously related to, but more elaborate than Basket-maker III figurines; by abundant pictographs of distinctive types; and by a number of minor features which tended to identify it as a Southwestern culture on approximately a Basket-maker III level, but which showed consistently a degree of divergence from corresponding features of orthodox cultures.

This maddeningly vague prescription launched a controversy that shows no signs of attenuating more than eighty years later. Some leading Southwestern scholars still don't buy Fremont as a separate culture from the Anasazi, or Ancestral Puebloans. When I asked University of Colorado archaeologist Steve Lekson, who was my most valued informant for *In Search of the Old Ones*, if he accepted the "Fremont" designation, he shook his head. "What would you call it, then?" I asked. "Northern Periphery" was Lekson's succinct answer.

It is true that the moccasins made from the lower leg skins of bighorn sheep, often with the dew claws still attached, that have been found in sites all over central Utah look nothing like the yucca sandals worn by the Ancestral Puebloans. The "Utah-style metate," a deep U-shaped grinding platform, sometimes with a connected shelf designed to hold the mano or grinding stone, looks very different from the shallower metates found all over the Ancestral Puebloan heartland. Granaries from the Fremont region tend to be top-loading, as opposed to the front-loading storage bins of the Ancestral Puebloans. And a distinctive rock art, depicting trapezoidal humanoids with headresses, their dangling arms often holding shields or "trophy heads" (thought to be the decapitated, deboned heads of enemies slain in battle), are never seen south of the Colorado River. (Two of the most striking panels bearing masterly petroglyphs in this style appear at McKonkie Ranch near Vernal, Utah, and at McKee Springs Wash, on the western edge of Dinosaur National Monument.)

Yet the variation in artifacts and structures found across the Fremont domain since Morss's time tends to make a mess of the culture's coherence. In their definitive 1998 analysis, "The Fremont Complex: A Behavioral Perspective," Madsen and Simms conclude, with wry frustration,

> The differences between the many small groups of the Great Basin and northern Colorado Plateau areas of western North America were often quite great, and Fremont specialists have had a difficult time defining just who these people were and how they related to each other. There are, in fact, only three things common to all these people: they grew maize [corn] or knew someone who did, they made or traded for pottery and they were not Anasazi . . .

Elsewhere, Madsen and Simms categorically state, "In short, it is impossible to categorize the Fremont in terms of material remains." And in his popular study of these ancients, *Exploring the Fremont*, Madsen confesses his own confusion: "I have studied the Fremont for more than twenty years, but the more I learn about them the less I seem to understand."

Despite such caveats, Simms and Madsen cling to "Fremont" as a meaningful cultural label. Their map of the domain of those ancients covers all but the southeastern sector of Utah and spills into eastern Nevada, southern Idaho, southwestern Wyoming, and a sliver of northwestern Colorado.

Where the Fremont came from remains one of the unsolved questions about these ancients, though most scholars would trace them back into the Archaic, an era loosely defined as stretching from 6500 to 1200 B.C. In this view, the ancestors of the Fremont hunted game with atlatls (spear-throwers) and gathered wild foods in their Utah-centered homeland long before they discovered how to grow corn, make pottery, or use the bow and arrow.

What became of the Fremont is a more vexing unsolved question. We know beyond a shadow of a doubt that thousands of Ancestral Puebloans who fled the Four Corners just before A.D. 1300 became the present-day Puebloans, living in some twenty-odd villages that stretch from Taos in northern New Mexico to Hopi in northeastern Arizona. Some kind of environmental catastrophe helped trigger their whole-sale migration to the south and east. Tree rings document a terrible drought that lasted from A.D. 1276 to 1299, and famine, deforestation, and the depletion of big game through overhunting played their parts.

That same catastrophe apparently afflicted the Fremont, too. After 1350, they all but disappear from the archaeological record. Yet recent discoveries in northwestern Colorado seem to prove that the Fremont hung on in such unlikely places as Douglas Creek—a virtually tree-less arroyo choked by tamarisk and cheat grass today, through which meanders an undrinkable brown trickle of a stream—at least as late as A.D. 1500.

Theories about the fate of the Fremont abound. They gave up farm-ing, migrated east to the Great Plains, and assimilated with nomads who hunted bison. Or they were wiped out by Numic peoples—Ute, Shoshone, Paiute—who surged into the Fremont heartland from the west around the thirteenth century. Or they were simply assimilated by the Utes or Shoshone. Or perhaps the Fremont starved to death and became extinct. All that we can say with certainty is that the Fremont cannot be convincingly linked with any living Native Americans.

Corn—and later, beans and squash—turned the Ancestral Puebloans into a sedentary civilization, capable of building such magnificent villages as Pueblo Bonito in Chaco Canyon. On the other hand, experts believe that the Fremont—out there on the edge of the reliable growing season, where late spring or early fall frosts all too often ruined a whole year's crops—never fully committed to a farming lifeway. Madsen and Simms evoke a strategy they call "switching." At any given time, they argue, full-time foragers lived side by side with full-time farmers. Or in any given year, a band of farmers "switched" to hunting and gathering. The Fremont built no major villages because it was essential to their survival to be able to pack up and move on. The nomadic spirit, according to Madsen and Simms, never ceased to course through Fremont veins. And because the sites and artifacts of nomads are so much harder to detect on the ground than those of agriculturalists, the Fremont may not have disappeared from the face of the earth so much as slipped into the anonymity of the myriad nomadic tribes that roamed the West in the centuries just before European contact.

For two years after my first visit to Range Creek, even while I returned again and again to that enchanted canyon, I roamed across Utah and into Colorado as I pursued my crash course in the Fremont. In doing so, I found magical sites. The limitless petroglyph gallery in Nine Mile Canyon, abounding in long-necked cranes and big-horn sheep, snakes with criss-crossed bodies and surrealistic, lizard-like humanoids. The spooky warriors carrying trophy heads on the McKonkie Ranch and McKee Springs Wash panels. Mantle's Cave in Dinosaur National Monument, out of which University of Colorado excavators dug a treasure trove of unique artifacts in 1939 and 1940. The magnificent red pictographs in Barrier Canyon style on sandstone cliffs all across the San Rafael Swell, painted several millennia ago by artists who may have been the ancestors of the Fremont.

As I did so, I became aware of the regional differences that so bedeviled Madsen and Simms and their fellow Fremont experts. What I would find in Range Creek between 2004 and 2006 indeed had its own idiosyncratic stamp. Eventually I would place it under the rubric that Jerry Spangler, director of the Colorado Plateau Archaeological Alliance, named the Tavaputs Adaptation. Yet even within the rectangle of the Tavaputs Plateau—a deeply dissected tableland roughly forty miles square, split down the middle by the Green River—Range Creek, I would come to see, had its own peculiar wonders. Nowhere else in the Fremont domain would I find a granary as mind-bogglingly inaccessible as Waldo's Catwalk. Or a hidden rock art panel that it took a roped climb to get to, which we named the Shield. Or the lofty butte-top ruin that Waldo himself had explored decades earlier and named the Fortress. It was there, the rancher believed, that the Fremont in Range Creek had made their hopeless last stand.

During the first wave of public excitement after news about Range Creek leaked out, Waldo Wilcox was cast as a hero of sorts. In Salt Lake City in February 2005, I attended an evening of public lectures about the newly revealed valley. From the podium, Utah state archaeologist Kevin Jones announced, "Range Creek is the best-protected place I've ever seen in my life. And the great irony is that it was protected by a single private owner, not by all the laws that we've passed to preserve our cultural heritage." Duncan Metcalfe, co-leader with his wife, Renee Barlow, of the UMNH team working in Range Creek, said, "Waldo knew the archaeology of the canyon really well. Ninety-nine percent of the sites we've seen so far, Waldo told us where to find." Bob Morgan, former director of the Utah Division of Natural Resources, had grown up in Carbon County, just west of the Tavaputs Plateau. He regaled the crowd by claiming, "You've heard of the proverbial 900-pound gorilla? Well, Waldo was the 150-pound Tasmanian devil." With his fellow teenagers, Morgan recalled, "We went into Nine Mile Canyon [looking for arrowheads, pots, and the like], but we never dared to go into Range Creek, because of Waldo Wilcox." Metcalfe explained why. "There was a fairly strong fear among the local populace about hopping those fences. Waldo was a good welder, and he knew how to use a shotgun."

Metcalfe predicted a rosy research future for Range Creek: "In the next ten to fifteen years, I can see twenty dissertations and twice as many research projects coming out of our work there. That'll be my legacy." Renee Barlow, with whom Greg and I would rappel to the Catwalk a few months later, waxed the most enthusiastic about Range Creek. Since the UMNH team had started surveying three years earlier, she said, "We've recorded seventy-five sites with rock art. We've recorded more than ninety-seven granaries. And so far we've only looked at 15 percent of the land. We want to view Range Creek as an outdoor museum of archaeology."

The "Outdoor Museum" was a concept championed by Fred Blackburn in the 1980s. An ex-BLM ranger on Cedar Mesa, Fred would become the mentor who taught me the most about Ancestral Puebloan ruins and rock art, as he guided me into Grand Gulch and several of its tributary canyons. The idea of the Outdoor Museum was that prehistoric artifacts found in the backcountry should be left in place, rather than gathered up and stashed in museum collections. Yes, there was always the threat that those objects would be looted, but the thrill of finding an arrowhead or a yucca sandal in some remote alcove was an experience, Fred believed, that later visitors ought to have the chance to repeat.

In *In Search of the Old Ones*, I had heartily endorsed Fred's manifesto, devoting a chapter called "The Outdoor Museum" to its idealistic practice. Not only had I never taken home anything I found in the backcountry (to do so would violate the Antiquities Act of 1906), I had never informed any BLM rangers or archaeologists about even the most remarkable objects I had discovered, such as the intact corrugated pot I found on the obscure ledge during my solo outing in October 1993.

On my first several visits to Range Creek, however, I wondered how what the UMNH team was doing could conceivably fit into Barlow's prescription of preserving Range Creek as an Outdoor Museum. In the field, Metcalfe and Barlow's grad students were plotting the GPS coordinates of every potsherd, arrowhead, and metate they found. But they were gathering up nearly all the artifacts for eventual curation at the UMNH. Metcalfe had defended the practice in his February lecture in Salt Lake City, when a person in the audience challenged him. "The end justifies the means," Metcalfe claimed. "We collect the information, and we save it for the future." He added, "You can't eliminate looting. All you can do is minimize the slope of degradation."

When I saw the teams in action in Range Creek, planting little red flags as they picked up potsherds and chert flakes and dropped them into plastic bags, I was dismayed. So, too, I soon learned, was Waldo. "I don't think what Ol' Duncan and his wife are doin' is right," he told me. "They should leave the stuff where it is. I think the canyon's the biggest and best museum the Indian stuff could be in."

Already, the tension between the cowboy and the professionals was tangible. Waldo inevitably referred to Metcalfe as "Ol' Duncan," even though the archaeologist was his junior by about twenty-five years. Barlow was reduced to "his wife," never identified by first or last name. Though Waldo had graduated from high school in Price, he had read none of the learned monographs in which professionals analyzed the Fremont achievement. During his decades of wandering through Range Creek, he had formulated his own theories about the Indians who had lived there. One evening, as we sat in the cinderblock house Waldo had originally built for his family, which now was serving as the cluttered headquarters for the archaeologists, he unfolded those theories to me. Metcalfe was sitting close by.

"The first people in here wasn't but four foot tall," said Waldo. "I call 'em the Little People. I don't think they could count above three, 'cause in their pictures chipped into the rock [petroglyphs], they never got more'n three fingers. I think the Fremont come in and killed off the Little People. Then later the Utes come in and killed off the Fremont.

"Every place you find an arrowhead, there was a dead Indian."

In his adjoining chair, "Ol' Duncan" kept a straight face, but I could smell professional dismissal wafting from his pores. I knew that Metcalfe, as well as all the other archaeologists who had looked at Range Creek, thought the place was solid Fremont, with as yet little evidence of violent conflict. And no professional would give much credence to Waldo's numerically challenged Little People.

Waldo perceived the dismissal. Later he told me, "I may not know what I'm talkin' about, but hell, them archaeologists don't know either. They're just guessin'."

A couple of years earlier, before the news about Range Creek had gone public, Waldo had directed two of Metcalfe's fitter grad students toward a site a thousand feet above Range Creek on the east. Decades before that, on a visit to the high site, Waldo had found a Fremont skeleton eroding, skull first, out of the ground. To protect it, he picked up a nearby metate—or "corn grinder," as he calls the kind of heavy stone basin the ancients used to pulverize their maize—inverted it, and laid it over the cranium.

The grad students, according to Waldo, came back from their all-day hike exhausted but exhilarated. "They told me," he recalled, "'we've discovered that the Fremont buried their dead with corn grinders covering their heads.' I said, 'Yep, and I bet I can tell you right where that was, too.'"

Even before our first trip into Range Creek, Greg and I had spent time with Waldo in and around Green River. He took us to three of his favorite rock art sites. In Sego Canyon, we beheld a dazzling array of pictograph and petroglyph panels looming over the dirt access road. "Only place I know," said Waldo with a sly smile, "where you got four different cultures." Pointing his finger, he enumerated them: "Barrier Canyon, Fremont, Ute—and hippie." The last designation embraced the appalling graffiti that locals and tourists had carved right on top of the ancient paintings.

A few days later, Waldo drove us up the lower canyon of the Green River, where we came upon a BLM sign indicating a tributary valley called Nefertiti Canyon. The rancher pointed up the steep hillside on our right. "Trail goes right out of the canyon there," he said. "My dad and my grandad built it. Called it the New Year's Trail. It'll always be New Year's Canyon to me. That's what it was before the damn hippies come in." "Hippies," I would learn, was Waldo's catch-all term for everybody from grad-student archaeologists to BLM rangers to the river runners who had slapped an Egyptian label on a side canyon that had had a better name for the good part of a century.

On another day, explaining why he had never disturbed the graves of the Fremont or the "Little People" he had stumbled across in Range Creek, Waldo inveighed, "I don't want some goddamned hippie digging up my bones after I die."

At a site not far from his house in Green River, a place he called Willow Bend, Waldo showed us some petroglyphs carved on a lonely boulder. Among the images was an unmistakably pregnant bison (the baby outlined inside the womb of the mother), but also a pair of surrealistic anthropomorphs, with drooping antlers sprouting from their faceless heads, their bodies adorned with mystic spirals and crescents. The carving of those two humanoids was exquisitely precise. "I never seen anything like these figures," said Waldo, "and I've seen as much rock art as anybody around here." He paused, staring at the hallucinatory panel. "I think they're gods," he ventured.

On the same boulder, some passerby had crudely gouged out the initials "D.S." and the date "1921." "Look at that," said Waldo, pointing at the graffito. "Whoever put their name here wasn't near as good as they was." His finger returned to the anthropomorphs. "How'd they do that?" *Without metal tools*, I silently annotated. *With only harder rock for carving stones.*

Waldo insisted that only once, as a youngster, had he carved his name on a cliff in Range Creek. "I heard about that from my dad," he added. "He'd put his initials once in Chandler Creek, and he felt bad about it ever since. I never did it again." On yet another day, as we drove along the Green River corridor, we stopped to look at a Fremont petroglyph panel along whose margins old signatures had been carved. One of the more prominent etchings read "F McP." "I hate to say it," Waldo offered, "but that's my aunt. My mother's sister, Fern McPherson."

A tall man with a slight stoop, curly white hair, and a ruddy, weatherbeaten face, Waldo walked with his hands clasped behind his back, like a clergyman crossing a heath. At seventy-five, his gait was hobbled by the bowlegged limp of a cowboy feeling a lifetime of aches and pains.

The more time Greg and I spent in Waldo's company, the more we realized that he was a walking encyclopedia of local lore, of knowledge that had escaped the historians and archaeologists, of understandings that would evaporate with his passing. Waldo knew it: that sense of impending loss, I guessed, was at the core of the vague sorrow he seemed to carry with him wherever he went, even as he told funny stories about the blatherings of self-styled "experts."

On our first trip with Waldo into Range Creek, as we drove in his pickup along the Turtle Canyon road, he suddenly put on the brakes, got out of the truck, hooked his thumbs in his jeans pockets, and stared at the skyline to the west. "This is where the old horse trail from Woodside comes in," he mused. "I oughta flag it. I'm probably the only one still alive who knows where it is."

Raising cattle for a living was always a tough and financially precarious business. Over the years, Waldo had used his cowboy skills in ingenious ways to augment his income. One trick was to capture mountain lions alive and sell them to zoos. (The going price in the 1960s was about five hundred dollars a specimen.) Waldo had trained his two dogs, Shardy and Dink, to track cougars, chasing them up the steep ledges and slopes that wall in Range Creek. When the hunt went right, the canny dogs would corner their prey on a tree limb or a rock ledge. Waldo would unlimber his lariat, lasso the lion, then somehow carry it down the mountain without getting mauled.

One February day around 1970—Waldo couldn't remember the exact year—Shardy, Dink, and their master were on the trail of the biggest mountain lion Waldo had ever seen, or would ever see. For hours, they pushed their prey higher and higher up a craggy ridge that towers over Range Creek on the east, negotiating a perilous gauntlet of sandstone slabs, boulder-choked gullies, and skin-shredding scrub oak thickets. The cougar angled relentlessly toward a square, lofty butte top that Waldo had seen from the ranch buildings every day he had spent in the valley during the previous two decades, but which he had never before approached.

At last, fifteen hundred feet above the valley floor, Shardy and Dink cornered the great animal, which took shelter on a ledge right beneath the caprock of the butte. Waldo pulled out a camera and took a fuzzy photo of the cougar crouching in its eyrie—the picture hangs mounted today on the rancher's wall in Green River. Then the wildly yapping canines closed in.

With two swipes of a paw, the mountain lion killed Shardy and tore out one of Dink's eyes. This was a cougar, Waldo realized, that was not destined to be sold to a zoo. He raised his rifle, fired, and killed the great beast with one shot. Then he wrestled the mountain lion down from the ledge, skinned it, cut off its head, packed up the booty, and prepared to hike with a hysterical dog down the opposite side of the mountain.

Yet now Waldo paused. In a glance, he saw that the cliff just to his right bore the vestiges of a fifteen-foot ladder made of upright logs. Evidently the Fremont had turned the butte top into some kind of refuge. Curiosity trumped the urgent need to retreat.

In cowboy boots, Waldo clambered up the ladder. For an hour during the too-brief February afternoon, he explored the bedrock oasis in the sky, which almost certainly no human had visited during the previous seven hundred years. He found arrowheads lying everywhere, potsherds strewn in the dirt of shallow runoff rivulets, four rings of upright stones marking anomalous above-ground pithouses, five or six big "corn grinders," and, on a ledge twenty feet below the rim, peering out over the butte's sheer south face, a dilapidated granary. On the opposite north rim, he discovered three rows of big stones that had been piled along the cliff edge. Waldo concluded that these were ammo with which to bombard an enemy trying to sneak up the log ladder, the only possible route of access to the butte top.

At once, this high refuge fit as a pivot point into Waldo's ideas about prehistoric life in Range Creek. The Utes, invading from the west, he was convinced, had wiped out the Fremont. And here, Waldo decided, was where the Fremont had made their last stand. The Fortress, as he nicknamed the butte top, was the scene of the Fremont demise.

Below the cliff, Dink was howling in pain and terror. Waldo shinnied back down the ladder, gathered up the mountain lion hide and head, and started descending, by a route he'd never reconnoitered, toward a tributary of Range Creek called Dilly Canyon. It was not long before, in the fading light of dusk, he came to a fifty-foot cliff that blocked his way. He found its only weakness, a tight chimney that more than thirty years later Greg Child and I would rate as 5.3 in difficulty. "I put my rope through Dink's collar," Waldo later recalled, "pushed him off the cliff, then lowered him down. Pulled one end and got the rope back up. Same with the lion skin and the head. Then I climbed down myself." It was after dark by the time Waldo regained his cinder-block cabin.

Thirty-five years later, the Fortress was high on the agenda of Greg, Renee Barlow, and me. One day in May 2005, through binoculars Greg and I worked out a long, devious route that we thought should get us to the site. Three times on the ascent, we broke out the rope to belay Renee up easy but dangerous cliffs. The butte top itself still had only that one possible line of access, the steep groove up which the Fremont had built their fifteen-foot log ladder.

We spent hours on top, discovering the same vestiges of the ancients Waldo had first seen more than three decades before. Whether or not the Fortress was the site of some Fremont last stand, it was plainly a hyper-defensive eyrie. "What a desperate place to live," Greg muttered. Meanwhile Renee, scribbling notes in her log, was in a taxonomic ecstasy. "Guys," she said, "this is one of the best days of my life!"

I belayed Greg down to the dilapidated granary twenty feet below the south rim. As he poked around, he was startled to find a 1967 penny lying beside the storage bin, as if pitched there from the butte top. At last we headed down the "back way" toward Dilly Canyon. Slithering down the 5.3 chimney, I was awestruck by the solo winter expedition Waldo had pulled off so long ago, returning with a lion skin and head and a badly injured dog.

Later, over the telephone, I told Waldo about our ascent. "How long did it take you to get up there?" he asked.

"Four hours."

"I coulda done it in two." There was a pause. "Well, maybe not anymore."

I told him about finding the 1967 penny. Waldo chortled over the line. "I told you you'd never find my name carved anywhere," he said. "But every time I got to a site, I'd flip a penny in there. You keep lookin', you'll find my pennies all over the place." Another pause. "I was too tight to leave a quarter."

The longer I hung out with Waldo in Range Creek, the more keenly I sensed the building antipathy between the rancher and the archaeologists. Duncan Metcalfe would outwardly compliment Waldo, but his rejection of the self-taught cowboy's theories of prehistory was hard to hide. For his part, Waldo saw "Ol' Duncan" as the very prototype of the stuffed-shirt academic. On a later hike in a different canyon, Waldo took Greg and me to a bizarre, ancient stone wall in the middle of nowhere that he had discovered decades before. Greg and I could make neither head nor tail of it.

"I was hopin' you could tell me what it was," said Waldo with feigned regret. "Now I'll have to bring in Ol' Duncan to explain it to me."

The cattle Waldo had run for fifty years had kept Range Creek grazed, but during the years since 2001, the grasses had grown thigh-high. The whole canyon had become a tinderbox. It infuriated Waldo that the archaeology team—more than half of whose members smoked, some even in the field—wouldn't institute a smoking ban, at least outside their ranch-building base camp.

"The whole place is gonna burn down," I heard Waldo inveigh more than once. And: "Ten years from now, when the canyon's ruined . . ."

I myself was not initially impressed by the quality of the UMNH team's work. With no apparent research plan in mind, Metcalfe's grad students were engaged in systematically GPS-ing every site and gathering up every chert flake and potsherd, dropping them into their plastic bags to take back to Salt Lake City. That was standard archaeological practice in the Southwest in the 1960s and '70s, but by 2005, it was hard to justify. A commonplace has it that to excavate a site is to destroy it forever; in the same way, to pick up a potsherd and carry it away is to rob it of its provenience (no matter how carefully the GPS coordinates are taken), and in turn to deny a future generation the chance to ask questions in the field that our own generation has yet to formulate. As I had seen with my own eyes on many a gloomy occasion, the storage drawers of famous museums all over the world are crammed with artifacts no one has bothered to look at in decades.

With the exception of Renee, the UMNH crew struck me as intimidated by the true challenge of Range Creek, as they puttered along the dirt road, tackling only the most accessible sites. The narrow compass of the UMNH investigation seemed to me particularly ill-suited to the landscape of Range Creek. The scale of the canyon is immense. The highest ridgelines tower a full four thousand feet above the creek, giving a vertical relief that approaches that of the Grand Canyon. But it was only when Greg and I began to hike and scramble that we recognized how rough the country truly was, with steep scree and talus, thorny jungles of bushwhacking, and cliff bands everywhere that demanded our canniest route-finding.

Had it not been for Renee Barlow's unbridled enthusiasm for the high, inaccessible ruins, Greg and I would have been confined, like tourists, to a perfunctory traverse of the twelve-mile-long dirt road that runs alongside the creek. The third ambitious scramble that the three of us took, after Waldo's Catwalk and the Fortress, was to the strange site that we had started calling the Shield.

Decades earlier, on a blank wall arching from a ledge six hundred feet above the valley floor on the west, Waldo's keen eye had spotted a big, circular, white-and-yellow pictograph. Over the years, he had gotten near the ledge without figuring out any way to traverse onto it to inspect the pictograph up close. Gifted scrambler though he was, the rancher had never aspired to be a technical rock climber. Many a time he had lowered himself off a tree trunk with his lariat, but the thought of rappelling made him blanch. As he liked to tell Renee, "I'd go to hell for a pretty woman, but not swingin' on the end of a rope."

In July 2005, it took Greg, Renee, and me a long, grueling day just to discover the right approach to the Shield site. We left our gear cached up high, then returned two days later. The traverse to the hidden ledge lay across a band of vertical purple rock, rotten in the extreme (every other handhold came loose in our grasp), above a sheer two-hundred-foot drop. Greg led this dicey passage, slotting one spring-loaded cam after another for protection into the only good horizontal crack. He later rated the pitch solid 5.8. As I came across, I could barely imagine the Fremont, unroped and in leather moccasins or barefoot, performing the same traverse.

The hidden ledge turned out to be a cranny about the size of a walk-in closet. Ten feet above us, an ancient artist standing on a secondary shelf had painted the Shield: a ring of white thirty-two inches in diameter enclosing a yellow ring twenty-seven inches across. During the several hours Greg and I spent there, we discovered the collapsed sticks and beams of what might have been a small granary, a three-inch-long scraper made of dark red chert, several potsherds, a broken black obsidian arrowhead (obsidian being very rare in Range Creek), and, most bizarrely, a huge Utah-style metate that must have weighed twenty pounds.

The site was utterly puzzling. No one had ever lived on this tiny shelf in space. If the ancients had hidden corn in the collapsed granary, why not grind it on easy terrain back around the corner, then haul it in in baskets? How in God's name had some daredevil "flashed" the 5.8 traverse not only unroped but lugging a twenty-pound metate under his arm? Later, when I mentioned our finds to Waldo, he said, "Everywhere they been, they took those big old corn grinders. Even if they was only goin' to be there a few days."

And what was the Shield all about? Was the ledge some kind of shrine? The day before, high on Locomotive Rock, through binoculars I had admired a masterly petroglyph—a triangle-bodied humanoid with deer antlers, holding up a fringed stick (spear?) in one hand, seeming to drag a net or snare in the other. The carving had been executed on the lip of a bulging scallop of caprock, sixty feet above the ground. There was no way that I could see to place a log ladder to get anywhere near that sandstone canvas, where the self-assured artist had pecked out his vision.

It made sense to build granaries in difficult places to get to. As Waldo put it, "It's like why you put your money in a bank. If you only got a little bit of corn, and everybody's hungry, you hide it away where other folks can't steal it."

But what sense did it make to execute rock art in the most inaccessible places? Did the Shield, then—and half a dozen other such barely reachable rock art panels in Range Creek—represent some sort of virtuosic deed performed for its own sake? Did the myths or magic those images conjured up gain in potency because some artist had risked his life to paint or pound them there?

At first, Renee had balked at the traverse. Instead she beseeched us to use her pocket saw to sever one of the beam-ends for tree-ring dating. I couldn't bring myself to commit such desecration, but Greg dutifully sawed away. Later, after I had traversed back to safe ground, Greg hectored Renee to give it a try, and after two retreats, with a tug or two on the rope, she gamely scrabbled onto the ledge.

That evening she admitted to me that she had bagged the obsidian arrowhead. I was dismayed and even a bit shocked. The arrowhead, I thought, should have stayed where we found it. It was part of the Outdoor Museum. But later, Renee was able to source the obsidian. The stone, she discovered, had come from the Mineral Mountains on the edge of the Great Basin, 250 miles west of Range Creek. It was a small revelation, but an important one, expanding our knowledge of the trade network of the Fremont who had lived in this isolated canyon.

A few days later, we stopped on the dirt road several miles north of the Range Creek ranch buildings, and Waldo pushed his way through a frieze of ferns and cattails to a hidden source bubbling from the ground. "Dilly's Spring," Waldo pronounced. "Taste it. Sweetest water you ever drank."

"Who was Dilly?" I asked as I filled my water bottle, remembering also the name of the side canyon by which Greg, Renee, and I had descended from the Fortress.

"Tom Dilly," Waldo answered. "He was one of them old outlaws. When he was hidin', he'd hang out here, right near the spring. He was a real ladies' man. Real smooth. He could talk anybody into anything. If I could of known any of them outlaws, I'd of picked Tom Dilly. He wasn't a bank robber, but he stole more cows than Butch Cassidy did gold."

"So did the Hole-in-the-Rock Gang come through here?"

"All the time."

"Butch Cassidy was in Range Creek?"

"You bet."

Waldo went on to say that his maternal grandfather, Jim McPherson, who had first homesteaded on Florence Creek in 1883, was suspected of being unduly sympathetic to the outlaws. "He had to be," Waldo quipped, "or he wouldn't have stayed alive. They needed him, and he needed them." Then Waldo added, "Grandad said Butch Cassidy never died in South America. He seen him up here."

A few days later, Waldo pointed out the bench at the mouth of Range Creek where in 1900 the Carbon County posse had cornered and shot to death yet another notorious outlaw and member of Cassidy's gang, Flatnose George Curry. "The old-timers said he got kicked in the nose by a horse, is how he got his name. After he died, my dad found his last camp."

But suddenly Waldo gave vent to an unsentimental stricture: "People look at Butch Cassidy like he was a god. But a thief is a thief is a thief. Butch Cassidy was just a damned thief who was too lazy to work for a living."

One day at his house in Green River, Waldo pulled the giant mountain lion pelt from 1970, head reattached by an expert taxidermist, out of his storage shed for Greg to photograph. "Biggest cougar ever captured," he boasted. "Beat Teddy Roosevelt's record by half an inch."

In the 1960s and '70s, to help make ends meet, Waldo supplemented his ranching income by running a rather exclusive big-game hunting operation. Clients would fly in to a dirt airstrip Waldo had bulldozed out of an alfalfa field; then he would guide them in the pursuit of deer, elk, bear, and even mountain lion. By then, he had perfected his technique of chasing a cougar with his dogs and bringing it back alive. The mountain lions he did not sell to zoos, he stowed in fifty-gallon "grease cans," then set them loose only hours in advance of his clients' pursuit. (One day during my visit to Range Creek, spying an old grease can that still stood in the yard of his former home, Waldo was stung with remorse. "If I go to hell," he murmured, "it'll be for how I treated them lions.")

How many men still alive in the West, I wondered, knew how to track a cougar, corner it on a ledge, and lasso it into submission? Even the skills Waldo had honed during his fifty years on Range Creek had lapsed into the limbo of lost arts. I would have given much to see Waldo wield his lariat in his prime, for he told me that he had once roped a stray bison that had wandered into Range Creek, then single-handledly castrated it, for fear the animal would interbreed with his cattle. ("Never did see that buffalo again.") For sport, he had roped a black bear or two ("If you give him a little slack, he'll pull the noose off with his arms, just like a monkey"), and, once, a bighorn sheep, just because when his dad had done the same thing back in the 1930s, it had made the newspapers, nobody in Utah ever having heard of a cowboy pulling off such a stunt.

In the vast labyrinth of the Tavaputs Plateau, I asked Waldo one day, were there other canyons with anything like the richness of the "Indian stuff" in Range Creek?

"Nothin' as good as Range Creek," Waldo replied; but then he named several canyons east of the Green River, over on the Ute Reservation. Later I telephoned the Uintah and Ouray headquarters. A spokesman told me bluntly, "Hiking isn't allowed on the reservation."

"How about with a Ute guide?"

There was a pause. "Nobody's ever asked before," the man answered. "I might bring it up with the tribal council." I knew better than to hold my breath.

Finally, in March 2006, Waldo shared another of his secrets with Greg and me, on the condition that we not name the place in print. We spent four days exploring that other canyon, two of them with Waldo, two on our own. The cowboy had first entered the valley way back in 1941, at the age of eleven, not for the fun of it but as he helped his father round up stray cows on the cattle drive between the Wilcox winter range near the town of Green River and their home on Florence Creek.

The secret canyon was no match for Range Creek in beauty—a stark, forlorn corridor between lumpy cliffs, it cut a long swath through the Tavaputs. The canyon looked to me like a poor place to live, with a scarcity both of firewood and of potable water (despite the silty stream that ran through it). Yet though the valley is uninhabited today, ranchers had tried since before the turn of the twentieth century to homestead here, and long before them, the Fremont (and for all I knew, the Little People) had found the barren place congenial, for its cliffs and boulders proliferated in rock art panels.

Waldo had told us that a good trail ran up the valley, but as we hiked the first few miles, there was no trace of it. "Where's your trail, Waldo?" I teased.

"It's growed over since I was here last."

Having just turned seventy-six, Waldo limped painfully as he hiked, but he was clearly having fun. "I never thought I'd come back through here," he announced after an hour, "and I knew for damned sure I wouldn't be walkin'!"

In a small stand of cottonwoods, we came upon a rusty stove going to pieces in the grass. Waldo touched it with toe of his boot. "That old stove," he said, "started out in Fisher Valley. Grandad had it. He give it to Dad. Dad took it to Range Creek, then to Bighorn. When he stopped runnin' cattle in Bighorn, he give it to some Eye-talian sheep-herders who brought it down here."

A mile farther up the canyon, we came upon the remains of a Navajo sweat lodge, a low pyramid made of forked sticks, the heating rocks still lying in a pile on the north side of the structure. "Melvin Adams, out of Blanding, had the permit in here," Waldo mused. "He brought in a bunch of Navajos to herd his sheep."

I was flabbergasted by the precision of Waldo's details. As we approached a huge, lone boulder, I saw a rusty shovel head lying at its foot. I picked it up. "I suppose this is yours?" I needled.

Waldo didn't miss a beat. "Yep. I used it to sand the ice in winter, so the cows could get across the stream."

Even farther up the canyon, Waldo pointed out the sagging ruin of a wooden house, half a mile away on the far bank of the stream. "Ellick Reed and Albert May built that, back in the twenties," Waldo soliloquized. "Ellick was the handyman in this country. He had his hand in about everythin' was built around here.

"Ellick come in, tried to help Albert take care of it, but they went bankrupt. Al ended up a pumper for the old steam locomotive out of Woodside. It just broke his heart goin' bankrupt here."

Waldo paused reflectively. "Come to think of it," he added, "except for my kids, there's no one I been in here with who's still alive. My dad's gone, and my brother, and everybody who worked for them, and both the old men who lived in that house over there are dead, and their kids are dead." The sorrow hung in the warm, windless air.

On one of our days in the canyon, Waldo stayed and shared our campfire before, late in the evening, driving his pickup back to Green River. I mixed up a salad while Greg cooked steaks over the fire and roasted corncobs in their husks in the coals. Waldo drank the single beer he allowed himself on the rare festive occasion. At the moment, Ol' Duncan and his entourage of hippies working their mischief in Range Creek seemed but a distant rumor.

Waldo took a bite of corn. "I hate to say it, but I think that's the best corn I ever ate," he told Greg. "You make a good oven, boy."

In the winter of 2005–06, the UMNH effort was dealt a serious blow. Under bitter circumstances, Duncan Metcalfe's marriage to Renee Barlow broke up. She obtained a legal separation and filed for divorce, though it would not become final until 2009.

Early in 2006, Metcalfe joined with the head of the anthropology department at the University of Utah to prohibit Renee from conducting any further research in Range Creek. For the first three months of the season, she was banished from the valley. It was August before she was allowed to return. After that, Renee tried to continue her fieldwork among the high granaries, even without access to the kitchen, toilets, or showers of the UMNH headquarters. Meanwhile Metcalfe's grad students continued their collecting, in an enterprise completely divorced from Renee's research.

An exhibition devoted to Range Creek opened at the UMNH in August 2006. Visiting it one day, I saw that in the displays, all credit for Renee's work among the inaccessible granaries was expunged even from the fine print of the acknowledgments. Ironically, the pièce de résistance of the exhibit was a surprisingly accurate fiberglass replica of Waldo's Catwalk, based on Renee's and Greg's photos. Quite by coincidence, Metcalfe was giving a tour to visitors when I arrived. Aware of my low opinion of the research the UMNH was conducting, an evidently startled Metcalfe seemed to be trying to ignore my presence. Eavesdropping, I heard the man blandly tell the tour group what "we" had found in the twin granaries, even though I was quite sure he had never seen the site except through binoculars from the valley floor.

Waldo himself was barely mentioned in the exhibition. And as Metcalfe gestured proudly at the fiberglass model, he told his audience, "We call this 'The Scaffold.'" "Waldo's Catwalk" was expunged along with the estranged wife who had named and first explored it.

In the spring of 2006, the DWR changed the locks on the gates at either end of the twelve-mile-long homestead in Range Creek. Perhaps inadvertently, neither the agency nor the UMNH team gave Waldo a key. State archaeologist Kevin Jones had told me, "Preserving Range Creek will be the most important thing I can do in my life." But now the rancher who had kept the place pristine for Jones and Metcalfe and the grad students to marvel over no longer felt welcome in the valley that for half a century had been his home.

After 2006, I let Range Creek drift away from the focus of my wanderings in the Southwest. It seemed that I had no choice, for with the banishment to Outer Mongolia of Renee Barlow, I had lost my permission to hike to the high, inaccessible sites that had so captured Greg's and my imagination. Renee snagged a job at the College of Eastern Utah Prehistoric Museum in Price, but left after three years. Currently, she works for the BLM office in Ely, Nevada. She took her Range Creek research with her, driving a deeper schism through the UMNH effort. None of her work in the canyon has been published, although she's submitted a number of papers to scholarly journals.

I got back in contact with Renee late in 2013, six years after I'd last communicated with her. To my surprise, she told me she'd continued working in Range Creek until 2010, authorized by a separate permit obtained through her College of Eastern Utah appointment. With Byron Loosle, then the BLM archaeologist for the state, Renee had backpacked high above the Fortress. "There are sites everywhere," she told me, "no matter how high we climbed. By now I've found 160 granaries, as well as a number of high habitation sites."

Her continued work in Range Creek, however, only intensified the rancor between Barlow and Metcalfe's UMNH team. After buying the land on which Renee was working from the state, the UMNH crew again tried to kick her out of Range Creek. She claimed to me that the ranch manager had chased her up the dirt road in a pickup truck. But a member of the team whom I contacted in 2013 pooh-poohed this allegation. "There was no chase up the dirt road," she said. "But Renee was definitely trespassing." Once again, the team changed the locks on the gates. Barlow hasn't been back in Range Creek since 2010. The team spokeswoman added, "It was odd, but even before the break-up with Duncan, Renee kept her data separate from ours. Even when we were working side by side."

Since 2003, the UMNH has run a summer field school in Range Creek, with the Wilcox ranch as headquarters. A bibliography prepared by Metcalfe's team runs to an impressive ten pages, but on closer perusal, the vast bulk of the work of the grad students has issued in the ephemeral forms of posters presented at conferences and talks given to various gatherings. (A sample of the former: "Excavation and Geophysics at 42Em2861 in Range Creek, Utah." Of the latter: "Archaeology in Range Creek—Presentation for the Lehi Elementary 4th Grade.")

Almost none of the research has been published. As of this writing, in March 2014, the sole contribution by Metcalfe himself is a short chapter in a book aimed at a general audience called *The Great Basin: People and Place in Ancient Times*, in which he admits, "We so far know very little about the Fremont occupation of Range Creek."

Perhaps the most interesting paper yet to come from the UMNH team is Shannon Boomgarden's "An Application of ArcGIS Viewshed Analysis in Range Creek Canyon, Utah" (2009). Viewshed analysis is a technical means of quantifying lines of sight between, in Boomgarden's work, the high granaries in Range Creek and the dwelling sites on the valley floor near the creek. Boomgarden enlisted the mountaineering skills of a University of Utah geologist, Larry Coats, who climbed and rappelled into many of the granaries perched on high ledges (though not Waldo's Catwalk), where he recorded GPS coordinates and photographed sites visible from above. All in all, Boomgarden analyzed seventy-two different granaries.

Her intriguing conclusion is that the granaries closest to the living sites and most easily accessed tended to be small and well-hidden in nooks and crannies. The higher granaries that were hard to get to were deliberately made visible from as many as eight residential sites on the valley floor. They also tended to be much larger than the handier nearby storage bins.

Boomgarden's premise is that the purpose of both types of granaries was to hoard food, and to guard it against thieves. The strategy of the Fremont in Range Creek was to parcel out small batches of food in the close hidden granaries, so that even if one was raided, there would be others still left full. The bigger granaries high on the canyon walls were defended by the difficulty of getting to them and by their sheer visibility, so that villagers going about their business on the valley floor could keep a watchful eye on those precious deposits of grain and wild seeds.

In 2013, Renee Barlow shared with me a paper she had been trying for years to get published. (None of the UMNH team had read it.) Titled "Farming, Foraging and Remote Storage in Range Creek," it argues that the high, inaccessible granaries such as Waldo's Catwalk were nearly all built in the period between A.D. 950 and 1050, in response to the threat of raiding and theft, at a time when the Fremont in the canyon were still semi-nomadic. Yet by 1100, according to Barlow, those granaries were abandoned in favor of a more settled lifeway in a small number of sites along the valley bottom, close to the creek. That, in turn, preceded an early abandonment of Range Creek, even while Fremont elsewhere in Utah were still flourishing.

Working with Ron Towner of the Laboratory of Tree-Ring Research in Tucson, Barlow got dendro dates from some twenty high granary beams. All the dates ranged between A.D. 930 and 1063. She also got radiocarbon dates from corn found in the granaries, which yielded a range from A.D. 1000 to 1040. But by A.D. 1200, Barlow argued, Range Creek had been abandoned for good.

In her paper, Barlow addressed the difficulty of climbing to sites such as Waldo's Catwalk that had so baffled Greg Child and me. Her provocative comments made me wish I'd stayed in touch with her after 2006, and gone on many another hunt for cliff-ledge storage bins.

Accessing these granaries, and hauling the loads of stone slabs, adobe, timbers and maize up the cliff faces to build them, probably posed a significant risk to prehistoric farmers. Prehistoric climbing aids have been recorded at several dozen sites, including pecked toeholds above or below granaries, wooden timbers and sticks jammed into crevices on cliff faces to form handholds or to support platforms, and a few Douglas fir tree boles up to ten meters that were apparently used by the Fremont as ladders. Several of these were probably hauled significant distances from Douglas fir forests to the sites, and set at the base of a cliff below a granary. They were debarked, stripped of limbs, and leaned against the cliff. Several yielded tree-ring dates consistent with the age of timbers used in the construction of granaries or platforms above them. . . . Sometimes pecked toeholds, jammed sticks or timbers, or natural handholds are found above these logs and directly below granaries, and sometimes they are simply found on the cliff face about four to five meters above the ground surface on cliffs below granary ledges, where a ladder tree may have been during prehistoric times. At one site, a possible Fremont "ladder" had been pulled up onto the ledge above the cliff and left beside the granary.

Barlow's paper, if published, will make a significant contribution to our understanding of the magical canyon that Waldo Wilcox so fiercely guarded all his life. In an ideal world, the breach between her and the UMNH team would be healed. Barlow and Boomgarden might collaborate on theories about farming, subsistence, and defense in Range Creek. But there is very little likelihood this will happen. The nasty divorce between Barlow and Metcalfe has driven a chasm through the heart of research in the canyon that, in the rosy optimism of 2002, promised to tell us more about the Fremont than seventy years of previous work all over Utah.

As of 2013, the UMNH team had been at work in Range Creek for twelve consecutive years. The "twenty dissertations and twice as many research projects" Metcalfe had gleefully predicted would appear in ten or fifteen years may yet come to pass. Boomgarden, in particular, seems to be doing interesting work, and she appears to be the most diligent and ambitious member of the team in terms of publishing and lecturing. But nothing like a synthesis of the Range Creek research has been crafted, or seems likely to be in the near future.

The history of Southwestern archaeology is littered with major excavations conducted by scholars who never mustered the self-discipline to publish their results. Yellow Jacket ruin, near Cortez, Colorado, was a massive, important village occupied by as many as two thousand Ancestral Puebloans between A.D. 630 and the end of the thirteenth century. For more than thirty years, University of Colorado archaeologist Joe Ben Wheat dug at Yellow Jacket, but by the time he died in 1997, he had published none of his results. According to his colleagues, Wheat was a respected scholar, a great guy, and a diligent worker, but his silence in print turned the excavation of Yellow Jacket into a fiasco—although present-day

CU archaeologists still hope to wring a good report out of Wheat's copious maps, photographs, and field notes.

Edgar Lee Hewett was a major figure in early Southwestern archaeology, the man responsible for the Antiquities Act of 1906. But he became infamous for large-scale digs that issued in no scholarly publications. At Chetro Ketl, one of the finest of the Great Houses in Chaco Canyon, Hewett led University of New Mexico field school excavations on and off for fifteen years, starting in 1920. He published a few superficial popular articles about the place, but no monograph. Even worse, the paperwork he left behind is so sparse as to leave Chetro Ketl all the more difficult for future scholars to understand. The same negligence stamped Hewett's work in other major ruins in northern New Mexico. A persistent rumor has it that the man directed his wife to burn his papers after he died.

The counterexamples validate archaeology at its finest. Harvard's J. O. Brew dug a series of mesa-top ruins on Utah's Alkali Ridge in the 1930s. Brew's 1946 report, *The Archaeology of Alkali Ridge, Southeastern Utah*, was a landmark work, establishing for good the previously elusive Pueblo I phase of Ancestral Puebloan culture, and with it, the continuity between Basketmaker and Pueblo—originally thought to be separate peoples.

No one would be happier than I if a magisterial synthesis such as Brew's ultimately came out of the UMNH work in Range Creek. But I'm not optimistic. The titles of the posters and papers listed in the team's bibliography betray a preoccupation with minutiae, with tiny questions timidly explored ("Smoke Signals: The Positive Effects of Fire on the Germination and Growth of Nicotiana Attenuata"). Indeed, during the last twenty years, grad students in archaeology have been encouraged to focus on niches so specialized that their findings run little risk of being criticized. The era of the big picture guys—J. O. Brew, Alfred Kidder, or for that matter, Steve Lekson, whose 2008 synthesis, *A History of the Ancient Southwest*, supplants all such previous works—seems to have come and gone.

In April 2013, Greg and I visited Waldo in Green River. We hadn't seen him in more than five years, and he hadn't been back to Range Creek once during that time. "There's nothin' left there for me," he lamented. "They stripped it all bare."

Though creakier than ever, Waldo was still up for a walk to Willow Bend and another look at the boulder with the surreal anthropomorphic petroglyphs that he thought might depict Fremont gods. The next day, he would turn eighty-three. "What are you going to do for your birthday?" I asked Waldo as he drove us back to his house.

"Get up and have breakfast," he answered.

Then, as if in a reverie our visit had induced, out of the blue: "The evil spirits are gonna get them archaeologists sooner or later."

Back in 2006, pushing hard and long on our two marathon hiking days in the secret canyon Waldo had introduced us to, Greg and I managed to traverse all but a mile of it. We found dozens of rock art panels, a few potsherds, and one perfect arrowhead, made of chert with intermingled streaks of gray-green, copper, and red.

On a hunch, Greg climbed the cliff band above the terrace where we found the arrowhead. We were far enough in that, in effect, we had reached the pole of inaccessibility of the long, winding canyon. While I sketched a pair of faint bighorn sheep petroglyphs, Greg climbed until he was a good five hundred feet above the valley bottom—halfway to the distant rim of the canyon.

Then I heard his cry of astonishment, and a distant command, "Hey, come have a look at this!"

I scrambled up to the high corner that jutted out in a major canyon bend. Greg stood beside a boulder whose upper surface was coated with the dark brown mineral accretion known as desert varnish. The whole of that upper surface had been carved—a millennium ago? or two, or three?—by some artist in the grip of a vision. The design was pure abstraction, an intricate mass of curved and intersecting lines, what some rock art experts call a "maze." It was the most masterly ancient image we would come across in the whole length of the valley, and it occupied a truly lordly niche overlooking miles of canyon forking north and east of us.

Waldo later admitted he'd never seen that petroglyph boulder. "One reason I brought you guys in there," he said, "was I figured there was at least ten times as much Indian stuff as I ever seen." Only then did it dawn on Greg and me that we might just possibly be the only Anglos ever to have seen the ancient maze graven on the obscure rock halfway up the canyon wall.

Whoever had carved the maze had known exactly what it meant. And his people had known, too. And they had known why he had carved it there, on that boulder, not the next one (which was utterly blank), at that high bend in that particular canyon.

The Hopi sometimes interpret petroglyph mazes as migration maps left by their ancestors, recording the people's wanderings from the time of the first emergence from the underworld to their present whereabouts. But there is only the faintest of possibilities that the Fremont are ancestral to the Hopi. Nor could Greg and I even be sure the maze was a Fremont petroglyph. The patina in the carved grooves was so dark that we knew the art was very, very old. Perhaps it was the work of an Archaic nomad long before the Fremont arrived, a shaman from some culture we have yet to identify.

It was this sense of lost meaning that ached inside me, linking with what I perceived as Waldo's sorrow. More than once, I had heard him say, "I figure I know Range Creek better'n anybody else ever did, 'cause them Indians didn't live so long." And one day in 2005, as Waldo, Renee, and I walked along the dirt road the Wilcoxes had improved after they bought the ranch, Renee had suddenly gushed, "So far we've found two hundred and eighty sites in Range Creek. Every one Waldo either told us about, or we found it on the way to a site he told us about. And we've only seen 15 percent of the canyon!"

"You ain't seen five percent, kiddo," Waldo rejoined.

The sorrow was intermingled with anger about what the archaeologists were doing to Range Creek. The neat cinder-block house in which the cowboy had spent his lonely winters had become, in the hands of the UMNH team, a rather squalid menage. "You spend your whole life keeping it up," Waldo mused, "only to have it tore down right before your eyes."

Some of the sorrow and anger Waldo directed against himself. "I oughta kick myself," he abruptly told me one day, "for sellin' the most beautiful place in the world."

When Waldo Wilcox goes, his life's store of wisdom and knowledge will go with him, and we will be the poorer for it. Range Creek is still there, of course, in all its glory and mystery. But its meaning is nothing you can put in a plastic bag.

Two

THINGS

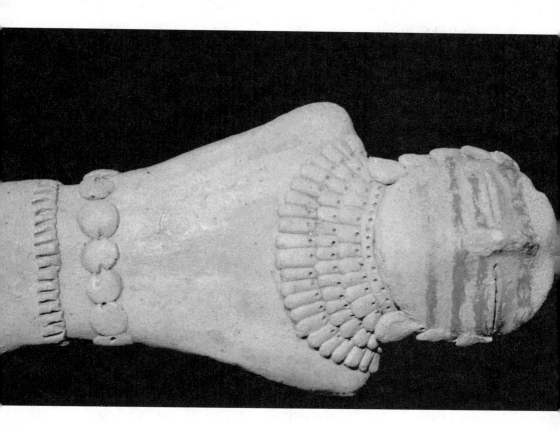

A common claim by professionals in the field, especially in recent years, is that "archaeology is not about things." Things—artifacts dug up in excavations—are of significance only for the light they cast on the cultures that produced them. As R. E. Mortimer Wheeler writes in *Archaeology from the Earth*, "We are concerned here with methodical digging for systematic information, not with the upturning of earth in a hunt for the bones of saints and giants or the armoury of heroes."

The retreat from "things" is in part a reaction to our age's enduring caricature of the archaeologist as adventure hero: Indiana Jones. In *Raiders of the Lost Ark*, Harrison Ford ransacks Nepal and Egypt in search of the Ark of the Covenant. In *The Last Crusade*, he's off to Italy and Turkey to get his hands on the Holy Grail. In *The Kingdom of the Crystal Skull*, he gallivants from New Mexico to Peru in quest of a crystal skull whose powers have something to do with extra-terrestrials. The bad guys trying to beat Ford to the treasure are either Nazis or Soviets.

And yet, when all is said and done, things—artifacts—can have a powerful numen. The intact corrugated pot that I found on the high ledge in a Cedar Mesa canyon in 1993 was far from unique. Museums are full of similar vessels. Yet the fact that numerous readers set out to look for that pot, guided by my fuzzy treasure map, testifies to their hunger for a transcendent moment such as the one I had had when I found the pot in situ, where its owner had hidden it in the thirteenth century.

The archaeology of things is an archaeology of loss. Is there any greater cultural tragedy in history than the burning of the Alexandria library, whether it happened once, in A.D. 391, as Gibbon believed, or several times between the reigns of Julius Caesar and Caliph Omar? The ambition of the library's founders was "to collect all the world's knowledge." In the hundreds of thousands of papyrus scrolls that went up in flames, no one will ever know what works of which geniuses vanished forever.

The tomb of Tutankhamun, unearthed in 1922 by Howard Carter, continues to fascinate us not because Tut was an important pharaoh, but because, almost uniquely among royal sepulchers in ancient Egypt, it had not been looted by vandals. The desecration of nearly all the other pharaonic tombs had been performed not by moderns in search of priceless relics, but by one dynasty after another trashing its ancestors' dream of celestial immortality.

Things dug up in excavations often brim with meaning, confronting us with questions we can only begin to answer. In my last thirty years of crisscrossing the prehistoric Southwest, no objects that I have seen were more astonishing than the Pilling figurines and the Telluride blanket. I found both in museums, having come 55 and 117 years too late, respectively, to have a chance of discovering them in situ. Attached to both the figurines and the blanket are incredible sagas, as, thanks to the greed and negligence of their putative owners, they came perilously close to vanishing as irretrievably as the Alexandria scrolls or the grave goods of Khufu, builder of the Great Pyramid at Giza.

Clarence Pilling owned a ranch just downstream from the Wilcox spread in Range Creek. One day in March 1950, the year before Waldo's parents bought their own ranch, Clarence, his two brothers, and two friends were out herding cattle in a side canyon. They poked inside a south-facing alcove, where they found a crude masonry room and red, white, and yellow pictographs painted on the back wall. It was an intriguing find, but nothing sensational. The men were headed out of the alcove when Clarence Pilling, who had made a hobby of hunting for "Indian stuff" since the age of sixteen, peered into a dim recess in the cave wall. There, laid out on a ledge, he discovered eleven unfired clay figurines, ranging in length from four to six inches.

As he carefully gathered them up, Pilling saw that each figurine was covered with exquisitely detailed ornaments: necklaces, pendants, waistcloths, and hairbobs made of tiny blobs of clay stuck to the torsos and further decorated with pinprick holes. The faces were round, with sculpted protruding noses, the eyes rendered as horizontal slits. The bodies were roughly trapezoidal, descending from broad shoulders to narrow waists and hips (the legs were not represented). In addition, traces of red, buff, and black paint still adhered to the figurines.

Recognizing how fragile these objects were, Pilling nonetheless determined to take them out of the canyon, so he wrapped them up and loaded them into his horse's saddlebags. It is a miracle that the figurines survived their jostling transport some forty miles out to Pilling's winter home in Price. As Duncan Metcalfe told me in 2005, "If you dropped one of the figurines in a glass of water, you'd have a puddle of clay in a couple of hours."

To his credit, the rancher recognized that the effigies he had found were not only beautiful and unique, but would be of great interest to professional archaeologists. A friend of Pilling's, Geneve Howard Oliver, was planning an auto trip back east. Pilling entrusted the figurines to her. Oliver took the precious objects first to Neil Judd at the Smithsonian Institution in Washington, then to Harvard's Peabody Museum, where they were studied by Noel Morss, the scholar who had first defined the Fremont culture in 1931. Morss later wrote a monograph about the objects.

As Morss observed, "On arrival at the Peabody Museum the specimens had suffered some damage and displacement of the applied elements, but careful work by Mr. Frederick Orchard of the Museum's staff resulted in the restoration of nearly all the available fragments to their proper position. . . . There has been no 'restoration' in the sense of renewing or replacing any of the original fabric."

Two years later, Morss visited the Range Creek alcove with Pilling, Oliver, and Oliver's niece, approaching by jeep and then on foot. The archaeologist was stunned by the figurines' survival. "It is remarkable," he dryly mused, "that such delicate objects should have remained, undisturbed and largely undamaged by humans, animals or the elements, in such a location for the several centuries which have undoubtedly elapsed since their manufacture."

Morss made several canny observations about the figurines. They were, he saw, distinguished by gender and apparently linked in pairs. (A potential twelfth figurine, possibly lost, might have been paired with "the odd female" that Morss designated as "No. 1.") "The females have breasts and wide hips and wear aprons," he wrote. "The men wear breech-clouts, except for No. 2, which has a sort of kilt. The women dress their hair in heavy bobs, bound with cord, hanging down over the shoulders." Morss believed that all eleven figurines were the work of a single artist.

The archaeologist also discovered that the objects, while still soft, must have been laid in baskets or trays, for the imprint of some kind of woven fabric was still visible on the back sides of several specimens. "The figurines," Morss concluded, "were intended to be viewed from the front only. They are too fragile to have been much carried about or to have been worn attached to the person, nor is it likely that they were suspended, or tied to anything in a vertical position."

In an effort to place the Pilling array in context, Morss surveyed the known ceramic figurines from all over the prehistoric Southwest, as well as kindred examples found as far afield as Mississippi and Mexico. As to their purpose, Morss concluded that the effigies most likely derived from an "increase cult," as objects used in rituals to invoke magical powers to ensure that women would be fertile. Morss rejected the idea that the figurines sprang from an agricultural increase cult aimed at guaranteeing a good harvest, because figurines not unlike the Pilling group elsewhere in the Southwest date back to the Archaic times, long before the domestication of corn.

It might have been a happy outcome had the figurines been curated at the Peabody. But Clarence Pilling wanted them back. The museum offered him a thousand dollars for the collection—just under ten thousand dollars in today's currency—but Pilling turned the offer down. Thus began an odyssey of ownership and display that would make any lover of the ancient Southwest cringe.

Back in Price, with Pilling's blessing, Oliver put the figurines on exhibit in the lobby of the Park View Motel, which she owned with her sister. There they remained for more than a decade. One can only imagine how vulnerable those clay statuettes must have been to damage or theft.

Had objects such as the figurines been discovered in Europe or Latin America, they would immediately have become the property of the government, as part of the country's cultural heritage. But in the United States, with our peculiarly American belief in the sanctity of private land, an artifact or a ruin dug on one's own property, no matter how valuable it might be to science, belongs to the owner. A rancher in Utah or New Mexico can with impunity take a backhoe to an ancient village and trash it beyond repair.

Enter, once more, Waldo Wilcox. Clarence Pilling had claimed that the alcove in which he had found the figurines was on his own spread. But Waldo, who had always believed in leaving the "Indian stuff" where he found it, thought he knew better. The alcove, he insisted, was on BLM land. If he was correct, that meant that Pilling had no viable claim to ownership of the objects.

"Clarence had them damn things sold to Japan for a million dollars," Waldo told me in 2005. It was a rumor I had heard elsewhere: the figurines had come within a whisker of being sold to some rich collector in either far-off Japan or Germany. At some point—once again, he could not pin down the year—Waldo took some BLM rangers to the alcove. With them they carried a photo someone had shot of Pilling in front of the cave. "There was Clarence," recalled Waldo, "with his hand held out just like Joseph Smith." (The allusion was to the founder of Mormonism and the purported golden plates he dug up in upstate New York and translated into the *Book of Mormon* with the aid of a "seer stone.") "I showed 'em [the rangers] that the cave was on BLM land. Clarence hated me ever after. But I kept him from sellin' the figurines to Japan."

Pilling, who died in 1990 at the age of ninety, is buried in the Price cemetery. I had come along fifteen years too late to get his side of the story. But in 2013, Blaine Miller, a longtime BLM archaeologist and one of the men Waldo had guided to the alcove (Miller thought it was in the late 1980s), told me that their visit had proven for good that the alcove lay on BLM land. Pilling may have had a grazing permit in that side canyon, but owned none of it. According to Miller, Pilling, threatened with a formal injunction to confiscate the precious collection, at last capitulated and admitted that the alcove was not on his own land.

More than two decades earlier, in 1961, when the College of Eastern Utah opened its Prehistoric Museum in Price, Pilling had agreed to lend them the collection. For seven years, the figurines lay on display under glass. But in 1968, Pilling got them back. For the next six years, he ran a kind of roadshow with the objects, displaying them in banks, courthouses, and other public places all over Utah. (It may have been during this period that the shadowy black market deal with the German or Japanese collector almost came to pass.) It is astonishing that all the handling of the clay objects during these years—packing them up in one venue, driving them to another, unpacking them and putting them on display—failed to damage them seriously.

In 1974, the CEU museum once again asked Pilling for the loan of the figurines, and the rancher agreed. (Having never met the man, I can only guess at his motivations, which seemed to veer from doing his best to serve archaeology and let the figurines be shown to the public, to using them for his own traveling vaudeville show, to contemplating dumping them in the lap of a foreign treasure-seeker for a million bucks. Ambivalence must have been at the heart of Pilling's character.)

After 1974, the figurines were on display at the CEU museum for two years before its curators, making an inventory of the collections, noticed that there were now only ten of them. The eleventh, Morss's No. 2, one of the finest of the male figurines, the one with the kilt instead of the breech-clout, painted with lines and swaths of red and buff, "the only specimen," Morss noted, "in which ear pendants seem to be unmistakably represented," had somehow disappeared. Comparing photographs, the curators pinpointed the loss as occurring between September 1973 and January 1974. Presumably, it was filched by some thief toward the end of Pilling's roadshow. The curators despaired of ever seeing the irreplaceable object again.

The surviving ten figurines stayed on display at the CEU for the next three decades. In all those years, only one significant addition to the research about those objects took place. In 2004, Renee Barlow, whom Greg and I had guided to the high, inaccessible sites in Range Creek, entered the Pilling alcove and took a core from one of the timbers used in the construction of the ancient room in the front of the cave. From it she got a tree-ring date of A.D. 995–1005. There is little reason to believe that the room and the figurines were not contemporary with each other. If so, the figurines are now fixed in time as a thousand years old, crafted during the peak of Fremont prosperity in Range Creek.

In the spring of 2005, when I first visited the CEU museum and gazed at the Pilling figurines under glass, I could not take my eyes off them. Their pristine condition, despite their extreme fragility; the exquisite precision that had gone into the shaping and affixing of each bead of a hanging pendant or each twist of an apron; the enigmatic touches of paint that still clung to the clay (all eleven, the scholars guess, had originally been painted); the powerful sense that, arranged together, they announced some profound but unknowable communion with the supernatural—all these qualities flooded me with awe. Later, in other museums, I would see further examples of Fremont figurines, none of which could hold a candle to the Pilling array. In the words of Bonnie L. Pitblado and her six colleagues in a 2013 paper titled "Archaeological Fingerprinting and Fremont Figurines," they loom as "the most significant find of Fremont portable art ever documented."

Yet for all that, the purpose for which some ancient artist lovingly fashioned the Pilling figurines out of unbaked clay remains, in the epithet of Pitblado et al., "enigmatic." Morss's 1931 monograph is still the only full-scale study of the statuettes to be published. Later scholars have noted the similarities between the way the figurines represent the human body and the anthropomorphs depicted in many panels of Fremont rock art, but since those petroglyphs and pictographs themselves defy interpretation, that linkage goes only so far. Morss's theory that the figurines were designed for some kind of fertility ritual in an increase cult is as good a guess as any—but it remains only that, an educated guess.

Out of the blue, in November 2011, came a turn of events that astonished everyone who cared about the figurines. In 2013, Blaine Miller explained to me how it came to pass. Ken Cannon is the director of Archaeological Services at Utah State University in Logan. In 2011, his wife, Molly, traveled to Lincoln, Nebraska, to defend her Ph.D. dissertation in geography at the University of Nebraska. According to Miller, a stranger approached Molly Cannon, knowing of her connection to Utah anthropology, and confessed to the possession of an artifact that he felt should be returned to the museum in which it belonged. "He didn't want money," reported Cannon.

The upshot was a box mailed to the USU Museum of Anthropology in Logan. Inside it was an object and an unsigned note. It read:

> Sometime between 1978 and 1982 I came into possession of this piece by way of a vagabond acquaintance. He had told of "acquiring" it near Vernal, Utah. I have great interest and respect for this continent's native culture and have always hoped to somehow return this to wherever it had come from. It has rarely been out of the soft leather covering I put around it and I have kept it in the condition in which I received it.
>
> Recently in conversation I mentioned its existence to a friend and told of my desire to find its original home. They offered to help and were able to find that it may be the missing piece of the Pilling Figurine set. I am very excited at the prospect of it being returned to its proper place. Thanks to all who are involved in making this happen.

The object, still in good shape, looked identical to the lost No. 2 Pilling figurine. But there was a fly in the ointment. Over the years, thanks to the vast popularity of the figurines, the CEU had started making replicas of them to sell in the gift shop. By 2011, there were scores of copies of Pilling No. 2 circulating through private collections. How could the USU archaeologists prove that the figurine mailed from Nebraska wasn't one of those replicas?

The then director of the Museum of Archaeology, Bonnie Pitblado, took on the challenge. Through an exhaustive series of high-tech testings, involving such arcane disciplines as production-attribute analysis, scanning electron microscope analysis (to try to find traces of the particular glue with which Morss had reattached the broken ornaments in the 1950s), and trace-element analysis, Pitblado and her colleagues (including Molly Cannon) scrutinized the figurine. Their arguments, published in "Archaeological Fingerprinting and Fremont Figurines," are too technical to summarize here, but their conclusion is definitive: the statuette mailed in the box from Nebraska was indeed the original Pilling figurine No. 2. Returned after being lost for almost four decades, it now resides beside its companions under glass in the Prehistoric Museum in Price.

If the archaeology of things is a chronicle of loss, here stands a rare, inspiring tale of recovery. In 2013, I went back to Price to look at the Pilling figurines again. It did my heart good to see the collection whole, as I had never seen it before. But where, I wondered, was the hypothesized twelfth figurine that Morss thought might have once existed, to complete the half dozen gender pairs—the male companion to Morss's lonely female No. 1? If indeed there had once been a twelfth figurine, could it still lie hidden in the dirt or a pack rat nest inside the Range Creek alcove? Or was it gone forever, like the Alexandria scrolls?

It was Fred Blackburn, my mentor for *In Search of the Old Ones*, who in the spring of 2013 put me on the trail of the Telluride blanket. Fred's championing of what he called the "Outdoor Museum" had sprung from a passionate crusade he and a handful of friends had waged in the late 1980s and early '90s. Although their number included Winston Hurst, a professional archaeologist based in Blanding, Utah, most of the gang, like Fred, were self-taught amateur or "avocational" archaeologists. They called their ongoing mission the Wetherill–Grand Gulch Research Project. The powerful tool they wielded was "reverse archaeology."

In the 1890s, self-taught archaeologists dug scores of ruins in the Four Corners area. Some of these men were ranchers from Mancos and Durango, Colorado. None was more successful than Richard Wetherill, the oldest of five Quaker brothers who had emigrated to Mancos from the Midwest. Though decried by some of the scholars of the day (and for most of a century afterward) as ruthless looters and pothunters—an unsubstantiated claim was that the Wetherills used dynamite to open up ruins—Richard and his brothers were genuinely interested in science. They sold the artifacts, mummies, and skeletons they had unearthed to museums back east. The Wetherill materials still anchor the Southwestern collections of the American Museum of Natural History and the Museum of the American Indian, though it has been many decades since any of those objects was on public display.

Richard Wetherill's greatest discovery came in December 1893 in a small, obscure alcove he called Cave 7. Beneath a crumbling ruin, he and his partners dug up a familiar scattering of Ancestral Puebloan pots and tools. Then, a few feet below the surface, they hit sterile soil. Something convinced Wetherill to keep digging. Five feet down, the men made a monumental find. The former floor of the cave might once have been riddled with bottle-shaped pits that had been used as burial cists, although traces of them had eroded away. But the team found some ninety skeletons strewn in the dirt. Four-fifths of them showed evidence of violent death, with fatal projectile points scattered among the broken bones.

Cave 7 had been the site of a prehistoric massacre. Important though that discovery would prove, it paled beside the keen observations that Wetherill wrung from the site. There was no sign of pottery among the deep-buried debris. What struck Wetherill most forcefully, though, was the shape of the skeletons' skulls. Most of the ancients he and his brothers had dug up at Mesa Verde and in southeastern Utah had crania that were flattened in the back. These skulls, however, were fully rounded.

Digging in alcoves in Grand Gulch, another rancher turned archaeologist from southwestern Colorado, Charles McLoyd, had independently come to the same conclusion that Wetherill now made—that the victims of the massacre were a different people from the ones who had built the cliff dwellings that filled alcoves all over the Colorado Plateau. Wetherill proposed the term "Basket People," which was soon regularized as "Basketmakers." And he reasoned that those people had lived many centuries before the ancients he had dug up nearer the surface.

Wetherill's distinction, verified by later scholars, would find its way into the Pecos Classification adopted by Alfred Kidder and his colleagues in 1927. In making the seemingly simple logical leap to conclude that the lower dead must have preceded the upper dead in time, Wetherill—as Kidder himself would acknowledge with a tip of the hat six decades later—had been the first to apply the principle of stratigraphy in Southwestern archaeology. In general, barring geologic or human upheavals, the lower an object is in the ground, the older.

In the end, Wetherill would be proved wrong. The Basketmakers, we now know, were the direct ancestors of the Puebloans who had flourished in the Southwest after A.D. 750. They were all one and the same people—Anasazi, as they were first called by Kidder. But it was not until J. O. Brew proved the continuity between Basketmaker and Pueblo phases with his work at Alkali Ridge and his brilliant 1946 synthesis that this continuum was demonstrated beyond a shadow of a doubt. The flattened skulls of the later Puebloans, it would eventually be deduced, were primarily due to the hard cradleboards in which infants were carried.

Although the Wetherill collections reached the eastern museums intact and in pristine condition, over the decades after their accession the actual locations of the discoveries got lost. As important as the objects themselves were the places they came from. But eastern curators by and large were ignorant of the topography of the Southwest. They didn't hike the canyons of Cedar Mesa on their holidays. Wetherill's own notation system—sequentially numbered sites, such as Cave 7—gave little clue as to where those sites lay on the map of the Southwest.

Thus in Frank McNitt's admirable 1957 biography, *Richard Wetherill: Anasazi*, a Wetherill photo of Cave 7 was erroneously captioned "Grand Gulch." Fred Blackburn and his cronies knew that that location was wrong, but they had no idea where the "real" Cave 7 lay. Yet Blackburn and company were all devotees of the backcountry Southwest. They had hiked scores of canyons in which the Wetherills, and other early self-taught excavators, had dug.

In proposing their Wetherill–Grand Gulch Research Project, Fred and his allies hoped to use Richard Wetherill's own copious notes and correspondence to rediscover the proveniences of those priceless collections—to link the artifacts back to the alcoves from which they had been extracted. But at first, the team was looked at askance by museum curators. They were "amateurs," after all, dilettantes from the Southwest, romantic idealists who didn't know their way around a museum archive. It took much lobbying and proving their mettle to win the cooperation of those eastern guardians of the past. And, by their own admission, on their first visits to the big cities, Fred and his colleagues were intimidated by such august institutions as the American Museum of Natural History or Chicago's Field Museum.

But the Research Project began making cardinal linkages, and in doing so, the team won the grudging admiration of the curators. No locus more stubbornly resisted their sleuthing, however, than the all-important Cave 7. It took years of false stabs and the ingenuity of a Sherlock Holmes in parsing Wetherill's notes before, one day in September 1990, in a tributary of Butler Wash in southeast Utah, Owen Severance and Winston Hurst swept aside the tamarisk and, 1893 photo in hand, came to the mouth of an unprepossessing alcove. Hurst stopped in his tracks and exclaimed, "Shit! This is it!"

The fruit of the Research Project labors has been chronicled in an excellent 1997 book by Fred Blackburn and Ray Williamson, titled *Cowboys and Cave Dwellers*. Yet almost two decades later, despite the disbanding of the team, Blackburn and Hurst continue to be passionately engaged in reverse archaeology.

No search of the backcountry in recent years would prove more maddening, yet in the end more improbably wonderful, than the effort to discover the site from which two ranchers in 1896 had removed the Telluride blanket, one of the most astounding "things" ever found in the prehistoric Southwest.

Mel Turner was one tough hombre. In the 1890s, to run cattle and homestead in the remote region in southeastern Utah that he chose for his domain meant living as close to the edge as a cowboy could. His regular partner (perhaps his only one) was his nephew Ed Turner. The Turners may well have preferred to keep the whereabouts of their open-range spread a hazy secret. One contemporary newspaper clipping placed Turner's stomping grounds no more precisely than "60 or 70 miles from Thompson Springs, Utah"—that locale being a bleak whistle stop on the Denver and Rio Grande Railroad line between Grand Junction, Colorado, and Green River, Utah. When "renegade Utes" escaped their reservation and began to infringe on Turner's range, the territory of Utah dispatched cavalry to help chase the Indians away. The captain in charge of that mission described the trail to Turner's outback as "fearful" and "beyond white men."

Latter-day archival research has dug up a few bare facts about Mel Turner. Born in Maine in 1851, he migrated to Utah sometime around 1880. His first domicile was a cave. A photograph of Turner in middle age reveals a handlebar mustache, a broad forehead, and wide-open, vacant-looking eyes. In a 1901 newspaper clipping, Turner was saluted as "a model of industry, thrift and integrity, honored and respected by all who know him." He was reputed to be prodigiously strong.

But in 1908, Turner had a horseback accident in which he suffered severe head injuries. He was never the same thereafter. Although he lived to the age of seventy-nine, he spent his last decade alone on another ranch near Paradox, Colorado. According to historians Lee Bennett and Bill Sagstetter, during these years,

> Because of strange behavior a guard had been hired to keep an eye on him. But he had managed to elude the guard and showed up at the Paradox general store demanding a rope with which to hang himself. The frightened customers and store owner managed to lock the doors, locking themselves inside and Mel outside. The sheriff was dispatched. The under-sheriff drove the old man to the hospital in Montrose for treatment. On the way there Mel commented, "When I came here there was nothing but Indians."

Mel Turner died in the Colorado State Mental Hospital in Pueblo, Colorado, on September 8, 1932.

Like many another rancher, Mel and Ed Turner made a hobby of searching for old Indian relics. One day in 1896, as they were out herding cattle, they caught sight of a shallow alcove in a cliff about three hundred feet above the range, a little more than a third of the way up the massive sandstone butte that loomed above them on the southeast. It looked to their trained eyes like the kind of place the Moqui (the cowboy term for Anasazi) might have inhabited, so they tied off their horses and scrambled up to the alcove.

When they got there, at first they might have been disappointed. A single dilapidated, poorly built mud-and-stone granary stood near the front of the cave. But in the dim recesses of the alcove, they saw that the ceiling was coated with centuries' worth of soot from ancient campfires. There was a substantial fill of dirt covering the sandstone floor, so the Turners started digging.

In 1896, it was still perfectly legal to probe for ancient artifacts in the Southwest, and to keep what you found, even on public land. The Antiquities Act would not be passed for another decade. It did not take long for the Turners to make the find of a lifetime.

Precisely what Mel and Ed found in the fill at the back of the cave is revealed only in a single, elusive document—a copy of the Telluride, Colorado, *Daily Journal* for August 14, 1896. A typed transcript of that article was incomplete, a big chunk evidently missing, so Fred Blackburn, as well as Bill and Beth Sagstetter, began an exhaustive search for the original—a search that lasted several years. In the musty archives of the Telluride Historical Museum, Fred found that the entire run of the 1896 *Daily Journal* had burned. At last the museum turned him loose on a stack of unsorted old newspapers. The very last paper that he turned over was the August 14 issue—on which the complete story of the Turners' find depended.

According to that account, the climb to the alcove three hundred feet above the plain "was reached by easy stages of terraces and projecting rock. The last terrace before the opening of the caves was out of reach, but [the Turners] managed to throw a rope around a rock and ascended without difficulty."

Mel Turner and his nephew Ed had strong connections with Telluride, even though the mountain town lies a good 120 miles as the crow flies (and much more as the trail wends) from their Utah homestead. In 1901, in fact, Mel would marry Maggie Dresser, daughter of the owner of the *Daily Journal*, the newspaper that five years earlier had published the account of the cowboys' discovery in the remote alcove.

According to that account, the Turners were digging through the fill at the back of the cave when they encountered a firepit.

A white, fleecy substance was seen protruding from the fine ashes. It was pulled out and found to resemble a mass of woolen strings. It had been used as a stopper to a large earthern vessel perfect in condition and of native workmanship. Scraping aside the ashes the vessel was lifted out and its contents deposited on the floor of the cavern.

The stopper in the mouth of the vessel—an olla, or large ceramic water jar—was a skein of cotton yarn. Inside the jar the men discovered a bone awl and an amazing sixteen-foot-long string of beads, seven thousand of them all told. No ordinary beads, they were "very small, black and red" and were "brittle as glass and shiny as ebony." But even more amazing was the blanket, neatly folded and tucked away inside the olla. In perfect condition, the tassels still attached at the corners, the blanket, when unfolded, measured fifty-seven by fifty-nine inches.

Perhaps Ed and Mel Turner failed to appreciate just how special the blanket was. Perhaps they were simply generous fellows. Or perhaps they needed money. In any event, sometime in 1896 or shortly after, the Turners either gave or sold the blanket to a Telluride banker named W. E. Wheeler, who was a collector of Indian relics. The blanket remained in Wheeler's possession until his death in 1935, though how many people knew about it is unclear.

One of them, however, was Jesse Nusbaum. Mesa Verde National Park, which lies about seventy miles by road south of Telluride, was established in 1906. But during its early years, the stunning cliff dwellings first discovered there by Anglos (including the Wetherills) in the late 1880s were haphazardly administered. Cattle still grazed all over the mesa, and no museum had been built to house the artifacts found in the ruins. It was not until 1921 that the Colorado-born Nusbaum, who had trained under Alfred Kidder, was appointed superintendent of the park. He became, in fact, the first archaeologist hired anywhere by the National Park Service.

As Fred Blackburn discovered in his research, about the time that Nusbaum directed the construction of the first Mesa Verde museum, he approached Wheeler. According to Blackburn, Nusbaum "received a handshake or verbal promise from Wheeler that at some point the blanket and its accompanying artifacts would become the property of Mesa Verde National Park. No documents were ever drawn and no legal claim to the blanket was ever established."

Wheeler's bank folded in the crash of 1929, and when the man died six years later, all his belongings reverted to his wife, Antoinette. Apparently sick of living in the derelict mining town, she promptly took off to travel the world, eventually settling down in the ritzy Brown Palace Hotel in Denver. Everything she didn't want to take with her, Antoinette packed into barrels, crates, and suitcases and gave to a fellow Telluridian to keep in storage. Among that baggage was the Telluride blanket.

Thus the priceless relic was relegated to a dusty corner of a dry goods store. For the first of several times, it came close to disappearing forever.

On my visit to his house in Cortez, Colorado, in April 2013, Fred told me the story of the Telluride blanket, about which I knew almost nothing. And he urged me to head up to the mountain town to see the blanket for myself, now that it had finally been properly curated and displayed by the Telluride Historical Museum. Ironically, Fred had been born in the same building in 1950, when it served as the local hospital.

I had spent a lot of time over the years in Telluride, hiking and climbing and participating in Mountainfilm, the spirited festival devoted to outdoor adventure at the end of May each year. But I had made only the most cursory tour of the museum, which is housed in a venerable brick building on Gregory Avenue, three blocks uphill from Colorado Avenue, the lively main drag. I think I dismissed the place as a parochial small-town monument to itself, the display cases cluttered with bric-a-brac from the mining days, with only a token nod to the Indians who might have roamed the box canyon before 1875.

It was raining and chilly when I left Cortez. Above 9,000 feet, the rain turned to snow. As I crested Lizard Head Pass, at 10,222 feet, visibility was down to fifty yards and the temperature stood at nineteen degrees Fahrenheit. I waved down a snowplow driver to ask if he thought I could negotiate, even in my all-wheel-drive SUV, the twisting descent past Ophir to the San Miguel valley without sliding off the precipice. Then I managed the rest of the drive at a 5-mph crawl.

Telluride was as dead as I had ever seen it, caught in the mudseason lull between the skiers' paradise of winter and the wildflower riot of summer. The museum was closed, but, thanks to Fred, Erica Kinias, the young executive director, had agreed to meet me there and show me the blanket. On a gloomy April afternoon, with the snowflakes still coming down, I was treated to that rare privilege—a museum all to myself.

The blanket now reposes under glass in a climate-controlled vitrine, half unrolled to show off its glories. At first sight, it took my breath away. Woven of cotton, a relatively rare crop in the prehistoric Southwest, in an exquisitely tight herringbone pattern, the blanket remains in pristine condition 117 years after the Turners dug it out of the Utah alcove. Bands of white, red, and dark brown repeat a longitudinally striped design down the length of the tapestry. The loose tassels at the corners, like handles, are as intact as the blanket itself. Peering close, I saw that the red bands were interspersed with solitary, minuscule threads of a single white filament, eight of them running through each red stripe.

"There are only a tiny handful of known intact Ancestral Puebloan blankets," Kinias told me. "The others are in private collections. And this is the finest of them all.

"In 2007, we radiocarbon-dated the blanket to 1040 to 1272 A.D.," Kinias went on. "But there's still so much we don't know. What was the blanket used for? I don't think it was utilitarian. I think it was an heirloom, passed down within a family. We're hoping to get a grant to study the blanket further. There are three things in particular that we want to learn."

Kinias enumerated them. "What were the dyes created from? Where was the source of the cotton? Experts argue that cotton could not have been grown anywhere near the alcove in which the blanket was found. But where was the source? And was the blanket woven in some far-off place and carried there, or was the raw cotton transported from somewhere else and woven near where the Turners found it? And you see this stain?" She aimed her finger at a faint brownish smear on the fabric, its only blemish. "It may be pack rat urine. We'd like to find out."

I spent an hour simply staring at the Telluride blanket, murmuring out loud between questions directed at Kinias. Yes, it was only a "thing." But an hour's perusal did not begin to assuage my curiosity. Not only had I never seen anything like it—the Telluride blanket, I decided, was the single most remarkable prehistoric artifact I had beheld anywhere in the Southwest.

Eino Pekkarine was born in Telluride in 1911. His family ran the local dry goods store. Having received the crates and suitcases that Antoinette Wheeler left behind in 1935, he simply stacked them from floor to ceiling in the store. At some point Antoinette wrote to him to say that, since she had never paid Pekkarine a storage fee, all the stuff was his to keep.

For some reason, Pekkarine never evinced any curiosity as to what the Wheeler boxes and barrels contained. In 1970, thirty-five years after he had agreed to store the discarded belongings, a newcomer to Telluride, Harriette Billings, befriended Pekkarine, whom she later described as "a small, cherub-like man who played the piano and was often referred to as the 'town intellectual.'" One day Billings asked Pekkarine, "What is in that room?"

"Oh, that is Mrs. Wheeler's stuff and she gave her belongings to me," Pekkarine answered. He added that not only had he never opened the crates and barrels, but he had no interest in them. Billings was free to open them up.

Most of the containers were nailed shut. Laboriously, Billings pried loose their covers one by one. Inside the barrels she found "rare china and crystal," but also all kinds of junk. She was able to open all the containers but one, a locked tan suitcase with a missing key.

In 1973, Pekkarine was hit by a car in the streets of Telluride. He died three days later in a Grand Junction hospital after a blood clot caused either a stroke or a heart attack.

The tan suitcase ended up at the historical museum, which had been founded seven years before. It was not until December 1974 that the museum finally opened the suitcase. Inside it was the blanket. The skein of cotton yarn that had served as the stopper in the olla was also there, along with an old photograph of an Ancestral Puebloan ruin. But the bone awl and the sixteen-foot "necklace" with the seven thousand shiny beads were not. Those objects, along with the olla itself, are apparently lost forever. Tantalizingly, however, when the blanket was unfolded, the faint impressions left in it by the awl and the beads could still be discerned.

For another fifteen years, the Telluride blanket floated in a perilous limbo. In the 1970s, Arlene Reid became the first curator of the museum. Almost singlehandedly, Reid built the collections of historic documents and prehistoric artifacts that gave the museum credibility. During those years, Fred Blackburn worked with her as a volunteer. He became familiar with all kinds of relics housed there, and he pored over the institution's research files, but he never heard a word about the blanket. In retrospect, Fred believes that Reid may have hidden it under her bed, to protect it against thieves.

Sharon Clark, a later collections manager for the museum, believes that Reid either did not appreciate the value of the blanket or did not let on to others that she did. According to Clark, "it sat for years [in the museum], unlabeled next to a couple of Navajo rugs." Somehow, the first professional textile expert to discover the blanket, Kate Peck Kent, got wind of the matchless artifact. Kent worked out a deal with Reid that she could publish a photo of the blanket in her monograph

Prehistoric Textiles of the Southwest (1977), only if she stated that the object was kept in an unspecified private collection.

In an unpublished manuscript, Kent waxed lyrical about the object:

> The blanket is not only in good condition, but is an exceptionally fine piece technically. The weave is expertly done. Weft stripes are very exact in width. The direction of twill ribs changes regularly with each shift from a red-white band to a brown one. The selvages are tight and flawless. The blanket could only have been produced by an experienced weaver. While fragments of brown/red/white twill are very common in Pueblo III Anasazi sites . . . no other complete specimen exists.

Despite this published encomium, the Telluride blanket would still come perilously close to vanishing—not into the rubbish bin, but into the hands of a private collector. It would take a heroic effort by Fred Blackburn, collaborating with another Telluride curator, Lauren Bloemsma, to rescue the irreplaceable artifact.

In April 2013, Fred told me, "Around 1992, I saw an article in the newspaper stating that the Anasazi blanket was on display in the Telluride Historical Museum. I said to Victoria [Atkins, Fred's wife], 'Let's go up and look at it.'

"By then, Keith Laquey was the curator. We saw the blanket in a display case, rolled up next to some historic Navajo blankets. Laquey took it out of the case and just flung it open across the table, like this"—Fred pantomimed a reckless unfurling of the blanket. "I said, 'Holy shit!' Victoria and I knew what we were seeing. We knew it was cotton, and we knew it was unique."

According to Laquey, when he took over as curator in 1988, he found the museum's collections in a shambles. In the summary of Beth and Bill Sagstetter, whose "Unraveling the Mysteries of the Telluride Blanket" is the definitive work on the subject,

Textiles and photographs were nailed to the wall. Coal dust was everywhere from the furnace. [Laquey] was shown an old jewelry case, full of dust, with several Indian blankets and rugs all wadded and mixed together. There was no security at this time. Worst of all, he noted that the back wall of the museum—where the blanket was stored—was starting to crumble.

Laquey's first priority was to raise the funds to restore the museum building itself. Recognizing the potential value of the Telluride blanket, he and some of the museum's directors pondered selling the artifact to raise that money. There was an undercurrent of feeling that since the blanket had come from a far-off part of Utah, it had nothing to do with Telluride history.

Blackburn and Atkins vehemently disagreed. Despite their opposition, however, Laquey and the directors secured a loan from a local bank. While the museum was being restored, the bank held the Telluride blanket as collateral. Atkins managed to convince both bank and museum to entrust the Anasazi Heritage Center in Dolores, where she worked as an archaeologist, to curate and conserve the blanket in the interim.

As Fred recounted, "Laquey really wanted to sell it. He thought he could bail out the museum. I tried to talk him out of it. Eventually Laquey quit as curator. For years, I kept encouraging the museum not to sell the blanket. I kept pestering them. Several others got involved. We thought we could make the blanket so famous, the museum wouldn't dare sell it."

In 2005, Lauren Bloemsma took over as curator of the Telluride Historical Museum. She knew nothing about the bank's having claimed the blanket as collateral, for by then, for reasons that remain murky, the artifact was stashed away in the museum's attic. Since the reopening of the building in 2000, five years had passed without adequate exhibit facilities being installed. The problem was money. According to Bloemsma, several museum professionals, one of them a colleague of Victoria Atkins at the Anasazi Heritage Center, declared that the Telluride museum should surrender ownership of the blanket because the institution was too rundown to care for it properly.

The museum's own board of directors was split down the middle on the question, half of them wanting to sell the blanket to raise funds for the other collections. But Bloemsma dug in her heels. Along with Blackburn and Sagstetter, she organized a public display of the textile, complete with local police guard, to raise awareness of the unique treasure and to raise enough funds to conserve it in state-of-the-art conditions. Among the attendees was Kent Erickson, chief financial officer of the Telluride Ski Resort, who had become aware of the blanket during the years it was not on display. On each visit to the museum, he would ask Bloemsma for another look at the ancient textile, and she would oblige. Now Erickson made a donation of $50,000 to the campaign, which secured its success.

Thus Blackburn, Bloemsma, and their allies ultimately won the day. In 2007, the Telluride blanket went on permanent display—in a climate-controlled case, with foolproof security alarms. After more than a century of coming perilously close to vanishing, one of the most extraordinary artifacts ever found in the Southwest has been saved for posterity.

It would take a monumental effort, however, to solve another essential mystery about the Telluride blanket. By the 1990s, no one knew where Mel Turner had run his cattle and built his homestead—only that it lay somewhere in San Juan County, the largest of Utah's twenty-nine counties, stretching across 7,820 square miles. The provenience of Mel and Ed Turner's landmark discovery—the location of the alcove in which they had found the olla that held the blanket—was utterly unknown.

The only possible clue, it seemed, was the old photograph of the Ancestral Puebloan ruin that had accompanied the blanket when it fell into W. E. Wheeler's hands, and that had stayed connected with the artifact ever since. A hand-lettered caption read, "Prehistoric Ruins in So. Utah Taken by E. Turner Given to W. E. Wheeler." Presumably, the photograph depicted the alcove in which the Turners had discovered the blanket.

At the tail end of their hugely productive Wetherill–Grand Gulch Research Project, Blackburn and Winston Hurst took on this new challenge. They scrutinized the photograph, looking for any clues to the location of the ruin. It was an unremarkable edifice, yet with enough distinctive features—a standing wall that adumbrated a second-story room that had fallen apart, two intact square doorways, and the crumbling remains of a T-shaped doorway—to give the site a unique fingerprint. The alcove itself had distinctive features, too: a thin roof that stretched evenly over the dwellings, a loose boulder resting atop its center.

Blackburn and Hurst were quite sure they had never seen the ruin. They showed the photograph to a number of friends who had hiked all over the canyon country, but none of them recognized the ruin. In 1991, Hurst put out a feeler in a copy of the *San Juan Advertiser*, which he followed up in the summer 1994 issue of *Blue Mountain Shadows*, a quirky but important journal devoted to the history and prehistory of the Four Corners area. The two-page article was called "The Mysterious Telluride Blanket." Reproducing the image of the ruin, Hurst pleaded,

> We urge the readers of this article to study the photograph in Figure 2 carefully, and help us locate the ruin. It appears to be easily accessible to cattle and other agents of change, and is probably in much worse condition today than it was when the photograph was taken. Tips regarding the location can be called in to Winston Hurst . . .

The article closed with Hurst's phone number and address.

The challenge went unanswered for a decade. The eureka moment that suddenly emerged in 2004 came in such an improbable fashion as to unfold like the convoluted plot of some fairy tale.

Residents of Georgetown, Colorado, Bill and Beth Sagstetter made regular excursions into Utah to hike the backcountry in search of ruins and rock art. As Bill Sagstetter later wrote,

In June 2004, Beth and I had just paid for several books at Edge of the Cedars Museum in Blanding, Utah. On the way out the door I picked up a copy of *The Blue Mountain Shadows* Magazine and saw an article by Winston Hurst (whom we had known since 1987), but since we had just paid for a stack of books, I set it down and walked out. But something made me go back in and buy the magazine.

Driving to Bluff, Beth was reading aloud Winston's article on "The Mysterious Telluride Blanket." I glanced over to see a photograph that almost caused me to lose control of the vehicle. Pictured here was the very first cliff dwelling I had ever found! I was immediately transported back to 1968. I remember looking for cliff dwellings using William H. Jackson's Hayden Survey Report. I was very discouraged because for several years I could not find a single cliff dwelling. Being young and inexperienced and being in a very remote area, I got lost reading the maps incorrectly. Running low on gas and water, I suddenly thought I glimpsed a window about a quarter of a mile away. This had actually happened frequently, and had never panned out. But still I hiked to it, losing it in the trees on the way, and then spotting it again. Then finally, there it was—my first cliff dwelling!

Sagstetter, however, did not immediately contact Hurst, as he assumed that more savvy explorers than he had long ago solved the "mystery." It was only after several weeks that he phoned his old friend. To his astonishment, Hurst reported that in the preceding ten years, no one had come forth with a positive identification of the ruin. Sagstetter mailed off his own photographs of the cliff dwelling from

1968. In an email, Hurst responded, "This is indeed a perfect match. I'm pretty stoked about getting out there with you in September. I've notified Fred . . ."

Because that first ruin had meant so much to him personally, Sagstetter had no trouble thirty-six years later recalling exactly where it lay. The upshot was that on September 17, 2004, Bill and Beth Sagstetter, Hurst, Blackburn, and their fellow desert sleuths Joe Pachak, Terry and Susan Tice, and John and Susie Mansfield set out from Blanding to drive for hours to the remote range where the ruin lay. Bill Sagstetter's memory was dead on. It took only a few minutes to hike across level ground to the old cliff dwelling, which, surprisingly, had deteriorated relatively little in the past 108 years. There, Hurst and Pachak started mapping the ruin and the alcove, while Blackburn searched the walls for old inscriptions—a pursuit in which he was leading expert in the Southwest.

Something didn't feel right to Hurst, and in a matter of minutes, he put his finger on the problem. The 1896 newspaper article had reported that Mel and Ed Turner had dug through five feet of fill to find the olla. But this cliff dwelling rested on a bedrock floor, with only inches of scattered fill deposited here and there. What was more, the alcove was too moist. Relics stashed inside it would not have survived the centuries of weathering. To the whole team's chagrin, Hurst concluded that the cave from which the Telluride blanket had been retrieved had to lie elsewhere.

As the Sagstetters later picked up the story,

> Terry Tice and John Mansfield had been studying the 1896 newspaper article. The article described a cave about 300 feet above the cliff dwelling ruin. John and Terry scrambled up the cliff. About an hour later they returned asking if a cave with an inscription dated 1896 and if the names of Ed T and M R Turner would be of interest? Fred said: "Are you jerking my chain?"
>
> They replied: "No! The signatures are there and written in red!"

The whole team scrambled up to the higher alcove. There they found the dilapidated granary and the heavily sooted ceiling in the deepest recesses of the cave, beneath which a substantial fill of dirt and ashes still covered the natural floor. Blackburn carefully studied the faded inscriptions and verified their authenticity. These latter-day sleuths had evidently found an easier route to the alcove than the one the Turners had climbed, for it required no lassoing of a projecting rock to gain entry.

After 108 years, the provenience of the Telluride blanket had been rediscovered. None of the coups of reverse archaeology that Hurst, Blackburn, and their teammates had pulled off in the previous years outdid the thrill and gratification of this one.

A month later, a kind of ad hoc advisory council met at the Telluride Historical Museum. The team agreed to document the great find, and the Sagstetters offered to compile the definitive narrative about the matchless blanket. But in the dim interior of the remote alcove, all the searchers had recognized that the deep fill might very well still conceal ancient artifacts. The team agreed never to identify in print the location of the alcove, for fear that pothunters might journey there and loot it. Only a proper excavation by professionals sometime in the future could responsibly cast new light on that nondescript but stunning prehistoric hiding place.

Having spent my hour in the museum in rapt admiration of the Telluride blanket, I was of course eager to visit the alcove in which the Turners had found it. Fred agreed to tell me where it was, as long as I promised not to disclose the location in print. (Even as I pledged my troth, a memory of the treasure map some of the readers of *In Search of the Old Ones* had conjured out of my book flashed glumly through my brain. This time, I vowed, I would be no more specific than "a place in southeast Utah.")

In late April 2013, I headed out there with two friends, Connie Massingale and Stephanie Scott. Connie, who lives in Castle Valley, only about a mile from Greg Child's house, had become a regular partner on backcountry prowls with Greg and his then nine-year-old daughter Ariann—the pluckiest wilderness hiker her age that I had ever teamed up with. Stephanie is a Colorado-based freelance photographer who had also caught the bug on three or four several-day outings with me in southern Utah.

With USGS topo map in hand, on which Fred had inked a tiny X, the three of us left the car parked on the obscure dirt road and headed through the bunch grass toward the cliff at the base of the massive gray butte that loomed ahead of us. What ensued was an exercise in prolonged frustration. For three hours we traversed right and left along the foot of the cliff. We found a couple of small ruins, but they looked nothing like the one that Bill Sagstetter had discovered in 1968. I scrambled two hundred feet up the slabs above in a vain search for an alcove—any alcove—that might resemble the deep cave with the sooted ceiling where the Telluride blanket had lain undisturbed for at least six hundred years.

"Goddamn it, Fred!" I said out loud. By late afternoon, it was clear that he had drawn his X in the wrong place. It had been nine years since Fred had made his own discovery of the Turners' alcove. Two scenarios sprang into my suspicious brain.

One was that Fred's memory was a little off. I myself had sometimes "misplaced" ruins, even to the extent of being unable to find again a site I had blundered upon by chance years before. Yet Fred had as keen a topographical acumen as anyone I knew. And that fact led naturally to the second, more fiendish possibility.

I remembered the occasion, more than twenty years ago, when I had started to put my own X on a topo map, after Fred had guided me to a little-known ruin. "That's a no-no," he had blurted.

"Why?" I asked.

"Keep it up here," he lectured, pointing to his head.

The second scenario, then, was that Fred had deliberately misplaced the X, leaving me to earn my own discoveries rather than follow his trail of crumbs. Another memory from 1993 came to me. Fred had guided photographer Terry Moore and me to an utterly nondescript bend of a canyon on Cedar Mesa. Then he had sat down on a rock and told us, "Okay, find it. It's within a hundred yards of here." (He didn't bother to tell us what "it" was.)

As Terry and I poked our heads under ledges and into crannies like kids on an Easter egg hunt, Fred cackled with malicious glee. But when we found the small, nearly intact gray pot stowed in a narrow crevice, we tasted a bit of the frisson of original discovery—as we would not have if Fred had simply led us directly to the crevice and the pot.

Camped out in a clearing among the piñons that evening, Connie, Stephanie, and I reread Hurst's *Blue Mountain Shadows* piece and the Sagstetters' "Unraveling the Mysteries," as we mused over the strange twists and turns of the history of the Telluride blanket. Neither Connie nor Stephanie had yet seen the object itself, but now they promised themselves journeys to Telluride to pay homage.

The next day, Connie had to return to Castle Valley. I apologized to her for the wild goose chase, but she was so enthralled by the remote region itself that she vowed to return a week later with her husband, Phil. Stephanie and I decided to stay on for three more days of exploring. I'd made visits to this outback twice before, so I knew that ruins and rock art were scattered all across it. The weather was holding splendidly, with warm, crisp, almost windless days alternating with cool, starry nights.

After saying goodbye to Connie, Stephanie and I hiked to a hallucinatory petroglyph panel I had visited before, where she shot off a good hundred digital pictures in half an hour of devout admiration. And halfway up another massive butte, we discovered a fine ruin that was all but hidden from below. Because it took a scary climb to get into the site, it was relatively undamaged, a two-story structure wedged into a vertical chimney, with many gorgeous sherds of Mesa Verde black-on-white pottery strewn across the ledge.

We camped again in our piñon grove, sorry that we had had to give up on the Turners' alcove, but pleased with the day's finds. For the morrow, I had my eye on yet another squarish butte farther west, about seven hundred feet tall, with ledge after ledge contouring toward the blocky summit. No ruins were visible from below, but the butte itself, which I hoped to traverse in its entirety, promised a challenging route-finding puzzle in its own right.

We started up a long, gradually ascending sandstone fin that formed the far end of the butte. Half a mile into our ramble, I spied a gap in the overhanging cliff above that would allow passage to the skyline notch just below the summit. But Stephanie, peering to our left, thought she saw, several hundred yards away, the tiny square of a window in some Ancestral Puebloan structure, tucked into a corner of the butte. I got out my binoculars and verified her hunch.

Twenty minutes later, we stood before a small Pueblo II or III structure. It looked as though it had been hastily and crudely thrown together. Stephanie's "window" was actually a big hole in the front wall that hinted at some pothunter's mischief. "It's too small to be a dwelling," I said to Stephanie, "but the door is in the ceiling, which would be weird for a granary." On the back wall of the alcove, some vestigial ocher handprints still clung to the spalling stone. Near them I noticed some modern graffiti—perhaps the "Kilroy-was-here"s of the pothunters themselves. Stephanie photographed everything in sight.

We wandered farther into the deep, narrow cave. The ceiling was thickly coated with charcoal. "It's a Basketmaker site," I murmured. "Much earlier than that structure out front." I touched the thick soil underfoot with my toe. "There could even be burials here. But of course it's not our right to find out." (In all the Ancestral Puebloan sites I had visited in the last twenty-five years, I had never succumbed to the itch even to scoop with my hands through the middens in front of the ruins or the dirt packed into the back crevices. That was a prohibition mandated not only by the Antiquities Act, but by a common-sense respect for the Old Ones.)

"Well, we found something," I said to Stephanie as we traversed back to the gap I wanted to climb toward the skyline. "A Snazi site, even if a mediocre one." (With a friend such as Stephanie, I felt comfortable using Vaughn Hadenfeldt's nickname for the Anasazi.)

"Yeah," she concurred. "I thought it was pretty cool, even so."

We were halfway up the butte when I suddenly flung my pack down. "Wait a minute," I said. "What were the names painted on the wall?" I had paid the graffiti so little attention, I couldn't recall them in any detail. "Did you photograph them?"

Stephanie scrolled back through the pictures she had shot in the alcove until she found the signatures. In red paint, they read:

M R TURNER

ED T.

"Shit!" I yelled. "That's the Turners. Mel and Ed."

"Of course!"

"I guess they went everywhere around here. Remember, they were supposed to have spent a lot of time looking for Indian stuff. So we found a Turner cave. That's pretty neat."

During the next four hours, we worked out a clever route, zigzagging from ledge to ledge, till we got to the summit notch. Then we found an even more devious route down the back side of the butte. But even though this side of the monolith faced south, the aspect favored by the ancients, we found not the slightest trace of the Ancestral Puebloans. Still, ours was a beguiling ramble.

Off the butte at last, I was trudging down a brushy ravine when I heard what sounded like a falling rock. In that instant, hiking behind me, Stephanie shouted, "David! Look!"

Only thirty yards away, on the far side of the ravine, a young black bear was dashing from ledge to ledge, panicked by our unexpected arrival. The sound I had heard must have been the creature falling off a short cliff, for now it slipped and fell again. "Whoa!" I muttered,

"Take it easy, buddy." But the bear had a mind of its own. Without a pause, it regained its footing and took off again, scrabbling across big stones until it disappeared around a far ridge.

"That's amazing," I said to Stephanie. "In all my time in the canyon country, I've only seen a couple of bears. Bear tracks, yes, but not the bears themselves."

"What a great day!" she rejoined.

Late that afternoon, worn out, we regained the SUV. In the passenger seat, Stephanie fell asleep, as I trundled back toward camp on the dirt road we had headed out in the morning. As we circled the butte we had climbed, I slowed to a crawl, wondering whether you could see the alcove with the structure and the Turner signatures from the level plain. And there it was, hovering above us on the right.

I slammed on the brakes. "Stephanie, wake up! Remember the old clipping." The crucial phrase was engraved in my memory: "It was a climb of three hundred feet or more, and was reached by easy stages of terraces and projecting rock." "That's about three hundred feet up!" I yelled at Stephanie. "Get out your camera again."

While she scrolled groggily back through her day's photos, I dug out the Sagstetter report and found the photo of the signatures on the wall in the blanket cave. "Here it is," said Stephanie. We stared at the Xeroxed photo and at Stephanie's image.

"It's a dead-on match!" I exclaimed. "We found the cave where the Turners dug up the blanket!"

"By accident."

"Yeah, we didn't even know we were there!" Both of us were reduced to idiotic laughter. "Goddamn it," I said when I'd recovered my breath, "if I'd known, I would have looked a lot more carefully."

Despite another search on the following morning, we never found the low alcove with the cliff dwelling in the 1896 photo that had rung bells of recognition in Bill Sagstetter's head, and that had led to the rediscovery of the blanket cave. Several weeks later, Fred Blackburn, who swore he hadn't intentionally sandbagged me with his misplaced

X, stuck his thumbnail on the map. "Here," he said, "you should've looked here." On the morning after our accidental discovery of the blanket cave, Stephanie and I had looked everywhere except the cliff corner where Fred laid down his thumbnail.

"Oh, well," I said to Fred. "We can always go back."

"Yeah," he answered, "and when you do, I'm coming along. There's a lot more to learn about that cave."

Three

CEDAR MESA REVISITED

titled one chapter of *In Search of the Old Ones* "In Praise of Cedar Mesa." By 1995 I had already made fourteen trips to that piñon-and-juniper-thick upland dissected by slickrock canyons in southeast Utah, on outings lasting between three and eight days, during which I had made scores of personal discoveries. But in the book I limited my narrative to two of the best finds of all, which occurred two weeks apart in late autumn 1993. The first happened when I was alone, in the middle of a four-day backpack; the second, with a single friend on a glorious one-day outing between chilly car camps on mesa-top benches.

Both were ruins that I found by accident, since in 1993 the secrets of Cedar Mesa were still closely guarded by a small number of cognoscenti. In my book, I did not name the canyons in which I stumbled across those small but stunning ancient sites. The second ruin, on a ledge one hundred feet above the twisting trickle of the stream, looked at first sight like a blank, windowless stone-and-mud wall festooned with carefully aimed loopholes through which the residents could spy on unwelcome intruders. But behind that façade, a row of pristine rooms, some of jacal construction (the walls made of sticks daubed with mud, rather than the usual laid and mortared stones), stretched from right to left, filling the deep recesses of the alcove. And those walls, both inside and out, were decorated with mystic bands and triangles, painted white with a clay-like substance called kaolin. Although I had never seen a photo of the place, I deduced at once that this must be the fabled Moon House, about which I had overheard devotees of the backcountry whispering to one another.

Two weeks earlier I had spotted the first ruin, the one I found on my solo outing, from the canyon floor six hundred feet below it, then had spent hours working out a devious scramble to reach it. Five nearly perfect masoned rooms, sharing common walls and stretching six feet from the bedrock floor to the brow of the overhang under which they nestled, stared south from the most majestic eyrie I had ever hiked to in Utah—a peninsula of sandstone hanging over vertical walls on all sides except the narrow ramp that gave access to it from the west. It is still the only Ancestral Puebloan site I have ever seen with a full 360-degree view of the horizon. Unaware of other searchers who might have visited the ruin before I did, I gave it my own nickname, Peninsula House. (Later I would learn that some of those others had bestowed on it a somewhat humdrum label, the Citadel.)

Twenty years on, Moon House and the Citadel are secrets no longer. Directions to both sites can be easily found on the Web. By now, those ruins have become so popular that the Bureau of Land Management officials who administer Cedar Mesa have seriously pondered closing them to visitation for good—as many other Ancestral Puebloan sites, including nearly all the cliff dwellings on Mesa Verde, have been for decades. Moon House is so accessible that the most casual hiker can get to it from his vehicle in half an hour, as a road delivers the ruin-bagger to the rim of the canyon directly overlooking the site. That road was originally a bare track used by archaeologists in the 1960s, after which the BLM closed it down. It happens to lie, however, on a "school section," an anomalous square mile of state land, so the San Juan County commissioners successfully forced its reopening.

To try to protect the extremely fragile ruin that is Moon House, the BLM has put laminated yellow signs inside the inner rooms forbidding entrance. On a bench outside the ruin, an ammo box contains a visitor register, a précis of the archaeological research that has illuminated Moon House's purpose as well as when it was built and abandoned, and a checklist of caveats for how to visit the place responsibly.

In 1993, it took me most of a late October day to get from my tent camp to the Citadel, via a route so circuitous and tricky that I'd hesitate to recommend it to others. But there's a much easier shortcut, as I discovered on my second visit—a nearly level canyon hike covering a mere two miles from the dirt road. There was no hint of a trail there in 1993, but by now the path is trampled solid with bootprints and festooned with cairns to guide those too lazy to read the map.

In my book, I wondered out loud whether I would ever see Moon House again, quoting Robert Frost: "Yet knowing how way leads on to way, / I doubted if I should ever come back." I ought to have known better. I've been back something like twenty times, and though I no longer hope to have the place to myself, as my friend and I did in

1993, it's still gratifying to show Moon House to other friends who have never seen anything like it, and to listen to their outbursts of incredulity.

Likewise with the Citadel, though I'm beginning to wonder if it's worth it. My buddy Vaughn Hadenfeldt, founder-owner of Far Out Expeditions in Bluff, Utah, used to make the Citadel a standard gee-whiz stop for his clients. But on a recent outing, he counted sixty-five visitors there—a nightmare apparition that made him want to flee in disgust.

One thing that keeps me coming back, however, is that for all the obvious glories of both sites, Moon House and the Citadel both possess subtle features that few visitors notice, but that profoundly enhance the power of those refuges. I wait till no one else is around before I show those hidden gems to my own friends.

Still, there's no denying the threat to both sites posed by the sheer numbers of visitors who flock there each spring and fall. Four or five years ago, as I approached the rim one day, I saw three hikers crawling through the small portal in the windowless façade at Moon House. I winced as I watched them yank hard on the edges of the doorway to pull their bodies through. But then I realized that they had brought their dog, and that the animal was unleashed, in violation of BLM rules. To my horror, the dog started scrabbling through the doorway, paws flailing away at the mortar.

"Get the goddamn dog out of the ruin!" I shouted at the top of my voice. The trespassers shooed Fido back through the doorway. The dog stood just below it, panting with its tongue hanging out, anxiously awaiting the return of its masters.

Twenty minutes later, as I climbed up the ledges to Moon House, I was preparing my diatribe. But the family had disappeared around the corner, no doubt to avoid my scolding. I thought better of chasing them down. *What's the point?* I mused. *I can't stand guard here day after day against idiots who don't know any better, and neither can the understaffed BLM.*

Within the last decade, websites giving GPS coordinates not only to Moon House and the Citadel but to many other ruins on Cedar Mesa have sprung up. Browsing through such postings recently, I came across a photo of a woman sitting on the sill of the doorway to one of the inner rooms at Moon House, holding her baby in her lap and beaming at the camera. Either she had failed to notice the sign prohibiting entry, or she and the dolt who took the picture (her husband?) had chosen not only to flout the interdiction but to celebrate her deed on the Web.

Of course, in writing a chapter called "In Praise of Cedar Mesa," I had no doubt put those ruins on the radar of folks who might otherwise never have heard of them. I could take refuge in the rationale my editor at *National Geographic* had thrown out to me like a life preserver years ago: "If a thing is worth doing, it's worth writing about." But the gloomy truth was unavoidable—*In Search of the Old Ones* had contributed to the damage Cedar Mesa was suffering at the hands of the family with the dog, the woman with the baby, and untold numbers of other visitors who tread heavily and take home souvenirs.

I might have been tempted during the last decade to turn my back on Cedar Mesa, for I knew that in other corners of the Southwest there were still many outbacks rich in ancient ruins and rock art that few people knew about. But I've done just the opposite. Since 1996, when my book was published, I've lost count of how many more trips I've made to Cedar Mesa, but the number is over fifty. At times, in fact, I believe that Cedar Mesa is my favorite place in the world. In this chapter, I'll try to explain why.

To be sure, desecration and disappearance are the inevitable fate of prehistoric wonders. The hooliganism of Napoleon's soldiers shooting off the nose of the Sphinx had its counterpart in the Southwest at least until the middle of the twentieth century. Cowboys and ranchers thought it good sport to use Ancestral Puebloan petroglyphs and pictographs for target practice. No matter how many times I've come across a panel on which the raw scalloped scars of bullets have obliterated the visages of the shamans and spirits whom the ancients invoked, I'm stung anew with shock and dismay.

Of course, weather and collapse take their toll on the monuments of antiquity, without the aid of human sacrilege. The fate of ruins is ruination—as with the statue of Ozymandias in Shelley's famous poem. The first time I found an unexcavated mesa-top pueblo, open to the air and the elements—at Yapashi, in Bandelier National Monument, a place that was once home to as many as five hundred people—I was deeply disappointed. Expecting something akin to a well-preserved cliff dwelling, I saw only mounds of rubble from which sprouted thickets of cholla. It was only after educating myself as to how to "read" these crumbled villages that I could delight in tracing the pattern of the roomblocks, or in roughly dating the habitation by the designs on the potsherds strewn everywhere, or in calculating where the nearest source of year-round water might be and how to get to it.

Sometime in the 1990s, Vaughn Hadenfeldt took me to a site on Cedar Mesa that he had discovered, which he called the Pottery Shrine. In an unremarkable bend of a shallow canyon in the nondescript middle of nowhere, I suddenly saw in the dirt all around me hundreds of sherds from broken ceramic vessels—not only grayware and smudged corrugated, but Mesa Verde black-on-white, Tusayan polychrome, and half a dozen other styles I couldn't name. I was astonished by the place. We spent two hours there, picking up sherds, dusting them off to bring out the color, turning them over in our fingers, then dropping them back exactly where we'd found them. Vaughn wondered out loud if the place was a special locus—a "shrine"—where the Ancestral Puebloans had come to break their pots, ritually "retiring" them. From the top of a short cliff, I could even imagine a woman throwing her vessel to the ground below, leaving its telltale scatter to testify to the act.

Just a year or two later, Vaughn took Winston Hurst to the Pottery Shrine. Having grown up in Blanding, Winston had spent many more years in the nearby canyons and mesas than had Vaughn, who had discovered southeast Utah only in his early thirties. Winston's reaction to Vaughn's special place was numb, even disconsolate. "Yeah," he told his friend, "when I was a kid, all of Cedar Mesa looked like this."

When I recently reminded Winston of that episode, he amplified in an e-mail, "It wasn't specific to Cedar Mesa. When I was a kid the sites around Blanding, even close to town, looked like that. Yesterday I was out on some sites in Comb Wash that get limited traffic, and their rich middens were so totally stripped of surface ceramics that I couldn't find a single diagnostic sherd to date the site from. As recently as the 1970s, they would have looked a lot like Vaughn's Pottery Shrine."

During the first years of my friendship with Vaughn, he was the mentor in things prehistoric, I the acolyte. But with far more free time to explore than he had, since guiding clients was the way he made a living, I started finding wonderful things on Cedar Mesa that Vaughn had never seen. We became colleagues in Snazi discovery, as we half-jokingly alluded to our passion.

One day I struck out solo on a trailless shortcut through the "p-j" (the piñon and juniper forest), trying to find a direct route to a ruin I had visited before. About a mile from the road, on the shoulder of a small sand dune, I discovered something amazing. A series of five or six flat sandstone slabs had been carefully laid out, as if to construct a gently descending staircase. The surfaces of every one were covered with potsherds and lithic flakes, in a dazzling variety of hues and patterns.

The pottery and flakes were Ancestral Puebloan, but I could not tell if the assemblage, the likes of which I had never seen elsewhere, was the work of a modern self-styled landscape artist, or even a New Age wacko. Recognizing that the spot—a shallow dune that looked like any of scores of others on every side—would be hard to find again, I stared carefully at the map before hiking on. (For various reasons, including my incompetence at things mechanical, I've never used a GPS in the Southwest.)

A few weeks later, I took Vaughn and his wife, Marcia, to the site, which I found again without much trouble. Vaughn, too, was dumbfounded, having never seen anything like it himself. We peered close at the lichens growing on the sherds, trying to guess the age of the construction from that botanical clue. Vaughn speculated that the site might conceivably mark a Ute burial. We started calling it the "Ute burial," but Marcia, bothered by the tendentious overtones of that name, suggested the more neutral "Pottery Steps" instead.

During the next few years, I returned to the Pottery Steps four or five times with friends I could trust. Once or twice it took a little circling through the p-j to find the site, but I never failed. None of those friends carried a GPS, or if one of them did, he kept it in his pack. All of my cronies were as stunned by the place as I had been on first discovering it.

Then, on perhaps my sixth return to the Pottery Steps, I couldn't find it. Irked at this hint of a lapse in my navigational skills, I resolved to make a more thorough search next time. And on that subsequent try, despite spending twice as long circling and meandering, I couldn't find the site again. Nor the next time.

It's barely possible that I've misplaced the Pottery Steps. But the far more likely scenario is that it's gone. On the last three tries, I found pottery scattered all through the forest, but nothing that even faintly resembled the careful assemblage of slabs, sherds, and lithics. It's gone completely, I believe. In recent years, some asshole (I choose the word advisedly) must have packed up all the goodies that had been laid out so lovingly, and then, to cover his crime, scattered the slabs themselves hither and yon.

The disappearance of the Pottery Steps is far from the only case of vandalism on Cedar Mesa I've witnessed over the years, but it's the one I grieve most deeply. The archaeology of things, to repeat, is an archaeology of loss—in this case, not simply of those beautiful sherds and flakes, but of what the whole thing meant, to whom, and when, and why.

Long before 1967, when archaeologists began to make systematic studies of Cedar Mesa, the place was a favorite cattle range. The path into Grand Gulch via its tributary below Collins Spring still sports a rusty, disused gate, as well as the dynamite gouges of the ranchers who in the early 1900s blasted a corridor out of the bedrock to blaze it as a livestock trail. Since 1968, cattle and sheep have been banned from the canyons, but ranchers still use most of Cedar Mesa as a lush open range. As I've learned firsthand, confrontations between those old-timers and us hikers can be less than cordial.

Many of the names strewn across Cedar Mesa date from the early cowboy days. I had long mused about their obscure origins, but in 2012, backcountry guide and author Steve Allen published his monumental two-volume *Utah's Canyon Country: Place Names*, the fruit of many years of dogged research. Allen lifts the veil from many of those quaint or forgotten appellations.

Collins Spring and Canyon, for instance, commemorate a pioneer cowboy from Bluff whose first name may be lost to history. Most likely, he helped dynamite today's trail. Pollys Pasture immortalizes either the wife of one of those early ranchers or a wayward mule that kept running away from its owner to return to the place of its birth. About Slickhorn Canyon, fourth longest on Cedar Mesa, Allen quotes old-timer DeReese Nielson: "My father told me that the first time he went there in that canyon [in the 1880s] there was Texans in there and they had these longhorn cattle and they left 'em in there a long time and none of 'em was branded and they just called 'em 'the slickhorn.'"

According to guide Pete Steele, who informed historian James Knipmeyer, Bullet Canyon got its name as follows: "In the lower part . . . the canyon is pretty much a straight shot to its junction with Grand Gulch. For a half mile or so you can see a small natural arch high on the west wall of Grand Gulch, as if someone had shot a huge rifle, making a bullet hole." (Bullet may also be an accidental variant on "bullocks," after the young bulls that once wintered in the canyon.) The Twist alludes to the fiendish switchbacks that the exhausted Mormon Hole-in-the-Rock expedition carved off the eastern edge of Cedar Mesa, as they dragged their wagons down to the San Juan River to establish Bluff in 1880. Salvation Knoll celebrates the promontory from the summit of which scouts from that expedition, lost in a blizzard, saw the Abajo Mountains and knew they were near the promised land. Cedar Mesa itself, in fact, was named by the Hole-in-the-Rock party, whose members, as was commonplace at the end of the nineteenth century, called the junipers that cover the mesa "cedars," even though the vaguely similar trees belong to different genera.

Some of the Cedar Mesa names are prosaic enough to suggest their origins without the need of Allen's exegesis: Water Canyon, Pine Canyon, Step Canyon, Owl Canyon, Long Flat, Brushy Flat, even Grand Gulch itself. Others have stories to tell. About Point Lookout, Mormon pioneer and author Albert R. Lyman wrote, "One may ride for hours at a stretch on the Cedar Ridge [Cedar Mesa] and see nothing but the standing or fallen trees immediately around him. A rise, therefore, affording a look at the distance, is a place of new inspiration." Hells Half Acre earned its pejorative label after a ranchers' fiasco. "There is just a small acre in the trees," DeReese Nielson told Allen. "They was holdin' the cattle there one time and they was noonin' the cattle, and the cattle got scared and stampeded out there, and after that, all the old cowboys called it 'Hell's Half Acre.'" Muley Point, offering one of the most sublime vistas on Cedar Mesa, likewise reflects a rancher's pragmatism. According to historian Walter Ford, "Old-timers say that Muley Point takes its name from the fact that it is shy of vegetation, like a Muley cow is shy of horns."

Here and there in the canyons, you run across old cowboy caches, with rusty shovels, crowbars, frying pans, and other debris tucked under overhangs or stashed inside wooden lockers. The signatures of early ranchers abound on the sandstone walls, and there are even several panels bearing cowboy petroglyphs, some of them obscene. It's strange, to my mind, that the old-timers seem to have been largely indifferent to the ruins and rock art of the Ancestral Puebloans, for none of the names they slapped on the landscape mirrors the legacy of the earliest inhabitants of all on Cedar Mesa. The cardinal exceptions are Richard Wetherill and his four brothers, ranchers from Mancos, Colorado, and their rivals in excavating ancient sites, Charles McLoyd, a rancher and miner from Durango, and his partner, Charles Cary Graham, a cowboy who lived near Bayfield, east of Durango. Whether we regard them today as pothunters or as self-taught archaeologists, those men dug up massive collections of artifacts, skeletons, and mummies among the ruins in the Cedar Mesa canyons during the 1890s. A good portion of what they retrieved ended up in museums.

In 1993, Fred Blackburn guided me via a shortcut side canyon to a major ancient ruin in Grand Gulch that the Wetherill brothers had dug a century before. After I had stared in awe at the inaccessible cliff dwelling that Richard's team had reached by using their lariats to tie logs end to end to craft a very shaky ladder, Fred led me to a fin of sandstone that protruded from the west wall of the six-hundred-foot-deep canyon. Reaching into a tiny cubbyhole at the base of the fin, he pulled out several old tin cans. Fred had found them lying in the open eight years earlier, and from their shape and design had deduced that they had probably once held the pork and beans and condensed milk that had fed the Wetherills as they worked away in the dead of winter. Inside one of the battered containers, I found Fred's note from 1985:

> This can may have belonged to Richard Wetherill. The solder at the bottom dictates to the late 1890s. Please leave as an important piece of the Outdoor Museum of Grand Gulch.

I wrote about that beguiling outing in *In Search of the Old Ones*, and for years after 1993, I guided friends on the shortcut hike Fred had taught me, culminating our visit by retrieving the cans. My friends and I marveled over those historic relics before carefully replacing them inside the cubbyhole.

Then one day about ten years ago, I reached into the cubbyhole and found—nothing. The cans were gone. Elsewhere in Grand Gulch, Fred had found the once easily legible carved signatures of Richard Wetherill's teammates from the 1890s rubbed out by recent visitors. One could imagine those effacements as the misguided work of self-styled conservationists who thought that all graffiti were deplorable. But whoever had taken the tin cans had ignored Fred's note. He, she, or they had packed up the cans and taken them home not to rid Grand Gulch of trash, but to loot it of treasure. I felt the same dismay as I had when I concluded that the Pottery Steps were gone forever.

Virtually all the names in common use for ruins and rock art on Cedar Mesa are unofficial, neither appearing on USGS topo maps nor winning endorsement from the U.S. Board on Geographic Names. Because of that fact, it's hard to trace their origins. Some may date back to the Wetherills, McLoyd, and Graham, although explicit references are hard to find. (In Richard Wetherill's field notes for Grand Gulch, the alcoves in which his team dug are alluded to mainly as Cave No. 7, Cave No. 11, and so forth.)

Most of the names we use today are descriptive, and it's not hard to discern their logic. Turkey Pen Ruin mistakes a dilapidated freestanding jacal room—a frieze of sticks still planted upright, with most of the mortar eroded away—for a cage in which the ancients might have kept their turkeys, one of only two animals they domesticated (the other being the dog). Split Level Ruin is adorned with a pair of well-preserved, connected rooms, the lower one thrust in front of the upper like the suburban split-level homes that came into vogue in the 1950s. Banister Ruin takes its name from a huge straight log (probably Douglas fir or ponderosa pine) suspended horizontally at chest height in front of the room block.

Moon House alludes to a pair of circles left blank in the middle of white painted bands on facing walls inside the finest room, which look very much like a crescent and a full moon. Jailhouse Ruin earns its name from a quadrangle of jacal in the front wall of one room from which the mud has eroded away, leaving crisscross sticks that suggest prison bars. The two Perfect Kivas on Cedar Mesa indeed feature kivas, circular underground chambers with doors in the roofs, that escaped the ravages of time to remain in pristine condition in the twentieth century.

The Green Mask Panel celebrates its most striking pictograph, a green-and-yellow-banded visage that may depict a severed, painted trophy head. Centering the Big Man Panel are spooky, hulking anthropomorphs that are taller than real humans. The Great Gallery is indeed great—probably the richest rock art assemblage on Cedar Mesa.

Over the years, Vaughn Hadenfeldt, Greg Child, and I have found scores of ruins and panels on Cedar Mesa that very few others seem to have discovered. We don't automatically name them, but shorthand labels have crept into our vocabulary. About ten years ago, Vaughn and I made our way to a beautiful, well-hidden, two-story ruin just under the rim of a canyon we thought we'd thoroughly explored. I jokingly called it Coat Peg House, because inside the largest room, a profusion of short sticks that had been mortared into the wall at head level stuck out like so many hooks to hang things on. Vaughn shortened the name to Peg House. We've both taken others to the place, but we would never insist that it be known henceforth as Peg House. So far, thank God, the ruin has escaped the Internet, by that or any other name.

And yet, an accidental poetry clings to place names casually bestowed. I have no idea who started calling a side canyon to Grand Gulch "Hardscrabble," or a plain bursting with stone outcrops "Hat Flat," but I relish those cognomens. About the history of another pair of unofficially named sites, Fred Blackburn filled me in. "The FBI Panel" is a cliff wall covered with some four hundred Ancestral Puebloan handprints. According to Fred, "It was named by either Pete Steele or Carl Mahon, who were among the first guides to take clients into the

Cedar Mesa canyons between 1940 and 1960." "Best Forgotten Kiva" is a wonderful, obscure ruin in a remote canyon bend. Fred: "Kent Frost did a lot of guiding in Grand Gulch in the 1950s and '60s and probably knew the country better than anyone, but he was secretive about it. When I found that ruin in the 1970s, I knew Kent had been there, but the site was so pristine it made the hair on the back of my head stand on end. As I looked at it, I thought the only hope for its preservation was if few people knew about it, so I called it Best Forgotten Kiva."

The enduring appeal of Cedar Mesa for me, after as many as sixty trips there, lies in the fact that I'm still finding ruins and rock art I've never seen before. And if I'm taking friends to sites I've previously visited, I know exactly how to choose a day-long hike full of prehistoric wonders during which we won't cross paths with a single other hiker.

I've also learned a trick of access that applies better to Cedar Mesa than to most other canyon systems anywhere in the Southwest. My first explorations there were backpacks and llama treks lasting as long as eight days. In the early 1990s, I hiked the length of Grand Gulch in two eight-day jaunts, the first from the trailhead at the Kane Gulch ranger station to an exit at Collins Spring, the second from Collins Spring down to the San Juan River and back. Those are standard itineraries today for newcomers to Cedar Mesa. But over the years, I figured out trailless shortcuts linking ledges and gullies that would allow me to get deep into the wilderness on a day hike from my car. That's my style nowadays. Ironically, for all the wild convolutions of the canyons and the generous scale of Cedar Mesa (about thirty miles from north to south by forty miles from west to east), there are relatively few places in any of the canyons that you can't get to and back from in a single day, if you're good at scrambling.

Cedar Mesa remains, I'm convinced, the richest region in all the Southwest for unrestored ancient dwellings and granaries, and for unvandalized petroglyph and pictograph panels. More than fifteen years ago, whenever Vaughn and I ventured farther afield to look for ruins and rock art and artifacts in other parts of the backcountry, we often ended up disappointed. As Vaughn first said to me on one such outing, and as we now regularly repeat to each other, "Cedar Mesa sure does spoil you."

There's no denying the fact, however, that in 2015, Cedar Mesa is teetering on the edge of a cultural and environmental crisis. The greatest threat to its antiquities may not, after all, be the casual visitors who don't know any better than to stand on ruin walls or take home potsherds. In a tradition dating back to the early years of the twentieth century, locals and nonlocals alike have dug illegally in the ruins and carted home precious vessels, grave goods, and even skeletons and mummies. Some of these "treasures" end up in private display cases or dusty attics, while others are sold on the black market to dealers. If you go on eBay and look up "Anasazi pots," you'll find scores of beautiful objects for sale at prices ranging upward to twenty-five hundred dollars or even higher. Each one comes with a certified disclaimer, insisting that the artifact was excavated legally on private land. Example: "The ancient pieces that I have listed were found on private land, with the owner's permission over 40 years ago. They were not found on any Indian, BLM, Federal or State land." There is no way, of course, to check the validity of such a claim.

In 2009, however, after a two-year undercover operation conducted by the BLM and the FBI, agents descended on the town of Blanding to arrest looters of Ancestral Puebloan ruins and grave sites on public land. Twenty-three miscreants ranging across four states were identified as participants in an organized ring of pothunters and dealers. The sting targeted 256 illegally removed artifacts worth an estimated value of $335,000.

However welcome as a corrective to the grave-robbing that had taken place on Cedar Mesa and in other parts of the Four Corners region for a century, the crackdown turned tragic after the key undercover informant and two of the looters (one of them the well-regarded Blanding physician Dr. James D. Redd) committed suicide. Blanding residents blamed the "Gestapo-style" tactics of the crackdown, and a backlash against the federal intervention spread across the West.

My own take on the eternal dilemma of the looting of antiquities is that there's no good remedy. One of the most stunning assemblages of prehistoric artifacts that I've ever seen is a collection of Ancestral Puebloan baskets in a glass case at the Edge of the Cedars Museum in Blanding. The signage tells the gloomy story behind the display. Blanding native Earl Shumway—the most notorious pothunter in Southwest history, a man who carried loaded guns to the sites he looted to scare off officers, and who openly bragged about his crimes—finally got busted in 1985 after DNA from a cigarette butt he left at the scene proved his identity. Shumway had removed thirty-four baskets from a ruin west of Blanding on national forest land. It was the first case in U.S. history of a successful conviction under the Archaeological Resources Protection Act of 1979 (ARPA). But Shumway turned snitch on his Blanding neighbors to avoid a prison sentence. Though ARPA teams subsequently raided other illegal stashes, all of the cases against the pothunters were eventually dropped.

Yet in 2005, when Duncan Metcalfe showed me some of the collections at the Utah Museum of Natural History, I was surprised to see old pots still bearing the label "Shumway." As Metcalfe explained to me, in the 1920s, University of Utah archaeologist Andrew Kerr actually hired Earl Shumway's grandfather to dig up pots from southeastern Utah to bolster the museum's collection. Kerr paid the man two bucks a pot—provenience be damned. Earl Shumway, then, came from a family legacy of ruthless vandalism not only sanctioned but paid for by the professional guardians of Southwestern antiquity.

There's no doubt that pothunting continues to be pursued on Cedar Mesa. In recent years, I've seen what look indisputably like fresh looters' pits in the soil of remote ruins, and the ATV tracks of these vandals, circling everywhere, smashing the cryptogamic soil, bear witness to their sport. The increasingly underfunded BLM rangers cannot possibly police the whole of Cedar Mesa. Scott Edwards and

Laura Lantz, who have manned the Kane Gulch ranger station for the past twenty-three years, along with a handful of unpaid volunteers, have their hands full issuing hiking and camping permits and giving advice to visitors so they won't get lost or caught in flash floods. To make matters worse, they're furloughed—put on unpaid leave—for six months from late fall to early spring, during which the Kane Gulch headquarters is closed. That's when the pothunters have their field day.

In the last few years, the idea of turning Cedar Mesa into a national monument has been bruited about. The great advantage of such a change in status would be a huge boost in funding, some of which could go toward policing the vulnerable ruins. Personally, I'm against the idea. National parks and monuments seem inevitably to create a self-sustaining bureaucracy, and rules meant to protect a place turn into finicky and arbitrary interdictions. A few years ago, at Chaco Culture National Historical Park, I got ticketed by a ranger on a bicycle who set off in pursuit of me as I hiked to the Great House ruin of Wijiji. Our exchange went something like this.

"You don't have a permit to hike to Wijiji," she admonished.

"I know. I wanted to see it at sunrise, in beautiful low-angle light," I answered.

"You need a permit."

"But the visitor center doesn't open until 8 A.M., and I can't get a permit the day before."

"Sorry, those are the rules." She handed me my citation. "Don't try this again."

What's more, turning BLM or National Forest Service land into a park or monument would inevitably mean multiplying the number of visitors many times over. I'd hiked the side canyons of the Escalante River in southern Utah both before and after Bill Clinton announced the creation of Grand Staircase–Escalante National Monument in 1996. Before, three of us had hiked for eight days up and down four separate canyons and across two mesas and run into not a single other wanderer. Shortly after the Clinton decree, I backpacked into another tributary canyon of the Escalante, expecting to enjoy a blissful solitary four days of rambling, only to share my riverbank campsite with eight other tents housing something like twenty-five people, whose chatter kept me from sleeping before midnight.

If Cedar Mesa is turned into a national monument, perhaps on a given day in early May you can expect to commune at the Citadel not with sixty-five strangers, but with two hundred. Or perhaps you will have had to acquire a permit the day before, as one does now for Moon House, to be able to visit the Citadel at all.

I was heartened to learn that Winston Hurst shared my skepticism. In an e-mail to me last year, with his inimitable flair, he wrote:

> Re the future of Cedar Mesa—all futures are sad or sadder. National Monument status is a form of death that's hard for me to stomach, like killing a place, painting the corpse and putting it on display for money. Proliferating uniforms and "Everything not compulsory is forbidden" signs, and don't step off the trail, and spies who speak in non-threatening rising intonations. Brings out the redneck in me big-time. That would no doubt help preserve certain natural elements, but I don't know in my gut which future I prefer. If I were God, I would make a future that follows the old Mormon adage, to teach people correct principles and let them manage themselves.

Although less dyspeptic, Fred Blackburn was equally gloomy. About the same time last year, he gazed into his own crystal ball, also by e-mail:

> National monument status is likely inevitable, but it may prove harmful as well. It endangers the resources to add even more rules, regulations, and visitors without a firm commitment to long-term funding, progressive management, interpretation, law enforcement, and innovative planning. The amount of cultural

destruction is only going to increase. So far, the commitment to and management of Cedar Mesa by the BLM have been dismal.

Fred waxed nostalgic for the early years, when he himself was a BLM ranger in the late 1970s:

The uniqueness of Cedar Mesa used to be the freedom to explore on one's own, by gut instinct, curiosity, or distinctive terrain. Campfires during cold nights, dogs, and a good horse or mule for your companions. But now, the proposed rules and regulations [of a national monument]—which I must say are necessary and inevitable—will make that experience impossible. The increasing numbers of visitors and their impact on the land will chip away at the souls of the curious who remember the Good Old Days.

In recent years, Vaughn Hadenfeldt seemed to me to be growing more and more bitter about what was happening to Cedar Mesa. Sometimes I wondered if he was suffering from guide's burnout. But more than any of us, he'd seen the changes firsthand. "The place is going to hell," he told me one day last September as we swigged beers in his house in Bluff. "The cattle are getting into the heads of the canyons, and all the way up to the crest of the Comb Ridge. In the canyon heads, they're trampling everything in sight, and their shitting and pissing are fouling the water sources for hikers. The cows are driven by drought and poor range conditions, and the BLM's questionable range management practices aren't working.

"The ATVers are increasing every day, and their lobby is a powerful one. The counties want to keep every scrap of road open, so as to minimize the chances that Wilderness Study Areas will be redesignated as true wilderness. They want jeep and ATV safaris. They want drilling for oil and gas. In fact, just this fall, an outfit called Wildcat Drilling bored a deep probe on Cedar Mesa, just west of the head of Fish Canyon. What they're doing, unfortunately, is perfectly legal, but we're all praying that they don't hit oil."

The threat to federal land in Utah is indeed an ominous one. In 2012, a fiendish new law was passed by the state legislature and signed by the governor. The Transfer of Public Lands Act (TPLA) mandates that all Forest Service and BLM land in Utah be transferred to the state within two years. That amounts to 57 percent of the whole state, including not only Cedar Mesa but such still wild outbacks as the San Rafael Swell, the Book Cliffs and Tavaputs Plateau, most of the mountain ranges of the Wasatch and Uintas, Elk Ridge, Beef Basin, Dark Canyon, and many other tracts. The only thing that can stop this movement is if higher courts declare the law unconstitutional. Meanwhile TPLA advocates and the legislature are amassing legal arguments to demonstrate that the law is constitutional and must be enforced.

If TPLA takes effect, according to David Gerbett, a lawyer for the Southern Utah Wilderness Alliance, "The only way the Utah legislature can generate money from the public lands is to ramp up development and hold a fire sale to clear inventory. That means that the places the public has come to know and love will be sold to the highest bidder and barricaded with 'No Trespassing' signs."

In Bluff, Vaughn went on, "Another major problem is the woodcutters. A lot of them are Navajos from the Monument Valley area, and Cedar Mesa is their nearest source of firewood. They have to get a permit to gather dead wood, but instead of parking their pickups on the road and hauling the trees out, they drive straight to them. The BLM puts up plastic stakes saying 'Road closed to vehicular travel,' but the woodcutters just drive around them. You've seen those tracks all over Cedar Mesa, especially on the southern end. I sympathize with the Navajos' need to stay warm in the winter, but those intrusive off-road tracks make a godawful impact on the landscape, and sometimes even on archaeological sites.

"Another thing—Cedar Mesa is old-growth forest. Especially with drought and climate change, I wonder how long folks can continue to harvest the wood. Where's the tipping point when the forest won't recover?

"I don't know about a national monument. But what I'd say to you and Winston is, can you think of a better alternative? There's got to be something better than the current status quo. I'm in favor of better protection. The so-called Wilderness Study Areas should be converted to true Wilderness Areas. RVs should be banned from parking at the heads of canyons. But the BLM is so underfunded, it can't protect or patrol the six hundred thousand acres of Cedar Mesa.

"There are rules the BLM could change. The current maximum size of a backpacking party—twelve people—is absurd. But outfits like NOLS and Outward Bound depend on that number for their business. You could ban dogs from all the canyons, but there are just too many dog-lovers who also like to hike. More important than rules is education. We need to educate the people who flock to Cedar Mesa how to treat sites with respect. Maybe that takes the form of a required debriefing at the Kane Gulch headquarters. The number of visitors per day to the more popular ruins maybe has to be limited, as it is at Moon House already. Of course, some hikers would simply sneak in and do their own thing, no matter what the requirements.

"A national monument would bring the hordes. But it would also bring more money for preservation and enforcement. Some of us in Friends of Cedar Mesa"—an activist group founded a few years ago—"would prefer a national conservation area over a national monument. We might get the same protection but attract a lot fewer people."

Vaughn took a sip of his beer. The look on his face was dour. "I don't know," he concluded. "There's just no goddamned good answer." Fixing me with his gaze, he added, "You like to say, 'If a thing is worth doing, it's worth writing about.' I say, 'If it's worth doing, it's worth preserving and protecting.'"

As mentioned in the prologue, after I published *In Search of the Old Ones*, the BLM officials in Monticello tried to ban me from Grand

Gulch. Over the years, my relations with those stewards of Cedar Mesa have improved somewhat, but they're still a little touchy. At the 2013 Pecos Conference, however, I met Don Simonis, the relatively new chief archaeologist for the BLM office, and we had a short but cordial exchange. In September, I traveled to Monticello to talk with him about the future of my favorite Southwest stomping grounds. We met for an early dinner at one of the town's only two or three open cafés.

Shaking my hand, with a sly smile, Simonis said, "As I'm sure you know, David, some people love you and some people hate you."

Taken a bit aback, I rejoined, "Are you unhappy that I'm writing a new book?"

He shook his head. "It's really hard to find anything decent that's been written about this region. But you can Google almost anything you want to find and get the GPS coordinates."

"And?"

"So what we'd like you to do is put out good information. To help teach your readers proper site etiquette."

That's what I thought I've always done, I said to myself. But as Simonis went on, carefully treading an invisible political line, I found myself sympathizing with the man's predicament. "We're government archaeologists," he said. "To keep our jobs, we have to go along with management. But 'multiple use'"—the catchphrase of the BLM, the NFS, and other federal land agencies—"is really insanity."

Another sly smile. "Some people in government," he added, "care more about cows than artifacts."

We talked ruefully about other Utah archaeologists who had lost their government jobs because they had too stridently advocated preservation at all costs. "There's no place in the Southwest like Cedar Mesa," said Simonis. "We need to get that message across to Congress. Over the years, we've lost hundreds and hundreds of artifacts. They're now in private collections. And the ATV lobby is really pushing hard. They want new routes and canyons opened up for their vehicles. Dogs are not allowed in any of the sites, even on leashes, but people ignore that rule all the time.

"We're trying to reach the young people in the country. The fifth-graders in Blanding. To train them in archaeology. A lot of people who live around here won't admit that today's Native Americans are related to prehistoric peoples.

"We'd really like to have Cedar Mesa become a national monument. Right now, it's just another piece of BLM land."

No, I thought, *I'm glad I don't have Simonis's job. I'm glad I don't have to manage Cedar Mesa. I'd rather just write about it.* "What do you foresee for the future of places like Moon House and the Citadel?" I asked.

"As you know, now you need a special permit to go to Moon House. In the future, we'll probably only have guided tours. The sooner the better, in my opinion. And sometime in the last three years, somebody knocked down a wall at the Citadel. There are only five windows now. There used to be six."

Why hadn't Vaughn told me about this desecration? Had it been three years since I'd last taken friends to the Citadel?

Now Simonis made a statement that dismayed me. "I'm no fan of the Outdoor Museum," he said, "not to the extent of leaving everything out there. When it comes to unique, diagnostic artifacts, people are going to take them from the sites."

The talk shifted to the corrugated pot I had found on the high ledge on my solo four-day backpack in 1993. "We get reports from visitors who have been there," Simonis claimed. "Somebody's put brush on top of the pot to camouflage it. Other people have left their business cards inside it. A photo of 'your' pot even appeared in the San Juan County phone book!"

"Christ!" I laughed.

"Two years ago we were going to go into the canyon and remove the pot."

I was shocked. "Have you been to the site yourself?"

"No."

"The pot's embedded in a layer of marl. If you tried to pull it loose, you'd break it into pieces." Simonis nodded. "So why didn't you remove it?" I asked.

"We got a call from Betsy Chapoose, on the Uintah and Ouray Ute Reservation. She said, 'What's going on with this pot?' I said, 'We're going in to collect it.' She said, 'I don't know if that's a good idea.' So we just sort of backed off."

I was nonplussed. How had Betsy Chapoose, whoever she was, even heard about the pot? And why did she care what happened to it? There was virtually no possibility that modern-day Utes had any cultural affiliation with a thirteenth-century pot in a Cedar Mesa canyon.

Later I would learn that Chapoose was the Cultural Rights and Protection Director for her tribe, so it was not surprising that she might have intervened with the BLM. But in the café with Simonis, I was ignorant of that fact. Instead, I whispered to myself: *Thank you, Betsy . . .*

The human history of Cedar Mesa stretches across millennia. Nomads in the Archaic period hunted and gathered there during five thousand years, from 6500 B.C. through 1500 B.C.. During Basketmaker II times, from 1500 B.C. to A.D. 400, the population markedly increased. In 1967, Bill Lipe, one of the Southwest's most brilliant and dedicated archaeologists, began a systematic survey of selected "quadrats" of land on the mesa-top and in the canyons that spanned nine field seasons. Lipe's teams deduced a curious pattern of habitation and abandonment after Basketmaker II—dense populations between A.D. 650 and 750 and again from 1100 to 1300, punctuated by the nearly complete absence of Ancestral Puebloans from 400 to 650 and again from 750 to 1100. The reasons for these fluctuations remain mysterious.

The rock art panels on Cedar Mesa that I've sought out during the last twenty-five years span the whole of those eight millennia, from the Archaic through the Pueblo III era. But the ruins that captured my imagination are cliff dwellings and cliff granaries, and they almost all date from the last two hundred years before the abandonment of the Colorado Plateau. The reason is unmistakable—during that final period, the Old Ones were driven by fear to build in alcoves and on high ledges. Fear of an enemy who would steal your corn and, if necessary, kill you to get it. And that enemy, as has been amply demonstrated during the last thirty years, was other Ancestral Puebloans. Famine, drought, deforestation, the hunting to near extinction of the big game, and other environmental factors drove the people to the edge of survival—until, just before A.D. 1300, survival was no longer possible anywhere on the Colorado Plateau.

If Cedar Mesa continues to lure me because of the abundance of new sites I keep finding, none of them are more enticing and baffling than the truly inaccessible ruins—mostly granaries—that it takes a diligent search to find even with binoculars. During the last ten years, with several friends, including Greg Child and Matt Hale, and sometimes alone, I've spent considerable time trying to figure out how to get to these hyperdefensive constructions. Some that I've succeeded in entering, I suspected, had seen no visitors during the more than seven hundred years since their builders left for good.

At their most extreme, the granaries perched on skimpy ledges on vertical and even overhanging cliffs in the canyons are as mind-boggling as Waldo's Catwalk in Range Creek. But on Cedar Mesa, the use of ropes to gain access to ruins is forbidden. Instead, I've worked out tricks involving scary traverses on the ledge systems that lead to these almost invisible granaries. Other sites, however, look so hard to get to that I can imagine reaching them only on rappel from the cliff rims above. But whether or not the Ancestral Puebloans had hefty coils of rope in their arsenal, I'm pretty sure they didn't rappel to those ledges.

Elsewhere in the Southwest—in the canyons of the Tsegi in northern Arizona, for instance—hand-and-toe trails carved with pounding stones abound, and it's clear that that was a standard technique for getting to the remote ledges where the granaries reside. But it's always puzzled me that hand-and-toe trails—Moqui steps, as the old-timers called them—are few and far between on Cedar Mesa.

From a climber's point of view, Cedar Mesa sandstone—a subset of what geologists call the Cutler Formation—is treacherous stuff. The rock is much softer than the Wingate sandstone that makes Indian Creek, just east of Canyonlands National Park, an international climbing mecca. On Cedar Mesa, handholds often come loose when you pull on them. And unlike Wingate, which glories in clean vertical cracks up which acrobats hand-jam and layback and in which they can place protection, Cedar Mesa is largely deficient of vertical fissures. Almost all the seams and cracks are horizontal ones.

Whether or not rope helped the Old Ones build their Cedar Mesa homes and storage bins, the key to those twelfth- and thirteenth-century cliff dwellings, I think, was virtuoso traverses linking one ledge to another with precarious log ladders. Proof of this theory abounds in the ominous structures I call "stopper walls." You'll be crawling along a narrow ledge toward a ruin you spotted hours earlier from below, and you know you're almost there, but then, just where the ledge gets narrowest, a blank masoned wall pinches closed the approach. Stopper walls were obviously constructed to keep the bad guys out. A raider trying to enter a site would be a sitting duck for arrows or even just a vigorous shove off the precipice as he tried to sidle his way around a stopper wall.

It's always vexed me that archaeologists, by and large, have paid so little attention to the inaccessible ruins that so intrigue me on Cedar Mesa. My pet theory is that because so few of the professionals are climbers, they fail to appreciate the accomplishment of the ancients not only in getting to those remote and dangerous places, but in building structures, storing grain, and even living in those outposts. In the 1990s, I spent considerable time in the Tsegi and Escalante canyons, where I found lots of hand-and-toe trails leading up wildly exposed cliffs. Many of them I tried to climb, sometimes donning rock shoes

Waldo Wilcox, who guarded and preserved Range Creek for half a century (© Greg Child)

Renee Barlow rappels toward
the double granary she named
"Waldo's Catwalk" (© Greg Child)

The mysterious Shield site, on a ledge high above Range Creek (© Greg Child)

The Pilling figurines, made of unfired clay (© USU Eastern Prehistoric Museum)

The Telluride blanket
(© Telluride Historical Museum)

The jutting promontory on Cedar Mesa that cradles the Citadel just under its summit
(© Stephanie Scott)

Moon House, perhaps the most remarkable ruin on Cedar Mesa (© Matt Hale)

Detail from the Great Gallery pictograph panel in Grand Gulch (© David Roberts)

An obscure, seldom-visited ruin on Cedar Mesa (© Greg Child)

Fred Blackburn (© David Roberts)

Greg Child (© David Roberts)

Vaughn Hadenfeldt (© David Roberts)

Matt Hale (© David Roberts)

Archaeologist Steve Lekson, retracing the route of the Chaco Meridian (© Bill Hatcher)

Paquimé, the astonishing adobe ruin in Chihuahua, Mexico (© Bill Hatcher)

Pueblo Bonito, finest of the twelve Great Houses at Chaco Canyon, as it would have looked to a pilgrim arriving from the north (© Bill Hatcher)

for the effort. And sometimes I chickened out and backed off—the sequences of shallow steps simply seemed too marginal to risk my life trying to navigate.

Back in Cambridge, Massachusetts, where I lived, I ransacked the journals in Harvard's Tozzer Library, trying to find out what the academics had written about the old Moqui steps. When my search came up empty, I queried archaeologists whom I knew. None of them could cite a single paper. Several misunderstood my question, directing me instead to studies of prehistoric pathways, like the network of Chacoan roads. As far as I could tell, no professional had ever seriously grappled with the phenomenon of hand-and-toe trails in the Southwest.

As a climber, I was deeply impressed with the severity of these nearly vertical staircases in the sandstone. But what was even harder to fathom was how the ancients had carved those steps in the first place, as they paved the way on their first ascents. Sometimes a route suddenly veered sharply right or left, as the craftsman sought out slightly less steep terrain. I tried to imagine an Ancestral Puebloan, standing barely in balance in his foothold depressions, reaching down to ankle level with his pounding stone to chip yet another hold off to the side. Ice climbing in Alaska or New Hampshire before the development of modern tools and crampons, I had often chopped steps on such a traverse. It was delicate, precarious work, even with a two-and-a-half-foot-long ice axe shaft for a handle, at the end of which a sharp metal adze did the gouging.

When I tried to explain my astonishment at these trails to archaeologists, they sometimes countered, "Well, the cliffs have weathered away in the last seven hundred years. Probably the steps were much deeper and more secure back when they were first made." A kindred dismissal explicated the granaries that looked impossible to get to today: "No doubt there were boulders and ramps of stone that made those places easier to get to once, and they've collapsed in the centuries since."

Bullshit, I said to myself. Yes, the cliffs have weathered in seven hundred years, but not to that extent. Sometimes I've felt the tiny cuplets shaped for individual fingers still in place in Ancestral Puebloan handholds. And several times I've seen ruins a hundred feet up a sheer cliff, directly above contemporary ruins at the base of the cliff. Had the "access ramps" collapsed since A.D. 1300, they would have crushed those lower dwellings to smithereens.

It's fashionable in Southwest archaeology to dismiss the hyper-defensive villages of the last-gasp Ancestral Puebloans as marginal, not worth concerted study. In a sense, such an attitude is a reaction against touristic enthusiasm for the spectacular cliff dwellings that captured Americans' fancy starting in the 1870s. About the prehistory of the Montezuma Valley in southwestern Colorado, I'd heard more than one scholar say something like, "Those folks who built Cliff Palace and Spruce Tree House up on Mesa Verde were hicks, hillbillies. The real action was down on the plains, at places like Lowry and Yellow Jacket and Yucca House"—huge amalgamated pueblos that today are reduced to mounds of rubble. Even Bill Lipe, who had grown to love Cedar Mesa and its canyons during his nine-year survey, regarded its inhabitants as weird outcasts. As he told me in 1993, "On Cedar Mesa, the Anasazi were really going their own way. These people were escaping the confines of normative thought."

Well, I believe, that mainstream dismissal of inaccessible granaries and dwellings as marginal and unimportant is archaeology's loss. The scholars generally agree as to why the Old Ones resorted to such desperate retreats: out of fear, to guard the dwindling supplies of food as the Ancestral Puebloan world fell apart in the thirteenth century. But the other question—How did they do it?—remains virtually unanswered. Over the years, I've tried to bring that question to the attention of Steve Lekson, my chief source of insight about the ancient Southwest, to little avail. Admitting he had a healthy fear of heights,

Lekson would wave away my probes, saying, "You wouldn't catch me dead trying to get to those places." But in 2007, when I showed Lekson Greg Child's dazzling photo of Renee Barlow spinning in space on rappel, twenty feet out from Waldo's Catwalk, he confessed, "I'm beginning to see what you're getting at."

In certain places on Cedar Mesa, freestanding buttes isolate their summits from easy access. In 1994, I led three friends, including Fred Blackburn, up a three-hundred-foot-high butte that had only one possible route of ascent. Several dwellings just under the rim, plainly visible from below, announced an Ancestral Puebloan presence. But to surmount a bulge of overhanging sandstone two-thirds of the way up, we had to climb a piñon whose topmost limbs almost brushed the lip of the overhang. Someone had tied a stick to the stoutest branch, making a perilous one-step gangplank leading to the ledges above. Nor did the difficulties end there, as we resorted to a shoulder stand to surmount an eight-foot blank wall just below the rim. I stood on the shoulders of two of my companions, seized handholds above, pulled myself up, then helped the others up after me.

I had expected that the summit, fully thirty acres in extent, would have housed some kind of defensive redoubt, perhaps even a minor fortress. But though we found a few collapsed buildings, a scattering of potsherds, and some interesting petroglyphs, the glory of the place was something else. All across the bedrock surface, we found hundreds of lithics—chert and obsidian flakes chipped from cores in the process of making projectile points, scrapers, knives, and other tools.

Bruce Bradley, an archaeologist who is one of the world's leading experts in lithic technology, as well as one of the best self-taught flint knappers, was in our party. He went into an ecstatic trance as, crawling across the stone surface, he picked up one flake after another, narrating his finds in a breathless outpouring of taxonomic rapture. Bradley could date the flakes by style, and he claimed to find debitage from every period from Basketmaker II through Pueblo III—despite Bill Lipe's conclusion that Cedar Mesa had been abandoned twice in that span for hundreds of years.

Bradley kept finding broken points—atlatl darts (earlier) and arrowheads (later)—that had been tossed aside after the ancient knapper made a tiny mistake. And he came upon an "eccentric," an extremely rare crescent of chert chipped into a design that looked like a parrot's claw. The function of eccentrics remains unknown. (As an old archaeological joke has it, in such cases one assigns the thing to the category of "ceremonial or religious objects.")

The top of the butte was virtually unique on Cedar Mesa, and deeply mysterious. Why should the Ancestral Puebloans, during century after century, have sought out such a difficult place to get to as the workshop for the creation of their chert and obsidian tools? Why was that the best place to make dart points and arrowheads?

Yet as extraordinary as the butte top seemed to us in 1994, it looked nothing like what it had a century before. In his researches, Fred and his colleagues in the Wetherill–Grand Gulch Research Project had learned that in 1891, those pioneering Durango-area ranchers Charles McLoyd and Charles Cary Graham had found their own way to the top of the sandstone plug, which they called Arrow Point. From that lithic atelier, the two men had retrieved no fewer than 120 intact projectile points from different eras. McLoyd and Graham had apparently sold the collection to the Field Museum in Chicago. What a treasure trove that assemblage would prove to archaeologists today! But to the horror of Fred's team, further research revealed that sometime in the early 1900s, the Field had sold all but two of the points to a curio trader whose shop was across the street from the museum. Much of the legacy of Arrow Point is gone forever.

Unbeknownst to us, in 1994, several BLM rangers from Monticello had watched our every move through binoculars from the opposite canyon rim. These were the same officials who deplored the prospect of the book that would become *In Search of the Old Ones*. A few weeks after our visit, the rangers recruited a climber who took them to the top of the butte, where, for all I know, they gathered up everything in sight. Once they had "documented" the site, they climbed back down.

On the way, they cut down the piñon, which may have been more than five hundred years old, so that no one after them could visit that island in the sky or marvel over the lithics as Bruce Bradley and the other three of us had on that special day.

There's another freestanding butte on Cedar Mesa that will stick like a burr under my saddle till my dying day. It lies in a certain part of a certain canyon that I had visited often, but one day around 2000, while my partners were checking out nearby ruins, I studied the butte carefully through binoculars, then headed for it alone. The key to getting started was a scary traverse across twenty yards of ledge tilted at an angle of almost forty-five degrees, above a hundred-foot drop. As I stepped carefully across that slab, I prayed that my boot soles would adhere.

Beyond that rite of passage, I pushed rightward, linking ledges with moderate scrambles. I hadn't really expected to find anything along the way, for my binocular inspection had discovered no ruins on the ledges, not even the most minimal granary. Yet here I found a few potsherds, there some worked flakes, and in one cranny, a shaped stick that might have been a digging tool. At every turn, I had expected to be stopped by a featureless cliff, but the ledges joined up so cleverly, you would think they had been designed by a master architect. And the vesitigial artifacts kept appearing, even as I climbed higher and higher.

After an hour's effort, I stood below the final cliff, having ascended five hundred feet of the butte's six-hundred-foot rise. There was a generous ledge halfway up that final cliff, but it was guarded above and below by overhangs. The butte had stopped me cold. A rope here, even if it were legal to use one on Cedar Mesa, would have been of no use, for there were no vertical cracks for holds and protection. But a series of log ladders might have made all the difference. I searched the ledge below the cliff for any remnants of dead recumbent piñon or juniper trunks, but I found nothing.

Reluctantly, I started down, breathing easy only after I had recrossed the angled slab near the base. Later that day, as I had several times before, I hiked the complete loop around the butte, staring up at the cliffs as I walked. There wasn't the ghost of a climbable route on any other side.

At the end of the day, hiking back to the trailhead, I thought, *There's got to be something on top. Why else would there be a trail of artifacts all the way to the final cliff?*

Yes, I believe today, there's something on top. Some Ancestral Puebloan shrine or hideout as remarkable as the lithic workshop on the summit of Arrow Point. But, alas, I'll never see it.

Four

CHACO MERIDIAN

By the 1990s, the prehistoric Southwest was pretty well mapped. Scholars still argued whether the Fremont culture deserved its separate domain or should be subsumed under the Anasazi as "Northern Periphery," and they wondered whether such localized variations as Sinagua and Salado really merited their badges of autonomy. But the three main cultures—Anasazi, Mogollon, and

Hohokam—claimed their distinct regions, with little fluctuation over almost three millennia dating back to 1500 B.C..

The textbooks reaffirmed this certainty. In Linda Cordell's comprehensive *Prehistory of the Southwest* (1984), a Venn diagram-like map indicated those domains, though according to Cordell, the territories of the cultures were contiguous but not overlapping. Cordell drew the Anasazi homeland as a curving blob, extending in the east as far as the New Mexico plains beyond the Sangre de Cristo range, and as far west as the Virgin River in the southwest corner of Utah. The northern boundary cut a rising arc to an apex a little north of present-day Moab, swooped into Colorado to include the Mesa Verde region, then dwindled south toward the headwaters of the Rio Grande. The southern frontier extended from Flagstaff, Arizona, past Gallup, New Mexico, only to die out southeast of Albuquerque.

Hohokam, on Cordell's map, was a pear-shaped blob embracing most of south-central Arizona. Mogollon, three or four times as large, took over where Anasazi left off in the south and where Hohokam gave up the ghost in the east, but it stretched pendulously deep into the Mexican states of Chihuahua and Sonora.

What eventually became of these peoples, and what kinship they bore to present-day Native Americans, composed a far thornier archaeological and ethnographic riddle. But the experts pretty much agreed on end dates. The Anasazi abandoned most of their homeland just before A.D. 1300. The Fremont hung on maybe fifty years longer (or even two hundred years in isolated pockets such as Douglas Creek in northwestern Colorado), the Mogollon perhaps until 1400, while the Hohokam may have faded away only about 1450. In any case, by the time Coronado marched into the Southwest in 1540, no living trace of the prehistoric cultures that archaeologists would later reconstruct remained. The sedentary *indios pueblo* and the nomadic *indios bárbaros* whom the Spaniards encountered, warred against, and tried to convert into good Christians apparently bore some kind of connection to the Anasazi, Mogollon, Hohokam, or Fremont, but just what linkages tied them to their ancestors, scholars fiercely debated.

Still, by the late 1990s, a kind of taxonomic orthodoxy hovered over the prehistoric Southwest. No scholar had advanced any radical new theory that would attempt to overturn the applecart of Cordell's Venn diagram. Not, that is, until Steve Lekson published a slender but explosive book called *The Chaco Meridian* in 1999. Sixteen years later, we're still picking up the pieces.

I first met Lekson in 1994, when he was director of the Crow Canyon Archaeological Center, a research institute based in Cortez, Colorado. Unlike some other professionals, who didn't want to waste their time with an inquisitive layman, Lekson was instantly approachable and generous with his time. As I would learn, he believed that it was important that the work he and his Southwestern colleagues undertook should reach a larger audience than that of their peers. If an author like me could "get it right," or at least mostly right, he was all in favor of spreading the word via books such as *In Search of the Old Ones*.

I also saw early on that Lekson was a born iconoclast, with a penchant for questioning received wisdom and for puncturing balloons. This trait emerged in the most casual exchanges. In 1994, as he and I walked through a ruin near Cortez, I noticed a bedrock slab scored with five vertical incisions. "Nice sharpening grooves," I commented. Every Anasazi textbook that I had read attributed such slits to hunters over the ages filing their axes and knives to keen edges.

But Lekson said, "Maybe they're sharpening grooves. Maybe not."

Surprised, I asked, "Why not?"

"Why do you need five of them, when one would do?"

"What else could they be?"

"I haven't got the slightest idea."

In 1988, Lekson had published a short paper in *Kiva*, a quarterly professional journal, titled (not coincidentally) "The Idea of the Kiva in Anasazi Archaeology." Beginning in the 1870s, Anglos exploring the ruins in the Southwest kept finding subterranean chambers, usually round, with doors in the roofs through which the ancients climbed via wooden ladders left in place. The interiors of these chambers typically bore a suite of standard features: benches in the walls interspersed with pilasters, a chimney adjoining an outside wall, a deflector slab to keep the fire from blowing out, log cribbing that built hexagonally from the upper walls toward the roof, and sometimes a small cuplike hole in the center of the floor. These structures were markedly different from the above-ground room blocks that were evidently living quarters.

Baffled as to the nature of the underground chambers, ethnographers in the 1890s asked Hopi informants to explain them. At once, the Hopi called them "kivas," even as they showed the scholars their own kindred structures at villages such as Oraibi and Walpi. Hopi kivas had doors in the roofs and ladders leading to the windowless interiors, like the underground chambers found in the ruins, but in other respects they were quite different—above-ground, usually rectangular in shape, often without such features as cribbing or benches and pilasters. Hopi kivas were used for ceremonial and religious purposes, and women were forbidden to enter them. In the 1890s, the going ethnographic practice was to take Puebloan informants, as self-evidently the descendants of the Old Ones, at their word. So the round, below-ground chambers in the ruins became Anasazi kivas. The Hopi further insisted that the cuplike depression in the floor represented the *sipapu*—the Hopi name for the sacred place of emergence of the people from the subterranean Third World to the present Fourth World in the creation myth.

By the 1930s, thanks mainly to New Mexico archaeologist Edgar Hewett—the same man who was instrumental in getting the Antiquities Act of 1906 passed—the belief that Anasazi kivas were religious and spiritual sanctums had become dogma. So certain were the scholars of this fact that they argued from an abundance of kivas at certain sites that they were religious centers serving far-ranging populations.

For half a century, no one questioned this orthodoxy, until Lekson, in effect, stroked his chin and said, "Now wait a minute."

How do we know Anasazi kivas were ceremonial, Lekson asked. What evidence was there beyond the word of the Hopi informants? Might the chambers instead be an alternative form of residence, echoing the underground pithouses of the Basketmaker people before kivas made their first appearance around A.D. 750?

Lekson's paper caused a furor. His critics dismissed his work as that of an image-smasher who delighted in riling up his colleagues. But subsequent research came up with all kinds of evidence supporting Lekson's hypothesis—a plethora of domestic ware and tools, as well as remnants of corn, beans, and squash, in the fill in previously unexcavated kivas. By 2015, Lekson's revisionism has pretty much won the day among Southwestern archaeologists. Romantic ideas die hard, however, and the signage at more than one restored ruin still touts the kiva as a religious sanctum and the *sipapu* as the place of emergence.

After our first meeting in 1994, Lekson and I became good friends. A few years later, he became a professor at the University of Colorado, so on every visit to Boulder, where I had grown up, I looked him up, booked a leisurely dinner at a quiet restaurant, and spent hours pumping him for the latest news and his latest ideas about the prehistoric Southwest—a ritual I continue to the present day.

Unlike nearly all his colleagues, whose prose inclines to dry, overcautious academic discourse, Lekson is a flamboyant, even a brilliant writer, though one with a weakness for bad puns. The very vividness of his writing, the humor and irony woven through his papers, earned him further disapproval from some of his more straitlaced colleagues. On top of that, Lekson is a generalist, a big picture guy, in an age when minute specialization and territorial possessiveness (jokingly referred to as the disease of "my-site-itis") rule the day.

Lekson reminded me of Carl Sagan, under whom I had studied at Harvard, another big picture guy who spoke and wrote with flamboyant style. For his very popularity, Sagan was punished by academe when Harvard denied him tenure. He ended up at Cornell, and after he became famous as the visionary guru of the TV series *Cosmos*, Sagan went out of his way to append to even an ordinary letter his résumé of professional papers, which ran to many pages. As I would later learn, Lekson has borne his own brunt of professional envy and academic snobbery, even as his popularity grew.

One day in 1999, as I was walking the streets of Santa Fe, I bumped into Eric Blinman. He had been a valuable source for *In Search of the Old Ones*, as five years earlier he had found himself in the crosshairs of a vehement local debate. At that time, Santa Fe archaeologists were agonizing over the ethics of cooperating with an art dealer turned self-styled excavator who had bought the land on which a huge, pristine fifteenth-century pueblo ruin lay, then proceeded recklessly to dig it up. When the art dealer blundered upon an incredibly rare cache of artifacts, including two intact but extremely fragile kachina masks, he at least had the sense to stop digging and call in some experts. Blinman had chosen to curate the cache rather than let it disappear forever, but in the eyes of some of his colleagues, that was making a bargain with the devil.

Now, without even bothering to say hello or shake my hand, Blinman blurted out, "Have you heard about this absolutely crazy new idea of Lekson's? He's writing a whole book about it!"

Thus, even before it was published, I learned about *The Chaco Meridian*, for Blinman had recently attended a talk that Lekson, a longtime colleague and friend, had given in Santa Fe. As soon as the book appeared, I got hold of a copy, then read it cover to cover.

Even for Lekson, the writing in *The Chaco Meridian* verged on over-the-top. I could see why some of his fellow archaeologists might be put off by the hints of arrogance in passages such as these:

This book is not for the faint of heart, or for neophytes. If you are a practicing Southwestern archaeologist with hypertension problems, stop. Read something safe.

If Southwestern archaeologists don't ask big questions, we will slide back into feeble provincialism—endlessly fine-tuning the record of a region where archaeology is easy and research over-funded. It's time to take some chances: Live dangerously, turn the page.

But as I plunged, at first skeptical but also enthralled, into the heart of Lekson's revolutionary new thesis, I thought, *He's earned the right to be brash.*

The idea behind the Chaco Meridian is not hard to explain, but it requires a little background. Archaeologists have long recognized that in the tenth and eleventh centuries A.D., something happened at Chaco Canyon, in western New Mexico, that was absolutely unprecedented in Southwestern prehistory, and unduplicated since. As far back as we can trace them, the Ancestral Puebloans seem to have been radically egalitarian peoples living in small villages virtually autonomous from one another. (The Pueblos today, from Taos to Acoma to Hopi, remain firmly egalitarian and autonomous, speaking a number of mutually unintelligible languages.)

Yet beginning around A.D. 1000, in the most unpromising of landscapes—the barren, shallow valley of Chaco Wash, where, now as then, almost no trees grow and the feeble stream flows only intermittently—the ancients built twelve separate Great Houses: massive, multistory pueblos shaped to preordained designs, with extraordinarily large rooms and the finest masonry ever crafted in the prehistoric Southwest. The most famous of the Great Houses is the dazzling Pueblo Bonito. Chacoan civilization climaxed between A.D. 1030 and 1125—the "golden century," as some scholars call it.

Radiating out from the central Great Houses is a mind-blowing network of "roads," many of them as wide as thirty feet, characteristically arrowing for miles at a stretch in dead straight lines, in defiance of topographic glitches like cliffs and canyons. Why would a people without either beasts of burden or wheeled vehicles need roads at all—let alone perfectly straight promenades as wide as ten yards? The Chacoan road system, so vestigial today that pieces of it are newly discovered every year, seems to connect with at least 125 and maybe as many as 200 "outliers"—isolated Great Houses built roughly to the plan of the buildings in "Downtown Chaco" (a Lekson coinage), yet as far away from that center as 150 miles.

Are we seeing in Chaco that unmentionable Southwestern thing—a true empire? Scholars rage politely at one another over the question, with Lekson the chief proponent of a hierarchical mini-empire. (He likes to tweak his adversaries by calling Pueblo Bonito and the other downtown Great Houses "palaces," and he insists that Chaco was ruled by "kings.")

Yet suddenly, around A.D. 1125, Chaco collapsed. Why, we still do not know. Other Ancestral Puebloan villages took up some of Chaco's slack. But it is only in the last twenty years that scholars have come to the consensus that the greatest post-Chaco center lay at Aztec, fifty miles to the north. Aztec flourished through the twelfth and thirteenth centuries. Then, sometime just before A.D. 1300, along with all the rest of the Four Corners area, Aztec was abandoned.

So what happened in the fourteenth and fifteenth centuries, before the Spanish arrived? On the Colorado Plateau, nothing. Along the Rio Grande and in southern Arizona, large inward-looking pueblos scattered here and there. Yet during this epoch, the grandest village of them all in the greater Southwest arose at Paquimé, in northern Chihuahua.

Lekson's "eureka" moment, as he calls it, came to him in a blinding flash one day in 1995 in his Boulder office. Squinting at a map, he realized that Chaco, Aztec, and Paquimé lie exactly on the same longitude—107°57' west of Greenwich. Could this be a mere coincidence? Lekson thought not. The truly revolutionary part of the idea, which came to the archaeologist almost in the next breath, was the notion that it was the same folks—or at least the same leaders—who, abandoning Chaco around 1125, marched north to found Aztec, then, almost two centuries later, moved 450 miles south to establish Paquimé, following some profound injunction that we may never fathom to move with utter precision along that imaginary north-south line. Whence (as Lekson would prefer to call it) the Chaco–Aztec–Paquimé Meridian.

What was it about this theory that so upset Lekson's more conservative colleagues, that led Eric Blinman to characterize it as "absolutely crazy"? First of all, the idea that an arbitrary line of longitude could be the key to more than four centuries of Southwestern civilization sounded to some almost like a wacko New Age belief, akin to the "vortexes" that spiritualists insist channel supernatural power into rock formations around Sedona, Arizona. But equally unacceptable to conventional thinking was the notion that Ancestral Puebloans might have become the founders of Paquimé. Lekson's "meridian" threatened to destroy the time-honored integrity of Anasazi and Mogollon as separate domains with little or no overlap. All previous scholars had regarded Paquimé as thoroughly Mogollon.

Thus the thesis of the Chaco Meridian could be neatly summarized as three successive centers of pan-Southwestern hegemony precisely aligned north and south: Chaco (1000–1125), Aztec (1110–1275), Paquimé (1250–1450).

As he marshaled the evidence that would go into *The Chaco Meridian*, Lekson did far more than trace longitude lines on the map. Back in 1976, as a newly hired "shovel bum," he had dug his first Ancestral Puebloan room, at Pueblo Alto, Downtown Chaco's northernmost Great House. By ten years later, he had become one of the leading experts on Chaco. Lekson had also spent much time at Aztec and Paquimé, studying the features and the layout of those two remarkable centers. Now, for his book, he itemized the structures and design elements that the three ancient villages had in common, and that obtained at very few other sites in the Southwest.

As soon as the book was published in 1999, the controversy burst into flames. *The Chaco Meridian*, as I learned when I read it, is more than a trellis on which to hang the vine of Lekson's central argument. It is also a kind of manic compendium of ancillary ideas and insights. It is not an easy book for the casual aficionado of the Southwest to comprehend. Many of Lekson's colleagues simply ignored the book. Others must have ordered their grad students not to read it, for according to persistent rumor, *The Chaco Meridian* is the book most often stolen from the Southwestern stacks of university libraries.

After 1999, the most vociferous attacks on Lekson's hypothesis focused on the improbability of ancients so precisely obeying a longitudinal mandate. To his critics, the north-south alignment of the three great centers is a coincidence, nothing more. After all, western efforts to calculate longitude failed abysmally until the invention of an accurate chronometer in the 1760s. But, as Lekson would demonstrate, in a desert landscape such as the Southwest, surveying long distances on a north-south axis is not such a tricky business. To find true north, for instance, simply plant a straight pole upright in the sand. Sight the sunrise and sunset from the pole, mark those lines at a uniform distance from the pole, draw a cord between the two points, and bisect the cord perpendicularly. Voilà—the line points straight north. Now set up three poles along that line, and you can sight a point on a ridge crest forty miles away that is exactly on the same meridian. It would not take so many such jumps to cover all 450 miles from Aztec to Paquimé.

In part because Lekson had furnished me with so many insights when I wrote *In Search of the Old Ones*, I was tempted to go along with the Chaco Meridian. For five years, I followed the debate over the radical theory as a fascinated bystander. Then, in 2004, I convinced Lekson to take a trip by car and on foot along the meridian, from south to north, as I recorded the journey and the theory in an article for *National Geographic Adventure*.

It was not easy for Lekson to take two weeks off from his teaching duties and his frenetic research, but the idea appealed to him. For all the time he had spent at Chaco, Aztec, and Paquimé, he had never done what I was proposing—to retrace the supposed pilgrimage route on the ground. We would not be following the Meridian in its historical sequence—starting in the south at Paquimé, we would actually be beginning at the end—but we would be able to see with our eyes and feel under our boots the logic of the peregrination.

In early October 2004, Lekson and I rendezvoused in Silver City, New Mexico, with photographer Bill Hatcher. What ensued during the next eleven days was the most intellectually stimulating road trip of my life.

In Hatcher's vintage Ford truck, we careened south, crossing the Mexican border at Columbus, where Pancho Villa attacked the United States in 1916, launching Pershing's army of ten thousand on a futile pursuit through Chihuahua. A few hours later, we alighted in Nuevo Casas Grandes at the Hotel Hacienda, where during the next two evenings, once our work was done—if you can call hiking and gawking and photographing "work"—we sat in the palm-shaded inner courtyard squirting lime juice into tequila *añejo*, then repairing to excellent *carne adobada* and *enchiladas rojas* in the cozy dining room.

Paquimé lies only a few miles from the Hacienda. Hatcher and I had been to the site before, but never in the company of a guide like Lekson. As we strolled through the ruins, the archaeologist delivered a free-associative tour of the colonnade, the T-shaped doorways, the bed platforms, the macaw pens, the ball courts, the great kiva with a ramp entryway, and the rest of the arcana that informed his Meridian thesis.

The most bizarre thing about Paquimé—an architectural conundrum so vivid that it strikes even the untutored eye—is that its northern and western precincts abound in formal "mounds," or raised platforms laid out in various shapes (plumed serpent, cross, pyramid), built of solid stone mortared with mud. Yet the southern and eastern sides of the great village amount to an adobe labyrinth, up to four stories tall, in which narrow corridors twist toward hidden rooms and puzzling nooks and alcoves. Why build only in adobe, if you have decent stone available? For adobe is structurally weaker than masoned walls, and it erodes with every rainstorm. Yet here the adobe maze still stands, seven centuries after its builders began to lay the gooey brown muck in place. "It's about the architecture of power," said Lekson, for the first of many times on our trip.

Paquimé lies less than one hundred miles south of the U.S. border, yet it remains woefully undervisited by gringos (we saw only six or eight other *norteamericanos* during our two days there). This, despite the fact that the grandest archaeological ruin in northern Mexico is not only a national park but a UNESCO World Heritage Site.

Before our trip, I had phoned Eric Blinman to tell him about our impending junket. He had let out an exasperated sigh, then said, "I hope you hold Lekson's feet to the fire."

"What do you mean?"

"You've been to Paquimé," Blinman spewed. "It doesn't look anything like Chaco."

It turned out that Lekson had never heard Blinman's strictures about the Meridian from his colleague's mouth. Now I recounted that telephone exchange.

In response, Lekson's voice rose to a querulous pitch as he apostrophized his absent colleague. "Nothing else in P II [the Pueblo II period, from A.D. 900 to 1150] looks like Chaco. Eric, what do you want?" Agitated, Lekson took another look at the adobe marvel before us, and had an epiphany. "It's a dozen Great Houses all jammed together! It's the Emerald City of Oz. This is Chaco translated into P IV [A.D. 1350 to 1600], with a good dollop of Mesoamerica thrown in."

The very name of Paquimé is of uncertain origin. One version has it that the first Spanish visitors in the sixteenth century, staring dumb-founded at the ruins, asked the local Indians who had built this city. In some Piman tongue, the seminomadic locals answered with a simple phrase. "Paquimé," as the Spanish ear heard the Indian formula, means "Nobody knows."

About half of the ruin was excavated between 1958 and 1961 by Charles Di Peso, who, though a gringo working out of Arizona, saw the anomalous village in the middle of a Chihuahuan nowhere as a frontier expression of ideas emanating from the mighty cultures of central Mexico, such as the Toltecs, the Aztecs, and the builders of Teotihuacan. As Lekson told us, "Di Peso sees people coming up from the south and saying, 'You guys don't know how to build, we'll show you how.'" The abundance of certain trade goods at Paquimé—notably copper bells, macaw feathers, and Pacific Coast seashells—argues for such a linkage. But there is an old Mexican bias built in here. In Lekson's paraphrase: "This is Gran Chichimeca, the howling north. Nothing but savages. Even among the INAH [Instituto Nacional de Antropologica y Historia] guys today, working up here is considered hardship duty. You want to be in Mexico City."

Yet Di Peso also pointed out remarkable similarities between Paquimé and Chaco—presciently, from Lekson's point of view. For today's leading experts in the Casas Grandes area work very hard to see Paquimé as a local, isolated outburst of a culture with few links to either the south or the north. As Lekson ruminated out loud, "Whole careers have been made out of pulling Di Peso apart. I call it 'devaluing Di Peso.'" (Hatcher and I groaned at the pun.)

On our second day in Chihuahua, the three of us set out before dawn to hike up Cerro Moctezuma, the highest hill in the Paquimé region. For thirty years, ever since he had first read in Di Peso's report about the mysterious pair of sites near and on the cerro's summit, Lekson had intended to pay a visit, yet had never gotten around to it. Sizing up the peak the previous afternoon, we had guessed it would take half an hour to hike to the top. But the desert landscape, devoid of scale, fooled us badly. That morning it took three strenuous hours to complete the trek, as we crested one false summit after another, wrenched our ankles staggering across fields of loose rhyolite talus, and wove our way through spiny thickets of ocotillo, sotol, mesquite, and prickly pear.

At last we reached the shoulder on which stood the village nick-named El Pueblito, surmised to be the home of the guardians of the "atalaya" on the mountain's summit. In borrowing the Nahuatl (Aztec) term for "watchtower," Di Peso had loaded his argument in favor of the Mesoamerican influence from the south.

Wiping the sweat from his brow, Lekson paced through the ruins in a state of delighted shock. "Even though I'd looked at the maps, this place is much bigger than I expected," he confessed. Bigger, and far more complicated, for the central block of masoned stone-and-mud rooms was counterpointed by an adobe complex as tall as eleven feet. "Why the hell adobe, up here?" Lekson muttered. "You'd have to haul water and mud, how far?"

"Three miles from the nearest stream, a thousand feet of altitude," I answered, consulting the field report Lekson had lent me.

The three of us wandered through the seldom-visited ruin in a collective daze. There were brown and orange potsherds strewn everywhere, dating from the Medio period, contemporary with Paquimé. Large basalt manos and metates for grinding corn sat where they had been abandoned more than five centuries ago. Mortar and pestle holes had been gouged in the bedrock.

The strangest feature of the site was a massive wall on the eastern side, beautifully masoned with stones ranging up to the size of true boulders; the wall stretched for more than fifty yards, stood as tall as six feet, and at its thickest, had a breadth of a remarkable seven feet. Far from precisely straight, the wall swayed in sensuous wriggles along a north-south axis. Scholars had puzzled over this structure since the time of Adolf Bandelier, the Swiss-American pioneer of prehistory who had visited Cerro Moctezuma way back in 1884.

"I haven't seen anything like this in the Southwest," I said to Lekson.
"Me neither. This is cool!"

A moment later: "This site looks like Aztec North, guys! Wait'll we get there."

As we trudged on toward the summit, Lekson turned to look down on El Pueblito, and was visited with another epiphany. "Jesus, it's a serpent! Pointed north. Just like the Mound of the Serpent at Paquimé." Was Lekson right? There was no one alive who could tell us—but once more, the archaeologist's lightning intuition had forked through the clouds of ignorance, flashing a possible truth.

The atalaya on the summit was another stunner—by far the biggest peak-top tower any of us had ever seen in the Southwest. A double-walled ring fully sixty feet in diameter, the atalaya had evidently been quite tall, judging by the tons of rubble that had collapsed on every side. We sat beneath the north wall and gazed at distant mountain ranges. Far below us, smudged in the lowland haze, Paquimé slumbered.

"If it's a signal system," Lekson mused, "you need somebody at El Pueblito to answer the phone. But why does it take a whole town to take care of the atalaya? What's that all about? It would be a miserable place to live, so far from water and arable fields. But the metates and manos mean they *were* living there."

Lekson stared at the northern horizon. "You put Great Houses up high so they can see each other and talk back and forth. 'Smoke and mirrors.' Bonfires and pyrite. With one repeater, you could be talking to Aztec in fifteen minutes. But somebody's gotta be here to answer the phone.

"Why's the atalaya so big? The architecture of power. Impress the hell out of people. The construction of it would have been an event people remembered. It's monument-building.

"And if that wall really is a serpent . . ."

Hatcher and I looked at each other, dazzled by the show. I thought, This is how science gets done—by tossing ideas into the air like pebbles, just to see where they land. And staring north myself, I began to imagine that I could see all the way to Aztec.

After recrossing the border, we meandered through New Mexico for four days, making our leisurely way up to Chaco. No roads today follow Lekson's Meridian for more than an accidental mile or two at a time. The pilgrim of A.D. 1300, heading south beyond ruined Chaco, would have had to march across the desolate plateaus of today's Navajo Reservation, graze the edge of the Zuni Mountains, traverse the sinister lava flows of El Malpais National Monument, wind through the craggy Sawtooth Mountains, burst across the Plains of San Agustín, and plunge into the ponderosa forests of the Gila Wilderness and the Mogollon Mountains—just for starters.

So we rambled along highways and back roads as Lekson conducted his tour of the Meridian's tangled corollaries. Most of the sites we visited, Hatcher and I would have been at a loss to find on our own. Now, as we strolled through the prehistoric wreckage, we kept our ears cocked as Lekson unfurled one baroque hypothesis after another.

What sites! Near the Gila River, an unexcavated Mimbres village: a streamside bench scored with room-block undulations, strewn with literally thousands of sherds, whose taxonomic tags (Three Circle red-on-white, Boldface black-on-white, Classic Mimbres black-on-white) do not even hint at the beauty of the finest and most cryptic pottery ever produced in the Southwest. Lekson: "This is the stuff they should have made at Pueblo Bonito. But look at this architecture." His toe tapped a sagging wall made of unshaped river cobbles. "I used to call this a bunch of bowling balls in Jell-O. But that's probably not fair to the Mimbres. A bunch of bowling balls in peanut butter, then."

The Dittert Site, near El Malpais National Monument, right on the Meridian, a classic outlying Great House, where even Hatcher and I could see the masterly masonry that linked the place to Downtown Chaco, seventy-five miles to the north. Nearby, the hallucinogenic lizard-men petroglyphs at the mouth of Lobo Canyon. Sites in the most godforsaken places: Candelaria, only a stone's throw from a frozen tidal wave of black lava; Kin Ya'a, a four-story spike of masoned meaning, surrounded today only by the derelict pickups and disused wells of the Navajo Reservation; the Rams Pasture herradura, the subtlest of twin curling benches of stone in the shape of a horseshoe, which Lekson and a handful of other scholars believe proves the existence of the long-suspected South Road out of Chaco, the North Road's mirror twin.

Like smart-aleck sophomores in the front row, Hatcher and I delighted in needling our professor. "How can you call this a Great House?" I protested, looking at the tumbledown walls of a pueblo atop a crumbling butte. "It's just a bunch of rocks."

"Yep," answered Lekson, not missing a beat. "A big bump. Up on top of something vertical. Two stories. There's no community living here. But it's right on the Meridian. Some people think you get these every twenty miles or so. Maybe it's a place to flop along the road."

On successive nights, in the Big Burro Mountains and the Mangus Mountains, we car camped in upland meadows, lingering late by the fire as we watched the constellations wheel overhead. I cooked up my favorite glops, which we washed down with draughts of merlot and pinot noir. Lekson had confessed that nearly every night back in Boulder he woke up at 4 A.M., "wringing his hands" over all the tasks his stern superego reminded him were still undone. Those nights in the piñon and juniper, however, we managed to get enough wine inside the workaholic professor to allow him to sleep until dawn.

During these days in the field, I came to see a fundamental paradox about Steve Lekson. For all the wit and flamboyance of his writing, he is essentially a shy, private fellow. When I asked him if that was a fair assessment, he confirmed my hunch. Despite decades of practice, he confessed, he hates public speaking. And he is uncomfortable in the limelight, going out of his way to credit the work of colleagues who lack his gift for the oracular utterance.

For all my enthusiasm for the Chaco Meridian, I was not equipped to make a true critical evaluation of Lekson's bold idea. Only his professional peers could attempt that appraisal. To that end, on the last morning of our four-day jaunt north toward Chaco, I lured Eric Blinman away from his Santa Fe duties to meet us for breakfast in Grants, New Mexico. We assembled at 7 A.M. in a truck-stop café called 4-B's, just off Interstate 40. Far from defensive, Lekson welcomed the confrontation with his friend.

The three hours that passed in the café booth, over spongy eggs and leathery bacon and too many cups of coffee, had an effect on me not unlike watching a world-class table tennis match on fast-forward. The initial pleasantries took all of two minutes; then the volleys, smashes, and high-looping returns commenced. Sitting opposite each other, the two archaeologists flung out such terms as "parsimony" and "equifinality" and "the null hypothesis" like curse words from the gutters of academe. "Is it a scalar phenomenon?" Blinman jibed. "Data doesn't come in bags," Lekson counterpunched. "Steve," Blinman purred, his voice dripping with irony, "have you completely dismissed Peterson's argument about climate?" And: "The correlation between village size and hierarchy follows the Johnsonian rule of six."

The debate turned nasty early on, as Blinman admitted he hadn't actually read *The Chaco Meridian*. His only knowledge of its thesis came from the talk Lekson had given in Santa Fe in 1999. "I can't believe you haven't read the stinking book!" Lekson fumed. "I don't have time to read stuff just for the fun of it," Blinman witheringly rejoined. Then: "Have *you* read Orcutt, Blinman, and Kohler?" For once, Lekson teetered off-balance, until the work alluded to was glossed as a fairly obscure symposium paper authored by the antagonist himself, his ex-wife, and another colleague. Lekson allowed as how he had skimmed it.

With the ping-pong ball too fast to follow, I let my attention drift to observe the man who had been camping and hiking and speculating with us for the past six days. Slender, six feet two, with sandy hair, a trim mustache, and the timid onset of a goatee, Lekson looked far younger than his then fifty-four years. Even in casual chat, he talked at the frenetic, unpunctuated pace of a play-by-play sportscaster. When he got agitated and passionate, as he did now, he spoke even faster, his voice climbing in pitch to a screech of disbelief: how could the sheer reasonableness of his ideas somehow fail to sweep away his critics' doubts?

I relished—and came close to following—some of the machine-gun volleys at the net. "So you have to argue that influence is moving without a material correlate?" Blinman stabbed.

"Shell," Lekson shot back.

"Shell moves. From California? Pottery doesn't."

"Who cares about pottery?"

"Pottery carries symbolic meaning."

"No. Clothes do. A bone through the nose. I just gave you a bag of evidence, Eric, and you don't like it."

During such crossfires, the two archaeologists did not quite pound on the table, but their voices rose and they resorted to more than a few undeleted expletives. At one point, a solitary codger in the next booth who was placidly chewing his oatmeal looked over in alarm, as if for fear that the two mild-mannered-looking gents nearby might actually come to blows.

At the end of three hours of haranguing, Blinman remained unmoved. In his book, Paquimé had nothing to do, culturally, with Aztec and Chaco. Exhausted, the two men rose from the table and shook hands. "This is the kind of intellectual excitement that makes our whole profession worthwhile," said Blinman. "It's always good talking with you, Eric," Lekson lobbed back. But for hours, even days, after the shootout at the 4-B corral, as we drove on north, Lekson would suddenly exclaim, "Damn it, I just realized what I should have said to Eric."

During the parts of three days that we spent at Chaco, we had time to visit only five of the dozen Great Houses that define the Anasazi marvel of the eleventh and early twelfth centuries. I had toured each of them several times before, but in a state (as I now realized) of relative ignorance.

One warm morning, we hiked the three-mile loop trail to Pueblo Alto, built on a lonely plateau north of Chaco Canyon itself. After crossing a short, level plain, we came to a hundred-foot sandstone cliff. A hidden chimney allowed us to scramble up to the rim. There we stood just after dawn and stared down at Pueblo Bonito, which some experts deem the most important prehistoric ruin in the United States—a village of between six and eight hundred interconnected rooms, the rear wall five stories tall, the whole town laid out in a perfect D shape.

"Imagine that you're a fourteen-year-old kid in the eleventh century, coming from the boondocks to Chaco for the first time," mused Lekson. "You've walked four days from the north across that desolate plain to get here. You look over the edge—"

All three of us stared down at Pueblo Bonito, awash in the orange sunrise.

"It would scare the hell out of you," Lekson concluded his whimsy. "They planned it as theater."

We hiked on to Pueblo Alto. There we time-traveled back into our mentor's youth, for here he had dug his first Chacoan room in 1976. Standing on top of the backfilled quadrangle where he had toiled a quarter century before, the archaeologist resisted nostalgia. "We should have dug the kivas first," he inveighed. "That's where they were living." Not lost on me was Lekson's impish allusion to his own 1988 paper that had revolutionized the understanding of kivas.

Over a picnic lunch, we took in the view from Pueblo Alto. "You can see most of the San Juan basin from here," said Lekson. "Every direction except southwest." He pointed toward the north. "That's Huerfano Butte. Keep that in mind when we get to Chimney Rock. And don't forget that the Great North Road starts right here. Where it ends, we're still squabbling about."

Lekson's digging in the late 1970s was part of one of the most ambitious programs ever undertaken in the Southwest: the Chaco Project, a ten-year-long intensive study, involving scores of archaeologists, that probed every aspect of the matchless but deeply enigmatic center of the near-empire that had flourished in this barren wasteland almost a millennium ago. It was no small irony that, eighteen years after the project's termination, Lekson had been charged with writing the impossible volume that tried to synthesize all that research.

So our seminar trundled on, as we poked through the Great Houses of Chetro Ketl and Pueblo Bonito, to a running commentary from our professor's overflowing brain. An example: on previous visits, I had walked right past the Chetro Ketl colonnade without even recognizing it for what it was. Now I not only saw the long, twin-columned passageway but divined its kinship with the one at Paquimé. "This is the only known colonnade in the American Southwest," said Lekson. "But I'd bet we'd find one at Aztec, if we dug in the right place."

Colonnades are unmistakably a Mesoamerican invention. As our guide now mused, "These guys go down to Mexico. Shake hands with the emperor. They come back and say, 'When I was down there, I saw one of these things.' So they build one here at Chetro Ketl, and in the process one-up the folks at Pueblo Bonito, next door."

"Why have we found so few burials at Chaco Canyon?" I asked Lekson at another point. The paucity of graves has puzzled every excavator since the 1890s.

"It's not a pueblo," responded Lekson. "It's a ritual center. That's my answer, anyway."

As this exchange suggests, Chaco is so mysterious that good scholars vehemently disagree on the basic question of just what it was all about. To build the colossal Great Houses, literally hundreds of thousands of timbers were carried as far as fifty miles, from forests in the Lukachukai and Chuska Mountains, to serve as roof beams. Shortly before our trip, it was discovered that corn found in storage rooms at Chaco had also been grown some fifty miles away.

Lekson's views about Chaco are on an extreme end of the scholarly spectrum. He sees the place not only as the center of a sprawling network of vassal villages, but as a hierarchical civilization that enforced its rule with violence and even cannibalism. As Lekson summed up the controversy, "My version of Chaco is a little more brutal and political than most people like. Most people want a kinder, gentler Chaco."

Supporting Lekson's take is a discovery made in a pair of adjoining rooms at Pueblo Bonito way back in 1896, by the cowboy turned archaeologist Richard Wetherill. In those otherwise ordinary chambers, two skeletons seemed to have been interred in the richest "status burial" ever found in the Southwest. These men were accompanied by a basket inlaid with a mosaic made of 1,214 pieces of turquoise, an exquisite frog carved out of jet, a shell trumpet, a quiver filled with eighty-one arrows, three hundred wooden staffs, several turquoise-inlaid effigies, and hundreds of scattered beads and pendants. One of the two skeletons wore bands of turquoise beads around his wrists and ankles, as well as a pair of chest pendants composed of some four thousand pieces of turquoise.

In *The Chaco Meridian*, Lekson writes of this astonishing pair of skeletons: "Were they chiefs, priests, kings, queens, duly-elected representatives? Who knows? And for now, who cares? They were elite leaders, Major Dudes; that much seems clear. If ever anyone in the Pueblo Southwest was elite, it was those two guys buried in the famous log crypts of Old Bonito. Those boys had power."

The "brutal, political" picture Lekson paints of Chaco is crucial to the whole Meridian argument, for only such a despotic, well-organized regime could have kept its cultural stamp intact across a migration on a north-south vector among three successive centers spanning 450 miles and five centuries. If Lekson is right, then what happened to that quasi-empire? Why are the Puebloans of today—the descendants of Chaco's builders—so egalitarian and autonomous?

I had heard Lekson outline the answer at 4-B's, in the middle of his tussle with Blinman. "All the Pueblos have legends today about the 'White House,'" he had explained. "Florence Hawley Ellis goes around in the 1960s and asks them, 'Is the White House Mesa Verde?' They say yes—partly, I think, because they themselves have heard so much hype about Mesa Verde.

"But there's a lot of evidence that the White House was really Chaco. In the legends, it was a place that was abandoned because something went wrong. Perhaps the rulers became too powerful. Today's Puebloans say, 'We don't talk about that place. Bad stuff happened there.' They'd seen guys throwing their weight around in unpleasant ways, and decided it was no good."

Onward into the north we drove, past more seldom-visited sites, each a piece of the Leksonian puzzle: Pierre's Ruin, Twin Angels Pueblo, the Kutz Canyon herradura, Salmon Ruins on the San Juan . . .

We spent but a single day at Aztec Ruins National Monument. Excavated, restored, and stabilized by the pioneering archaeologist Earl Morris between 1916 and 1921, Aztec revealed itself as a three-story complex of some 353 contiguous rooms, as well as twenty-nine kivas. The place had long been recognized as a major Ancestral Puebloan center that flourished in the twelfth and thirteenth centuries (right after the demise of Chaco); but it was not until about twenty years ago, thanks largely to the work of Lekson's colleagues Peter McKenna and John Stein, that scholars acknowledged Aztec's preeminence in its era. For the Aztec that Morris dug and rebuilt—the Aztec that the tourist visits today—amounts to a mere one-fourth of the gigantic site.

Aztec West, as Morris's creation is nicknamed, stands mirrored by Aztec East, a wholly separate pueblo two hundred yards away, which looms as a jumbled, sprawling pile of weed-covered rubble. If excavated, it would doubtless produce as many rooms, burials, and artifacts as Aztec West. It was Aztec North that nobody seemed to suspect (Morris must have known about it, but he never mentions it in his reports).

On a raw, rainy afternoon, I drove back roads with Lekson to circle around to Aztec North, which stands on a shelf some hundred feet above Morris's ruin. We zigzagged on foot across an ugly bench clustered with sage and prickly pear. There were potsherds everywhere, but little else to see. "Where are the room blocks?" I asked my guide.

"It's adobe," Lekson answered.

"My god. Why?"

I flashed on Paquimé—the adobe labyrinth balanced by the Mounds of the Serpent, the Cross, the Heroes. Lekson did not need to remind me of the parallel.

Only in the last few years, thanks to such techniques as ground-penetrating radar, has the vast extent of Aztec North begun to be glimpsed. There are no plans at the moment, however, to excavate its hidden secrets. But Lekson and his like-minded cronies believe that, taken as a whole, Aztec must have been the largest Ancestral Puebloan center in the Southwest for about 175 years, from A.D. 1125 to 1300—smaller by one order of magnitude than Chaco, but larger than Paquimé.

Late that same day, we sat inside the great kiva at Aztec West, one of the most astounding prehistoric structures in the Southwest. As restored by Morris in the mid-1930s, it stands seventy feet in diameter by a daunting sixteen feet tall. Four giant masonry columns, each mounted on four heavy disks of limestone hewn to the task (the rest of the ruin is sandstone), support the massive roof. A pair of "foot drums"—coffinlike floor vaults big enough to hold several reclining adults—may have been covered with planking and stomped on by masked dancers to create an impressive, booming report. The red-and-white-painted walls match the colors Morris found on the flaking plaster inside the ruin.

Unlike the twenty-nine smaller kivas at Aztec West, the great kiva was unmistakably a ceremonial chamber, one that would have tied together a far-flung community that came to Aztec for special occasions of worship and celebration. "This is the only restored great kiva in the Southwest with a roof," Lekson explained. "I think it's really cool. Morris was a smart guy—he knew what he was doing. But I've come here with Puebloans, and they're ambivalent at best. They're polite, but their take on this place is that they're not sure it should have been rebuilt. Ruins are supposed to be ruins, to fall apart and return to the ground."

For Lekson and me, however, the magnificence of the great kiva was an enduring testimony to the brilliance of Ancestral Puebloan civilization. Blinman was still rattling around in Lekson's head. "You know," he said now, "Eric's 'parsimony' seems like a sure way to be wrong." Again and again at 4-B's, Blinman had invoked "parsimony"—the notion that the simplest, most reductionist explanation of a phenomenon was the most likely to be right. The alignment of Aztec, Chaco, and Paquimé was thus a mere accident. "The ancients were doing so much more," Lekson added, holding his palm open toward the architectural wonder before our eyes. "All we're seeing is a fraction of a fraction of the material culture."

The wildest surmise in Lekson's book is tucked away in a five-page appendix. There, the author slyly notes that when the first conquistadors pushed north from central Mexico into present-day Sinaloa in the 1530s, they found a massive, flourishing Indian civilization at a site they called Culiacán. Guess what? Culiacán is awfully close to 107°57′ W. With the demise of Paquimé around A.D. 1450, could the same visionary migrants have carried their civilization another four hundred miles straight south, across the towering ridges of the Sierra Madre and the plunging chasms of Copper Canyon, to found the last of four great centers on the Meridian?

Even Lekson is too cautious to assert such a claim without evidence. He has never been to Culiacán. The only archaeology ever performed among the ruins there was that of a Berkeley team in the 1930s, who barely scratched the surface. Are there T-shaped doorways, colonnades, bed platforms, and great kivas—features that appear together only at Chaco, Aztec, and Paquimé—at Culiacán? No one seems to know.

Instead, Lekson closes his book with a subversive tease: "Was Culiacán the last hurrah? . . . Or is Culiacán another beautiful fact, killed by an ugly theory? Sing the benediction: More research is necessary."

Ever since our road trip in 2004, I've teased Lekson with the suggestion that we should go to Culiacán together and check out the ruins. But especially in recent years, that town, the center of the Sinaloa drug cartel, has become one of the most dangerous places in North America. A recent government travel advisory warns, "With the exception of Ciudad Juarez, since 2006 more homicides have occurred in the state's capital city of Culiacán than in any other city in Mexico."

For now, we're taking a raincheck.

In the years since *The Chaco Meridian* appeared, however, Lekson has come across new discoveries that he believes further bolster his radical thesis. A 2009 paper that he published in the journal *Archaeology*, titled "Amending the Meridian," gives a glimpse of these revelations. One came during a visit to a place formerly called Sacred Ridge, just south of Durango, Colorado. There, a "rescue" excavation called the Animas–La Plata Project (ALP) was taking place in advance of the construction of a dam and a reservoir. Shown around the site by the director of the excavation, Jim Potter, Lekson, as he writes, "was immensely impressed by the size and complexity of the pit-house sites, which dated to the eighth century A.D. There was nothing in the ALP area immediately before the eighth century, and nothing after. It was a big—but short-lived—bang."

A further tour of the eight-mile-wide swath of the project convinced Lekson that "there were more eighth-century sites than in any other area in the northern Southwest. It was a continuous blur of houses and villages. . . . ALP excavators found things on Sacred Ridge that no one had ever seen at eighth-century sites, such as the 10-foot-wide base of a two-story tower. Nobody built towers in the eighth century!"

The tour, Lekson wrote, "got me hopping-up-and-down excited again," for a glance at the map confirmed his hunch: Sacred Ridge lay very close to the 107°57' meridian—not precisely on it, but close.

Could the ALP excavation have revealed the center of the Meridian-based civilization two hundred years before Chaco got started? Lekson liked to think so.

That epiphany jogged Lekson's encyclopedic memory of Chaco Canyon. As he writes in "Amending the Meridian":

> The "Chaco" of *Chaco Meridian* was the grouping of stone-masonry Great Houses of the 11th and 12th centuries, like Pueblo Bonito. But there had been strange doings at Chaco Canyon long before those famous photogenic structures. In the sixth and early seventh centuries, Shabik'eschee Village and another unnamed pit-house site . . . flourished in the canyon. These sites were not visually spectacular . . . but they were big, indeed the biggest pit-house sites of their times in the Pueblo region. Each had more than 80 houses, and each had a Great Kiva. . . . The next largest sites of that period had about 20 pit-houses.

Was Shabik'eschee the Meridian center before Sacred Ridge? Near the end of his paper, Lekson drives home his amended thesis. (As I read it for the first time, I could see Eric Blinman rolling his eyes.)

> Shabik'eschee, Sacred Ridge, Chaco, Aztec, and Paquimé—five unique points in a line, each the biggest and most important site of its respective era. The chances of that happening by accident are minuscule. There has to be history—human decisions and human intentions—behind the Meridian.
>
> So, for seven centuries, the center of the Pueblo World bounced back and forth over (only) 80 miles, from Chaco Canyon to Sacred Ridge and back again—and then to Aztec Ruins. The southern extension to Paquimé is still a matter of doubt and debate, I admit. But the new data from Shabik'eschee and the ALP complex give me some confidence that the Chaco Meridian was real, and that it meant something to ancient Pueblo people.
>
> What exactly did it mean? I don't know—yet.

In 2009, Lekson published his magnum opus, *A History of the Ancient Southwest*. It was at the same time a comprehensive synthesis that, in my view at least, supersedes all such prior efforts, and, like *The Chaco Meridian*, a dazzling compendium of asides, tangents, skating-on-thin-ice probes into the *incognita*, and leaps of connectivity between realms that had never before been linked. It shares with Edward Gibbon, the great historian of the fall of Rome, the quirk that the endnotes—ninety-seven pages of them in very small type—are at least as exhilarating and deep as the text itself. Reading it, I found myself thrilled, challenged to the limits of my intelligence, and provoked to outright laughter by the wit, the high-wire riffs, and yes, even the bad puns of Lekson's prose.

As I had learned over the years, the labels of "gadfly" and "iconoclast" that his critics have pinned to him vex Steve Lekson, because they minimize the substantive breakthroughs of concerted research on his part that have transformed our understanding of the prehistoric Southwest. Just as the revolutionary idea that kivas were domestic living rooms rather than ceremonial or religious chambers has by now gained general acceptance, so has the belief—so radical in 1999 that it was widely denounced by his peers—that Chaco moved to Aztec after A.D. 1125 won the day. Paquimé will prove a tougher sell. As Lekson sardonically wrote in a recent paper,

> The Four Corners crowd spun and sputtered and denied absolutely that Chaco had moved to Aztec Ruins. They didn't mind so much about Paquimé, that was beyond their horizons. The Paquimé gang wanted no part of Chacoans from the north.

However,

> Today, two decades later, almost everyone accepts three of those four points: Chaco moved north to Aztec Ruins. Paquimé, the fourth and final point on the Meridian, is still in play. Lots of evidence, few believers.

When all is said and done, Lekson is not so much an iconoclast as a synthesizer, a scholar who always tries to see the big picture. His sort doesn't come along very often. So it was a rare privilege to ride the Meridian with him in 2004.

On our last day together, Lekson's tour took Hatcher and me to Chimney Rock, near Pagosa Springs, Colorado. High on a sharp ridge that soars toward twin pinnacles Chacoans had built the most northeasterly outlying Great House of their vast network, fifty miles beyond Aztec, twice that distance from Downtown Chaco. At 7,600 feet above sea level, Chimney Rock is also the highest of all the Chaco outliers. At first blush, it seems an absurd place to live: the nearest water, in the Piedra River, flows four miles away and twelve hundred feet below.

Now we stood beside a Great House, whose floor plans and splendidly fitted masonry had a cookie-cutter affinity with the Great Houses at Chaco. Said Lekson, "I'd like to take the Chaco skeptics from Arizona up here." Some archaeologists, surprisingly, still doubt the very existence of a network of Chacoan outliers. "I'd say, 'Okay, make this one go away.'"

Tree-ring dates from the pueblo demonstrated that it was built in two phases, in 1075 and 1094. Lekson's University of Colorado colleague, Kim Malville, has elegantly demonstrated that those two dates were not only the years of the lunar standstill—the farthest northern points on the horizon of the rising of the full moon, which wanders through a cycle of 18.6 years—but also that near the winter solstice in both of those years, the full moon, as viewed from the Great House, appeared exactly in the notch between Chimney Rock's twin pinnacles. Of what use is such esoteric knowledge? Malville argues that Chacoan astronomer-priests could have used the standstill to guarantee that there would be no solar eclipses during those years. To the humble denizens of this far northern outpost, the Chacoans must have been seen as communicating directly with the gods.

Now Lekson pointed at the southern horizon. "Huerfano Butte," he said, like a math teacher writing "QED" on the blackboard. "It took a high school student, Katie Freeman, to prove that you need only two lines of sight from here to Pueblo Alto, more than a hundred miles away, with Huerfano Butte as the relay station. And there are structures all over the top of the butte." The professor smiled. "She did it as a school science project."

As I gazed at the blue horizon, I saw myself, Hatcher, and Lekson standing, some ten days before, atop the atalaya on Cerro Moctezuma, a good five hundred miles away. I flashed through all the obscure, diminutive sites we had visited on our meandering journey north from Chihuahua, then on the prodigies of Paquimé, Chaco, and Aztec. The Meridian stretched south from beneath my boot soles. I was ready to believe.

Five

WANDERING THE REZ

Open the Automobile Club of Southern California's beautifully drawn Indian Country map—the favorite chart of the Southwest for many of us devotees. Near the center sprawls a huge, zigzag-bordered tract of land, shaded in light purple. It's the Navajo Reservation, established in 1868, its borders adjusted through the decades since. Occupying most of northeastern Arizona, with a broad swath in northwestern New Mexico and a lumpy band stretching across southeastern Utah, it's the largest Native American reservation in the country, covering 27,425 square miles, or 1,755,200 acres. The 2011 population of the Navajo Nation was just over 300,000, making it, along with the Cherokee, one of the two largest tribes in the United States. Not all Navajos live on the Rez, as it's called by natives and Anglos alike. No precise count of the residents of the purple tract has been made, but estimates hover around 175,000. If that number is accurate, it means that the Rez is actually sparsely populated, with only about one Navajo per ten acres.

The land of today's Navajo Reservation was also prime territory for Ancestral Puebloans during thousands of years dating back into the Archaic. As a result, ruins and rock art abound all over the Rez. The relationship between Navajo and Ancestral Puebloan forms a complex and fascinating nexus, still not well understood. Obviously, the reservation, so rich in the abandoned sites of the Old Ones, is a great place to hike and backpack in search of prehistoric wonders. Yet for various reasons, relatively few Anglos undertake such ventures. To hike anywhere in the backcountry, you need an official permit issued by the Navajo Nation headquarters in Window Rock, Arizona. During the last decade, those permits have become harder to obtain. And more and more regions have been declared off-limits to intruders. The reasons are not always made explicit, but they tend to center around the notion of respecting the privacy of Navajos who live near the sites.

No locus of Ancestral Puebloan presence on the Rez is more dramatic than Canyon de Chelly, a national monument in northeastern Arizona. Ruins such as White House, Antelope House, and Mummy Cave are as splendid as any in the Southwest, but entering them has been forbidden for decades. Likewise, a more recent prohibition forbids hikers to approach such rock art galleries as the Narbona panel or Ceremonial Cave. For that matter, only a single self-guided trail, an easy two-and-a-half-mile round-trip stroll to a vantage point below White House ruin, is open to non-Navajo visitors.

Which is why, one bright, warm day in the spring of 2008, photographer Dawn Kish and I found ourselves in the company of Kalvin Watchman, a fit, forty-three-year-old Navajo guide, who was leading us down the White Sands Trail, an improbable, wildly exposed ancient shortcut from the southwest rim of Canyon de Chelly down to the valley bottom. It's not my style to hire a guide in the Southwest, but according to national monument regulations, that's the only way to explore the intricacies of this immemorial sandstone fortress.

Halfway down the trail, we paused for a lunch break. At our backs the sheer wall rose vertical, eclipsing half the blue sky. Four hundred feet below us, a ribbon of green—willows and tamarisk—traced the whimsical meanders of Chinle Wash. Against the far wall, a grid of peach trees in early bloom identified a longtime resident's orchard. The south wind that torments the canyonlands every spring was in full force; later that day, it would batter us with gusts of forty miles an hour. But the wind cut the heat of late May, and as I caught my breath, I realized that at that moment, there was no place on earth where I would rather be.

Over to the right, a hundred yards from the trail, I spotted a pile of stones neatly stacked on a small ledge. "What's that?" I asked Kalvin.

"When the people come up," he answered, "they carry a stone, and they pray to the canyon."

"Pray for what?"

"For safety. Not just to get out of the canyon okay, but safety in general. And fertility."

I'd made five or six previous trips to Canyon de Chelly, on each one hiking to places that were new to me. What brings me back, besides the beauty of the landscape and its ancient sites, is the unique and paradoxical status of the monument. In the Southwest, there are some seventeen national parks and monuments devoted to preserving the ruins and rock art of prehistoric Americans. They range from Mesa Verde to Bandelier to Hovenweep. Other jewels in the park system, such as Arches or Canyonlands or the Grand Canyon, enfold such vestiges of the ancients almost as an afterthought—*mérite le détour* for the tourist in search of natural sublimity. Among them all, only Canyon de Chelly tries to balance the recreational agendas of visitors who flock to the place from all over the globe with the needs of the Native Americans who live there.

For at least the last 250 years (some would say longer), the twin gorges of Canyon de Chelly have formed one of the most sacred locales in the Navajo universe. This was the stronghold in which the Diné (as the Navajo call themselves) believed they could never be conquered by enemies. It was the refuge where, during the cruelest droughts, the water would always flow and the corn grow. And it was the dwelling place of Spider Woman, the deity who taught the Diné to weave and who gave the Hero Twins the power to overcome monsters.

Needless to say, by the time President Herbert Hoover signed Canyon de Chelly National Monument into being on April 1, 1931, the government had not bothered to consult many Navajos about such a designation. More than eighty years later, the friction and misunderstanding that arose with the establishment of the monument seep to the surface in cultural ambiguities that play themselves out daily.

There's a tradeoff involved in trying to apprehend the wonders of Canyon de Chelly. It's frustrating not to be able to walk, however carefully, through the ruins, or to peruse the rock art panels up close. And it's confining to be restricted to the itinerary and the timetable of a Navajo guide. Those trip leaders vary widely in savvy and enthusiasm; some of them are barely going through the motions. Twice I'd been stood up by a guide I'd reserved in advance, when the man in question apparently found something better to do with his day. But Kalvin Watchman, I'd already concluded, was as good as they get.

The benefit of going with a skilled Navajo guide lies in seeing the landscape from the Diné point of view, and in gaining insight into the ambivalent and puzzling Navajo take on the Ancestral Puebloans.

The contrast could not be more blatant. Navajos claim that they have always lived within the quadrangle formed by the four sacred mountains: Sierra Blanca in southern Colorado, Mount Taylor in western New Mexico, the San Francisco Peaks just north of Flagstaff, Arizona, and Hesperus Mountain, north of Mancos, Colorado. The creation myth details with rich specificity the religious significance of virtually every topographic feature within that quadrangle.

Yet most anthropologists argue that the Diné are Athapaskans who migrated from subarctic Canada, close cousins to such tribes as the Chipewyan and the Dogrib or Kutchin who even today inhabit the Yukon and Northwest Territories. And archaeologists have concluded that the Navajo did not enter the Southwest before A.D. 1400, and most would set the date closer to 1500. Thus, in all likelihood, when the Diné arrived in the homeland now consecrated by the reservation, the Ancestral Puebloans had already abandoned it.

Just after lunch, as we pushed on down the White Sands Trail, Kalvin volunteered, "'Navajo' is a Tewa word. It means 'cultivators of the field.'" That was exactly what I had gleaned from anthropological treatises: conquistadors in New Mexico in the seventeenth century had first heard the term on the lips of Tewa Indians from such pueblos as San Ildefonso and Santa Clara, as they referred in hushed terms to "savage" marauders to the north. But then Kalvin went on, "In Spanish, Navajo means 'thieves.'" That was news to me.

We reached the foot of the trail and emerged onto the canyon floor. Across the Chinle, shelving from a high ledge in the southwest-facing wall, stood Sliding Rock Ruins. I asked Kalvin, "Can we at least go to the foot of it?"

"Nope," our guide answered evenly. "Ned Yazzie's got it fenced off."

Kalvin gazed across the homestead spread in front of us. "He lives three seasons in here. Comes out the White Sands Trail at first frost each fall."

I spent long minutes staring at Sliding Rock through my binoculars. The ruin contained at least fifty rooms, most of them shored up with stone-and-mud footings to give each dwelling a level floor. Behind the dwellings, on the overhanging cliff, I thought I could make out the vestiges of cryptic pictographs.

Leaving Sliding Rock behind us, we headed east, hiking upstream along the bank of Chinle Wash. As we walked, Kalvin told Dawn and me something about himself. He had grown up near the mouth of the canyon, not far from a place called Duck Ruins. We learned that he had six kids, two of them stepchildren, ranging in age from toddler to twenty-three.

As we moseyed along, Kalvin narrated the landscape. Indicating a sagging hogan on our right, he said, "Chauncey Neboyia lived right there. He was one of the code talkers in World War II." A little later, Kalvin paused to point out a desperate-looking chute snaking down from the rim to the south. "That's the Zuni Trail. Zunis used to come in and out that way in the 1700s, to trade with the people."

The wind was picking up. I could taste grit in my teeth. We turned a corner, and as I peered at the skirt of the massive cliff on our left, I shouted, "Edward Curtis!" Kalvin smiled, perhaps approvingly.

The scene before us matched every detail in one of Curtis's most famous photographs, shot here in 1904. In the picture, seven mounted riders and a dog—black silhouettes in the middle distance—move with solemn purpose from left to right toward some secret destination. We dropped our packs and spent half an hour cavorting about this canyon bend. A forty-foot Ancestral Puebloan hand-and-toe trail led us up the fifty-degree skirt to a blank dead end. Dawn posed us as she tried to duplicate the iconic black-and-white photo from a century before.

"His picture was a fake," Kalvin declared. "They were actors."

"Who?"

"The guys in his photo. He used the family of the guide who took him in here. They passed the story down to us."

We moved on. High on an obscure left wall, almost hidden by foliage, Kalvin pointed out a painted frieze of white *yei'bi'cheis*—slender stick humanoids representing the supernatural beings who are personified by the dancers in the nine-day Nightway healing ceremony. Once more, I used my binoculars as I absorbed a panel I would never have seen without Kalvin's nudge.

Farther on, we passed by a traditional female hogan—a hexagonal dwelling made of stone, mud, logs, and sticks. "This was the Henrys' place," Kalvin annotated. "They built it in the 1960s."

"Do the Navajos still abandon a hogan after somebody dies in it?" I asked.

Kalvin nodded. "Sometimes they knock down the west wall to let the spirit escape." Out loud, he counted the horizontal timbers, from base to roofline: ". . . seven, eight, nine. One for each month of a woman's pregnancy."

By mid-afternoon, we had rounded five bends in the deep defile, each one opening a new vista in the east. Now in the distance we could see the natural arch called the Window, the goal for our day's ambulation. "How long have the Diné lived in Canyon de Chelly?" I asked Kalvin.

"Since the 1300s."

That's not what the anthropologists think, I was tempted to say. But I kept my silence.

According to archaeologists, who have tree-ring-dated hogans and other structures, the Navajo first appeared in the Southwest in a region they call Dinétah—a series of shallow canyons southeast of Farmington, New Mexico. Forced out of Dinétah by disruptions caused by the Spanish reconquest of the Pueblo world after 1692—so say the experts—the Navajo made their way south and west, fetching up in Canyon de Chelly only around 1750.

"Were the Anasazi still here when the Navajo arrived?" (In 2008, I had yet to succumb to the p.c. insistence on "Ancestral Puebloans.")

"No," said Kalvin.

"What happened to the Anasazi?"

"They angered the Holy Ones."

"Chelly"—pronounced "Shay-ee"—is a Spanish rendering of *tségi*, the Navajo word for "canyon." Canyon de Chelly, then, means "Canyon Canyon."

Chinle Wash, a major southern tributary of the San Juan River, has its headwaters (as does its northern companion, Tsaile Creek) in the pine-clad forests of the Chuska Mountains. Both rivulets trickle westward across a nondescript plateau before deciding to carve diminutive canyons that commence with mere thirty-foot walls. In the next twenty-five miles of Canyon de Chelly proper (Chinle Wash) and thirty miles of Canyon del Muerto (Tsaile Creek), those streams plunge with a vengeance, scraping out gorges whose walls rise to a dizzying thousand feet.

Four miles short of a western gateway, the two canyons converge, but by then, their geologic mayhem is spent. The walls diminish, then peter out entirely as the Chinle meanders into a tumbleweed badlands, where it turns north to keep its appointment with the San Juan. At the canyon's mouth sprawls the dreary town of Chinle—trailer parks, prefab "government housing," McDonald's and KFC, a Basha's supermarket, three or four motels—and the monument headquarters, where tourists alight to design their visits. Shaped like a three-fingered mitten that covers all the canyon wonders, the monument contains eighty-four thousand acres, on most of which live Navajos today, including the more traditional fam[i]les who dwell in perpetual fear that the federal government will make new rules to circumscribe their ancient lifeways, or even kick them out of the canyon for good.

In 2007, the year before Dawn's and my hike with Kalvin, Canyon de Chelly headquarters counted 94,582 visitors. The total number of tourists is considerably higher, since many passersby never stop to chat with the rangers. In late spring and summer, the Chinle motels and campgrounds teem with Europeans and Japanese. Among this country's national parks and monuments, however, it is hard to think of one that less readily lends itself to the appreciation of the serious visitor. Thanks to the paradoxes of bureaucracy, something like 99 percent of the tourists embrace the monument in only three ways. They

> Drive the rim roads, stop at the pullouts, and take their postcard snapshots. The views from the overlooks are indeed majestic, but after all, a postcard is only a postcard.

> Ride up the canyon in the open back of a six-wheel jeep with some twenty other tourists, never dismounting, as they listen to a drive-through spiel. In the lower canyon, the trucks have a habit of getting mired in quicksand. (On our second day, in the midst of a chilling rainstorm, we heard the whine of gears ahead of us. "Here comes the shake-and-bake," said Kalvin, using the guides' ironic term for the big trucks, an epithet that has been in use for more than two decades. The jeep bounced past us, all twenty-odd clients outfitted with black garbage bags in lieu of ponchos, staring forlornly at one another or their feet. No "bake" that drizzly day, but rather "shake-and-soak.")

> Take the self-guided hike from the south rim down to White House. It's a wonderful trail, and the ruin is a stunning and important one. But the outing tends to get trivialized by the hordes of other hikers, and by the Navajo vendors who set up jewelry and curio stands just below the ruin.

Despite those vendors, according to anthropologist Jeanne M. Simonelli, who spent several summers as a ranger in the monument in the 1990s, "The typical visitor comes to see the canyon's archaeology and scenery. Interaction with Navajo residents is minimal. In fact, many visitors are unaware that the canyon is occupied." The average tourist's stay at Canyon de Chelly is less than a day.

Four hours into our hike, we came to the Window. A massive ovoid arch with its own capstone bridge, it soared into the sky halfway up the eight-hundred-foot precipice on the north. We had hoped to circle around back and scramble up to it, but from the valley floor we could hear the wind roaring through the arch, and could imagine ourselves ejected therefrom like so much sandstone debris. Instead, Dawn framed the Window every which way with her camera. An excellent climber as well as a first-rate photographer, Dawn is an exuberant, tall, red-haired ex-model who communicates in a cowgirl drawl. Now she said to Kalvin, "Darlin', hold this lens a minute, will ya?"

"Yeah, but that'll cost you extra." A thin smile creased our guide's stoic face. (Dawn, I had come to know, calls everybody "darlin'," as in the Andrews Sisters' song.)

Now Kalvin pointed northwest. "Way up there, just under the rim. Beehive ruin."

Again I trained my binoculars. Far above us, the crumbling walls of forgotten dwellings hid inside a small, dark alcove. Surveying the cliff, I guessed that it would have taken me half a day to work out a route up to that strange eyrie, even though an ancient trail supposedly solved the passage. I knew about Beehive from my reading. Way back in 1904, a local Indian trader named Sam Day—little better than a pothunter, though the Department of the Interior appointed him "custodian" of Canyon de Chelly—ravaged the ruin for artifacts to sell to tourists. Some of the relics, fortunately, ended up in the hands of Jesse Fewkes, one of the leading archaeologists of the day. Fewkes identified fragments of kachina masks, ritual paraphernalia used by various Pueblo peoples after about A.D. 1350. Fewkes further linked the masks to the Asa Clan at Hopi. It was a stunning confirmation of an old oral tale.

We know that the Hopi descend in part from the Ancestral Puebloans. A decade before Sam Day's scavenger hunt in Beehive, members of the Asa Clan had told an ethnographer about how their ancestors, in times of drought, had returned to Canyon de Chelly long after the abandonment, lived for two or three generations there, planted the first peach trees, and intermarried with the Navajo. Skeptics had dismissed the story as a fanciful hodgepodge, until Fewkes verified it with the fragile pieces of kachina masks.

Musing upon these fugitive intersections in the past, I wondered if Kalvin might be right, after all, and the anthropologists wrong. Could the Navajo have been here as early as the 1300s?

Book learning might, after all, dovetail freakishly with oral tradition. But on our way out, a mile back down the Chinle, Kalvin told us another story that no amount of library time could have confirmed or contradicted.

Again he pointed to the cliff on the north. "See that little wall, 'bout two hundred feet up, standing in front of that little cave?"

We squinted and found it. I raised my binoculars for the fortieth time that day. The wall was evidently man-made. We would never have noticed it had Kalvin not called it to our attention.

"In the winter of 1863," our guide elaborated, "the U.S. Cavalry came in here, hunting people down. There was a man up there with his family. He built that little wall for protection. The soldiers fired at him, but he and his family hid in the cave. In the night, they fled up the Beehive Trail. The soldiers went up to the cave in the morning, but there was nobody there."

I was familiar with that cavalry invasion, having read the smug army reports from the "Roundup." But Kalvin's account of the family, the cave, and the flight in the night, I knew, could be found nowhere in the government archives.

"The story was passed down to us," Kalvin concluded.

The reason that Ancestral Puebloan ruins on the Rez tend to be pristine and unvandalized, as well as why so many artifacts still lie scattered on the ground, has to do with the Navajo fear of the dead. After a person dies in a hogan, the dwelling will be abandoned, with the door boarded closed, or (as Kalvin had told us), the west wall will be knocked down to let the spirit escape, or in some cases, the hogan will be burned to the ground. For the same reason, the dwellings of the

Ancestral Puebloans that the Diné discovered all over their "home-land" were to be avoided, as places of the dead. Navajos who have been conscripted to work on archaeological digs will often flee if a skeleton is unearthed.

In 1996, on a backpack trip into a canyon in the Lukachukai Mountains, north of Canyon de Chelly, one of my companions was a young Navajo named Wilson King, who lived in Cove, on the eastern edge of the range. When I found a remarkable ruin that could be entered only by climbing a sketchy hand-and-toe trail, I used a rope to belay my friends into the alcove. Very reluctantly, Wilson tied in and climbed up. But then, when I found a human leg bone sticking out of the dirt below the dwellings, Wilson freaked out.

"When I go home," he told me, "I'll change clothes, and wash everything I have before I handle my kids. And I won't tell a lot of people about the place—just a few friends. I'll keep it to myself." As I belayed him back down the hand-and-toe trail, Wilson suddenly felt a stab of pain in his knee. He was sure it was caused by his error in visiting the ruin.

At the end of that trip, I developed pain in my own knee and swelling so intense that I was barely able to hobble out, sedated by heavy painkillers. In the emergency room in Cortez, Colorado, my ailment was diagnosed as an anaerobic infection caused by a tiny splinter that had lodged in my knee as I bushwhacked down a steep slope. If it had gone untreated, I might have lost my leg to amputation. Instead, antibiotics restored me to health. But Wilson knew better what had happened to both of us.

In general, the Navajo regard the Ancestral Puebloans as having possessed extraordinary and even magical powers. The deepest exploration of this cultural cross-bedding by an Anglo scholar is in the pages of Robert S. McPherson's 1992 book *Sacred Land, Sacred View: Navajo Perceptions of the Four Corners Region*. As research for his treatise, McPherson interviewed many old-timers on the reservation, a good portion of whom are no longer alive. The results are intriguing.

Just as the first Anglos were in the 1870s, the Navajo—whenever they first entered the Southwest—were stunned by the inaccessible ruins their predecessors had left behind. To the Diné, those high dwellings and granaries proved not only that the Ancestral Puebloans had been master climbers, but that they could fly. McPherson learned from one elder that the ancients had special "sticky feet" to aid their ascents; another told him that the Old Ones "used shiny stones to slide up and down the rock walls." Yet others insisted that lizards and horned toads—noted for their ability to scuttle up vertical walls—were the descendants of the Ancestral Puebloans.

As McPherson may have been the first scholar to discover, the Navajo adamantly deny that today's Hopi are at all related to the Ancestral Puebloans. In the Navajo view, they are two distinct peoples—no matter what the Hopi say about their forebears. The Ancestral Puebloans, traditional Navajos insist, died out completely.

What might have led to this belief? The answer is clear. The Navajo are convinced that the Ancestral Puebloans abused their magical powers, angering their own gods, and were destroyed in retribution. (As Kalvin had told us, "They angered the Holy Ones.") Just as intriguingly, a majority of the elders whom McPherson interviewed believed that Anglo America was headed along the same arrogant path toward its own destruction. As one informant, Fred Yazzie, told McPherson in 1987:

> Just like now, the Anglos are designing many things. They are making big guns and poison gas. Whatever will harm humans, they are designing. What happened then [with the Ancestral Puebloans] I am relating to what is happening now. . . . Now the Anglos are going up to the moon and space. Whatever obstacle is in their way, they will not allow it to stop them. Some are killed doing this and others return from their quest. Do these people believe in the Holy Beings or God?

According to Yazzie, "The Anasazi built with ease houses in the cliffs. Their mind probably did all this and this was like a big competition between them. They started to fly and then got jealous of each other."

Said another informant, "They learned to fly . . . that is why their houses are in the cliffs . . . [but] the Holy Beings had their feelings hurt by it . . . [and] said it was not good and killed them off."

In the view of some elders, Ancestral Puebloan rock art itself betrays the ancients' abuse of their power. Of the petroglyph and pictograph panels in Canyon de Chelly, Mae Thompson told a scholar in 1986 that the depictions of "abstract" things such as wind and air, as well as "caricatures of animals," were particularly offensive. "The gods became angry, sent a whirlwind and fire, and destroyed life in the canyons and mesas. The black streaks of desert varnish that cover cliffs and rocks in the area are from the smoke and fire of this destruction."

The next day, Kalvin led us along another trail, one that plunged down a steep fissure from the north rim of Canyon del Muerto 850 feet to the bed of Tsaile Creek. Unlike the White Sands Trail, this path involved real climbing, or at least scrambling, as we tiptoed down hand-and-toe trails cleverly gouged out of fifty-degree sandstone slabs. Here and there, an upright log ladder had been wired in place.

"Is this an Anasazi trail?" I asked Kalvin.

"Navajo."

"From when?"

Kalvin considered the question. "'Bout the 1500s."

Not far below the rim, we came across some small petroglyphs: a mountain lion track, two flute players, an upside-down man. "They say that means death," said Kalvin, indicating the latter figure. "But nobody knows."

A little farther down, we discovered a massive petroglyph depicting a slithering snake, its head crowned with horns. I had seen the Avanyu, or plumed serpent, in New Mexico, but never in Arizona or

Utah. Rock art experts link it to Toltec imagery from central Mexico. What the hell was it doing here?

Our guide waved his forefinger at the petroglyph. "They say the canyon itself is a big snake, with all the turns and corners."

"But Kalvin," I interjected, "these are Anasazi petroglyphs, aren't they?"

Kalvin looked away. "Maybe it was an Anasazi trail before it was a Navajo one."

Dawn was in her element, frictioning off the trail sideways to frame snapshots of our guide in profile. The descent was pure giddy play. Kalvin had admitted that he wouldn't take most clients on such a trail. I might have been tempted to feel special had I not learned a few details about the daily commute practiced by scores of Navajo schoolkids.

Many of the Diné live on Middle Mesa, or the Peninsula, as they call it—the high, protruding neck of land that separates Canyon del Muerto from Canyon de Chelly. By rutted dirt road, it is as far as fifty miles from home to the schoolhouse in Chinle. Rather than subject their parents to the arduous drive, kids happily climb down and up any number of hand-and-toe trails connecting the Peninsula to lower Chinle Wash, completing their trek in a mere ten or twelve miles. In midwinter, the braver kids brag about cruising the trails when the steps are glazed with ice.

Once we had reached the canyon floor, we headed downstream to the base of Navajo Fortress Rock. A freestanding, seven-hundred-foot-high butte of sheer sandstone, connected to the south rim of Canyon del Muerto only by a V-notch on the east, the Rock is the most important place in the whole monument in terms of Diné cultural pride. (Its Navajo name, of which the English is a direct translation, is Tsélaa'.) I had been here before, but I wanted to absorb Kalvin's story about the tragic and heroic events that had taken place on Tsélaa' a century and a half earlier.

In 1863, after a decade of murderous depredations on both sides—an era the Diné still refer to as the Fearing Time—General

James H. Carleton, in charge of the U.S. Army in New Mexico, decided to settle the "Navajo problem" for good. He put Colonel Kit Carson in charge of a force that would lay waste to the Diné heartland. Carson's official orders were as follows: "The men are to be slain whenever and wherever they can be found. The women and children may be taken prisoners."

Weary of a life of Indian fighting, Carson radically tempered Carleton's orders: he won the surrender of Navajo men, instead of killing them. Yet Carson's scorched earth campaign, as he burned all the cornfields and hogans that lay in his path, driving the Diné into desperate refuges, proved devastatingly effective. (For his pains, Carson is bitterly reviled today by the Navajo, most of whom have never heard of Carleton.)

Thus began the Long Walk, as the captured Navajo were forced to march three hundred miles to a concentration camp called Bosque Redondo on the bleak plains of eastern New Mexico. During the next four and a half years, the fatality rate among the prisoners was monstrously high.

The climax of the campaign came in the winter of 1863–64, as Carson sent contingents of soldiers to sweep the length and breadth of Canyon de Chelly and Canyon del Muerto. The government reports are bland and self-congratulatory: a few resisters killed here, nineteen starving women and children captured without a fight there. As they marched away from Canyon de Chelly, the troops believed the Roundup was over.

Navajo Fortress Rock is not even mentioned in the army annals. In the tales preserved by the Diné from one generation to the next, however, the inaccessible butte looms as the enduring symbol of the people's fierce resistance.

Dawn went off to explore the nooks of Black Rock Canyon. I sat down on a bedrock slab with Kalvin as I asked him to tell me about Tsélaa', which towered above us on the north.

Our guide stuck a leaf of grass between his teeth, then stared into the distance. "Before Carson got here," Kalvin began, "warriors went into the deeper canyons to find big tall pine trees. They brought seven of them back. They came around to the south side of the Rock, and climbed with the logs up to the notch." (Perhaps for my unlettered benefit, Kalvin did not use the name Tsélaa'.) He pointed upward. "Four of the logs were used to make a bridge across the notch, so even the old people could cross.

"We had ropes from the Spaniards. We carried up corn, peaches, squash, water. There were natural tanks on the top, which the people sealed with clay to make them watertight. The two biggest trees were propped up right below the top, to make a ladder. People came from a long distance. One at a time, they lined up and climbed the poles. Some people slipped and fell to their deaths, because they were rushing.

"When our people first saw the soldiers, they were told, 'Be quiet. No noise.' But some soldiers walking along the south rim saw the Navajo on top of Fortress Rock. They looked like ants, trying to hide. The soldiers shot bullets, but they were too far away.

"Soldiers came down the canyon. They camped on both sides of the Rock. 'We'll starve 'em out,' they said. Some of the soldiers tried to climb up, but the warriors pushed boulders down on them. The soldiers were afraid of getting shot. On top, the Navajo sang all night long, just to keep the soldiers awake.

"It was really cold that winter. For firewood, the people had only a few evergreens that grew on top. They couldn't build many fires. They had bearskin and deerskin robes, but it was still cold. They made their corn into mush. They camped up there for three months. But eventually they ran out of water.

"Everybody got desperately thirsty. So, one night when there was no moon, some men climbed most of the way down the northwest corner of the Rock. They formed a human chain. With ropes, they passed clay pots down. They lowered the pots a hundred feet and dipped them in Tsaile Creek to fill them up. There were sentries sleeping right at the base of the cliff, but the people were so quiet, the soldiers never woke up.

"Finally the soldiers got tired and left. The Navajo stayed on top another month, in case the army came back. At last two warriors climbed down, and when it was safe, all the people came down.

"They scattered into different canyons, where they hid out for four years. They were never captured. They never went on the Long Walk."

How, I wondered, could such a dramatic siege and feat of endurance have entirely escaped the American record?

In 1999, I had made my first trip to Tsélaaʼ, guided by Dave Wilson, who, as luck would have it, turned out to be Kalvin's uncle. I had come in a skeptical frame of mind, which my approach hike did nothing to dispel. My source for the Navajo legend then was the vivid account by Teddy Draper, Sr., published in 1973 in *Navajo Stories of the Long Walk Period*. Draper had the story from his grandmother, whose own mother had been one of the refugees atop the Rock in the winter of 1863–64. Draper's account dovetailed perfectly with what Kalvin had just told me.

To get to the south side of Navajo Fortress Rock in 1999, I had walked right under the nearly vertical cliff of the butte's northwest corner. Here, indeed, Tsaile Creek swept tight to the precipice, where a lowered pot might well scoop up the flowing water. But the cliff looked utterly unclimbable for four hundred feet off the ground. Nimble though those warriors must have been, I did not believe they could have descended the northwest corner to within a hundred feet of the creek.

On the south side of the butte, however, I was beguiled to discover two neatly chiseled inscriptions: "U.S.A." and "U.S." Did those graffiti betoken the siege of the winter of 1863–64?

To my disappointment in 2008, as we approached the chimney on the south side that led up to the V-notch, Kalvin told me that not only was climbing anywhere on the Rock strictly forbidden, but that I could not even approach the base of the chimney. This had not been so in 1999. Then, as Dave Wilson napped in the grass, I had spent a magical hour scrambling solo two-thirds of the way up Tsélaa'.

Three hundred feet off the ground, I had come to the gunsight notch. All that remained of the bridge was a single thirty-foot timber, wedged tight across a hundred-foot void. I rehearsed the moves several times before I dared climb through the dizzy gap.

From there I followed ledges and chimneys until I was only two hundred feet below the top. I found a cave big enough to hold about twenty people, reinforced with a stone wall guarding its mouth, and, perched on the edge of the cliff, a number of breastworks—piles of flat rocks behind which warriors could have crouched to fire their rifles and arrows at the soldiers below. The last two hundred feet of the climb would have been severely technical. But right below the rim, I saw the two huge poles still in place, leaning against the nearly vertical wall—the ladder that the refugees climbed that long-ago winter.

Perhaps it was right that by 2008, the superintendent of Canyon de Chelly National Monument had declared Navajo Fortress Rock off-limits to nosy trespassers like me. Yet as I sat listening to Kalvin's story, staring up at the butte, I felt the insatiable itch to head back up there, to touch with my feet and hands the vestiges of a saga that Anglos had chosen to forget. And in Kalvin's face I saw the unquenchable pride of the Diné in those ancestors who had never surrendered, and whose deeper secrets I would never fathom.

While we sat talking, the sky had darkened ominously, and now a pelting wind came out of the west. As soon as Dawn returned, we headed out.

Earlier that day, I had asked Kalvin, "Do you ever get clients you simply can't stand?"

"Yes."

"What are they like?" Spoiled kids, I wondered, with no attention spans? Obese adults for whom a mile-long hike was torture? Shutterbugs who couldn't put down their point-and-shoots?

"Folks who say, 'That's not what I've read in books,'" Kalvin answered. "They think they know more about the place than I do."

"How do you deal with them?"

"Even if we've only been out on tour for an hour, I tell them, 'That's it. We're going back.'"

By the time we reached the foot of the trail to the north rim, the temperature had plunged twenty degrees and it was raining hard. The hand and toeholds would be slippery, even a little dangerous—though nothing a fourth-grader from the Peninsula wouldn't handle in stride.

Just before we started out, I flirted with the notion of carrying a stone up to the rim, where I would add it to the pile we had found on the way in. But then I thought better of the idea. I was no Diné, and this was not my canyon.

During the last two decades, I've made about sixteen backpack trips into various corners of the Navajo Reservation, lasting as long as twelve days. Several of my trips were solo outings, during which I ran into not a single other Anglo hiker or Navajo sheepherder. Besides those backpacking forays, I've headed out on more than thirty day hikes to out-of-the-way corners of the Rez.

Most of those journeys, like my ramblings on Cedar Mesa, were in quest of ruins and rock art left behind by the Ancestral Puebloans. But in September 2013, with Greg Child, I set off on a quest whose goal was to probe a Diné mystery, not a prehistoric one.

The doleful story of the Long Walk—the darkest chapter in Navajo history—has been often told. Of the 9,000 captives who were forced to march to the Bosque Redondo, more than 2,000 died within the next four and a half years. Some perished on the march, some even before starting out, of dysentery and exposure. At the Bosque, others died of starvation when the corn harvest failed two seasons in a row. Some women were fatally infected with syphilis by the soldiers guarding them. Some were killed trying to escape. Others committed suicide.

The alkaline water of the Pecos River running through the Bosque afflicted the prisoners with severe intestinal and stomach ailments. By the second year, the Navajo had to walk from twelve to twenty miles each day to gather firewood. One survivor of the famine later recalled, "The U.S. Army fed corn to its horses. Then, when the horses discharged undigested corn in their manure, the Diné would dig and poke in the manure to pick out the corn."

In 1868, forced to admit that the Bosque Redondo was a failure—even his own officers had begun to deride the general's squalid concentration camp, calling it "Fair Carletonia"—the government freed the surviving Navajos. Without horses, they had to retrace the three-hundred-mile walk to regain their homeland. Each adult was given a pitiful allowance on which to build a new life: two sheep and some seeds for planting. The leaders of the returning tribe, Manuelito and Barboncito, were broken men.

Ever since my first visit to Tsélaa' in 1999, I had been fascinated by the deeds of the Navajos who had hidden from Carson's pursuit and escaped the Roundup. No one, not even Diné elders today, knows how many they were, and their stories are far more evanescent than those of their brethren who survived the Bosque.

The greatest and most legendary of all the Navajos who eluded capture was a headman named Hoskinini, who lived near Monument Valley. About thirty-five years old in 1863, when the Roundup began, he fled with sixteen companions—men, women, and children—as Carson's mounted cavalry pursued them. They had a single horse, one rusty rifle, and twenty sheep.

Hoskinini's band came to the banks of the San Juan River. And there, miraculously, they escaped. In all likelihood, the Navajo knew of a secret ford by which they crossed into the wilderness, while Carson's troops waited three days for the flooding torrent to subside, then gave up. An old Navajo legend insists that Hoskinini escaped through a secret tunnel *under* the San Juan.

For the next four and a half years, the small group of refugees hid out in what even today is one of the most rugged and remote corners of the Southwest. No soldier or scout ever discovered their sanctuary, though many tried. During those years, through brilliant raiding, hunting, and husbandry, Hoskinini nursed his people back to health and then to an unprecedented prosperity. And though he lived on until 1909, Hoskinini never revealed to any Anglo the location of his hideout.

For 150 years, the secret hideout has remained pristine wilderness. Prospectors and explorers have tried, but no Anglo has yet conclusively rediscovered that sanctuary among the sandstone domes and slot canyons. For more than two decades, I had studied the scraps of history and the threads of oral tradition about Hoskinini's escape. And by 2013, I thought I knew where the hideout was.

To reach our jumping-off point that September, Greg and I drove a rental SUV deep into the canyonlands of the Navajo Reservation. Old ruts of dirt roads branched everywhere, most of them ending at isolated houses where some of the more traditional Diné live today. I flagged down a car that was creeping toward us from the west. Two young Navajo men got out. I could smell booze on their breath. I asked for directions to a trailhead just north of the maze Greg and I hoped to explore.

"You're in the wrong place," the shorter of the two men said, squinting at me. "There ain't no trail there." The subtext was tangible: *White boys, go home.* Instead, we trundled on, then left our vehicle, with a copy of our official Navajo backcountry permit on the dashboard, parked next to boulders that barred further progress except on foot.

The wilderness ahead of us, where I was convinced Hoskinini's band had hidden, lies southwest of the massive lacolith of 10,387-foot-high Navajo Mountain. That towering peak itself is sacred to the Diné, who call it Naatsis'áán, or Head of Earth Woman. There, in the creation myth, Monster Slayer, one of the Hero Twins, was born. All hiking or climbing by Anglos on Navajo Mountain is forbidden today.

Our first day's hike turned into a fiasco. In the week before our trip, it had rained nearly every day in southeastern Utah, where I was hanging out. Expecting to find water in the creeks that bisected our route, we carried only two liters of H_2O apiece. But when we crossed a pair of major side canyons only to find them bone-dry, we were forced to dump our loads, hike back to the car, and pack up the five gallons of water we had left there. At the end of a six-hour day, we had back-packed nine miles to gain a measly three.

We cooked dinner in the dark. But it was a beautiful night, with the Milky Way striping the sky from the southwest horizon to where it collided with Navajo Mountain at our backs. The next morning, we pushed on, groaning under seventy-pound loads that included two gallons of water each. An interminable trailless shoulder pitched us 1,800 feet down toward the canyon in the distance where we had planned to set up base camp. Hiking in shorts, we had our shins and calves lashed by thickets of thorny blackbrush. At one rest stop, Greg flung his pack down, cursing, "It's just too goddamn much weight!"

But as we neared the canyon, I shouted, "Water!" There it was, a pothole full of clear rainfall, hidden under a small tree that had saved it from evaporation. And when we got to the canyon itself, we found pool after pool of the blessed stuff—enough to drink for a month or more. Later I would learn that the Navajo name for the canyon means "Water under the Rocks." If we'd known that, we'd probably have taken the plunge on the first afternoon.

That day, moreover, we made our first major discovery. As we zig-zagged our way into yet another dry, thorny creekbed, Greg spotted it. "Look," he said, raising his binoculars. "Hogan."

We approached the old Navajo dwelling, which had been built on a stony bench beside the creek. It was well camouflaged by trees and bushes and by the folds of the canyon itself. We could easily have missed it altogether. No doubt the hogan had been built here because at least part of the year, the stream beside it ran. But camouflage was its blueprint—as if the people who lived here were hiding from some-thing, or someone.

The design was classic Diné, the walls forming an octagon of juniper cribbing rising six feet toward a central smokehole in the roof. The narrow door faced dead east, and a girdle of sandstone blocks protected the walls from weather or collapse. Ominously, however, the door was blocked with leaning juniper poles. This meant that someone had died inside the hogan. In the explanation of anthropologist Leland C. Wyman, "A 'no fireplace place home' in which death of a younger person occurred, and which . . . has had the entrance and smokehole blocked with timbers as a warning that a burial had been made in it, is avoided. No Navajo will even approach the site. It is tabu, the home of death."

Not being Diné ourselves, we surveyed the exquisitely preserved hogan from the outside. The logs, we saw, had been hewn with an axe, not a saw, and not a single nail had been used in its construction. I had found enough old hogans in the backcountry to know that this one almost surely dated to the nineteenth century. With mounting excitement, I allowed myself to wonder: *Could this refuge have been the work of Hoskinini's people?*

In 1925 historian Charles Kelly interviewed Hoskinini's son, who was five at the time of his small band's escape across the San Juan. According to Hoskinini-begay,

> We traveled many nights, sleeping in the daytime. We were all footsore and hungry, as we had not brought any food. We lived mostly on grass seed and sometimes a rabbit. . . . The country was very rough and we were all worn out climbing down into deep canyons and out again. Water was very hard to find.

Hoskinini forbade the slaughtering of any of the sheep, so that they might breed and multiply. "We had no bullets for the old rifle," remembered his son, "and hunted in the old way"—i.e., with bow and arrow. Wild game was woefully scarce, so the fugitives gathered seeds and piñon nuts to sustain them through the first winter. As

Hoskinini-begay recalled, "He drove everyone all day long and would never let us rest, knowing that we might starve. He always seemed to be angry with everyone for being lazy. So he was given the name Hush-kaaney, which means 'the angry one.'"

In their flight after crossing the San Juan, Hoskinini searched constantly for the perfect oasis to anchor the survival ordeal he knew his band must face. But in the end, it was not he who decided. Recalled Hoskinini-begay,

> Finally we reached the south end of Navaho Mountain and came to a nice little stream with grass. Mother sat on the ground and said she would go no further. Father tried to make her go on but she would not, so we made camp there, and lived in that place for six [actually four and a half] years.

The cold months came and went. Heartened that they had passed the first winter without a single death, the people dared to build their hogans. Led by Hoskinini, they found batches of stray sheep and drove them back to the hideout, and on far-reaching raids they stole horses from under the noses of unsuspecting soldiers. They also contacted other solitary fugitives and brought them into their hideout. On one reconnaissance, Hoskinini supposedly discovered a vein of silver, so pure that "he could shape it without melting." In four and a half years only one stranger stumbled upon the hideout—a "renegade Ute," said Hoskinini-begay, "who did not betray us."

In 1868, on learning of the return of the captured Navajos from the Bosque to their homeland, Hoskinini's band came out of hiding. By now, their numbers had swelled to scores, they had a thousand head of sheep, they had shorn wool to make robes and blankets, and they had harvested an abundance of corn from fields they had planted in the wilderness. They had become, according to Hoskinini-begay, "the richest Navahos in the whole country." The refugees returning from the Bosque were stunned to greet them.

At once, Hoskinini gave those wretched Diné corn, sheep, wool, and skins from the vast store he had accumulated during the years in hiding. And the recipients of these gifts were dazzled by the abundance of silver jewelry the headman had crafted from the vein in his secret mine. Out of awe and gratitude, the refugees bestowed on Hoskinini a second nickname, "The Generous One." Twenty-five years after his death, he was still remembered by that name on the northern part of the Navajo reservation.

Greg's and my base camp occupied an idyllic setting, on a sagebrush bench next to the clear pools of "Water Under the Rocks." Orange domes, gleaming in the low-angle sunrise, nestled our camp on all sides. As we peered west down the shallow canyon, we could sense how it deepened and twisted out of sight in the distance. That second day, we had made two more important discoveries: another pair of hogans, built to virtually the same design as the first one we had found, equally well preserved, and also crafted by axe blade, without nails. The third, tucked under a looming vertical cliff only two hundred yards from our tents, was the most perfect of all. Hexagonal in shape, twelve feet in diameter, six feet high at the smokehole, it bore the imprint, in the furred ends of each carefully fitted juniper log, of loving craftsmanship.

The cookie-cutter similarity among the three hogans suggested to me a powerful leader dictating the architecture. Once again, I dared to guess: *Was this the work of Hoskinini?* Or was wishful thinking getting the better of my habitual skepticism?

Even today, Navajos rarely build their hogans close to one another. The three we had found lay as far as two miles apart. But this would have been the pattern of Hoskinini's people, even while they hid out from the soldiers, each family planting its own corn, gathering wild plants, and hunting for game with bow and arrow. One thing was clear, however—the valley bottom of "Water Under the Rocks" did not fit Hoskinini-begay's description of the center of the sanctuary, where his mother had sat down and refused to go farther, for here there was no "nice little stream with grass."

Having studied the maps for weeks, however, I had a hunch where that elysian place might lie—in another, broader canyon three miles west of our base camp, of which "Water Under the Rocks" was a tributary. The maps also made it clear that to get from here to there would require difficult scrambling and inspired route-finding—if we could make the traverse at all. Sixteen years earlier, I had caught a distant glimpse of this slickrock maze that had confirmed my belief that there was no more tortured topography anywhere in the Southwest.

In 1997, on an eight-day llama trek on the seldom-used Rainbow Bridge Trail that goes west and north of Navajo Mountain, a clever path blazed by the veteran Indian trader and explorer John Wetherill as he guided the Bernheimer Expedition of 1922, I had gazed from above and afar upon the trackless labyrinth that Bernheimer's crew called the Kettle Country. Of that wilderness, Earl Morris, the archaeologist on the expedition, had written, "An adequate conception of the ruggedness of this particular region cannot be conveyed in words . . . [It] might be likened to a sea driven in the teeth of a hurricane, the waves of which at their height had been transfixed to salmon-colored stone."

Starting in 1909 and lasting well into the 1920s, John Wetherill explored the country on all sides of Navajo Mountain, blazing not only Bernheimer's "Northwest Passage" but the brilliantly engineered Rainbow Bridge Trail that passes north of the mountain. In 1997, we had found a lonely upright stone on which the explorer had carved the inscription "JW—1911." During all those forays, Wetherill had approached the Kettle Country from all sides, but he had never made his way into that labyrinth.

Greg and I set off early on our third day to explore the maze west of our camp. The sky was still blue, but a biting wind out of the southwest grew through the hours until it was almost a gale. The bends of "Water Under the Rocks" forced us in and out of slots, as we improvised bypasses on the steep arroyo banks that crisscrossed our path. An hour into our wandering, Greg suddenly said, "Look at that. It's a cairn."

I stared at the skyline on my left. Atop a large boulder sat a single stone. Anglos typically stack flat rocks to make a cairn, but as we learned that day, Navajo herders had been content with widely spaced route-markers, each composed of a single stone perched atop a big rock. And gradually we found the overgrown trails that linked the Diné cairns. Each vestigial patch of trail was strewn with desiccated sheep and horse dung—not from 150 years ago, but clearly many decades old.

A mile and a half from camp, "Water Under the Rocks" plunged into an impassable slot. From the map, I deduced that we were still another mile and a half east of the broader canyon that might have been the central oasis, the "nice little stream with grass," of Hoskinini's sanctuary. We struck out instead toward the south, climbing benches and scuttling across slickrock slabs, making a blind stab to solve the labyrinth.

Almost at once, we hit another dead-end slot. "Looks like we're boxed in," I said to Greg. "I don't think we can get from here to the bigger canyon." Frustration and defeat throbbed in my weary shoulders. But then we noticed an unpromising narrow corridor angling southwest. "What have we got to lose?" I muttered, as we entered the gloomy ravine between vertical walls so close together you could almost span them with open arms.

There were two reasons why, during the last forty-one years of his life, Hoskinini refused to tell any Anglo where his band had thrived after escaping Carson's Roundup. One was the constant fear that another government crackdown on the Diné would force him into hiding again. The other was the silver mine. Even his own son remained ignorant of the mine's precise location.

After 1868, the first Anglos who dared enter the northern reaches of the Navajo Reservation were prospectors. Some of them had heard rumors about Hoskinini's silver vein. In 1880, two men named Charles Merrick and Robert Mitchell set out from southeastern Utah in search of the treasure. When their return was overdue, a party of Anglos rode into Monument Valley, where Navajos directed them to the recent graves of the two prospectors. The Navajos claimed that Utes had killed the men, while Utes blamed the Navajos. It is not hard to imagine Hoskinini's hand in the killings.

To this day, no one has rediscovered Hoskinini's purported vein of silver so pure that "he could shape it without melting." Even the most traditional Diné apparently have no idea where it might be. Starting in the late 1850s, prospectors much farther south in Arizona, around Bisbee, Globe, and Tombstone, extracted millions of dollars' worth of silver from the ground, but geologists have found scant evidence of either gold or silver deposits on the northern reaches of the reservation. Could the lost Hoskinini mine be merely another tall tale? Unlikely—for Hoskinini-begay swore that the vein was real, and the returnees from Bosque Redondo were awestruck by the silver jewelry the headman had fashioned from his lode.

In 1906, more than four decades after Hoskinini's escape from Carson's troops, John Wetherill decided he wanted to build the first trading post in the northern part of the reservation. "Don't go," the rancher from Mancos, Colorado, was warned. "There are bad people there. They will kill you." Unfazed, Wetherill rode to Oljato, "the Place of Moonlight Water." There, met by hostile headmen, including Hoskinini-begay, the rancher stalled for three days as he parlayed over rabbits caught and cooked by the Navajo, coffee, sugar, and biscuits served by the intruder. At last Hoskinini himself, almost eighty years old, gave his benediction to the trader.

Louisa Wetherill, John's wife, quickly became so fluent in Diné that Hoskinini swore she was his long-lost granddaughter, descended from a beloved wife whom the Utes had stolen many years before. The great headman lived only another three years, but during that time Louisa got to know Hoskinini better than any other Anglo ever did. Upon his death, he bequeathed her his thirty-two Ute slave women. Dumbfounded, Louisa tried to set them free, but they refused to leave.

Instead, she built them a hogan and gave them useful chores to perform when they begged to work.

In his old age, Hoskinini was the most revered of all Navajos, still known as "the Generous One." Yet he was also feared. "He can almost kill you with his eyes," testified a younger member of the tribe. A spacious mesa and a towering pinnacle in Utah are named after Hoskinini. For his staunch resistance to the American military, he deserves to be as celebrated as Geronimo or Crazy Horse, but most Anglos today have never heard of him.

Threatening to pinch off at any moment, the corridor went and went. And then, to our joy, we found another one-rock cairn, followed by a downed tree trunk in which someone had hacked footholds with an axe.

Before our trip, several friends had asked me why I didn't hire a Navajo guide to lead us into the Kettle Country. The answer is that there simply are no such folks available. Even the Navajos who live not far from the canyons seem to have little knowledge of this wilderness. With the road into Navajo Mountain now paved, the supermarkets of Tuba City are a lot more accessible than the cornfields of the Kettle Country that had once sustained the Diné.

The narrow corridor led us on and on. Sometimes we had to backtrack to find a higher ledge to proceed, or bash through willows and tamarisk to avoid lush thickets of poison ivy. It was hard to imagine horses or even sheep making this passage, but the Diné must have used it regularly to get from one part of their wilderness to another. From the map, I could see that we were close to the bigger canyon, and then Greg crowed, "It goes!"

We burst out of the corridor into the main canyon, then followed it northward. Twice we had to chimney across deep pools in V-shaped slots, but within half a mile the canyon opened up. Now we had easy hiking on the sandbar, and on either side, broad terraces of alluvium hinted at fields where corn would grow. And yes, we now walked beside a "nice little stream with grass."

I stopped for a moment to stare at the horizon. On all sides but one, nearby cliffs towered over the meandering canyon, hiding it from all but the most dogged of invaders. Only from the west, where the distant rim of Cummings Mesa loomed three thousand feet above us, could a scout with field glasses have spied on this Navajo enclave. But no soldiers in the 1860s ever reached the top of Cummings Mesa, which was first climbed by Anglos—led by none other than John Wetherill—only in 1919.

"You know, Greg?" I said with mounting exhilaration. "This could very well be the hideout." He nodded in agreement.

Gazing around me, I pictured Diné men planting the seeds they had gathered the previous fall. I saw sheep grazing on the tall bunch grass that greened the sandy benches. I imagined women, huddled in that nearby alcove before a smokeless fire, weaving robes from skeins of wool, and a hunter coming over the brow of that hill to the north with a fresh-killed deer slung over his shoulders. I conjured up Hoskinini, deep in thought, plotting his next raid for horses, or slipping away with the three or four men he trusted to get more silver from his perfect vein.

We pushed down to the junction with "Water Under the Rocks" itself. It looked as impassable on the west end as it had at the eastern entry. We had apparently found the only hikable route from the tributary canyon to the main one. It might very well have been the passage Hoskinini had opened in 1863. But it was now 2:30 P.M., and the darkening sky threatened rain, while the wind shrieked between the high surrounding walls. We took a long last look and turned back in our tracks.

By late afternoon, we were within what should have been a mile of camp. But I stopped and said to Greg, "This doesn't feel right. We didn't come this way."

"Yeah," he reluctantly agreed, as he peered at the reddish sand ahead of us. "No footprints."

We were not truly lost, I thought, just somehow off-track. It was half an hour before sunset. We'd been going for eight and a half hours straight, and we were dog tired. The third-quarter moon wouldn't rise until midnight. We had headlamps, but even in the fading blur of daylight, all the sandstone domes and walls and slots through which we poked our way were starting to look the same.

To make matters worse, we'd left our tents pitched too close to the slickrock bed of "Water Under the Rocks." A flash flood could wipe out everything we owned, except the jackets and scraps of lunch in our daypacks. I felt the first prickle of adrenaline.

Our only recourse was to backtrack. Just after sunset, we found our footsteps and recognized the wrong turn we had made, thanks to my confusing a tributary canyon with the principal branch. At dusk we regained our camp. To my dismay, the wind had uprooted my brand-new tent and slammed it against a piñon tree, tearing holes in the fabric.

A spattering of rain deepened the gloom. "We gotta move camp," said Greg. "It could still pour."

With our last spurts of energy, we crammed all our gear and food into our backpacks, then hiked a quarter of a mile west. Making a misstep on a boulder, I slipped off and badly scraped my right leg. On a safe bench at last, we pitched our new camp, then cooked our freeze-dried dinner in the dark. In spite of the wind and rain and our exhaustion after a ten-and-a-half-hour marathon, we were supremely happy.

There was no way, of course, to prove that we had indeed discovered Hoskinini's sanctuary. Should an archaeologist take a dendro core from a juniper log in any of the three ancient hogans we came across, and the tree-ring date turn out to be sometime between 1863 and 1868, that would furnish a stunning corroboration. Elsewhere in the Navajo heartland, cores from hogans have yielded building dates as early as the seventeenth century. But obtaining permission to sample those hogans could launch a bureaucratic tangle, and besides, there aren't many dendrochronologists willing to make a trip as rugged as Greg's and mine just to confirm a hunch.

Yet everything seemed to fit Hoskinini-begay's description of the hideout. On our two-day approach, we could agree that "the country was very rough and we were all worn out climbing down into deep canyons and out again. Water was very hard to find." And the "nice little stream with grass" was an apt characterization of the far point we had reached where the bigger canyon broadened. If I had had to hide out for almost five years in the Kettle Country, and if I knew how to live off the land as those resourceful Navajos had, that was the place I would have chosen.

On our fourth day, we hiked back into the tributary canyon where we had gotten off-route the day before. Half a mile in, we found a bench backed by a smooth cliff facing south. The cliff itself was a Navajo bulletin board. Herders of sheep and cows had recorded their visits, some with a precision bordering on the absurd: "4–9–69 at 10:30 A.M. on Saturday." Others had carved "ONE COW" and "TWO COW." The graffiti dated back to 1904 and ranged up into the 1970s. But there seemed little indication that the Navajo had lingered here during the last three decades. Most oddly, compared to other such Diné "Kilroy was here" panels, not a single visitor had recorded his name or even his initials. A hundred years after the Long Walk, did this remote sanctum still pulse with the old fear of being found and captured?

It was not surprising that no dates preceded 1904. Virtually all the Diné of Hoskinini's era were preliterate, speaking no English and having no written language, despite the incredible richness of their oral history. (Even today, Diné elders living far from the main roads do not speak or understand English.) In the hideout, Hoskinini would not have carved his name on a sandstone wall.

On our last morning in the Kettle Country, I woke early, tied open the door of my tent, and lay snug in my sleeping bag as I watched the summits of the sandstone domes turn from gray to orange. *Hideout or no*, I thought, *God, what a beautiful place.*

But I had spent some time over the years in the reservation back-country with traditional Navajos, and I knew that they saw the landscape in a very different way from mine. Now I lapsed into a reverie, as I traveled back in time to 1865 and into the head of a young man in Hoskinini's band.

Was the corn in the field two benches away ripe for picking? The fresh deer tracks that I had followed yesterday until I lost them on the slickrock—was it worth another search? Should I stir the fire to life in the hogan, or save the piñon sticks for a colder day? How soon would the first snows fall?

And even before rising to stand in the doorway and greet the sunrise with my prayer, I must scan the horizons, checking to make sure the apparition my people have feared every day for the last two years has not come to pass—the silhouettes of bluecoats who have finally found our refuge, and who would march down to kill us all.

The reverie faded. Greg and I were twenty-first-century Anglos, not nineteenth-century Diné. We were intruders in this slickrock paradise. We had found our way into it, but we could never have begun to scratch out a living here. The skills of Hoskinini's band were beyond our ken. Like John Wetherill before us, we had penetrated this wilderness in search of adventure and discovery—a far different thing from survival.

Still, I mused, for all the worries that had daily plagued the Diné under Hoskinini, they must have basked in the wholeness of their freedom. They lived in the old way, before the coming of the Spaniards and the Americans. The world the Hero Twins had saved by turning monsters into stone was theirs, in all its goodness and harmony.

Six

LAND OF ENCHANTMENT–I

M ost of the canyons that have lured me on my quest for the ancients have been in Utah and Arizona, where the geology lends itself to soaring sandstone walls and slickrock terraces. But the Ancestral Puebloans (as well as the Mogollon) also flourished for thousands of years in what is now New Mexico. In places such as Bandelier National Monument or the Galisteo Basin or the shallow canyons of the Dinétah (Largo, Carrizo, Gobernador, et al.), you don't find the beautiful slickrock, but there are ruins and rock art to stir the most jaded seeker to awe.

What is more, of the twenty-one pueblos inhabited today, nineteen are located in New Mexico—all except Hopi, in Arizona, and Ysleta del Sur near El Paso, Texas, founded by a group that splintered off from Isleta shortly after the Pueblo Revolt in 1680. The ancestral linkages between today's residents of Taos or Cochiti or Acoma or Zuni and the Old Ones who abandoned the Colorado Plateau in the thirteenth century will never be definitively unraveled, even by the Puebloans themselves. Yet to explore prehistoric sites in the Southwest while ignoring the wisdom and heritage of today's Pueblo people would be irresponsible. Starting in the 1880s, pioneering ethnographers such as Adolf Bandelier, Frank Cushing, and Jesse Walter Fewkes vigorously endeavored at every turn to consult Puebloans about their past.

Easier said than done, however—especially nowadays. Time and again, the Puebloans at the end of the nineteenth century and the beginning of the twentieth saw their trust in those scholars—whose curiosity about native cultures at first seemed such a welcome alternative to the punitive depredations of the Spaniards—woefully abused. At Zia Pueblo, for instance, in 1888, ethnographer Matilda Coxe Stevenson and her husband essentially stole a sacred vessel from the Snake Society, as they decided, against the firm protestations of their hosts, that the vase would be better off in the Smithsonian Institution than in the cave in which the Zia stored it. (Ninety-four years after the theft, in 1982, the vessel was repatriated .)

Similarly, native informants who shared their sacred knowledge with the apparently kindly researchers who spent months and years in their midst were horrified later to find every last facet of that lore published in monographs issuing from Washington, D.C., or Cambridge, Massachusetts. For the Puebloans, the harm was irreparable. There was no way to make those books disappear.

The outcome of all this conflict emerges in the fact that, by and large, the Pueblos have never been more secretive and xenophobic than they are today. I ran smack on into this obstacle in 2002 and 2003, as I tried to research a book about the Pueblo Revolt.

Fifty-eight years after Coronado's *entrada*, in 1598, the ruthless conquistador Don Juan de Oñate succeeded in conquering the Pueblo world as he marched up the Rio Grande, establishing his colonial capital on top of the San Juan Pueblo, known today as Ohkay Owingeh. In 1610, the capital was shifted to Santa Fe. During the eighty-two years after the conquest, Puebloans from Taos to Hopi suffered grievously under a succession of Spanish governors, some of them abysmally corrupt. In addition, the natives were caught in the crossfire of the struggle for power between those governors and the Franciscan priests who installed themselves in the villages as they strove to save the heathen from eternal damnation. The more iron-willed of these priests believed that torture was a useful tool for conversion.

On a single day in 1680—August 10—in a brilliantly orchestrated secret plot, using knotted ropes carried by runners to coordinate the action, all the pueblos under Spanish rule rose up against their oppressors, killing priests, soldiers, and civilians alike. The revolt succeeded in driving all the Spaniards out of the Southwest. During the next twelve years, the Puebloans hung on doggedly to their autonomy, thwarting several ill-conceived attempts at reconquest.

As I embarked on my research, I assumed, perhaps naively, that today's Puebloans would be willing to talk about what remains arguably the greatest triumph in their post-contact history. The extraordinary feat of driving all the Spaniards out of New Mexico in a single thrust, I thought, should shine with the kind of lasting glory that adheres to our country's own American Revolution in 1776.

The Pueblo Revolt is well documented in Spanish annals, though badly distorted by the colonialists' apoplexy over how the Indians whom they had so benevolently governed should have had the ingrati-

tude to rise up and murder them. I wanted to balance that take on
history with the Puebloans' own oral traditions about the revolt.

Every effort I made, however, to gain an audience at the pueblos
where I could ask the people about that dramatic chapter in their history was rebuffed. When I showed up at the tribal headquarters of
a pueblo to tender my request, a clerk would murmur, "You'll have
to take that up with the governor [of the pueblo]." Phone calls and
e-mails went unanswered. In the end, the only voices in my book that
spoke for the Puebloan view of the revolt came from the mouths of
five unique individuals, men and women who had grown up in their
pueblos but had gone on, usually through graduate study in universi-
ties, to gain a wider, more conventionally anthropological perspective
on the past.

Realizing I could not begin to hope for a pan-Puebloan grasp of
the revolt, I focused my effort on Jemez, the Towa-speaking community of some eighteen hundred souls located on the Jemez River about
forty miles north of Albuquerque. Jemez had figured prominently in
In Search of the Old Ones, as I attended a flint-knapping workshop
there led by Bruce Bradley, consulted with then tribal archaeologist
Bill Whatley, and hiked the high mesas north of the pueblo to discover magnificent ancestral Jemez ruins. I also knew that Jemez had
played a pivotal role in the Pueblo Revolt and in the resistance to the
Spanish reconquest, which finally succeeded in the 1690s.

In 2003, it took me two months to arrange a single meeting with
the Jemez Cultural Committee to present my request. In the end,
that meeting could hardly have gone worse. On the designated evening in May, I arrived half an hour early, but the committee members
straggled into the conference room in the governor's office as long as
forty-five minutes after our scheduled start.

Eager to launch my spiel, I was delayed when the tribe's head of
resource protection apologetically asked the two Anglo archaeologists
present—good friends of his—to leave the room. Apparently the discussion we were about to have was too sensitive for their well-trained

ears. At last, a bit nervously, I made my pitch. Explaining the difficulty I was having getting the Puebloan point of view on the great revolt, I pleaded that that episode in Native American history deserved to be better known by all Americans.

As I spoke, eight blank faces stared at me. When I finished, there was a long, painful silence. At last a fellow opposite me at the conference table, slouched back in his chair, asked, "What's in it for Jemez?"

Taken off guard, I answered, "Nothing, financially." Then, a bit lamely, I mentioned the scholarship donation I had made at Zia Pueblo, six miles down the Jemez River, the week before.

"We're not interested in 'donations,'" my antagonist sneered.

Sensing that I was getting nowhere, I said, somewhat provocatively, "I'd hate for Joe Sando to be the only person speaking for Jemez in my book." Sando was one of my five well-educated informants. Seventy-nine years old when I had met him in Albuquerque a few weeks earlier, Sando had been born at Jemez in 1923, but had gone on to get a B.A. from Eastern New Mexico University and attended graduate school at Vanderbilt. He had taught at the University of New Mexico, served as the director of archives at the Pueblo Cultural Center in Albuquerque, and written a number of books, including *Nee Hemish*, a history of his home pueblo. At our meeting, he had spoken generously and insightfully about the Pueblo Revolt.

In the conference room, at the mention of Sando's name, the reaction was electric. "Did you tell the governor you talked to Joe Sando?" one member of the Cultural Committee asked me. I didn't get a chance to explain that I had never been able to get the governor on the phone. The slouched-back man added bitterly, "Joe Sando wrote his book. He got rich and famous. And he didn't give anything back to the pueblo."

I doubted this aspersion. *Nee Hemish* had been published by the University of New Mexico Press, and had long since gone out of print. But I realized that my Anglo take on "rich and famous" might be quite different from the Jemez concept of that status.

Now the committee members started talking animatedly to each other in Towa, a language almost no Anglos have ever mastered. I was shut out. Finally, the fellow opposite me, still leaning back in his chair, fixed me with a stare as he said, "The thing that really bothers me is that you keep talking about 'my book.' This is all about you. Where are we in all this?"

The man on my left gave me a more earnest look. "We just don't want to get screwed," he said, "again."

At the end of the exhausting confrontation, I made a half-hearted promise to put my requests in writing in a letter to the lieutenant governor. I knew better than to hope for a response to that probe. On my way out of the governor's office, I gave a rueful smile to the two archaeologists, still waiting patiently in the lobby. They smiled ruefully back.

No source was more valuable to me in my research than *Archaeologies of the Pueblo Revolt*, a collection of scholarly essays edited by Robert W. Preucel, a professor of anthropology at the University of Pennsylvania. And no paper in that volume, which was published just as I began work on my own book, struck me as more brilliant than Matthew Liebmann's "Signs of Power and Resistance: The (Re) Creation of Christian Imagery and Identities in the Pueblo Revolt Era." It was well known that Popé, the shadowy mastermind of the revolt, had ordered the Puebloans, after the Spaniards had been driven out of New Mexico, to rid themselves of anything that had the faintest taint of Spanish influence. Popé's campaign of purification was so extreme that he forbade the eating of wheat and of fruit from trees the Spaniards had introduced, such as cherry and peach. The Puebloans were also commanded to turn loose all the livestock that had originally come from the Old World, including not only cattle, mules, and pigs, but invaluable horses. To undo the curse of baptism that the Franciscan friars had imposed on them, the Puebloans were urged to wade into the Rio Grande and scour their skins with yucca root.

Liebmann, then a grad student of Preucel's at Penn, deftly argued that even as they cast off most of the Catholic iconography—burning all the statues of Christ, the Virgin Mary, and the saints—many of the Puebloans subtly incorporated Catholic imagery and even material culture in their post-1680 productions. This practice, Liebmann argued, was not so much unconscious as ambivalent, or even a deliberate repudiation of Popé's edict.

The cardinal instance of this incorporation of Catholic imagery that Liebmann cited was a design engraved on the sooted interior of a cavate—a dwelling carved out of soft bedrock tuff—in Bandelier National Monument. From potsherds found nearby, Liebmann deduced that the scratchings must have been executed about the time of the Pueblo Revolt. And in a tour de force of artistic analysis, he showed how a prominent human face engraved on the west wall of the cavate mingled the iconography of the kachinas (the supernatural beings whose masks the Franciscans ordered the Indians to destroy) with colonial depictions of the Virgin Mary and the Virgin of Guadalupe.

I got in touch with both Preucel and Liebmann as I did my research, and they pointed me in useful directions. At Bandelier, monument archaeologist Rory Gauthier took me to the cavate Liebmann had analyzed, even though that whole section of cliff dwellings was closed to the public. During an enchanted hour inside the dim recess of the hollowed-out living space in the rock, I trained my headlamp across all kinds of fugitive images scratched in the soot, and saw with my own eyes the powerful duality of virgin saint and kachina that Liebmann had discovered.

In a phone call with Liebmann, I learned that the focus of his doctoral study was Jemez Pueblo. Not only had he been to all the ancestral sites I would explore as I did my research, as well as many I had never visited, but he was somehow working with the pueblo even as he gained permission to study some of those sites.

After earning his Ph.D. from Penn, Liebmann got a job at Harvard as an assistant professor of anthropology in 2009. I meant to seek him out and meet him in person, but the messages I left at the Peabody Museum got misplaced, and it was not until late in 2012 that we finally made contact. That same year, his book about the Pueblo Revolt, an expanded version of his dissertation, was published. I read *Revolt: An Archaeological History of Pueblo Resistance and Revitalization in 17ᵗʰ-Century New Mexico* with growing admiration and even envy, as I recognized how much deeper he had probed into the mystery of New Mexico between 1680 and 1692 than I had been able to do in my own book, which, after all, was aimed at a popular rather than a scholarly audience. Liebmann's masterly study now stands as the definitive history of the Pueblo Revolt.

In the field, the man had performed the kind of collaborative research that I had come to believe was impossible in the twenty-first century. At Patokwa, for instance, a Jemez village built on a low bench above the junction of the Jemez and Guadalupe rivers, constructed immediately after the Pueblo Revolt and once home to between six and nine hundred people, Liebmann was able to enlist Jemez helpers to map and survey the ruin in 2003 and 2004 . I had hiked across the site a couple of times just before Liebmann did his work, and had winced as I saw the hollows left by pothunters over the decades and the brutal rupture in the ground that a bulldozing backhoe had gouged. If ever a ruin looked truly ruined, I thought, this was it. Patokwa seemed beyond the rescue of archaeology.

That was not how Liebmann felt about the place. As part of his project, he marked out four different five-by-five-meter quadrats at Patokwa and gathered up every potsherd and artifact that lay on the surface. In old-school archaeology, that stuff would have gone straight into the collection drawers of some museum or university. But, as I read with astonishment, after washing and analyzing the two thousand potsherds his team had picked up, Liebmann and his Jemez associates had returned every single one to the place where it had lain, "leaving the site," as Liebmann wrote, "exactly as it had been prior to our analysis."

I was stupefied. Not only did this incredibly rigorous work seem to herald a new standard of noninvasive field archaeology, but it was obvious that where I had run into a brick wall with the Jemez Cultural Committee, Liebmann had slipped through a back door (or given the right knock on the front door) and somehow won the confidence of a pueblo so distrustful of outsiders that today no non-Puebloan is permitted to spend a single night inside the village limits.

In the spring term of 2013, I started sitting in on Liebmann's popular Harvard undergraduate class, "Encountering the Conquistadors: The Archaeology of Native American Responses to the Spanish Conquest." As he ranged across the Americas from Columbus through the Inca and the Maya and into his special expertise in the Southwest, I saw that Liebmann was a gifted teacher, although many of his students didn't quite catch the sly ironies he injected into his lectures.

What I really wanted to know was how he had performed his high-wire balancing act at Jemez, so one day in March, we met at a campus café where he narrated the saga of his long journey to the New Mexico pueblo. Raised as a Catholic, Liebmann had majored in English and theology at Boston College, after which he had wondered what to do next in life. A stint as a teacher on the Pine Ridge (Lakota) Reservation in South Dakota made him realize, as he told me, "how much I didn't know about Native American history."

After toying with the idea of law school, Liebmann enrolled for graduate study in anthropology at the University of Pennsylvania, where he came under the sway of Robert Preucel. His mentor had done a landmark survey in the 1990s at Old Kotyiti, a refugee pueblo on a high mesa to which many of the Cochiti people had fled during the Spanish reconquest. I had visited that haunting ruin with archaeologist Mike Bremer, as, with Preucel's map in hand, we walked across the site, identifying the room blocks and trying to imagine the savage attack launched there by Don Diego de Vargas in April 1694, when the Spaniards took 342 women, children, and old men prisoner. Of the thirteen warriors captured, Vargas blandly recounted, "As soon as one of the two reverend missionary fathers and chaplains who came from the camp had absolved them, I ordered them shot without delay."

"One day Bob [Preucel] said to me," Liebmann recalled, "'Nobody's worked at Astialakwa. You might consider that for your dissertation.'"

Like Old Kotyiti for the Cochiti, Astialakwa was a high, mesa-top refugee pueblo for the Jemez. Vargas's attack on it in July 1694 was every bit as brutal and tragic as his assault on Old Kotyiti three months earlier. And more than any other encounter during the reconquest, it broke the back of the Puebloans' resistance.

Liebmann jumped at his mentor's suggestion. But at first, he confessed, he went about it the wrong way. "I wrote to Bill Whatley, the tribe's Anglo archaeologist. I said I wanted to do a survey at Astialakwa. Bill wrote back, 'Great, come on up!'

"In retrospect, I should have asked the governor first. When I got in touch with Mehrdad Khatibi, he was more cautious. He said, 'Okay, but do you have permission from the governor?'" Khatibi, the Iranian-born Department of Resource Protection (DRP) officer for the tribe, had been the person who facilitated my meeting with the Cultural Committee.

"When I got out to Jemez—this was in 2000—I went up to Astialakwa with the students. And I hired a Jemez intern to help me map the site. Mehrdad was welcoming—I even stayed at his house. Meanwhile, I prepared a slide presentation about my project for Vince Toya, the governor, and members of the Tribal Council.

"I got one slide into my presentation, when Toya raised his hand and said, 'Whoa! Whoa! Who gave you permission to do this?'

"I answered, 'Bill Whatley.' The conversation stopped dead. Then Toya and the other Jemez men had an intense exchange in Towa. When the governor spoke to me again, he asked, 'What's in it for us?'" It was the same chilling rejoinder the slouched-back fellow from the Cultural Committee would accost me with three years later.

Liebmann went on, "I answered, 'The work I want to do is completely noninvasive. I want to help save the site from looters.'"

Unlike myself in 2003, Liebmann was not shut down cold. Or perhaps he simply had the patience to keep trying, as I had not. The upshot was that he kept returning to Jemez every summer for the next three years. "I got to know some of the people pretty well," he explained, "like Tom Lucero, a specialist for the DRP. I never asked questions about religion. Instead, I asked questions like, 'What museums might have Jemez stuff? Geez, you guys should have summaries from those places.' In the end, Mehrdad and I wrote up a grant proposal to compile a database of Jemez materials in the various museums around the country. And then Mehrdad asked me to work with Jemez on a NAGPRA grant."

NAGPRA, the Native American Graves Protection and Repatriation Act, passed in 1990, requires institutions to provide all the tribes in the United States with inventories of their holdings of human remains, funerary objects, sacred objects, and objects of cultural patrimony that might be affiliated with those tribes, and provides federal funding to enact the return of those items. Among archaeologists, NAGPRA has driven a deep divide. Some fear the loss for good of artifacts that might cast light on prehistoric puzzles. In a few cases, Native Americans who have received repatriated objects have turned around and sold them on the black market.

Liebmann, however, told me, "For me, NAGPRA is completely constructive. I feel the native peoples' need to get all their human remains back in the ground. And oddly, NAGPRA has opened doors to a more anthropological understanding of the past." Doors, I thought, like the one the Cultural Committee had seemed to slam in my face in 2003.

In the end, it came down to patience and persistence. "I've been going out to Jemez every summer for two to three months for the last thirteen years," Liebmann said in the café. "And I'll be going out there this summer." He smiled wryly. "Almost nobody gets the chance to

spend ten years in this business. At a place like Jemez, you're in a foreign culture that completely understands you, but at first you don't
understand them at all. Even now, I'm not completely accepted. There's
a new administration at the pueblo every year. I could be kicked out
at any moment.

"I've made fantastic friends at Jemez. Most archaeologists have
their heads stuck in the dirt. But this is what anthropologists do. I
like to think we've opened up new avenues of research. It's genuine
collaboration, not just filling out a p.c. checklist. We can spend time
together and get good work done without realizing that we neverthe-
less come from completely different worldviews."

I came away from my talk with Liebmann with a heightened admiration for his humanity as well as his intellectual acumen, even as
I recognized that I could never have spent thirteen years trying to
understand any other cuture. At the same time, I could locate his style
of collaborative archaeology in a historical perspective.

The earliest ethnographers such as Cushing and Fewkes went overboard, taking everything the Puebloans said as literal truth, even if
it purported to elucidate mysteries that were thousands of years old.
Starting in the 1920s with men such as Alfred V. Kidder, a more rigorous generation sought objective evidence in the dirt. That backlash,
though necessary for good archaeology, went overboard in the opposite direction, discounting Native American testimony as fable and
superstition. As University of Arizona tree-ring expert Jeffrey Dean
told me in 1993, in a sardonic oxymoron, "I don't think the Hopi oral
traditions are worth the paper they're written on."

The Matt Liebmanns of the Southwest are pushing the pendulum
back to plumb, combining scientific rigor with a newfound respect for
Native American oral history. What revelations their work unfolds,
the next generation will get to see.

Yet already, in *Revolt,* Liebmann has marshaled his collaboration
with Puebloans to tease out understandings of that profound but mysterious episode in Southwest history that no scholar before him had

grasped. In particular, he insists on avoiding the polar oversimplifications that would have us see, in Liebmann's words, the period from 1680 to 1694 as either "a romanticized Native victory" or "a tragic indigenous defeat." (As I read this stricture, I realized that in my own book I had been guilty of both reductionist views.) Even though the Spaniards managed to "reconquer" New Mexico after the Puebloans had driven them from the territory, the revolt changed that world for good. As Liebmann points out, after 1694 a new rapprochement "tacitly emerged" between the former enemies. Gone for good were the hated practices of the *encomienda* and the *repartimiento*, first introduced by Oñate. The former gave Spanish settlers the right to demand tribute from the indigenes in such forms as corn or animal hides, the latter a similar tribute in forced labor. And after 1694, instead of going to such extremes as torture to abolish the kachina religion, the Franciscan friars grudgingly tolerated it.

Liebmann invokes the phenomenon of catechresis, in its specialized anthropological sense, by which a colonized people transforms the "value-coding" of practices and images imposed by the colonizers, creating something altogether new. His own cardinal example, first explicated in the paper about the petroglyph inside the Bandelier cavate, sees the image as neither simply a kachina nor the Virgin Mary, but as "a hybrid fusion . . . a transformation of Santa Maria into the Virgin–Kachina."

The religious syncretism of the pueblos today had always been hard for me to wrap my mind around, as when my tour guide at Acoma had insisted that the original *shibop*—the place of emergence from the underworld—lay both in the waters of the Little Colorado River and in Siberia. I was inclined to see such paradoxical dualities as evidence of ambivalence or even confusion, without recognizing the condescension embedded in my own hyperrational way of thinking.

Liebmann cites other examples of catechresis wrought by the Pueblo Revolt. For some reason, after 1680, the Jemez suddenly stopped making their characteristic pottery, called by taxonomists Jemez black-on-white. Instead, they produced a new pottery without designs, called by the specialists Plain Red. At Patokwa, for instance, a substantial portion of the sherds that Liebmann and his Jemez associates picked up were Plain Red. This style, curiously, had first been introduced to the Jemez by Franciscan missionaries. But the Plain Red that Jemez potters started making was strikingly similar to the pottery in use at other pueblos in northern New Mexico. The transformative effect of this universality, Liebmann argues, was to reinforce the pan-Puebloan consciousness first solidified in the brilliantly coordinated rebellion that struck the colony on August 10, 1680.

Thus even though the Spaniards, after Vargas's *reconquista* in 1694, took nominal control of the Pueblo world again, that was a world that had been remade by the revolt. The uprising, in this sense, was not a simple defeat or failure. In his deeply perceptive book, Liebmann concludes, "As the archaeology of the Pueblo Revolt era demonstrates, the phenomena of cultural revitalization weld previously separate groups together, forging new alliances and identities among Native communities." It was not that from 1680 to 1694 the people were too fond of or familiar with the things the Spanish had brought to the New World, from horses to pigs to peach trees, to obey Popé's strict injunction to forsake them forever. It was rather, as Liebmann writes, that "the Pueblos usurped and transformed the things the Spaniards had introduced to their world, reworking them in innovative ways that promoted a pan-Pueblo cultural revitalization during that decade."

What strikes me as so radical about Liebmann's approach is that he depends not mainly, as so many previous historians did, on oral traditions and ethnographic lore, but on archaeology, as he wrings his insights from broken pieces of pottery lying on the ground and from scratchings on the sooted walls inside dwelling places carved by the Puebloans out of the soft tuff of the canyons. It's a tour de force of science wedded to empathy.

In August 2013, I spent two days with Liebmann in Jemez Springs, the gently touristic town about ten miles upcanyon from the pueblo. There I met Maria, Matt's smart, beautiful wife, and their eleven-month-old baby, Stella. I stayed in the appropriately funky Laughing Lizard Inn, and we ate burgers and drank beer at Los Ojos Saloon, whose motto is "Serving cowpokes, city folk, hikers, bikers, drifters 'n' debutantes . . . since 1947."

On the second day we drove to Santa Fe Canyon, downstream from the state capital, to look for petroglyphs. Matt's passion of the moment was a search for Puebloan images carved in the rock that might record the arrival of Oñate's army in 1598. In 2003, I had found petroglyphs in that canyon that looked very much as though they limned that dolorous and apocalyptic event, since we know that that was the route the Spanish forces took to breach La Bajada, the escarpment that separates the lower plains along the Rio Grande from the upper plateaus. Approaching the canyon by car, however, is a tricky business, as one weaves through a maze of dead-end dirt roads in La Cienega, a Latino hamlet whose owners tend to block access with barbed wire fences and "keep out" signs. By the time we found a way to circumvent the private holdings as we hiked up the rocky shoulder of a ridge on public land, I was pretty sure we were not in the same stretch of canyon where I had found graven images of swords and conquistadors on horseback ten years earlier.

The rock was a dark brown basalt, and the steep slope up to the crowning rim proved treacherous underfoot. Matt and Maria took turns carrying Stella in her baby backpack. Peering over each parent's shoulder, Stella took the outing, as it were, in stride.

All at once, on the summit of the pointed butte above La Cienega, we found a dazzling array of petroglyphs. Lizard-like humanoids, handprints, concentric rings, chimerical beasts, abstract designs made of triangles and squares and wavy lines . . . Some of the faces bore the hallmarks of kachina masks, with rectangular mouths and diamond-shaped eyes. The Kachina Phenomenon, which first appears in the Southwest around A.D. 1350, anchored the religion of the Puebloans at the time of the Spanish *entrada*. It was those false gods that the Franciscans were so zealous to eradicate.

I turned a corner and suddenly saw an entirely different image. "Hey, Matt," I shouted, "come have a look at this!" On the wall above me, a Puebloan had pecked out a man on horseback, left hand holding the reins, right hand raised in greeting . . . or threat? The rider wore a broad-brimmed, crowned hat, just as the conquistadors had. The tail of the horse overlapped a more ancient abstract "net" of interlinked loops.

Without even pausing to park Stella on the grassy shelf below the cliff, Matt scrambled up the boulders to peer at the petroglyph up close. The baby lurched ominously in her pack but cooed contentedly, as if she were being rocked in a cradle. "Wow," said Matt, "that makes the day worth it right there." Using his iPad, he photographed the image, then typed in notes and a GPS location. Ever the skeptic, however, he commented, "The trouble is, I can't tell if it's contact period or eighteenth-century."

On the saddle east of the butte top, I found a grid of stones adumbrating massive walls. I assumed it was the habitation site of early Puebloans, perhaps the very ones who had carved the petroglyphs, but when Matt studied it, he came up with a different explanation. "I think it's a corral," he said. "See the smaller enclosures? The Spanish penned up the baby sheep in them. This looks like the corrals on Guadalupe Mesa."

My initial disappointment was tempered by the realization that this was what was so great about going out into the field with a professional. Too many of today's archaeologists would rather sit in their labs, fiddling with computer models of migration patterns and agricultural sustainability. What a treat it was to hike in the Southwest with an expert who got as jazzed about what we saw as I did, but who could counter my intuitive leaps with the wisdom of his discipline.

I remembered the joy of my eleven-day road trip along the Chaco Meridian with Steve Lekson and Bill Hatcher.

We plunged down the slope to the Santa Fe River. Just as the Ancestral Puebloans had dumped their trash in the middens below their dwellings, so modern American towns get rid of their refuse. Ten years earlier, the citizens of the hippest, most affluent, most environmentally conscious town in New Mexico had used the Santa Fe River as the effluent for their collective sewer system. The poorer Latino settlements downstream bore the brunt of that disposal. In 2003, you could smell it. But now the stream ran clear and odorless—apparently Santa Fe had gotten this part of its act together in the last decade.

All the way up the facing slope to the north rim of the canyon, every third or fourth boulder bore petroglyphs. Here the kachina imagery abounded. We found a chute through the butte-top cliff and scrambled up to the rim, where we paused for lunch. It was a sublime day, about seventy degrees with a light wind, and views in every direction to distant horizons. Maria fed avocado slices into Stella's mouth. The infant promptly fell asleep, still sitting upright in her backpack.

I walked west along the rim of the cliff. All at once I caught sight of a snake, stretched out in curves half hidden under shelving ledges, with its head thrust motionless over the void, as if about to sting some invisible prey in midair. The snake's body was striped in red and white bands. Its ruddy head bore intricate trapezoidal markings. I had never seen a red snake in the Southwest before. Later I deduced that it was a red racer—*Coluber flagellum piceus*, an aggressive hunter of rodents, birds, and other snakes, but non-venomous for humans.

From ten yards away I took pictures and stared through binoculars at the serpent. Then I waved Matt and Maria over. They too had never seen a red racer anywhere.

And at that moment, a kind of epiphanic juxtaposition occurred. "Oh, my God!" I exclaimed, pointing at the base of the cliff eighty feet below us.

On the upturned surface of a lone basalt boulder, an ancient artist had carved a snake, its body stretched in a pattern of nine zigzag bends, the head a stylized diagram, two horns and two slit eyes. The stone snake lay poised to strike in exactly the same direction as the red racer above, its prey another illusion in empty space.

It was enough to make you believe . . . in what? The kachinas? The magic of the moment hung in the air.

Seven

LAND OF ENCHANTMENT–II

The day after our romp in the petroglyph-rich canyon, I drove to Santa Fe, where I hoped to absorb both sides of an intense controversy that has been simmering among Southwestern archaeologists for more than a century, but that has heated up in recent years. Like so many other puzzles about the Ancestral Puebloan world, this one hinges on the abandonment of the Colorado Plateau in the thirteenth century, and it pits Four Corners archaeologists against those working in the Rio Grande Valley.

Abandonments in general have a way of capturing the public imagination, and in the Southwest, the big one just before A.D. 1300 has all too often been misconstrued by the popular media as a "disappearance." I once agreed to be filmed as a talking head in a TV production under the rubric "Encounters with the Unexplained." My segment was luridly titled, "Ancient Anasazis: What Really Happened at Mesa Verde?" To my chagrin, the reasonable and tempered commentary that I (as well as other devotees, including Fred Blackburn) offered up got trumped at the end of the show by a dotty old New Age mystic, who delivered *the* answer. The Anasazi, she claimed (and the producers seemed to concur), were actually aliens from outer space who had come to the Southwest to try to set mankind straight, but had given up in disgust and returned to their home galaxy.

Nothing irks today's Puebloans more than the misconception that their ancestors vanished. In *In Search of the Old Ones*, I quoted Leigh Jenkins (who has since changed his name to Leigh Kuwanwisiwma), the prickly cultural preservation officer for the Hopi tribe, about a 1991 scholarly conference focusing on the abandonment to which he claimed he was invited at the last minute. "All these professional archaeologists," he told me, "were debating the question 'What happened to the Anasazi? Where did they go?' I said, 'They didn't go anywhere. They're still around. I can tell you exactly where.'"

In the same vein, Alfonso Ortiz, a man from San Juan Pueblo who became a professional ethnographer and whose 1972 book *The Tewa World: Space, Time, Being, and Becoming in a Pueblo Society* is a landmark in the field, famously quipped, "The Anasazi didn't disappear, they're running bingo parlors in the Rio Grande Valley."

Despite those clever assertions, the mapping of Ancestral Puebloan culture onto today's pueblos is a complex and uncertain business. The biggest stumbling block is language. The people who live in today's twenty-one pueblos speak a number of different dialects that belong to four distinct language families. The six pueblos immediately to the north of Santa Fe—San Ildefonso, Santa Clara, Tesuque, Pojoaque, Nambé, and Ohkay Owingeh (formerly San Juan)—speak a single language called Tewa. Pueblos on either side of the Tewa world—Sandia, Isleta, and Ysleta del Sur to the south, Picuris and Taos to the north—speak Tiwa, although Southern Tiwa and Northern Tiwa are nearly unintelligible to each other. Towa is spoken only at Jemez, southwest of the Tewa world on the other side of the Jemez Mountains.

As their names suggest, Tewa, Tiwa, and Towa are related languages, though not mutually intelligible. They belong to a larger family called Kiowa–Tanoan. The inclusion of Kiowa in the group is itself surprising and mysterious, for ethnographers trace those plains nomads back to a homeland in the upper Missouri River basin. As recently as 1650, the Kiowa were centered in the Black Hills of South Dakota, far from any New Mexico pueblos.

Five pueblos west of the Rio Grande—Cochiti, Zia, San Felipe, Santa Ana, and Kewa (formerly Santo Domingo)—speak a language called Keres. And farther west, at Acoma and Laguna, a slightly different Keres is spoken. Despite the present-day proximity of their pueblos, there is virtually no resemblance, save for the occasional loan word, between the Keresan and Tanoan languages. Even farther west, the Zuni speak a language that has no cognates anywhere in the world. Like Basque, Zuni is what linguists call an isolate. Finally, the Hopi in Arizona converse in a Uto-Aztecan tongue, related to the languages of such northern peoples as Shoshone and Ute as well as to the languages of southern peoples all the way to the Aztecs in Mexico.

In short, the linguistic diversity of today's pueblos is deep and baffling. As Steve Lekson says, "It's one of the most intractable problems in all of Southwestern prehistory."

We have no idea what language or languages the Ancestral Puebloans spoke. It is conceivable that their own linguistic diversity was as rich as that of today's Puebloans. But languages do not rapidly mutate, and completely distinct tongues such as Finnish and Russian have disparate roots that extend thousands of years into the past. Thus any attempt to draw vectors on the map of the Southwest that would argue, say, that the Ancestral Puebloans simply "became" the Hopi (or the Zuni or the Jemez) are doomed to failure from the outset.

The white-hot scholarly wrangle that brought me to Santa Fe in August 2013 has to do with where the Tewa came from. The basic positions of the two camps can be simply stated. One side sees the Tewa as migrating to the Rio Grande from the greater Mesa Verde region in the thirteenth century. The other side says, in effect, "Non-sense. They were always here, close to the Rio Grande, as far back as we can trace them."

Each camp has a corps of adherents, but I chose to focus my inquiry on the two archaeologists who seemed to be their leaders in battle. On the Mesa Verde side was Scott Ortman, who had come to the Santa Fe Institute via a Ph.D. at Arizona State University and years of work at the Crow Canyon Archaeological Center in Cortez, Colorado. His in situ antagonist was Eric Blinman, director of the Office of Archaeological Studies at the Museum of New Mexico, the same man who had stopped me in the streets of Santa Fe in 1999 to rail against Lekson's "absolutely crazy" new theory, and whom five years later I had lured to the café in Grants to debate the Chaco Meridian.

At first blush one might think, Why not ask the Tewa where they came from? Some of the early experts did just that. In the 1920s, archaeologist Jean Jeançon was told by a Puebloan at Santa Clara about his people's migration from "a great village in southwestern Colorado in the dim past." The informant drew a map of that long-lost village with such precision that, several years later, Jeançon was able to carry a copy to the Montezuma Valley and match the features perfectly with an ancient pueblo called Yucca House. In the 1920s, Yucca House—now a seldom-visited national monument just south of Cortez—was little more than a mound of rubble, but Jeançon's trained eye could discern its architectural layout. Since the

Santa Claran informant had never been near the site, Jeançon concluded that oral tradition had carried a fundamental truth about the Tewa homeland across seven centuries.

Some recent scholars, however, are skeptical. Other Tewa origin stories collected by early ethnographers bore no hint of a connection to the Four Corners region. And just as Steve Lekson's bombshell 1988 paper exploded the idea of a kiva as a religious and ceremonial sanctum analogous to Hopi kivas shown to ethonographers in the late nineteenth century, so a number of today's archaeologists tend to put little faith in the veracity of oral lore across as many as seven hundred years. Matt Liebmann's work with the Jemez was of a different sort, for he was investigating a dramatic campaign that had occurred only 320 years before, and that had written correlatives in the Spanish record.

The skepticism today about oral tradition over such long periods has always made sense to me. If you asked me what my ancestors in Wales, England, and Ireland were doing in A.D. 1280, I wouldn't have the faintest idea.

Nonetheless, in April 2014, I made my own casual probe into Tewa oral tradition, in the form of a tour of Puyé, the extensive clifftop ruin north of Los Alamos that is ancestral to the people of Santa Clara Pueblo. Puyé was excavated (against the protestations of the Santa Clarans) early in the twentieth century by teams led by Edgar Hewett, who, characteristically, never wrote up a formal report of his diggings. (The archaeologist is still reviled by Santa Clarans today.)

One can visit Puyé now only on a guided tour. Our docent that chilly, blustery day was a short, plump, lively woman named Judith Harvier. As we waited for the tour to begin, I perused the exhibits in the small museum on the grounds. A caption leapt out at me: "The Santa Clarans believe that their ancestors came from Mesa Verde, Chaco Canyon and other communities in the Four Corners region. Possibly due to persistent drought a migration to the east began."

That statement seemed to settle the debate over Tewa origins firmly in favor of Scott Ortman and his allies. But when I mentioned the claim to Harvier, she scoffed at it, explaining that the pueblo had hired an Anglo to write the signage for the museum. (*Why?* I wondered.)

Harvier told us that, though born a Puebloan, she had become "a bible-based Christian." Thus, as we climbed into a restored kiva and I asked her about the *sipapu*, the cuphole in the floor symbolic of the people's emergence from the underworld, she said, "I think that's a myth. I believe we came from the Garden of Eden."

Harvier claimed that Puyé had been occupied since A.D. 1100. (Most archaeologists date it only from 1275.) She insisted that it was abandoned in 1580, just before the Spanish conquest under Oñate—a date with which the scholars agree. But while archaeologists believe the Puebloans left Puyé to move a mere eight miles to their present site on the banks of the Rio Grande because of a drought, Harvier bridled at the notion. "The people joyfully moved east to where Santa Clara is today," she declared. "It was a wonderful time. It had nothing to do with drought, despite what the books say. They found more fertile ground along the Rio Grande."

At last I got up the nerve to ask Harvier where her people had come from. "I was told," she answered, "that we came from the Alamosa area [in southern Colorado], not from Mesa Verde." While I was puzzling over that piece of lore, she added a gloss that completely flummoxed me. "There *were* some who came from Mesa Verde, Chaco Canyon, all over," she said. "Everybody came, blacks, Asians, they all came."

It would take a far shrewder mind than mine to untangle the threads of oral tradition that had gone into Harvier's understanding of her people's past. Instead, I admired the stunning ruin as we strolled through it—the orderly room blocks on the summit, the cavates carved out of tuff in the south-facing cliff, the deep paths worn in the tuff by generations of Puebloan feet, the cryptic petroglyphs carved in the soft stone. Puyé as a whole looked supremely defensive, but when I uttered that adjective, Harvier rejoined, "How silly is that? They moved here because they had ready-made housing." She waved her hand at a handsome, deep cavate dwelling nearby. "It's nothing like what you read in books. There's a lot of Hollywoodizing in those books."

I met Eric Blinman at the spiffy new research center the Museum of New Mexico (MNM) had built on the outskirts of Santa Fe. He proudly gave me a tour of the lab, introducing me to one colleague after another. Then we settled into a conference room where he delivered a three-hour tutorial that was so sophisticated, I felt like a dim-witted grad student on the verge of flunking out.

In 2007, at the Society of American Archaeology annual meeting in Austin, Texas, a symposium titled "New Light on the Thirteenth-Century Depopulation of the Northern Southwest" was organized by a pair of scholars. The symposium was dominated by staff members and research associates from the Crow Canyon Archaeological Center in Cortez. The presentations were well received, and the symposium was awarded a book contract by the University of Arizona Press.

A follow-up conference took place the next year at the Amerind Foundation in Dragoon, Arizona. Blinman, who had not been present at the original symposium, was invited to provide a missing Rio Grande archaeological perspective. Blinman had read the symposium papers from the Austin symposium and passed them out to his staff to review. Their reaction: "This is nuts! All of us here were in shock." When Blinman met with the original authors at the Amerind conference, he told them, "We don't think any of what you're saying is true." To me, he added, "Ours was the first objection to their ideas by any professionals. I felt like I was the skunk in the room."

Blinman went on to air a long-standing grievance. "Rio Grande archaeologists in general are kept out of the loop. We do plenty of archaeology on the ground, but we're not in the Club. At the Amerind, when I objected to the others' papers, people actually got angry. How could I disbelieve, they seemed to imply. The passion of the debate was intense. This isn't a blood sport, but there are casualties."

The papers from the SAA and Amerind symposia were collected in a 2010 book called *Leaving Mesa Verde: Peril and Change in the Thirteenth-Century Southwest*. Five years later, it remains the definitive discussion of the rupture that rent the Ancestral Puebloan world at the end of the Pueblo III era. The paper that most disturbed Blinman and his colleagues was by Scott Ortman, titled "Evidence of a Mesa Verde Homeland for the Tewa Pueblos."

Blinman had known Ortman since the 1990s, thanks to the former's frequent visits to Crow Canyon. Before Amerind, Blinman was aware that Ortman had been doing interesting work with pottery design styles and "metaphor," but now, as Blinman told me, "This was the first time we'd seen any of the details."

It would not be an exaggeration to say that the Blinman camp felt blindsided by Ortman's thesis. Except for the paper that Blinman and five colleagues contributed to *Leaving Mesa Verde*, somewhat innocuously titled "Remodeling Immigration: A Northern Rio Grande Perspective on Depopulation, Migration, and Donation-Side Models," the proponents of the thesis that the Tewa had been in the Rio Grande Valley for as long as we can trace them had published little in support of their argument. The Santa Fe archaeologists assumed that arguments dating back to 1972 for cultural continuity in the Rio Grande Valley were generally accepted.

Meanwhile, Ortman was turning his dissertation into a book, which he submitted to the University of Utah Press. When the book won a prestigious $3,000 prize for that year's "best book-length, single-author manuscript in anthropology," Ortman was assured of publication. *Winds from the North: Tewa Origins and Historical Anthropology* came out in 2012.

Blinman et al. were caught off guard. At the time of my visit in August 2013, Blinman insisted that his team was trying to turn their research into a book of their own. But meanwhile, Ortman seemed to have seized the upper hand in the debate. "People tend to have a vested interest [in Ortman's argument]," Blinman complained,

Kalvin Watchman, our Navajo guide in Canyon de Chelly
(© Dawn Kish)

A prehistoric trail used as a shortcut in and out of Canyon de Chelly
(© Dawn Kish)

Navajo Fortress Rock, on top of which many of the Diné successfully avoided capture by U.S. Army troops in 1864 (© Dawn Kish)

The finest of the three nineteenth-century hogans we found in the wilderness where Hoskinini's band may have hidden out to avoid the Long Walk (© Greg Child)

The convoluted Kettle Country—Hoskinini's refuge? (© David Roberts)

Matt Liebmann, with eleven-month-old Stella aboard, searching for petroglyphs in Santa Fe Canyon (© David Roberts)

Sev Fowles demonstrating the all-but-invisible Comanche rock art near the Rio Grande

(© David Roberts)

Next four photos: Pre-historic rock art, some-where in the Southwest

(© Stephanie Scott)

(© Greg Child)

(© Matt Hale)

(© David Roberts)

Kaiparowits Plateau (© Macduff Everton)

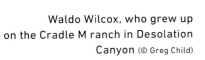

Waldo Wilcox, who grew up on the Cradle M ranch in Desolation Canyon (© Greg Child)

Mary Tobin, my companion on
Kaiparowits (© David Roberts)

Our gang in Desolation
Canyon (© Matt Hale)

Ariann Child, in her element on the trip to the basket
(© David Roberts)

Our camp on the rim, the night before our return to the basket (© Stephanie Scott)

The basket, still *in situ* (© Matt Hale)

"because, thanks to the book, it comes to them as an anointed idea."
Even worse, according to Blinman, "Mainly by interacting with the
people at Santa Clara Pueblo, Scott has shaped the Tewa perception of
their own history."

Blinman added, "In our own projects we've consulted with Tewa
Pueblo representatives, and without breaching confidentiality, I can
summarize their position as, 'We've had this place [the northern Rio
Grande] as our home forever.'

"Archaeology is a science only because our stories are intended to
be criticized. Someone like Scott lays out all the evidence he can in
support of his thesis. It's my job to work as hard as I can to disprove
it. I'm like a defense attorney in the face of an overzealous prosecutor.

"But we also need to come up with our own model to explain the
prehistory of the Rio Grande."

How do you prove or disprove a migration? It's a far more complicated and ambiguous business that you might think.

For all its rational rigor, archaeology, like other sciences, goes
through phases that are only tangentially linked to the phenomena its
practitioners spend their lives untangling. During more than thirty
years, from 1960 through the early 1990s, migration itself fell out of
favor. In a manifesto near the end of their 1973 treatise, *The Archaeology of Arizona*, Paul S. Martin and Fred Plog unequivocally declared
that migration "is an old, stale, overworked concept. It has fallen into
disfavor precisely because it has been employed without discernment
or due caution."

Martin and Plog were part of a movement called processual archaeology or New Archaeology, which sought to infuse a new rigor by using
the scientific method to study ancient cultures. The Old Archaeology,
these revisionists argued, had given up on trying to understand how
artifacts had been used in the past, content instead simply to cata-
logue and date them as dead relics disconnected from their makers.
In part, the New Archaeology was a reaction against such romantic

and outdated theories as those espoused by the Pan-Egyptian School around 1910, which saw all of world culture as emanating from the glorious fountainhead of the Egypt of the pharaohs.

The repudiation of migrationism (and its close cousin, diffusionism—the spread of cultural traits across wide geographical expanses not by human movement but by the interchange of ideas and technologies), however, went too far. In the Southwest, migrationism was first rehabilitated in 1994, at a Southwest Symposium session organized by Catherine Cameron (who happens to be Steve Lekson's wife), which focused on the movement of people from the Mesa Verde region to the Rio Grande in the thirteenth century.

If archaeology is swayed by intellectual fads and fashions, some of them may have unconscious roots. Historians of Southwest scholarship have pointed out that during periods in American history when there was a strong antiwar sentiment, such as during the last years of the Vietnam imbroglio, analyses of Ancestral Puebloan culture tended to minimize violence and warfare. Other trends stem from politically correct impulses. Just as "Anasazi" became a tabu designation, so in recent years some experts have urged the abolition of the word "prehistoric," ostensibly because it slights the achievements of peoples who had no written language but maintained rich oral traditions. (Linda Cordell's synthesis, published in 1984, was titled *Prehistory of the Southwest*. Twenty-four years later, in 2008, Steve Lekson called his own synthesis *A History of the Ancient Southwest*.)

Some younger p. c. scholars have even argued that we should retire such words as "warrior" and "raider." This simply goes too far for me, as it hints at a whitewash of any aspect of native cultures that has the faintest negative overtones. On the way from Cortez to Bluff, as I drive with friends through the small town of Montezuma Creek, almost one hundred percent Navajo, I like to mention this revisionist spasm as we pass by the high school, whose signboard proudly salutes the football team: "Home of the Whitehorse Raiders."

There is no getting around the fact that scientists become emotionally attached to theories in a way that exceeds disinterested objectivity. As a teenager in Boulder, Colorado, in the late 1950s, I keenly followed the debate between the two leading theories about the expanding universe. Fred Hoyle was the champion of the steady-state hypothesis, which postulated that galaxies were constantly being created out of nothing, so that their distribution would always remain much the same. George Gamow beat the drum for the big bang theory, which had the whole universe created in a primordial explosion 13.8 billion years ago, launching galaxies that were doomed forever to fly farther and farther apart.

My father, an astronomer, was friends with both Gamow, who taught at the University of Colorado, and Hoyle, who, though an Englishman, regularly visited our house in Boulder. Dad unhesitatingly put all his eggs in the steady-state basket, even though Hoyle could not cite laws of physics that would allow matter to be spontaneously created out of nothing. It was an emotional choice, based on Dad's aesthetic leanings: the steady state was elegant and reassuring, the big bang (as its name, derisively bestowed by Hoyle, suggests) crude and gloomy. As a loyal son, I too rooted for the steady state. It felt like the choice between the Dodgers and the Yankees.

Well, Hoyle and my father lost the debate. The steady-state universe now resides in the dustbin of cosmological theory, while every schoolboy knows about the big bang.

As I waded into the Santa Fe debate about Tewa origins, I couldn't help wondering if a regional prejudice played a small but significant role in the choosing of sides. Blinman and his closest allies had spent their whole careers in Santa Fe. Perhaps they had a vested interest in seeing the Puebloans who lived nearby as having deep roots in the Rio Grande past, needing no reinforcements from Mesa Verde to enhance their accomplishments. Ortman, on the other hand, had formed his theory while he worked at Crow Canyon, in the center of the Mesa Verde homeland. All those refugees—"our folks," for Crow Canyon— who took off in the thirteenth century must have gone somewhere, and the impact of the sophisticated culture they carried with them must have transformed the societies to the east and south into which they merged.

I had seen such regionalism at work, I thought, in other areas of Southwest archaeology, such as the question of where the Kachina Phenomenon first arose in the fourteenth century. The scholars who worked in New Mexico were sure the kachinas first popped up there, while their Tucson colleagues placed the wellspring in Arizona. When I researched my book about the Pueblo Revolt, I ran into an equally lively debate about what happened in the Dinétah, the Navajo homeland in northwestern New Mexico, during the 1690s, when the Spaniards finally reconquered the Pueblo world. Experts from Santa Fe and Albuquerque argued that Puebloan refugees fleeing into the Dinétah taught the Navajo to plant crops, to make rock art and pottery, and to build butte-top "pueblitos," defensive redoubts crafted out of stone and mortar. The BLM archaeologists based in Farmington, on the other hand, were having none of it. The Puebloan influence on the Navajos in the Dinétah was absolutely minimal, and rock art, agriculture, and pueblito architecture were indigenous Diné inventions.

Back to the crucial question: How do you prove a migration?

A couple of days after my seminar with Blinman in the MNM lab, I met Scott Ortman at the Santa Fe Institute. Founded in 1984, the multidisciplinary think tank occupies a hilltop complex of buildings on the northern edge of town, with a splendid view of the plateau stretching southwest toward La Bajada, the escarpment Oñate's army had surmounted to steal the Puebloan world from its natives in 1598. There could hardly be a greater contrast between the two institutions. Blinman's lab felt high-tech, cluttered, and energetic. If it were chemistry instead of archaeology the savants were pursuing there, you would expect to hear the bubbling of test tubes and the whirr of centrifuges.

The Santa Fe Institute, on the other hand, had a contemplative serenity about it. As Ortman gave me his tour, I glimpsed scholars politely discussing existential questions as they sipped coffee, reclining in comfortable armchairs. There was hardly a chalkboard in view, let alone the machines of scientific inquiry.

And there could hardly be a greater contrast in the demeanor of the two champions of the Tewa debate. Blinman, in his early sixties, is a tall fellow with a trim, graying beard and short cropped hair. His eyes crinkle as he tells a hearty joke, but when he gets going on archaeological theory, his voice rises to an agitated pitch, mingling outrage and triumphal demonstration. I could imagine him as a chess grandmaster. Ortman, forty-three when we met, is clean-shaven, of medium build, and unfailingly calm and polite. Dressed in blue jeans and short-sleeved shirt, he could have passed for a high-school social studies teacher. When Blinman explained his ideas to me, the sub-text was, *Pay attention, and you'll be able to understand.* Ortman's sub-text was, *I'm sorry this is so complicated. Thanks for your interest, though.*

A few days before our meeting, I had finished reading Ortman's *Winds from the North,* so I had his published exegesis to reinforce the arguments he now laid out at the institute. It's a brilliant book, but a dense and even technical one, and I had struggled to follow its more arcane lines of reasoning. The hallmark of Ortman's approach is a seemingly fair-minded willingness to consider the very objections that would undermine his central argument. But, to reverse the metaphor and see Ortman as the chess master, his technique is to offer those pawns up for sacrifice, only to come crashing down to the eighth rank with rooks and queen.

If the Tewa migrated in large numbers to the northern Rio Grande in the late thirteenth century, we would expect a surge in population there. But how do you measure the population of a region in prehistory? Basically, it comes down to counting rooms in ruins that date to the right era. Here Blinman and Ortman, not surprisingly, disagree. Blinman showed me a chart that estimated the number of households in three different segments of the northern Rio Grande.

In his count, the La Bajada–Velarde surge, covering the locales of today's six Tewa-speaking pueblos, occurred not in the thirteenth century but steadily through the tenth to twelfth centuries. He attributed this to better farming techniques and favorable climate, not an influx of refugees. A mere one percent increase per year in human fertility, according to Blinman, could account for that surge.

Where Blinman did see a surge was in the Albuquerque–Cochiti segment, where today's seven Keresan pueblos reside, but according to him, the surge started in the late twelfth century and accelerated in the early thirteenth century. No one denies that the Colorado Plateau was abandoned in the thirteenth century, and those folks had to go somewhere. As Blinman succinctly told me, "Everything we think of as Anasazi is Keres." But he added, "In the 1280s around Mesa Verde, a lot of people were killed. The society was decimated."

A whole chapter of *Winds from the North* is devoted to "Population History of the Tewa Basin." The arguments are complex, but Ortman's blunt conclusion is that by the end of the thirteenth century, fourteen thousand more people lived in the Tewa Basin than had at the beginning of the century.

A potential stumbling block for Ortman and his allies who favor a huge in-migration to the northern Rio Grande from Mesa Verde lies in the realm of material culture. The pueblos along the Rio Grande built in the thirteenth and fourteenth centuries don't look anything like the Mesa Verde villages that preceded them. They lack the Mesa Verdean towers, "keyhole kivas," and cookie-cutter family-household layouts known as "unit pueblos." Rio Grande kivas tend to be oriented to the east, Mesa Verde kivas to the south. Instead of rows of linear room blocks and kivas, the Rio Grande pueblos tend to feature clusters of room blocks facing in on large central plazas.

If the Tewa came to the Rio Grande in the thirteenth century and transformed a rather sparse and straggling population that was already there, why didn't they impose their architecture on these "country bumpkins"? Here, Ortman's argument invokes Chaco. If, as

Steve Lekson and others now believe, the collapse of Chaco around A.D. 1125 led to a lasting repudiation of hierarchical, grandiose, empire-building societies, then Ancestral Puebloans who turned their backs on Mesa Verde as a failure would have turned their backs on its material culture as well, adopting new styles, Ortman writes, "as a negative commentary on the society they had recently chosen to leave behind." Coming to the Rio Grande, they would have assimilated with the folks they met there, not lorded their own culture over them.

I asked Ortman if he wasn't in danger of making a circular argument here: if something you might otherwise expect doesn't show up, you claim the Old Ones deliberately did away with it. (Indeed, Blinman had complained, "Scott ignores data that refute him, and accepts data that support him.") Now Ortman nodded, smiling because he'd heard that complaint before, then went on to add, "What I try to suggest in my book is that when migrations occur, the traces of continuity in the culture are not predictable. Archaeologists tend to look for predictable continuities, but that can be a dead end."

Why, if the Tewa came from Mesa Verde, didn't they at least bring their pottery with them? Here the debate becomes thornier than ever. The most distinctive pottery style from the Mesa Verde region just before the abandonment is a vivid carbon-painted design called Mesa Verde black-on-white. At about the same time or shortly before, a new style crops up in northern New Mexico—Galisteo black-on-white. It looks, some experts think, an awful lot like Mesa Verde black-on-white. But for the last eighty years, ceramicists have argued whether they're the same (or whether the New Mexico variety is merely a local adaptation of the Mesa Verde one), or instead completely distinct and thus only accidentally similar. Blinman: "Galisteo black-on-white doesn't look anything like Mesa Verde black-on-white!" Ortman, in effect: Yes, it does.

It's not only the design style of the pottery that matters, but the very shape of the vessels. At Mesa Verde, mugs were common. They never appear in the Rio Grande, nor among the Keresan pueblos or Hopi.

Why? Some strange mixture of repudiation of the past while clinging to its vestiges may be at work.

One pueblo ruin, in particular, forms a keystone of Ortman's Tewa thesis. It's a place called Tsama, built on a low bench above the Chama River, about forty miles north of Santa Fe. The site was excavated by a field school led by the legendary Florence Hawley Ellis in 1970. Two archaeologists whom I met at the Pecos Conference in 2013, Tom Windes and Peter McKenna, had been eager young grad students at Tsama forty-three years before; now they were somewhat wizened sages of Southwestern prehistory. Both sat down with me to reminisce about that long-ago summer. Recalled McKenna, "On the drive back to Albuquerque, ten boxes of artifacts flew off the back of the truck. Everything was shattered. We lost important pots. A lot of paperwork blew away, too. There we were, out on the highway, picking up pot-sherds one by one."

Tsama was Hawley's last major dig, and she never wrote it up, although a 2006 paper by Windes and McKenna, called "The Kivas of Tsama," helps rescue the excavation from oblivion. The West Plaza at the site, earliest in terms of construction, would turn out to be crucial to Ortman's thesis. Despite the catastrophe with the truck en route to Albuquerque, the potsherds from Tsama were archived at the University of New Mexico. At Crow Canyon in 2000, Ortman "borrowed" the collection and analyzed the sherds in minute detail. He found that the pottery pieces from one special kiva in the West Plaza bore striking similarities to Mesa Verde designs: "rim ticking," X's and zigzags, patterns that mimicked the weaving in Ancestral Puebloan basketry, and the like. That part of the ruin, moreover, dated from between A.D. 1250 and 1275. Here, Ortman argues, was rare proof of linkage to Mesa Verde, almost as if its potters were memorializing a lost homeland.

On a windy day in August 2013, after a couple of false stabs, I found the unsignposted terrace above the Chama across which spread the ruin of Tsama. It wasn't hard to locate the West Plaza, and there I found potsherds that Ellis's crew had failed to scavenge. I held them in my palm, trying to discern the patterns that had lit flashbulbs in Ortman's brain, but the designs were too subtle for me to grasp. Gazing across the barren bench, I thought, *What a forlorn place this seems. And yet, what a vibrant home it must have been for the Puebloans who built it in the thirteenth century, wherever they came from.*

The intricacy and complexity of Ortman's and Blinman's dueling theses about Tewa origins can only be hinted at here, and I confess that there are many sides to each man's argument that I have not grasped. Several close readings of all 485 pages of *Winds from the North* (including forty-five pages of appendices) might turn an idly curious bystander into a staunch partisan for Ortman's thesis—as indeed I found myself becoming that August. But to do justice to the debate, one should also make several close readings of the massive opus that Blinman and his colleagues have yet to write.

Still, I was grateful that both archaeologists were willing to take so much time to try to explain to me how their theories worked. And in those intellectually challenging sessions, I felt the burning passion of both men for their beliefs.

The tour de force of Ortman's research, as well as its most technically complicated thrust, is a meticulous attempt to reconstruct Proto-Tanoan, the hypothesized root source for today's linked languages of Tewa, Tiwa, Towa, and Kiowa. By tracing similarities in Proto-Tanoan to the names of places far to the north mystically alluded to in Tewa origin stories, Ortman seeks to link the Rio Grande pueblos to a Mesa Verde homeland.

One of those mystical places has come down to us in the oral tradition of Tewa as "the lake of Copala." Ortman identifies it as a place hundreds of miles to the northwest of the Rio Grande, perhaps as far away as central Utah. But Blinman disagrees: "It's not northwest, just north of here. And not very far—still within the Rio Grande valley."

Says Ortman, "I don't understand how you can ignore oral tra-

ditions. Written literature changes everything, because it allows us
to preserve knowledge in libraries. But I'll bet that a few centuries
ago, you *could* ask Europeans where their ancestors came from.
Puebloan stories are sacred texts, and they are deeply attached to the
landscape."

When I mentioned Ortman's reconstruction of Proto-Tanoan to
Blinman, however, his eyes crinkled in his habitual "gotcha" smile,
as he said, "That's the part of Scott's work I like best. Unfortunately, it
doesn't support his thesis."

Even as I plunged into the controversy, I heard a mocking imp
whisper in my ear, *Does your average reader give a damn where the
Tewa came from?*

Maybe not. But I give a damn, although I'm not sure why. In *Winds
from the North*, Ortman makes his own case for why the truth about
Tewa origins matters, as it bears on the ability of a stressed-out people
to survive catastrophe.

> If the Mesa Verde population scattered, declined in place, or
> destroyed itself in a spasm of warfare, it would suggest an utter
> failure of a well-established society to cope with the challenges
> it faced and would present a cautionary tale of just how apoca-
> lyptic such failures can be. If, on the other hand, some fraction
> of Mesa Verde society responded to these challenges by moving
> to the Tewa Basin and developing a new society there, it would
> present a somewhat more optimistic view of human adaptability
> and resiliency.

One could plead that all scientific knowledge is worth pursuing,
not only for its own sake but for the fruits it may unexpectedly bear
in the future. In the late 1950s, I don't think most of my classmates at
Boulder High School gave a damn whether the steady-state or the big
bang explained the receding galaxies, but nowadays the expanding
universe is the stuff of *Nova* specials. I cannot even imagine what a

Higgs boson really is, but when scientists in 2012 confirmed its existence forty-eight years after Peter Higgs proclaimed its likelihood, I was thrilled, and I have no doubt that profound implications will unroll from its discovery.

Darwin with his finches, Mendel with his pea plants, Wegener with his tectonic plates . . . The incunabula of a lonely scientist's brain and lab can transform our understanding of the world. So, perhaps, someday, in some way, Blinman and/or Ortman with their Tewa. Origins are inherently interesting, and the fact that memory alone is incapable of retrieving them turns archaeology into a noble endeavor.

Just as I thought that I was getting a handle on the Tewa controversy, Steve Lekson brought me up to speed on another bombshell he had thrown into the migration battlefield in 2002. A team led by Lekson and New Mexico archaeologist Karl Laumbach had been running a field school excavating a butte-top village called Pinnacle ruin. The site overlooks the Cañada Alamosa, a steep-walled, twisting canyon whose stream forms a northwestern tributary of the Rio Grande a few miles above Truth or Consequences, New Mexico. It's a beautiful place, sacred to the Chihenne Apache under Mangas Coloradas and Victorio, who regarded Ojo Caliente, the small hot spring at the upper mouth of the canyon, as the center of their homeland.

Pinnacle ruin had been a major site for the Old Ones, a village composed of between 100 and 150 rooms. The various strata through which the team dug disgorged a wide variety of pottery styles from Glaze A through Reserve Indented Corrugated. But there was also an abundance of Magdalena black-on-white, named for its type site, a small town west of Socorro, New Mexico. That stuff sure looked like Mesa Verde black-on-white. In fact, H. P. Mera, the first ceramicist to study the ware, in 1935, simply called it Mesa Verde black-on-white. To Lekson and Laumbach, this seemed to argue for a migration by a band of Ancestral Puebloans all the way from the Mesa Verde region to the Cañada Alamosa, where they built the defensive redoubt of Pinnacle ruin. The trouble was, that site lies a good 100 miles south of the assumed southern limit (as specified in Linda Cordell's Venn-diagram map and many other textbooks) of the Ancestral Puebloan realm. The Cañada ought to have been one hundred percent Mogollon.

As Lekson pointed out, two other sites well south of that border, Gallinas Springs and Roadmap ruin, also yielded quantities of Magdalena black-on-white. Roadmap is even farther south than Pinnacle.

The problem was the same as with Galisteo black-on-white. Skeptics argued that Magdalena and Mesa Verde black-on-white were really two completely distinct styles, their similar look a mere coincidence. But Lekson and Laumbach also noted other Mesa Verdean features at Pinnacle, such as carefully coursed masonry, utterly unlike the surrounding Tularosa or Mimbres architecture ("bowling balls in peanut butter," as Lekson so vividly characterized the latter).

The two scholars came to an unambiguous conclusion: "Based on limited testing at Pinnacle Ruin, extensive but underreported excavations at Gallinas Springs, and survey data from the Roadmap site, we think these three large sites represent migrants from the Mesa Verde region of the Four Corners area." If they're right, the thirteenth-century migration map of the Southwest needs to be radically redrawn. Along with possible arrows redirecting the refugees from the Colorado Plateau to Hopi, to the Keres pueblos, and maybe to the upper Rio Grande, a much longer arrow would push them far into southern New Mexico, where they lived side by side with their Mogollon neighbors.

Lekson's bombshell reignited in 2008. He and Laumbach had initially thought Pinnacle ruin had been occupied only at the end of the thirteenth century and into the fourteenth. But new accelator mass spectrometry dating of kernels of burnt corn from the ruin pushed habitation way back to at least the early thirteenth century. If this is true, the dating implies that migration out of Mesa Verde may have begun well before the catastrophic last few decades, climaxing with the severe drought from 1276 to 1299. In fact, in recent years, more and more scholars are refining their conception of the famous abandonment, seeing it not as a sudden last-ditch upheaval but as a series of tricklings out of the homeland stretching across the whole of the thirteenth century, and perhaps beginning in the twelfth.

That in turn raises a host of new questions about the Ancestral Puebloan desertion of the Colorado Plateau. It's a field of inquiry and speculation that Lekson takes up with relish in his magisterial *History of the Ancient Southwest.*

Lekson agrees with Ortman that the population of the northern Rio Grande grew dramatically through the thirteenth century. And he ponders the same paradox about material culture. As he explains,

> We want to see Mesa Verde people (with Mesa Verde pottery, Mesa Verde kivas, Mesa Verde arrowheads, and so forth) suddenly appear in the Rio Grande, but (with a few exceptions) they are hard to spot. Two things were probably happening: migration of very small groups and—far more importantly—a conscious rejection of Chaco and Aztec and all they entailed. They no longer wanted to *look like* Mesa Verde people.

Lekson underscores the new research that sees the abandonment as occurring in sporadic migrations throughout the thirteenth century, not as a precipitous last-ditch desertion: "The conventional story holds that the Four Corners region was abandoned between 1275 and 1300—the period of the Great Drought. But it turns out that people were leaving in large numbers in the middle 1200s and perhaps even earlier. By 1250—twenty-five years before the Great Drought—the rush was on."

Lekson makes a further point, one that few of his predecessors had raised:

> here's the kicker: our most advanced environmental modeling . . . shows us that *they didn't all have to leave.* Even the worst

periods of the Great Drought could have supported numbers of people, and . . . they could have shifted gears and built canals. The Hohokam had been doing just that for a thousand years, and the Mimbres for several centuries. . . .

When the last villagers left the Mesa Verde area, sometime after 1280, the homelands were truly empty. If anyone stayed behind, we can't find them archaeologically. The totality and finality of the evacuations suggest to me political rather than environmental processes. Complete depopulation is unusual in history. When it happens, it often follows immense natural calamities, disasters of biblical proportions, not just a drought—"great" but no worse than several the Anasazi had previously weathered. The disaster that ended Chaco and Aztec was at least in part, and I think largely, man-made: failure of the political system.

When I was researching *In Search of the Old Ones*, between 1992 and 1994, Southwestern experts were already talking about a "pull" that must have reinforced the "push" of environmental hard times to convince all the Ancestral Puebloans to leave the Four Corners area. The theory in vogue then was that the pull was the emergence of the Kachina Phenomenon farther south—a radical new religion that put a premium on aggregating people in the kind of large pueblos that emerge along the Rio Grande (and elsewhere south of the Four Corners) in the fourteenth century. In Cortez, Bruce Bradley had succinctly summarized for me that theory: "The Kachina Phenomenon, by integrating clans and kinship groups, allows socialism to flourish. It's worked in the pueblos for several hundred years. It still works. Down there, the Anasazi found an answer about how to live together. They didn't find one up here. Surprise, surprise—up here they're all gone."

The trouble is that during the last twenty years, no one has found any evidence of the Kachina Phenomenon—neither the distinctive and vivid rock art nor the actual paraphernalia of the ceremonies, such as fragile masks—that predates A.D. 1350, or at the very earliest, 1325. The new religion that still anchors today's pueblos appeared too late to be the pull of the abandonment. The theory that Bradley so confidently outlined for me in 1994 has been almost entirely discarded.

An explanation for the total abandonment such as the one Lekson espouses is very hard to prove or disprove. Political upheavals leave almost no evidence in the ground for archaeologists to dig up. And because the time span is too great—not to mention the disparity in concepts of history—oral tradition can be of little help. If an archaeologist asked a Santa Claran or a resident of Ohkay Owingeh today, "Did you guys come to the Rio Grande because you got really fed up with Chaco and Aztec?," he would be met, most likely, with a blank stare—or a "none-of-your-business" evasion.

Lekson's naysayers, skeptics such as Eric Blinman, might point out that the author of *The Chaco Meridian* is using his own unproven theory about successive centers of Southwestern hegemony to argue the causes of the abandonment. Circular reasoning, they might sneer. But, as pointed out in chapter four, the idea that Chaco "became" Aztec around A.D. 1125, so radical when Lekson proposed it in 1999, is now commonly accepted. And we know that Aztec had collapsed by 1275. Whether or not its leaders took off for Paquimé then—the far more radical idea embodied in the Meridian thesis—Aztec may well have bred a contempt and bitterness among the far-flung commoners on the Colorado Plateau (vassals, perhaps) that made them not only want to flee their homeland for good, but to start life over far to the south and east without even a Mesa Verde mug to remind them of the bad times of the thirteenth century.

In July 2013, Lekson asked me in an e-mail, "Have you looked into Sev Fowles's work on Comanche rock art on the upper Rio

Grande?" I did a mental double-take. Comanches in New Mexico? I thought they were Plains Indians, nomads who had roamed across Texas, Oklahoma, and Kansas. Comanche rock art? And who was Sev Fowles?

Google directed me to Severin Fowles, who taught anthropology at Barnard College in New York City. The man himself was hard to locate, though. His office phone message box was full. Apparently he spent his summers in a house he had bought in Dixon, New Mexico, a sleepy little hamlet about twenty miles southwest of Taos.

Meanwhile, I got hold of his book, *An Archaeology of Doings*, which had been published only three months earlier. Browsing through it, I saw that it was another brilliant but difficult treatise, like Ortman's *Winds from the North*, that it would take my undivided attention to fathom. Its thesis somehow claimed that, before the arrival of the Spanish, the Puebloans had had no religion at all. Suspicious, I wondered, *Is this mere postmodern sophistry?* But I was intrigued to learn that one of Fowles's summer field schools in the Rio Grande Valley had excavated and analyzed a hippie commune from the 1960s.

When I finally reached Fowles by phone in Dixon, he welcomed me to come out so that he could show me the Comanche rock art, which he had discovered only in 2008. On a hot day in late August 2013, we met at the café and gift shop jauntily named the Pilar Yacht Club, halfway between Dixon and Taos. In the meantime, I had read a pair of papers Fowles had published about his findings. They whetted my curiosity. And a remark in one of them validated my Comanche ignorance. Before 2008, Fowles noted, not a single verifiably Comanche site had ever been found in New Mexico.

The archaeologist I met at the "yacht club" could have passed for a cowboy. Slender, obviously fit, he wore blue jeans, a long-sleeved shirt, and a battered cross between a Stetson and a safari hat, the brim curled up on either side above his ears. Nor did he talk like an East Coast academic, as he poured out his enthusiasm for the rugged landscape of his field work. I asked him how he had discovered the rock art.

"People had seen it for years," Fowles answered, "but they thought it was graffiti."

We headed into the canyon in his pickup. After crossing the Rio Grande on an old bridge, we parked in a turnout and started hiking northeast on a trail that led across a grassy terrace. I had a sudden hit of déjà vu, for I realized that I had hiked this same trail in November 2008—probably only months after Fowles and his students had discovered the rock art. And when we came to the first basalt boulder, I remembered my dismissal of five years ago: *Yes, scratchings, doodling, teenagers' graffiti.* A little farther on, we came to a design on another boulder that I remembered thinking was probably Ancestral Puebloan, but I had dismissed it, too, as crude, barely etched.

On that same shelf, other basalt boulders bear unmistakably Ancestral Puebloan petroglyphs, some apparently Archaic, for the patina in the spirals, wavy parallel lines, and wheel-like webs is as dark as that of the surrounding rock. It has also long been known that this stretch of the Rio Grande canyon was an encampment for Utes and Jicarilla Apaches in historic times.

In 2008, as Fowles studied the "scratchings" on the scattered boulders more and more carefully, he realized that what others had mistaken for graffiti was actually a series of very elaborate panels, the details so faint as to be almost invisible. "At first we thought it was Jicarilla," Fowles said as we stood beside one boulder. "We started to look for parallel examples in the rock art literature, but we couldn't find any."

Something else bothered the archaeologist. "Ancestral Puebloan rock art is pecked with a pounding stone or a stone chisel," Fowles said. "Ute and Jicarilla Apache rock art is also pecked. But these"—he waved his hand at the surface of the boulder—"are scratched with a metal tool, perhaps a knife. I started looking at Plains Indian rock art.

All of a sudden, I saw a panel from Alberta, in Canada, a thousand miles away from here, that looked just like this stuff. It's called the Plains Biographic Tradition."

As we moved from boulder to boulder, Fowles pulled out several pages of exquisite drawings he had made of the scratched panels, which are too subtle to photograph well. The demonstration that followed was like a sorceror's magic trick. As Fowles pointed out the details in his drawings, I peered closer at the panels, shading the scratchings from direct sunlight, or playing my headlamp sideways across them to highlight the grooves. To my astonishment, the "graffiti" transformed before my eyes into real objects. And those objects were tipis, horses, feathered lances, bows and arrows, and mounted warriors.

Once Fowles concluded that the rock art must be Comanche, he got in touch, through an ethnographer friend, with Jimmy Arterberry, a historian and artist working in the Comanche Nation Tribal Historic Preservation Office in Lawton, Oklahoma. "In 2009, I sent Jimmy this picture"—Fowles held out the detailed drawing of the panel we stood beside—"and he flipped. 'It screams Comanche!' he said. Jimmy first came out here in 2011. It's thanks to him that I could interpret the scenes that are depicted here."

From the iconography, Fowles was also able to date the rock art to the narrow window between 1690 and 1740. "It's post-horse, pre-gun," he neatly summarized. "Only after the Pueblo Revolt period, from 1680 to 1694, do the Comanches get horses. The Revolt liberated horses from the Spanish, and many of them turned feral. That's how they fell into Comanche hands. By 1740, the Comanche had guns traded by the French. There are lots and lots of horses on these boulders, but no guns."

As we strolled across the long bench on the north side of the Rio Grande, Fowles pointed out other signs of the Comanche presence that I never would have fathomed on my own. Tipi rings from "cold camps," where no fires were built (I would have seen only scattered stones half-buried in the soil). "Marker trees," where Comanches had tied down the limbs of junipers to contort their growth so that the trunks pointed in a certain direction. According to Arterberry, the Comanches call these bonsai-like junipers "trees that help us."

Along the trail, we ran into a pair of hefty, middle-aged gents wielding a metal detector. Searching for relics with such a gizmo is illegal, and Fowles later told me how much he deplored TV shows such as the National Geographic Channel's *Diggers*, which advocates and even glorifies digging for artifacts located by detector. Yet now he went out of his way to explain to the men what we were looking at. They nodded absently, eager to get on with their treasure hunt.

Once they were out of sight, I asked, "How come you were so nice to those yahoos?"

Fowles shrugged. "I can't stop them. Also, on one of my field days a couple of years ago, I lost my wedding ring right along this trail. I went back over it again and again, and even asked the students to search, but we never found it." He grinned ruefully. "Maybe those guys with their metal detector will locate it."

Returning to his explication of the rock scratchings, Fowles said, "The Plains Biographic Tradition is a narrative art—of which there's very little anywhere in North America. It tells the stories of particular individuals, recording their successes and failures in a given year. The tellers are making the art to show off what they've done."

In a landmark paper published in 2013, titled "Gesture and Performance in Comanche Rock Art," Fowles and Arterberry develop their theory of how the scratched panels served their people. We tend to assume that rock art is made to be seen, that it's like a gallery in an art museum. But the Comanche panels, in Fowles and Arterberry's view, are about "gesture and performance." The artist carves his scenes as he tells the story of his exploits, like a professor writing equations on a blackboard. His audience, sitting around the narrator on the ground, listens with rapt attention. Once the telling and carving are finished, the art has served its purpose. It's not necessary to come back later to admire the panel and remember the story. As the authors write, "Had the Comanche rock artist wanted to create a visually impressive finished product, he could have done so. . . . The Comanches scratched rather than pecked their images, however, presumably because the performed gesture was as, or even more, important than the icon produced."

I had encountered a similar phenomenon on the Cape York peninsula in northern Australia. There, in a series of sandstone alcoves scattered through the eucalyptus forest, Aborigines had painted an amazing congeries of pictographs mingling animals, humanoids, and supernatural beings called *quinkans*. What makes those panels so hard to comprehend, however, is the massive superimposition, one figure painted on top of an earlier figure on top of a yet earlier one. We know from elderly informants in Cape York, whose knowledge reaches back to the last living painters in the tradition, that the purpose of the Aboriginal rock art was not to be seen, but to be executed. Gesture and performance, indeed.

I held Fowles's drawing in my hand as he explicated a particularly rich panel whose details slowly blossomed before my eyes. A central human figure, his body obscured by a huge shield-like circular object, held a recurved bow (shaped like a sideways cursive "m") with an arrow on the string ready to fire. Facing him was a much smaller warrior with a single-curved bow, firing back. According to Arterberry, the Comanche warrior was wearing a missionary hood stolen from Spanish priests. "You wear it in battle," said Fowles. "It's a kind of 'in-your-face' to the Catholics." A recurved bow, Arterberry had explained, was more powerful than the conventional model the man's enemy was wielding. Toppling toward the central figure's feet were several broken bows, signifying weapons used up in battle. A series of diagonal strokes kept score: the Comanche had gotten off twenty-two arrows to his enemy's paltry seven.

"And see," Fowles added, "the big guy has a backup." Sure enough, behind the central warrior stood another shield-holding figure. But Arterberry had commented, "This guy doesn't look Comanche to me.

He could be a Ute ally of the Comanche." The artist-historian had also interpreted a barely sketched animal rearing behind the Comanche. "That's a bear," Arterberry had insisted. "A symbol of power."

The whole panel, then, commemorated an important battle between Comanches and some other Native American tribe. The man who had scratched it was most likely the central warrior who had emerged victorious. Said Fowles, "It took us half a day just to draw this panel. Other panels have taken us three days to draw."

We walked to another boulder. Here, the rock art had been scratched on the topmost surface, facing the sky. As I got in position to look at it, I realized how complicated the panel was, but I couldn't begin to understand what I was seeing—until Fowles performed a masterly job of explication. Some modern graffiti had been carved right on top of the Comanche art, including the initials "CM," the name "Jose," and the immortal boast, "JER FUCKED YOUR MOM." Fowles handed me a drawing in which the graffiti were sketched in red, so that they could be distinguished from the complex array of blue Comanche strokes. A second drawing was all in blue—the panel minus the graffiti. I could see horses everywhere, but the scene was still confusing. Then Fowles handed me a third drawing, saying, "We finished this just in the last two days." It subtracted the apparently random or abstract scratches from the panel.

Suddenly it was clear. The story the panel told was about a single mounted warrior on the edge of the panel capturing feral horses as they grazed near a spring. There was even a scattering of hoofprints on the rock. And the spring was represented by a natural hole, a tiny cup-like indentation in the top of the boulder. Fowles grew excited. "Hey, take a picture of that, will you?" he asked me. It had rained the day before, and now the hole that represented the spring was full of water—as Fowles had never before seen it.

The whole day's tour dazzled me. I had seldom, if ever, had a site in the Southwest that, left to my own devices, I would have overlooked entirely or dismissed as unimportant suddenly spring to life as this one had. The tapestry before my gaze was a narrative documenting deeds and stories that until the last few years, no anthropologists or archaeologists even knew existed. In and of itself, the newfound Comanche rock art was a startling phenomenon. But now Fowles put it in a larger context.

"In the Spanish record," he said, "the Comanches are always 'coming out of nowhere,' and they're always seen as ruthless destroyers, leaving villages in 'smoldering ruins.' That caricature has caught on. It's what you see in John Ford's movie *The Searchers*.

"It goes hand-in-hand with the received idea that the Spaniards 'conquered' New Mexico. But in recent years, Puebloans have increasingly criticized that idea, pointing out that, especially in the eighteenth century, those Spanish colonists were economically and militarily dependent on the indigenous people, with little actual power to impose their will.

"Very few historians have tried to see this period from the Comanche point of view. But the Comanche transformation was extraordinary. At the start of the colonial era, they were horseless hunter-gatherers living in small camps scattered around northern Colorado and Wyoming. By the end of the seventeenth century, they had become the most skillful equestrian warriors and long-distance traders in North America. Their domain stretched from the Canadian plains into northern Mexico."

Fowles referred me to *The Comanche Empire* by Pekka Hämäläinen, a revionist history published in 2008, which I later read. In it, Hämäläinen makes the remarkable claim that in the eighteenth century and the early nineteenth, the Comanches built a genuine empire that outdid the Spanish and French empires in military and economic power, as well as cultural influence.

"Hämäläinen may go a bit too far," Fowles told me, "but it's a valuable corrective. Unfortunately, even though *The Comanche Empire* won all kinds of prizes, it was published by a university press, and it won't get nearly as many readers as S. C. Gwynne's *Empire of the*

Summer Moon, which was a bestseller. Gwynne repeats all the old stereotypes about Comanches as wild barbarians bent on destruction."

In their paper "Comanche New Mexico," Fowles, Arterberry, and two colleagues quote a typical sentence from *Empire of the Summer Moon*, about how the Comanches transformed the Southwest into a veritable war zone, "an open and bleeding wound, a smoking ruin littered with corpses and charred chimneys, a place where anarchy and torture killings had replaced the rule of law, where . . . Comanches raided at will."

Hämäläinen sees the empire as collapsing only in 1875, after a number of defeats at the hands of U.S. Army forces. But Fowles would date the end of true Comanche dominion to the 1780s, with a peace treaty that succeeded the death of their greatest leader of the day, Cuerno Verde (or Tabivo Naritgant), in a battle with the Spanish in southern Colorado in 1779.

A curious fact about the rock art on the Rio Grande benches is that none of the enemies depicted are Spaniards. As Fowles et al. conclude in "Comanche New Mexico,"

[T]he truly consequential political relations for most communities in the colonial Southwest were between indigenous nations. And it is in this sense that we might look to a time and place like the northern Rio Grande during the eighteenth century and begin to tell the story of a very different sort of colonial setting, one in which the Comanches stood in the position of the expansionist polity and in which local residents—native and non-native alike—were forced to adapt to the politics of these powerful interlopers.

I came away from my tour with Sev Fowles in the Rio Grande canyon stupefied by how much new understanding about the Southwest I had gleaned in a single day. The man's enthusiasm was infectious, as I recognized that the rock art his teams are deciphering stands on the verge of launching of a whole new field of inquiry. Best of all, thanks to the collaboration of Jimmy Arterberry, Fowles's work represents a reengagement with Native American oral history of the sort that archaeology had turned its back on for decades. As Fowles told me at the end of our wonderful day among the basalt boulders, "I feel truly humbled before the knowledge of Native American tribes."

Eight

EXPLORING THE FIFTY

Forty-five miles down the Hole-in-the-Rock Road, I coaxed the rental 4x4 up a rough track that gained Fiftymile Bench, a broad terrace halfway up the Kaiparowits Plateau in southern Utah. Three miles farther on, just before the road petered out, I parked at the foot of the unmarked Lower Trail. With a groan, I hoisted my heavy pack, which included an extra gallon of water in case we failed to find a spring that evening. Mary Tobin hoisted her own pack, and we set off. In less than an hour, we climbed nine hundred feet up the cattle trail, admiring the craft with which it wended its way among spooky hollows in the cliffs to emerge on top of the plateau.

Ranchers had built a pair of four-foot-high cairns to mark the crest of the trail, but except for that homey touch, the summit of Kaiparowits immediately struck me as an alien place. In all my hiking in the Southwest, I'd grown used to the bend in the canyon ahead, or the mushroom-shaped hoodoo balanced on the bedrock shelf, to give the universe an intimate touch. Here, though, I saw only a limitless stretch of tableland, greened with clumps of juniper and piñon but otherwise almost featureless. The plateau seemed to sweep into the sky itself, detached from the world below.

It was April 2002. During the previous nine years, I'd hiked many of the tributary canyons of the Escalante River, including the Gulch, Wolverine, Horse, Little Death Hollow, Harris Wash, Red Breaks, and the slots of Peekaboo and Spooky. Seldom had I run into another visitor. In 1996, however, President Bill Clinton had announced the establishment of Grand Staircase–Escalante National Monument— outraging the locals in the towns of Escalante and Boulder, who saw the edict as another federal land grab that might ultimately curtail oil and gas exploration, cattle and sheep herding, and the time-honored pastime of riding jeeps, ATVs, and dirt bikes through the wilderness.

The new monument was huge, covering 1,880,461 acres that stretched from the boundary with Capitol Reef National Park in the northeast to the Arizona border in the southwest. It didn't take long for hikers and backpackers to swarm to the place, though for various reasons, the newcomers tended to focus their play on the most popular of the Escalante tributaries. By 2002, I knew that I could no longer have Peekaboo or Spooky to myself on a warm day in April or October.

In 1998, searching for clues to the mystery of the lost vagabond

Everett Ruess, I had spent a lot of time out near the end of the Hole-in-the-Rock Road, particularly in Davis Gulch, where the visionary twenty-year-old artist and writer's last camp had been found by a search party in 1935. Each time I drove out that lonely dirt road, which gets rougher and rougher as it nears the cliff above the Colorado River, I was acutely aware of Kaiparowits Plateau hanging twenty-five hundred feet above me on the right. The Mormon old-timers in Escalante called the almost treeless wasteland the road traversed the Desert, and they referred to Kaiparowits as Fiftymile Mountain, or more simply, the Fifty, for the plateau ranges fifty miles from northwest to southeast. Frowning over each of my drives across the Desert, the Straight Cliffs, a band of sheer sandstone strata, blocked access to the plateau in an almost unbroken sweep.

Before 2002, I'd never been on top of Kaiparowits, even though it too was part of the new national monument. Nor, it seems, had any of the desert-rat cronies I'd asked about the place, including several men and women who made a living guiding clients out of Escalante and Boulder. The reason for that neglect was hard to come by. Veteran after veteran told me, "I've always wanted to go up there, but . . ." Something about the sheer immensity of Kaiparowits, I suspect, had daunted all of us. And the Escalante canyons gave the casual visitor a much speedier gratification. As late as 2002, I realized, only a handful of Mormon ranchers, most of them ready for the rocking chair, knew Kaiparowits well.

Mary Tobin, my friend during the previous several years, worked as a publicist for museums first in Worcester, Massachusetts, then in New York City. But the nine-to-five rat race cramped her soul. In her early twenties, two journeys to Africa had steeped her in the glories of wandering and discovery, and she'd never gotten over it. An expert equestrian, she longed to set off on horseback across the fenceless ranges of Wyoming or Mongolia. Instead, she had to content herself with weeklong truancies from her job. On Cedar Mesa she'd made an ideal companion, for her delight at finding Ancestral Puebloan wonders was boundless. When I proposed Kaiparowits, Mary jumped at the invitation.

Now, at the top of the Lower Trail, we dropped our packs to search for a campsite. A forest fire had turned the grove of junipers around us into an ashen, Dantesque diorama in gray and black. Soon we were bushwhacking through sage and rabbitbrush down a ravine called Trail Hollow. A mile from the rim, we found a pair of crystalline pools fed by an invisible spring. "Too brushy and ugly for a camp, don't you think?" I asked Mary.

"Yes," she agreed. "Let's keep going."

We pushed on toward the southwest. According to the map, Kaiparowits was only two miles wide here. We ought to come soon to its southern rim. In the creek bottom, we found bobcat tracks in the mud. We turned a corner, hiking past weird sandstone gargoyles, towers twisted by rain and wind. Suddenly the rim leapt upon us. The level shelf of orange bedrock plunged into a vertical cliff. Beyond and below, spangled in the afternoon sun, lay the beautiful abomination of Lake Powell, with the long slot of Dry Rock Creek slithering up toward us. It should have been—it was—a magnificent vista; yet so narrow was the cleft in which we stood, so sudden the precipice below us, that I felt a shiver of gloom rather than joy.

The abyss beneath our feet was called Harveys Fear Cliff. Way back in the early years of the twentieth century, a ranch hand named Harvey Watts was chasing cattle in the vicinity. An ornery old cow suddenly reversed direction and pushed Harvey's horse off the edge. Harvey managed to grab a small bush and dangled there, a slip away from a fatal fall, while the cow deliberated whether to finish the job or go back to munching grass. Since then the cliff has been named for the cowboy's terror.

"It feels almost claustrophobic," said Mary.

"Let's go back and camp on the north rim, where we left our packs," I said. "It'll mean we'll have to hike to get water, but it's by far the best campsite we've seen." Mary nodded in agreement.

That evening, over a campfire of small juniper sticks, we watched the Escalante canyons twenty-five hundred feet below us dim from orange to dusky purple. Sixty miles to the north, the Henry Mountains were painted with alpenglow. Before dinner, I had hiked the mile down to the brushy pools and filled three liter water bottles and my gallon jug. Timing the operation for future reference, I noted that the chore had taken thirty-nine minutes round trip. A minor annoyance—for now Mary and I sat by the fire, as tired and happy as we had ever been on Cedar Mesa, basking in our solitude and in the grandeur of the world spread out before us.

Before the trip, I'd read the handful of reports and testimonies that my predecessors on the plateau had produced. The meaning of the name "Kaiparowits," I learned, was uncertain. It may be a Paiute word for "mountain lying down," though some sources argue that it means "one arm" in Paiute, in tribute to Major John Wesley Powell, who had lost his right arm at the battle of Shiloh but went on to lead the legendary first descent of the Colorado River through the Grand Canyon in 1869. Other glosses on the mysterious Paiute name include "Big Mountain's Little Brother" (in reference to Navajo Mountain, across the Colorado to the southeast) and "Son of Table Cliff." The Navajo call the plateau Tsèndoolzah, or "Rock Point Descending Jaggedly."

To the early Anglo ranchers, Kaiparowits was known as Wild Horse Mesa. In 1923, Zane Grey failed in a dogged effort to get on top of the plateau from the south.

Instead, he wrote *Wild Horse Mesa*, a novel about the upland he could only imagine. Echoing the lore of the cowboys, Grey wrote, "Where it got the felicitous name we could not learn; perhaps from the Mormon wild-horse hunters. Wild stallions . . . were known to disappear and not be seen again; and it was certainly a thrilling and satisfying assumption to believe they had a way to surmount this mesa."

The nominal hero of *Wild Horse Mesa*, one of Grey's most romantic novels, is a cowboy loner named Chane Weymer. But the real hero is a horse named Panguitch (Grey borrowed the name from the Mormon town sixty miles west of Escalante), an extraordinary white stallion, the leader of a vast herd of feral steeds that roam free on the mesa. It is Chane's lifelong ambition to capture Panguitch, but when at last he does, he is so moved by the horse's indomitable spirit that he sets it loose.

Whether or not there are wild horses still roaming on top of the Fifty is a matter of current debate, though most of the locals doubted it. That was another mystery I hoped to probe during my own forays across Kaiparowits.

On our second day, Mary and I rim-walked southeast three miles to reach a sharp promontory, where we found a quadrangle of stones embedded in the hard ground. It was our first discovery of the vestiges left by the Ancestral Puebloans sometime before A.D. 1300. I guessed that the quadrangle had been the base of a rudimentary dwelling. It stood at least a mile from the brushy spring we had found the day before. Here I felt a linkage to the Old Ones, for they too had decided that a good view—in their case, of potential enemies rather than glorious sunsets—was more important than a convenient source of year-round water.

We decided to make a marathon day of it by rim-walking all the way to Navajo Point, at the vast plateau's extreme southeastern corner. There are no hiking trails on top of the eastern half of Kaiparowits, only cattle tracks that meander through the scrub or zero in on some fetid seep only a thirsty cow could love. Yet rim-walking was easy, across lapping bedrock shelves interspersed with groves and hollows. Through one half-mile stretch, every juniper or piñon older than about twenty years had been shattered by a lightning bolt—stark testimony to the violence of the late summer storms. In another nook, we came across a cattle graveyard: dozens of disarticulated skulls, femurs, and vertebrae bleached white by the sun. In years when winter strikes early, stray cattle get lost on the Fifty. Lacking the wits to find their way off, they succumb to the cold and snow. "I wonder," I said to Mary, "if this boneyard is the remains of a band of lost cows that huddled together in one of those winter storms."

By mid-afternoon, five hours out, we'd reached Navajo Point, where we stood on a knob of sandstone and stared out over one of the most spectacular prospects in the Southwest. But during the previous several weeks, a leaden haze had bleared the landscape. A freak windstorm in Mongolia had sent so much Gobi dust into the atmosphere that halfway around the globe it was taking months to settle out. No matter. Sitting on our perch as we ate a leisurely lunch, we gazed across the nearer slot canyons, across the bays of Lake Powell dotted with insectlike houseboats, toward the massive bulks of Navajo Mountain and Cummings Mesa, the latter even more remote than Kaiparowits. On this prong in the sky, unapproachable from the south, we were a solid ten miles from our rental car at the trailhead to the north. "Think how few people have ever been here," I said. Mary smiled, serene in her contentment.

The report that had most fired my imagination about Kaiparowits was not Zane Grey's cowboy romance but a memoir published in 1933, called *Beyond the Rainbow*. Its author was Clyde Kluckhohn, who would go on to become a Harvard professor and the leading Navajo ethnographer of his day. But in 1923, he was a sickly Princeton undergrad packed off to recover his health on a New Mexico ranch. That summer, only eighteen years old, Kluckhohn and several buddies rode twenty-five hundred miles on horseback in a looping pilgrimage to Rainbow Bridge, which had been first discovered by Anglos only fourteen years before.

One day on the Rainbow Trail, a seasoned guide told Kluckhohn, "When you get on top of that little rise where you'll find your last Navajo hogan, look off to the north and west and you'll see a big high mesa stretchin' back a hundred miles into Utah. . . . They say no white man's ever been on it."

From a basin a few miles short of the colossal arch, Kluckhohn first caught sight of the "big high mesa." His quest to reach its summit, an endeavor that spanned three summers from 1926 to 1928, would turn out to be the greatest adventure of his life. On their first try, Kluckhohn and his buddies got nowhere near Kaiparowits, ending their recon- naissance at Canyon de Chelly, 120 miles southeast of Navajo Point. By the summer of '27, they had figured out a circuitous approach that required fording both the San Juan and Colorado Rivers—the latter of which nearly took the life of Kluckhohn's pal Jim Hanks. That close call wrote a finis to their second effort.

Having read everything he could about the Anasazi (as they were then called), Kluckhohn nursed a fantasy that drove him into his third year of exploration. It was the notion that up on Wild Horse Mesa there might lurk great prehistoric pueblos such as Mesa Verde's Cliff Palace or Spruce Tree House. Yet in the summer of 1928, at the last outpost of civilization he would encounter before he plunged into the maze of canyons that guard Kaiparowits on the south, Kluckhohn made an "infinitely . . . disappointing discovery." The Indian trader at Navajo Mountain, Ben Wetherill (John and Louisa's son), casually mentioned that he and his father had been on top of Wild Horse Mesa in 1915, when they had guided the geologist Herbert Gregory. Even worse, as Kluckhohn wrote in *Beyond the Rainbow*, "to our horror we learned that Mormon cattle grazed upon it, and hence occasional Mormon cowpunchers must have roamed over nearly all its surface."

In their dismay, the Filthy Five, as Kluckhohn and his friends now called themselves, considered abandoning their pursuit. Instead, they hired a reluctant Navajo guide named Hosteen Dogi ("Mister Mous- tache"), rented Navajo mules and horses, and pushed on. They fought quicksand fording the San Juan, then Dogi found an abandoned Mor- mon boat, which the team used to ferry their gear across the Colorado at the Hole-in-the-Rock cleft. At last they reached the foot of Kaip- arowits, then spotted "the one break in the bastion" of the Straight Cliffs above. Kluckhohn's description is vague (he had no map), but I believe that the Filthy Five rode up the same stock trail that Mary and I would backpack seventy-four years later. In the early afternoon of July 31, 1928, Kluckhohn's dream was fulfilled: at last he stood atop Kaiparowits Plateau.

Instead of the barren, rocky crest they had anticipated, the Five were delighted to find themselves surrounded by "sagebrush as high as a man's head" and "the finest stand of piñon and cedar [juniper] we had ever seen." That first blush of discovery Kluckhohn later recalled as one of a series of "fleeting instants, treasured forever in memory, when the soul's longing is completely satisfied and the spirit soars."

With food and gear for a month's stay, the men set out to search for a spring-fed glade to make camp. Within hours, they found the perfect place. Yet during their first week on the mesa, the fivesome found themselves more disappointed than delighted. There were no Cliff Palaces atop Kaiparowits. It was not until the second day that the young men found even a few small flakes of chert; not until the third day, their first potsherd; not until the fifth day, their first panel of rock art. Whatever the presence of the ancients had once meant, by now its traces were subtle and evanescent.

The signs of the Mormon cattlemen were much more obvious. Not only did Kluckhohn and crew find blanched cow bones and old livestock trails crossing the sage flats, but they also came upon numerous sets of initials and signatures carved into aspen trees and on the cliffs. "Most of the dates were from 1925 and 1926," wrote Kluckhohn. "There was one from 1918." The graffiti were a taunting confirmation that the Filthy Five were far from being the first white men to explore Wild Horse Mesa.

So discouraging was this revelation that the young men almost aborted their outing only a few days in. Hosteen Dogi claimed to exchange smoke signals with his "squaws" somewhere on the plains below, so he deserted, saying that the women demanded his return.

Despite their guide's defection, the Filthy Five stayed on top of Wild Horse Mesa for the full month. And gradually they realized that whether or not Mormon ranchers had preceded them, they had discovered an idyllic paradise. As Kluckhohn summed up the adventure in *Beyond the Rainbow*, "Here in the cool sunlight and cold nights of a high altitude, under such stars as only Southwestern heavens can hold, we spent wonderful weeks. . . . Fresh, taunting smell of pine needles blowing across the face; the hills smooth, soft-rolling, strokable; trees, shrubs, grass, and sky a hundred shades of green grading into blue and yellow; tall sentinel pines making a clean-pointed arch over the trail; wind and sun giving a cool caress. . . . No automobiles, no smoke, no road signs, no stores, no bridges, no concrete. Alone and free."

Despite its standing as one of the classics of Southwestern adventure, *Beyond the Rainbow* is not only out of print today, but exceedingly rare. (A used copy on Bookfinder.com sells for $1,505!) Neither before nor after our trip was Mary able to find the book in any of the New York City libraries. I had checked out the only copy from Harvard's Widener Library and taken it with me to Utah. The book was in my pack as we trudged up the Lower Trail. Around the campfire and in the tent, I read the book out loud. On our second evening, I mused, "I wonder if we're the first people ever to carry the book about Kaiparowits back up onto Kaiparowits."

"I'll bet we are," she answered. "Maybe we should leave it here. Dig a hole and bury it, so somebody else can find it in the future."

I was tempted.

That second evening, Mary volunteered to fetch the water. I'd performed the task as efficiently as I could, but I hadn't reckoned with Mary's competitiveness. As I heard her footsteps approaching the tent, she called out, "How long?"

I looked at my watch. "Thirty-eight minutes. You beat my time by a single minute."

She crawled inside. "And not only that, David Roberts," she boasted, "I spilled a little from one of the bottles, so I had to go back and refill it."

The wind blew all night, and in the morning the air had a cold bite to it. We set off at 8:45 A.M., hiking northwest along the rim, the opposite direction from the day before. The finest discovery made by the Filthy Five during their month on the mesa was a cliff dwelling they called Pictograph Cave. Kluckhohn was vague about its setting, and the endpaper sketch map in his book proved useless in our search. He claimed that the ruin could not be seen from above. The Five had discovered it only by bushwhacking along the bench below the cliff face that soared up to the rim.

From my first reading of *Beyond the Rainbow*, I had been determined to find Pictograph Cave. What it took was scraping Kluckhohn's text for the faintest hints of location, then applying those hints to the logic of the landscape. In the end, I caught sight of the ruin not from above or below, but from a cliff spur a quarter mile away. To get to it, however, we had to circle as far again beyond the site, climb down a hundred feet, and thrash through maple and scrub oak.

The only approach to the alcove was a narrow ledge entering from the right, forty feet above the base of the sheer cliff. I went first, crawling on my belly. At its narrowest, the ledge was only eighteen inches wide, and the overhang above threatened to push me off the cliff. Plainly the site had been a hyperdefensive one, for beyond the crawl a low "stopper wall" blocked entry. The Filthy Five had been sufficiently daunted that only their best athlete, Lauri Sharp, made it into the alcove, "after many a trial and some breathless climbing." The other four had to admire the find by squinting up at it from below.

My cries of enthusiasm lured Mary onto the ledge, where she gamely replicated the scary crawl. We spent an hour inside the site, cataloguing its details. A cozy room with an intact roof was surrounded by other, half-collapsed structures that might have been granaries. All across the ledge lay scattered potsherds and corncobs, as well as the broken half of a granary door and a fine metate on which the Old Ones had ground their corn. The most intriguing structure was a freestanding oval building about six feet wide by twelve feet long, with no windows or doors, though part of its thatch-and-adobe roof was still in place. "I wonder if it's a kiva," I said, knowing that very few kivas had ever been found on Kaiparowits. For the most part, the mesa lies at or above the highest altitude at which the ancients had been able to cultivate their crops—which explained the paucity of habitation sites. Pictograph Cave may well have been the pinnacle of Ancestral Puebloan achievement on Fiftymile Mountain.

Kluckhohn had raved about a solitary pictograph in the alcove. Painted in red hematite, "it suggested," he wrote, "a great female goddess with a plumed helmet cap. We thought of the old tales in Navajo legend of 'the white warrior woman who came up from the south' and 'the Bride of the Sun on whom no other man ever looked.'" Kluckhohn was so enamored of the image (which he saw only from a distance) that he reproduced it on the spine of *Beyond the Rainbow*. To me, that design looked like a plumed warrior holding a fending stick (to ward off arrows) in his left hand, a shield or a trophy head dangling from his right. Curiously, it conjured up Fremont rather than Ancestral Puebloan art.

In Pictograph Cave, however, all that Mary and I could find was a vaguely anthropomorphic swath of red paint on the back wall. Had the Filthy Five let their imaginations run away with them? Or could the rock art have severely deteriorated during the previous seventy-four years?

As Lauri Sharp discovered that August day in 1928, Mormon cowboys had found the site first. Their signatures, mostly undated, scratched with a blade or scrawled in charcoal, decorated the back wall. I found "Daryl Q.," "Duston G.," "Gene Q.," "Ken Allen," "T. Jacobsen," "Cecil G.," and—probably a legitimate tribute to a fearless canine—"Cecil's Dog." Another name, simply "DeLane," rang bells of recognition in my head, and would spark another adventure on the Fifty in the days to come. Some of these graffiti no doubt postdated the 1928 party's visit, but they were vivid evidence of the climbing skills of early-day ranchers, akin to other cowboy "Kilroys" I had found all over the Southwest in hard-to-get-to alcoves. To their credit, the Mormon visitors had resisted the urge to damage the structures or pilfer the artifacts in Pictograph Cave—though who knew whether they had pocketed arrowheads or hauled out pots even before 1928?

Reluctantly, we crawled back along the ledge, bushwhacked west, and regained the rim. Pushing on, we came to a promontory known as Blondie Knoll. We found a few faint petroglyphs and more Mormon names. In an apparent frenzy of tagging, "Ken" had left his three-letter signature on five different sandstone walls. Whether this was the Ken Allen of Pictograph Cave was uncertain, but twice the man had added the date, 1926. Whoever he was, the Mormon cowboy had preceded the Filthy Five by a couple of years.

On our way back to camp, Mary and I headed "inland," following a meandering cattle trail. We came across several other spring-fed rivulets. I wondered where the base camp for the Filthy Five had been, the perfect place they had found within hours of first reaching the top of Wild Horse Mesa. Could it have been in one of these glades?

Meanwhile, I had a growing hunch that the cattle trail was taking us off-route, and for the first of three or four times on top of Kaiparowits, I felt eerily disoriented. Amidst the juniper and piñon, there were no visible landmarks by which to regain my bearings. Then, suddenly, the domed summit of Navajo Mountain hove into view. It was in entirely the wrong place, some 120 degrees farther left (north?) than it should have been. Of course, I realized with a chill, it was Mary and I who were in the wrong place, not the sacred peak of the Diné. Had we been wandering in circles? Were we on the verge of getting lost?

By late afternoon, we were back in camp. The view over the Escalante canyons all the way to the Henry Mountains restored my faith in a rational universe.

Even in the 1920s, there was talk about creating a national park around the junction of the Colorado and San Juan Rivers, to include Navajo Mountain, the Rainbow Plateau, Rainbow Bridge, and Kaiparowits. Its chief proponent was the Anglo who knew that country best, John Wetherill. Not surprisingly, Kluckhohn was swayed by the idea. In *Beyond the Rainbow*, he extolled the beauty of Wild Horse Mesa, comparing it to Mesa Verde, which had been made a national park in 1906. Admitting that the ruins on Kaiparowits were no match for Cliff Palace and Spruce Tree House, he added, "But it is Mesa Verde on an exaggerated scale. The panoramas from the rim are more magnificent. Indeed for sublimity of scenery Wild Horse Mesa surpasses even Grand Canyon."

Yet the comparison with the Grand Canyon gave Kluckhohn pause. In a passage that, eighty-two years later, seems astonishingly prescient, he wrote:

It must be remembered that this is not a cheap scenery; it must be bought with time and sweat. But at Grand Canyon one does get cheap scenery in this sense. One can look down into Grand Canyon without having abandoned a single comfort or luxury, while the view from the rims of Wild Horse Mesa is purchased at high price, and perhaps is therefore understood and appreciated the more.

That is why I wonder if we want to make Wild Horse Mesa into a National Park, after all. . . . It suggests too much carefully built roads and elaborate regulations. Simply turn the Mesa into a national preserve denied to settlement. That is not a fantastic suggestion. The area of land involved is large, but is economically not of great value. Since there are, of course, no settlers on it now, there would be no question of land rights to be bought. All that would be necessary would be an Act of Congress withdrawing these public lands from the areas that may be homesteaded, and forbidding the building of roads. The last thing wanted is an appropriation for "developing" the area and for upkeep. . . . The one regulation that would be necessary would be: NO ROADS, NO BUILT TRAILS.

Viewed from the hindsight of 2015, Kluckhohn's vision reverberates with historical irony. By the 1960s, geologists had proved that hidden under the piñon–juniper forest on top of Kaiparowits lay one of the richest coal deposits in the world. A consortium of energy companies launched a plan to build a huge power plant on the mesa. Burning the promised yield of four billion tons of coal would, claimed the companies, supply the electrical demands of Phoenix, Los Angeles, and San Diego for decades to come. The Escalante locals were all for it. But environmentalists, stung by the recent loss of Glen Canyon to the dam that created Lake Powell, allied with federal agencies to defeat the proposal, which was abandoned in 1975.

Still, hopes for turning Kaiparowits into a gigantic coal mine did not die easily. It was only in 1996, with the creation of Grand Staircase–Escalante National Monument, that the would-be developers folded their cards. (In 2002, the bitterness about Clinton's fiat still rankled in Escalante. A billboard on Main Street announced, "Public lands are for all the people. Wilderness is only for a few people.")

As Kluckhohn never could have foreseen, it took the inclusion of Kaiparowits in a national monument to save the plateau from the kinds of commercialism and development that had made Grand Canyon a "cheap scenery." And in 2015, thank God, there are no plans afoot to build scenic drives through the Straight Cliffs up to the rim of Kaiparowits, nor to move the visitor center any closer to the plateau than it is now, on the western outskirts of Escalante—population 783 in 2012, down about 250 from the Depression-mired town through which Everett Ruess rode in November 1934.

To her dismay, on May 1, 2002, Mary felt the nagging pull of her job back in New York City, so we descended the Lower Trail and regained our rental 4x4. I wasn't finished with Kaiparowits myself, however. A week later, launching my probe out of Page, Arizona, I started up the Croton Road, a rugged old four-wheel-drive track that performs the remarkable feat of traversing another part of the Fifty from south to north—seventy-three miles of white-knuckle lurching up and down stony zigzags, often with a frightening drop inches from the edge. (In its whole fifty-mile expanse, the Croton is the only road that crosses Kaiparowits.)

Near the beginning of the drive, I saw the only warning sign posted along that lonely byway: ROAD NOT MAINTAINED. Later, a park ranger at monument headquarters estimated that only one vehicle a month drives the Croton Road. "If you'd come in here beforehand," he said, "we'd have told you not to do it."

The crux of the drive lies a good thirty waterless miles in from the southern end, as the road loops around a sandstone bluff in the appropriately named Burning Hills. My palms were sweating as, in low low gear, I spun my tires over boulders that rotated and slid a few inches from the void. I had a few gallons of water with me, but if I put the car in a ditch (or worse, over the cliff), I would face a grim hike out to the highway.

Earlier, I had had my sole encounter with another motorist in those seventy-three miles. I turned a bend to find an SUV with Alberta plates parked ahead of me, the roof rack bearing a pair of kayaks. Beside the vehicle, shading his eyes to peer at the horizon, stood a slender man in his mid-thirties, naked except for his sandals. On seeing me, he sprinted for the SUV, apparently pulled on his shorts, and roared away in full flight, bombing along at three miles an hour, which seemed to be as fast as his driving nerve would allow. Puzzled, I tailgated him for a quarter mile before he gave up, stopped, rolled down his window, leaned out, and asked, "Do you know this country?"

"Sort of," I said.

"I'm trying to find Lake Powell."

It did no good to tell him he was headed in the wrong direction, to point out the canyon walls in the southern distance that enfolded the reservoir he so ineptly sought. He trusted my advice no better than the crumpled road map he was powerless to read. He let me pass, however. As I caught a last glimpse of him in my mirror, I uttered a silent plea for his safety, rendered somewhat insincere by the relief I felt at shaking the Canadian nudist.

Fifty-seven miles and four hours in, I parked my 4x4 and started hiking down a tributary creek toward Rogers Canyon, one of the main streams that flow south off Kaiparowits. An old rut of a road, probably first built for horse-drawn carts, took me to the junction of the two drainages. The walls on either side were made of a mottled brown sandstone full of hollows and niches. But on the east wall of Rogers, I saw a huge alcove I could climb up to and enter.

It was, I suspected, an Ancestral Puebloan site, but a distinctly weird one. Lacking room blocks, with a heavily sooted ceiling, it had the dark gloomy feel of a Basketmaker lair, sporadically inhabited perhaps two thousand years ago. The strangest feature was a trio of big dead logs laid pointing west and covered with rock slabs. Was it a burial site? I had never seen the like.

That night, I camped on the highest bend of the eight-mile ridge that ranges across a sagebrush flat called Collett Top. I was twenty-five miles as the crow flies west of the mesa where Mary and I had rambled the previous week, but I was still on the summit of Kaiparowits. I drank a beer as I watched the sun expire over the craggy skyline of far-off Zion National Park, then, after dinner, lay on my back watching Castor and Pollux race Jupiter through the purple sky. After midnight, I half-woke to hear coyotes complaining to the rising moon.

By and large, Kaiparowits Plateau has been overlooked by archaeologists. The only serious investigations were conducted by teams in 1958 and 1961, as part of a heroically doomed project to survey all the lands adjacent to Glen Canyon, which would soon be flooded by Lake Powell. Those hardworking scholars recorded more than three hundred sites and excavated parts of eleven of them, collecting potsherds and other artifacts. They also brought back timbers used in the construction of the dwellings, but were unable to get tree-ring dates from them.

Instead, Florence Lister, one of the most diligent of all Southwestern archaeologists, performed a tour de force of ceramic analysis on the sherds to try to draw a broader picture of prehistoric life on the high plateau. She concluded that Kaiparowits had been settled for a mere 150 years, from about A.D. 1050 to 1200. Those dwellers were Kayenta Anasazi, migrants from northern Arizona. When they gave up on Kaiparowits, they evidently returned to their homeland. (The possibly much older Basketmaker alcove I found in Rogers Canyon lay outside the teams' survey area.)

No dwelling site the teams discovered contained more than thirteen rooms, while the norm was only two or three. Nor could the archaeologists find more than a few possible kivas. At altitudes ranging above seven thousand feet, agriculture was marginal at best on top of the mesa. Lister was puzzled by the knowledge that on the north and east, those Anasazi had been surrounded by Fremont peoples, but there was no evidence of warfare or even contact between the two cultures.

Poring over the dry technical reports from the surveys, I tried to imagine the plight of these "third and fourth generation provincials," as Lister called them. Were they refugees from the Kayenta heartland, men and women from the "wrong" clans, exiled to the northern frontier? Or were they pioneers, striking out into unexplored territory? My fondest fantasy was that these long-lost bands were wanderers and outlaws, tough men and women who gladly traded spindly crops for the glorious hunting the plateau must have afforded, for whom the building of well-wrought dwellings was a waste of time. Anasazi Vikings, if you will.

During their month on top of Wild Horse Mesa, the Filthy Five found no graffiti dated earlier than 1918, so they believed that Herbert Gregory, with John and Ben Wetherill, must have been the first white men to top the plateau. But Gregory himself, a famed geologist, knew better. He had come across the notes of one Almon Harris Thompson, a member of John Wesley Powell's survey party, who claimed to have ascended the mesa in 1875. Thompson's deed remained so shadowy that it could well have been dismissed as apocryphal—until 1985, when a trio of Escalante men, out on a day hike, came across a cairn containing a crumbling survey note from the 1875 expedition.

Just as the prehistory of Kaiparowits has yet to be fully elucidated, so, to this date, no one has seen fit to publish the more recent human history of the Fifty. By 2002, the definitive work about the place was not only unpublished; it existed in a single copy. That was a well-thumbed scrapbook belonging to Escalante rancher DeLane Griffin, seventy-nine years old that year, a memento lovingly composed over the decades to be handed down to his grandchildren.

I had interviewed Griffin in 1998 when I was researching Everett Ruess, for DeLane had been a twelve-year-old when the vagabond came through Escalante in 1934. Like the other boys whom Everett entertained during his several-day stopover in town, DeLane had never forgotten that meeting.

Mormon old-timers in Escalante tend to be leery of outsiders, especially journalists from the East Coast, but DeLane greeted me warmly on the phone and invited me over to his house. A short man, as bowlegged as a rodeo cowboy, his face creased by sun and wind, he showed me out to his veranda, where we drank Cokes while he regaled me with tales of the Fifty. Then, to my astonishment, he let me borrow the precious scrapbook overnight. In my room at the Prospector Inn, I read the thing from cover to cover.

A collage of mounted snapshots, cowboy verse written by DeLane and his son Quinn, and prose reminiscences pecked out on an old manual typewriter, the book distilled a lifetime of close scrapes and halcyon outings up on Kaiparowits, where DeLane had run cattle for sixty years, starting in 1942. (He would lead the grueling drive every summer, getting his herd up in June and down in October.)

Rounding up his cattle and pushing them up the Lake Trail to the top of the mesa could prove an ordeal. "The cattle had to go single file because the trail was so narrow," wrote DeLane.

Sometimes a cow would turn around in the trail looking for her calf. When she did that, it blocked the trail for the oncoming cattle. We'd have to get off our horses and edge around the sides of the mountain and throw rocks up to turn the critter around. Have you ever tried throwing rocks straight up all day long? By the end of the day you've got a limp arm hanging by your side. I think that some of the names hollered up at those old cows caused them to move along faster than the rocks, sometimes.

Many of the tales in DeLane's scrapbook were accounts of epic captures of wild cattle. Of one wild cow met on the Fifty: "She was as streamlined as a gray hound. Gaunt in the belly and thin as a bean. They can go on a high trot all day long. They go under trees in a straight line where the horse and rider have to go out around. You have to have a good dog, maybe two, before you can stop and handle those old gals."

One year—date unspecified—DeLane tried to capture a "wild spotted bull," the largest he had ever seen. "His head was the size of a no. three wash tub so it seemed, with pig eyes that were red rimmed and glowed like the devil himself. . . . Those big feet were the size of paper plates." At the end of a marathon battle, DeLane and his ranch hands subdued the beast, only to have it apparently die in the struggle. But when the bull revived a few minutes later, the men set it free because the animal was too much to handle.

In Lake Canyon in 1975, DeLane's family built a cabin to use as a base camp. The aspen trunks they used in the construction had to be hauled from two miles away by horse. DeLane and his father spent a cold Thanksgiving there in 1976, prompting this reminiscence:

I hung the nose sacks on the horses while Dad was a fixin' the pancakes, the fried eggs, and the ham. So, while the horses were getting their breakfast, we were getting ours. Dad got pretty good at making sour-dough pancakes. You might say them pancakes were a lot better than the first ones we tried to feed ol' Sammy, the cow dog, when she just sort of wrinkled up her nose and walked away.

On that same trip, a cantankerous steer knocked DeLane off his horse and into the bushes. As he tried to get to his feet, the steer charged. DeLane's father felled the animal with a single rifle shot.

In mid-May, I hiked both the Lake and Navajo trails through the Straight Cliffs to reach the top of Kaiparowits, on routes some ten miles farther west than the Lower Trail that Mary and I had first tackled. On top of the mesa, I was seized with the same agoraphobic disorientation that had addled me on the first trip, when the meandering cattle trail had wreaked havoc with the compass in my head. Hiking solo, I felt the weird sensation of almost getting lost all the more acutely.

In Moqui Canyon, I found many of the small Ancestral Puebloan dwellings and granaries that the 1958 and 1961 survey parties had discovered, and that the Filthy Five had never come across. They testified not to magnificence but to the marginal existence Florence Lister had imagined her "third and fourth generation provincials" eking out.

And in Lake Canyon, I found the cabin DeLane's family had built. Inside it, as I waited out a brief rain squall, I marveled at the clutter: homemade whips, bridles, and lariats hung from nails, bedrolls and sneakers drooping from the rafters, a rusty but unopened can of Van Camp's Beanee Weenee on the counter.

DeLane had told me about Llewellyn Harris and the legend of the golden Jesus, a tale so outlandish that Zane Grey might have invented it. Harris was a renowned Indian scout and Mormon missionary whom Brigham Young had sent to convert the Hopi and Navajo in northern Arizona starting in the 1870s. "There was one story," DeLane said, "that Harris went in among some Hopi who had chicken pox. He ministered to 'em. They all got well except one, who was a Ute. Made fun of Harris and wouldn't let Harris give him his blessing. He died."

While living with the Navajo, Harris was befriended by an elder who told him the legend. Long before, the Hopi had stolen the "golden Jesus" from the Spaniards—presumably a statue of Christ from the altar of some mission. Learning of this prize, the Navajo began to covet it. To keep them from stealing the golden Jesus in turn, the Hopi spirited it off to Fiftymile Mountain. "They said it was so heavy it took seven braves to carry it," DeLane added. In a secret place on the summit, the Hopi buried the icon.

According to DeLane, the Navajo elder gave Harris a map of Kaiparowits etched on deerskin, showing the hidden route by which his people climbed the mesa to hunt wild horses. Fired with the legend, Harris ascended the plateau in 1888, then, a year later, spent the whole summer on top, camping with his family, searching fruitlessly for the golden Jesus.

As corroboration of the tale, DeLane told me where I could find Harris's name carved into the plateau's bedrock. It was to be found on Window Wind Arch, one of the very few natural bridges on the whole summit of Kaiparowits. The arch is neither named nor indicated on the USGS topo map, but DeLane told me how to get to it.

On May 12, I dashed up the Navajo or Middle Trail to the mesa top, marveling again at the craft of the ranchers who had built a route that wound its clever way through the Straight Cliffs, resorting to dynamite only on two short stretches. Then I rim-walked west. In only half an hour, I stood beneath the arch. Its inner walls on both sides were covered with Mormon inscriptions, ranging from 1911 through the 1990s. Two of them, Norm Christensen and Edson Alvey, belonged to men who had figured prominently in the mystery of the disappearance of Everett Ruess.

It took me five minutes to discover "Llewellyn Harris." The carefully chiseled block letters of his inscription were larger than anybody else's, but the patina had faded to a brown hue that perfectly matched the surrounding rock. No doubt the missionary had recorded his deed the very day he had become the second white explorer to top out on the Fifty:

L HARRIS
APRIL 14
1888

History books pay scant attention to this early missionary and scout. Only the local old-timers still gossip about the golden Jesus. But as I later studied the maps, I realized that Llewellyn Canyon, just south of Window Wind Arch, and Llewellyn Gulch, which winds toward Lake Powell on the flats below the southeast corner of the Fifty, pay tribute to his flamboyant passing.

Before heading out to Utah, I had hoped to see the wild horses of Zane Grey's Wild Horse Mesa. On one of his last days on Kaiparowits, out tracking runaway mules, Clyde Kluckhohn had run into a band of horses, some of which had Mormon brands, some not. "None would let me approach them," he wrote.

But DeLane Griffin dashed my hopes. Yes, in the early days, a pioneer named George Wilson had put his horses on top of the Fifty, and some of them had gone feral, spawning the bands that were spotted over the following decades. But by 2002, DeLane insisted, there were no more wild horses on the mesa. The only ones left in the region could be found on the desolate benches south of Kaiparowits.

On my final afternoon on the plateau, I was hiking regretfully back toward the top of the Lake Trail. The sun was drying the willows after a rainstorm. In the corner of my eye, I spotted a flash of white. I peered, then caught my breath.

Four sleek horses, led by a majestic all-white stallion, loped through the distant bushes, then disappeared. I hurried ahead, hoping for another glimpse, and came to the rim of a large hollow. They were below me, stepping slowly now, pausing to snag mouthfuls of grass. The horses moved north, then wheeled and headed south, the other three always following the white stallion's lead. For five or six glorious minutes, I watched them in my binoculars. The horses had no brands. They looked fit and lean, and they behaved as if they knew the place well.

This is too good to be true, I thought. *This is the kind of corny ending Zane Grey would write.* Nonetheless, as I hiked down the Lake Trail, bidding goodbye to Kaiparowits, I was aglow with the grace of the providential.

A few days later, I called DeLane to tell him of my sighting. "Couldn't be wild horses, not up there," he said laconically.

"They didn't have brands."

"Around here, most of the ranchers don't brand their horses. Everybody knows each other's animals. What'd they look like?"

I described the white stallion. "Nope," said DeLane. "Only wild ones down on the benches is grays and sorrels."

Fighting my disappointment, I said, "But whose could they be?"

"I'll ask the lady who leases the spread just west of ours. Maybe they were tourists' horses." To DeLane, anybody not from Escalante was a "tourist." I protested: I'd seen no one else on the mesa on any of my outings, no hoofprints going up or down the three livestock trails. To no avail: DeLane was certain, and the man knew the Fifty.

So much for fantasy, I mused. There is no Cliff Palace on Kaiparowits Plateau. In all likelihood there is no golden Jesus. There may not be a single wild horse left on top—let alone the Panguitch of my dreams. But I had found something even better: a place where I could still get lost; a world in which solitude seemed magical, not lonely; a tableland so vast and complex that it made a mockery of my ambitions to dent it.

A few weeks after I got home, I called DeLane again. The horses were bothering him. He hadn't yet talked to his neighbor, but, he said, "There's no way her horses could've got through the fence 'tween our spread and hers." Uncharacteristically, he hesitated. "Up by Cougar Knoll, huh?"

"Just east of Cougar Knoll."

"You know," DeLane said slowly, "it's just possible if he was old enough, a wild horse could be all white."

That was good enough for me.

Nine

DESO DAYS

My trips into Range Creek between 2004 and 2006 had sparked a keen interest in the Fremont, a culture I had previously all but ignored. And though my chance to explore the high granaries and lookout posts of that extraordinary canyon had seemed to expire with Renee Barlow's exile from the UMNH team, my curiosity about the Fremont persisted.

So much less was known, after all, about those northern ancients than about the Ancestral Puebloans. So little, in fact, that quite a few scholars dismissed them as Northern Periphery—Anasazi hillbillies, in effect. Yet I had seen so many impressive cliff-ledge structures and so much rock art all over Utah that I was convinced the Fremont deserved their status as a separate people. The deep mystery of their ultimate fate abided, for no persuasive hypothesis linked the Fremont to any tribe living today. Had they truly gone extinct?

Other Fremont puzzles continued to tantalize me. Why had archaeologists discovered so few true villages, or even family-size habitation sites, and yet so many granaries? Why so little pottery? (One theory, advanced in recent years, is that there *were* sizable Fremont villages, but they all lie under towns founded by Mormon settlers in the nineteenth century.)

Yet if the Fremont left behind no cliff dwellings to rival Keet Seel or Pueblo Bonito, no vessels to match the Tusayan polychrome or Mimbres pots and bowls that dazzle visitors to many a Southwestern museum, still, their rock art was every bit the equal of that painted and pecked by Ancestral Puebloans farther south. At Sego Canyon, McKonkie Ranch, and Clear Creek Canyon, I had stood transfixed as I tried to fathom the trapezoidal humanoids with their shields and trophy heads, the chimerical animals and surreal lizards, the dot matrices that Fremont artists had carved into the sandstone.

No gallery anywhere in the Southwest is richer than the vast array of petroglyphs (nearly all of them Fremont) in Nine Mile Canyon, northeast of Price, Utah. In its forty-five-mile length, the number of panels on the canyon walls is estimated at around ten thousand, the number of individual images as at least one hundred thousand. Nine Mile, in fact, contains what is regarded by experts as "the largest concentration of rock art in North America." Both during and after my pilgrimages to Range Creek, I drove the long dirt road (now paved) that ranges along the creek bed in Nine Mile, armed with Jerry and Donna Spangler's superb guidebook, *Horned Snakes and Axle Grease*. Some of the assemblages, including the masterly Great Hunt Panel, are as fine as any rock art in the Southwest. Alas, the connoisseur of Nine Mile must try to ignore the nonstop traffic and noise of the trucks and wells that have turned the canyon into a bonanza of natural gas extraction. Nine Mile is a patchwork of public and federal land, but the BLM, with its "multiple use" policy, has given carte blanche to the corporations that want to suck every ounce of the estimated one trillion cubic feet of available natural gas out of the ground.

All across the Fremont domain, a much older rock art, called the Barrier Canyon style, proliferates on cliffs both alongside paved highways and in remote, trailless canyons. Polly Schaafsma, the leading expert on Southwestern rock art, dates Barrier Canyon art to the late Archaic, though it may range in time from as early as 2000 B.C. to as late as A.D. 500. The great question is whether the Barrier Canyon culture was ancestral to the Fremont, as many believe.

So distinctive is Barrier Canyon art that it cannot be mistaken for anything else. Most of it was executed in paint, with red by far the dominant color. The anthropomorphs, some of which are even bigger than today's humans, are elongated, with either vestigial arms and hands or none at all. The heads are ghostly, some with blank bug eyes; horns, antlers, "antennae," or sharp spikes sprout from the scalp; sometimes the heads bear crowns that radiate pulsing dots. Snakes abound, both dangling from tiny hands or writhing within the anthropomorphic bodies. Birds and tiny animals (sometimes called "spirit helpers") flit about the heads of the humanoids. Yet the vision that gave birth to these bold and spooky figures lies in the realm of some long-lost collective trance.

The common belief that history is progress has done a great disservice to art. In Europe, Romanesque art and architecture (from about the tenth to the twelfth century A.D.) was long regarded as a crude prefiguring of Gothic—until revisionists started recognizing the brilliance of the frescoes from tiny chapels in Catalonia or in such cathedrals as Cluny and Autun. Barrier Canyon rock art, painted by artists who had no permanent dwellings, had yet to cultivate corn, and were ignorant of pottery and the bow and arrow, is as splendid as anything that came later in the Southwest.

When the Paleolithic art inside the Grotte Chauvet was discovered in the Ardèche region of southern France in 1994, it was instantly classified as contemporary with Lascaux, or about seventeen thousand years old. I traveled to France to write an article about Chauvet, and though I knew better than to expect to be allowed inside the cave, I was able to interview the three amateur *spéléologues* who had made the amazing discovery. In the Musée de l'Homme in Paris, I perused the exhibits that summed up the current theory about the origins of art in Europe. Around thirty thousand years ago, the first crude female effigies—obese lumps of clay with grooves indicating vaginas—gave birth to the notion of art. Slowly over the millennia, according to the scholars, cave art developed, until it floresced in the glory of Lascaux, Peche Merle, Niaux, Altamira in Spain, and other grottoes during the high Paleolithic.

Then the radiocarbon dates came back from Chauvet. The paintings inside that magnificent underground cathedral were thirty-two thousand years old! The dating blew away all the theories of the so-called experts. The earliest art we can find in Europe is as sublime and evocative as anything that comes later. (Go figure . . .)

The same is true of Barrier Canyon art. A trip to the type site—the Great Gallery in Horseshoe (formerly Barrier) Canyon in southeastern Utah, protected by a small outlying square of Canyonlands National Park—will knock your socks off. There, thanks to erosion that has left the paintings beyond the reach of vandals and graffiti scrawlers, the pristine pantheon of hallucinatory gods or beings stretches along two hundred feet of the canyon wall.

Where, then, to broaden my acquaintance with the Fremont? An obvious answer had been stuck on my exploratory back burner for years: Desolation Canyon.

My mentor in Range Creek was not an archaeologist, but Waldo

Wilcox, the rancher who had guarded his twelve-mile-long spread for fifty years, keeping out trespassers and leaving all the "Indian stuff" in place. But Waldo had moved to Range Creek only after a government-mandated expansion of the Uintah and Ouray Ute Reservation had evicted his family from their home at the Cradle M Ranch. That homestead, first built in 1887, stood at the mouth of Florence Creek, an eastern tributary of the Green River, thirty miles north of the town of the same name.

In Desolation Canyon, the Green cuts a massive gorge through the Tavaputs Plateau, eighty-five river miles that bisect one of the largest roadless tracts in the Southwest. At its deepest, Desolation equals the Grand Canyon in vertical relief. Its gloomy name was bestowed on it by John Wesley Powell's rafters in 1869, who entered the unknown chasm with heavy foreboding. A few days in, spooked by the soaring walls, as Powell wrote, "We are minded to call this the Canyon of Desolation."

During my visits with Waldo, both in Range Creek and in his current home in Green River, he had told me many a tale about his boyhood days in Desolation, for he had thoroughly explored the canyon on foot and horseback as he helped his father drive cattle along its banks and over looping trails that crisscrossed the Tavaputs. Yes, he averred, there was Indian stuff all over the canyon, especially in its numerous tributary streams.

I am not, however, a river runner. Despite having to take a remedial swimming class my freshman year in college, despite the helpful efforts of several chums over the years to school me in backstroke and doggy paddle in the safe confines of motel pools, I have an ineradicable fear of bodies of water bigger or deeper than a bathtub. In counter-phobic flights of adventurous bravado, I have taken part in first descents of wilderness rivers in New Guinea and Ethiopia undertaken by pros from the rafting company Sobek. (On the genuinely terrifying Tua River in New Guinea, I asked my captain, Mike Boyle, what my role in the raft should be. "Shut up and hang on," he answered.)

The way for me to explore Desolation, then, was to hire a rafting company to take me down the canyon. About fifteen years ago I signed up for a commercial float down the first half of the Colorado River in the Grand Canyon, taking out at the Bright Angel Trail. Crashing through the big rapids was thrilling enough, as I managed to hang on and whoop out loud rather than shut up, but I felt like a tourist the whole time. What I really wanted to do was get out of the boat and hike up the side canyons, but for various reasons, our guides forbade such folly for more than fifteen minutes at a stretch.

If I were to sign up for a commercial trip on Deso (as the rafters affectionately call the canyon), it would have to be on terms that I could dictate. After several inquiries, I approached Sheri Griffith Expeditions out of Moab, for the consensus was that that company ran state-of-the-art river journeys. Over the phone to Arlo Tejada, its marketing manager, I explained my desiderata. "I'm not interested in running the river per se," I said. "It's not rapids that would be the point of the trip. I want to maximize our time on shore, so that we can spend as many hours as possible exploring the side canyons. The whole point of the trip would be to look for Fremont ruins and rock art."

I expected Tejada to scratch his head and utter a rejoinder such as, "Well, that's not the kind of trip we're in the business of running." Instead, he blurted out, "Geez, that sounds great! I wish I could go myself."

Tejada and I agreed on a nine-day trip, the maximum allowed on Deso by the BLM. When I mentioned the upcoming journey to friends, they were ravenous to join. Our crew ended up numbering eight. On backpack trips or even day hikes during the previous twenty-odd years in the Southwest, I had seldom set out with more than four companions. The ideal group size, I thought, was three or fewer, and many of my happiest outings had been solo ones.

But spread among three rafts on the river and six tents on shore, our group of eight—eleven, counting our three guides—made as ami-cable a congregation as I could have wished. On board from the start was my wife, Sharon, who had shared many of my Southwestern larks since 1991. So was Greg Child, my fellow sleuth in Range Creek, the

Comb Ridge, Cedar Mesa, the search for Hoskinini, and other junkets during the previous decade. Likewise Matt Hale, my climbing partner since 1962 and Southwestern compadre since 1993, as he had also become a passionate devotee of the Old Ones.

We rounded out the group with Charley LeCompte, who had been turned on to ruins and rock art on a weeklong trip to Cedar Mesa with Sharon and me a few years earlier, as well as the trio of Judi Wineland and Rick Thomson, Sharon's and my best friends in Watertown, and their twenty-three-year-old daughter, Erica Wineland-Thomson.

The great advantage of a raft is that it can carry huge amounts of stuff. On llama treks, I had added a bottle of wine per night to our evening glops, but Sheri Griffith invited us to supply all the libations we thought we might need. After all, our flotilla would carry 115 gallons of drinking water alone (the Green being too brown to drink)—920 pounds right there. After consulting with our team, Matt and I shopped at the Moab state liquor store the day before our trip where we bought scandalous quantities of beer and wine.

Before the trip, I did all the homework I could on the archaeology and history of Desolation Canyon. I reread Powell's gloomy account of their seven-day plunge into the unknown. The men's mood had not been helped by alkaloid poisoning incurred from eating potato greens planted by the Ute agent near the mouth of the canyon. Just before entering the gorge, Powell wrote, "one after another of our party is taken sick; nausea first, and then severe vomiting, and we tumble around under the trees, groaning with pain."

James M. Aton's handsome and erudite *The River Knows Everything: Desolation and the Green* proved an invaluable guidebook to the canyon. Ellen Meloy's rhapsodic *Raven's Exile* distilled the moods and joys of eight summers spent accompanying her husband, Mark, who was the seasonal ranger for Desolation between 1989 and 1996. In Bluff I chatted with Mark, who was nostalgic for those halcyon days on the river, even while he still grieved the loss of Ellen, who had died of a heart attack in 2004 at the age of fifty-eight.

The most serious survey work in Desolation had been undertaken during extended field sessions between 2006 and 2008 by teams from the Colorado Plateau Archaeological Alliance (CPAA) under the direction of Jerry Spangler. I had interviewed Spangler when I was working on Range Creek, and now he was kind enough to send me a redacted copy of the comprehensive 2009 report, called "Land of Wildest Desolation," that he and then state archaeologist Kevin Jones had written up. Spangler's BLM permits for Desolation had stipulated that the exact locations of the sites his teams discovered not be disclosed, so in copies available to the public, black swaths eclipsed the on-the-ground directions to the ruins and rock art. Even so, the report gave us a stunning window into the archaeological richness of the canyon, and the dry prose of the text whetted our collective appetite every day on the river.

Thus we had an arsenal of research to carry onto the Green River: Aton's excellent history-cum-picture book, Ellen Meloy's lyrical tribute to the canyon, and the CPAA survey report. Not to mention the USGS topo maps, with the exquisite precision that goes into the compiling of 7.5-minute quadrangles that cover every square foot of the United States except Alaska, where the project is still in the making.

To complement our printed matter, we would benefit from two oral sources. Every rafting company builds up a shared lore from their many runs of their favorite rivers. Our three guides on the Green, I knew, would regale us not only with tales about special places in the canyon handed down from one generation of rafters to the next since Sheri Griffith had founded her company in 1971, but also with anecdotes about absurdities, near disasters, and feats of derring-do they had witnessed or performed on previous trips. Finally, a few days before we launched, Greg and I visited Waldo Wilcox once more, where I pumped him for all kinds of knowledge about Desolation Canyon that perhaps no one else still alive possessed. On the river, I would be beguiled by the ways that Waldo's stories contradicted not only those of our guides, but even those of Aton, Meloy, and Spangler.

The put-in on Deso is at a place called Sand Wash, 32.5 miles downriver from the small town of Ouray, the last settlement on the Green River before its current enters the chasm it cuts through the Tavaputs. We could have driven our cars from Moab to Sand Wash, but that peregrination would have meant traversing 144 miles on paved highways followed by some 30 on a dirt road that gets progressively worse as it nears the river. And then, at the end of the trip, we would have had to repeat that circuitous jaunt to retrieve our vehicles.

Instead, we paid a little extra to fly from Moab to an old uranium-era landing strip on a bluff overlooking Sand Wash. The flight, in a snazzy new Quest Kodiak piloted by Nick and Troy from Red Tail Aviation, took a mere thirty-five minutes—all of it breathtaking, as we flew directly up the canyon and saw it for the first time. I was able to pick out the tiny rectangles of what is left of the Cradle M Ranch, where Waldo had spent the first eleven years of his life. Meanwhile our guides and their drivers, on flatbeds carrying the rafts and all our gear and food, performed the bone-rattling journey in eight hours, delayed by the breakdown of a brand-new distributor that required an emergency fix in Price.

It was a cool, beautiful morning. Our hike down eight hundred feet and a mile and a half from the landing strip to the beach where our guides were inflating the rafts gave us splendid views of the Green winding across scrubby flats to the north and between mud banks and small cliffs where it started to carve Deso to the south. Even before our "debriefing," we hiked upstream to check out some boulders that lay stranded on a bench above the river. Sure enough, five of them bore petroglyphs. The bighorn sheep and circles looked solidly Fremont, but the dark patina of the grooves that adumbrated other abstract designs hinted at Archaic. On the fifth and last boulder, we found a true rarity—faintly pecked, bug-eyed, elongated, armless human torsos, unmistakably Barrier Canyon in style, but rendered as petroglyphs rather than red-painted pictographs. The proximity of this boulder (not indicated in the CPAA report) and the Fremont images seemed to me a strong argument for ancestral linkage, but who knows?

Our trip leader, Marshall Dvorscak, was a tall, fit thirty-two-year-old who, growing up in Cody, Wyoming, knew from his first inner tube floats at age ten on Sage Creek that all he wanted to do in life was be a river guide. He'd run Deso about a dozen times before our trip, but showed no signs of getting jaded. Forty-year-old Utah native Brenda Milligan, the company's operations manager, had been down Deso forty or fifty times before, but she too was jazzed about the unusual design of our trip. Rounding out our guide trio was twenty-two-year-old Stephanie Berg, from upstate New York, who had drawn the plum assignment of training on this trip to become a trip leader.

That first day's run was pure lazy delight. As it enters the canyon, the Green is so placid that we tied the three rafts together and fired up the outboard motor to putter downstream like a floating patio. Rowing was unnecessary, and so benign was the river that we weren't even required to wear our life preservers. As the rafts spun gently, we trained our cameras and binoculars on the cliffs and buttes that slipped imperceptibly by us on either side.

The river corridor teemed with wildlife. On the first day alone, we spotted wild horses, a juvenile bighorn sheep, majestic blue herons, gaggles of geese and ducks, and a flock of eight pelicans that we chased downstream. Swifts and swallows flitted overhead. A dead bison—Marshall speculated that it might have broken through the ice attempting a winter crossing—floated down the river with us, lapping and being lapped by our rafts.

Only three miles into our journey, we pulled over to stretch our legs at Nutters Hole, a broad basin where a sand island divides the Green into separate channels. The place is named after Preston Nutter, who started a cattle business in Colorado in 1886, moved his operation to Utah shortly thereafter, and soon became one of the leading land barons in the West. Nine Mile and Desolation Canyons were centers of his far-flung empire. The man made enemies right and left, but even while they branded him a "land hog" and a "crook" in court depositions, those enemies admitted that he was a brilliant businessman. During his forty-plus years in the livestock trade, he all but bankrupted his rivals, especially those who ran sheep rather than cattle.

Nutter died in 1936, but it was his daughter Virginia who sold the Range Creek spread to Budge Wilcox, Waldo's father, in 1951. Waldo had told me that Virginia sent her son-in-law to close the deal with the Wilcox family at the elegant Hotel Utah in Salt Lake City, telling him, "Let 'em order anything they want, but if they order mutton, make 'em pay for it themselves."

With Marshall leading the way, we bashed a corridor through the tamarisks on the west bank to arrive at a pair of half-collapsed log cabins that Preston Nutter had built around 1902. The rusted bric-a-brac of homesteading still adorned the wooden shelves, and a dozen different cattle brands had been carved into the cabin's beams over the years. Dangling from nails in the ceiling were a couple of faded one-dollar bills, but whoever had left them there, perhaps as a testament to the transience of Nutter's erstwhile wealth, was a mystery.

Back at the rafts, I surveyed the canyon walls. Here, in 1916, the Utah Light and Power Company had proposed a two-hundred-foot-high dam to create an upstream reservoir—one of several dam projects in Desolation Canyon that, thank God, never came to pass. The Green River actually has two sources: the Green itself, flowing from the northern ramparts of the Wind River Range in Wyoming, and the Yampa, whose headwaters lie on the western slopes of the Gore Range in Colorado. The Green was dammed beginning in 1958, and its backed-up waters slowly filled Flaming Gorge Reservoir on the northern border of Utah. But the Yampa has never been dammed. Today, the approximately five-hundred-mile-long watercourse of the Yampa and the Green through Desolation and Labyrinth Canyons, joining the Colorado as it passes through Cataract Canyon, adds up to the second longest free-flowing river in the American West, after the Yellowstone River, 692 miles in length.

Guides in Deso have their favorite hidden gems to show to their clients, so a few miles farther downstream we pulled over again so that we could visit what Brenda and Marshall called the Cowboy Cache. In a small alcove about fifty feet above the river, someone had stashed a curious collection of relics. We saw two ornately embroidered wooden trunks starting to decompose, a huge sledgehammer, picks made out of truck axles, a rusty shovel, and a number of pots. Said Brenda, "We have no idea who cached this stuff here, or why. I'd guess it was in the 1940s. They may have been cattle rustlers."

In mid-afternoon, we floated past the mouth of Tabyago Canyon, a major eastern tributary of the Green. Although the stream lies inside the boundaries of the Ute reservation, Sheri Griffith's permit allowed us to hike up it. I was tempted, especially because the CPAA teams, out of respect for Ute sovereignty, had surveyed none of the eastern tributaries on the reservation. But already I realized that I was going to have to sacrifice all kinds of places I would have loved to search for ruins and rock art, because we had only nine days on the river. Mark Meloy had told me that during his ranger days, he and several friends had made a loop hike up Tabyago and over a saddle, regaining the river upstream, without finding anything "cultural."

Still, it was painful to float past that tributary without stopping to have a look. The name itself was intriguing. Tabyago was a Ute who, sometime early in the twentieth century, went insane and died a wretched death. A 1965 source cited in Steve Allen's *Utah's Canyon Country Place Names* declared that Tabyago frequently visited the ranchers farther south in the canyon, but in his demented condition managed to starve to death. His body was supposedly found in a naturally mummified state. Waldo Wilcox had a different story. As he had told Greg and me, "They long-roped him to a tree and he died there. Them Utes was real superstitious about crazy men."

We camped in late afternoon on a lovely beach in Rock House Bottom. At 6 P.M., the air was warm and dead calm. Late sunlight bathed the west-facing cliff across the river. We had covered only thirteen miles on our first day, having launched just before noon. Yet even at that leisurely pace, we would cover the eighty-five river miles in six and a half days. We could afford to slow down.

A rafting camp requires a prodigious amount of unloading and loading. We formed a bucket brigade to haul all the impedimenta our luxury accommodations required, from picnic table to camp chairs to buckets full of water to bundles of store-bought firewood to the "groover," the ingeniously designed toilet that would capture all the human waste that eleven people could produce in nine days, every ounce of which we would carry out with us. But then, as our guides prepared dinner, we were free to loll in camp around the fire, or write entries in our diaries, or photograph the matchless scenery, or just lie back and meditate.

On the morning of May 5, instead of an early launch, we prowled the shore for vestiges of the Fremont. Almost at once, we were rewarded with some of the most striking rock art we would see during the whole trip. At the mouth of Rock House Canyon, we pondered a petroglyph in the form of three crooked lines converging at a common vertex. Dangling from the bottom line was a circle. I saw it as yet another undecipherable Fremont abstraction, but Marshall said, "I think it's a map. Of the river."

He waved his finger close to the panel. "There's the Green coming around the bends we rafted yesterday. Here's Rock House Creek, coming in from the left. And there's the river ahead of us." The fit of the curves grooved in the sandstone, I had to admit, remarkably mirrored the actual topography. "So what's that circle at the bottom?" I asked.

Marshall chuckled. "Something pretty special."

"The place of origin from the underworld?" I teased. The Hopi interpret some abstract rock art "mazes" as migration maps of the routes the people followed after emerging from the subterranean Third World. But we were far from the Hopi domain, and in general, petroglyphs as maps of the surrounding terrain are virtually unknown in the Southwest.

Our second day in Desolation was even more idyllic than the first.

On shore excursions, we hiked to a mushroom-shaped pinnacle with Archaic designs on the base, then later discovered a weird dry-laid room perched on a promontory with great views up and down the river. "It could be a watchtower," I mused out loud. "If it's a habitation site, it's the first one we've seen in Deso." Indeed, by now we had found eight or ten granaries, but not a single site that unambiguously announced a Fremont dwelling. That pattern, persisting in the days to come, became a central focus of the Desolation enigma.

On our rafts, we floated past two bold landmarks that Powell's party had named. Lighthouse Rock, a huge pinnacle high on the western wall, looked indeed very like a warning tower for fog-bound mariners. A high arch Powell's team called The Outlook of Desolation conjured up the mood of the men as they glumly endured a gorge that to us, nearly a century and a half later, seemed a paradise.

We camped that night at the upper end of the beach formed by the fan of Cedar Ridge Canyon. Belknap's waterproof *Desolation River Guide* identified the spot as Mile 66. Sand Wash had been Mile 95. Twenty-nine of our eighty-five river miles were behind us. I felt the adventure already slipping through my fingers—I wanted to make the journey last forever. I thought of Edward Abbey's lyrical chapter in *Desert Solitaire* about his float through Glen Canyon with a single buddy just before that elysium was drowned by Lake Powell. "The time passes slowly," Abbey wrote, "but not slowly enough." On the final morning, "We . . . take a last lingering look at the scene which we know we will never see again as we see it now: the great Colorado River, wild and free, surging past the towering cliffs, roaring past the boulders . . ."

That night a big wind came up. I slept blissfully through it, but Charley's tent collapsed and he had to repitch it in the dark, while Erica, who had eschewed her tent to doze under the open sky, slept fitfully, worrying about falling rocks and bears. In the morning, while the others feasted on a lavish breakfast, I walked two hundred yards to the mouth of the canyon. There I found something that shocked me.

A Fremont artist had pecked a single bighorn sheep, facing left in pro-file. Some vandal had taken a chisel or a knife to the wall and tried to cut loose the panel to take home. He had evidently given up when the bottom half of the panel had fractured loose. (Had there been another sheep on that missing piece of sandstone that the thief was content to steal?) The chisel marks left behind were vivid proof of the vulnerabil-ity of prehistoric art.

On our second day on the Green, we had left behind the calm current along which we could glide as a tied-together flotilla of three rafts. Now occasional rapids interrupted our path, and for the rest of the journey we wore our life jackets, and usually our spray gear. The rapids in Desolation Canyon aren't terribly serious: a number rank as Class II, a couple ratchet up to Class III. Each one has a name, bestowed over the years by explorers and river runners: Moonwater Rapid, Firewater Rapid, Last Chance Rapid, Chandler Falls, Fretwater Falls, Log Cabin Rapid, Stone Canyon Rapid . . .

Yet as Marshall pointed out, every flash flood sent new boulders tumbling down the side canyons, changing the rapids in unpredict-able ways. Especially on this, their first float of 2013, our guides could take no rapid for granted. And indeed, as Sharon and I rode Mar-shall's raft while he maneuvered it through Joe Hutch Canyon Rapid, pulling hard, he broke an oar. "Hold on!" he yelled, while he deftly unslung a spare, slotted it into the oarlock, and cranked us to safety. "We always could have high-sided," he said, wiping his brow.

A few days later, we stopped to scout Coal Creek Rapid, the most treacherous in the canyon. Standing on shore, Marshall and Brenda plotted the narrow line between a hole on the right and dangerous rocks on the left. "If we go into the hole," said Brenda, "we'd wrap for sure, maybe flip." Holding on for dear life, I saw only frothing white-caps as we bounced and glided through the maelstrom—the three rafts taking three different lines. We emerged wet but unscathed.

The big wind that had come up in the night of May 5 was typical for the spring season. Always, it seemed, it came out of the south, blowing upstream. As Ellen Meloy writes in *Raven's Exile*:

> Desolation's spring windstorms never begin with a benign nuzzle of tamarisk fronds or thin clouds veiled across canyon rims, portending an imminent front. They never curl around the nape of the neck, softly lifting tendrils of hair, teasing the nostrils with the pungent aroma of sagebrush. Desolation's spring winds erupt with an abrupt, thunderous bellow of jet engines. They funnel upriver, gain speed in the narrow chasm, careen around bends and oxbows, shriek down straightaways, rouse sand clouds hundreds of feet in the air. . . . They can also blow for a week without ceasing.

Near the end of the trip, Marshall told us that we were lucky, for sometimes his parties had had to lay over for two or three days because rowing downstream in the teeth of a gale was impossible. And on a warm, pleasant day, as we slid around an innocuous bend on flat water, Brenda told us about another trip on which she watched as the raft she was trailing flipped completely upside down, dumping passengers and guide alike, as a sudden gust overturned hundreds of pounds of cargo, not to mention the weight of the humans on board and the raft itself. Brenda had already acquainted us with what the guides call "the 'W' word"—as if the rafters' perpetual nemesis could be kept at bay by euphemizing its name.

Powell's party had its own problems with the wind, made worse because they had neither tents nor sleeping bags. On the night of July 12, 1869, "The wind blows a hurricane; the drifting sand almost blinds us; and nowhere can we find shelter. The wind continues to blow all night, the sand sifting through our blankets and piling over us until we are covered as in a snowdrift. We are glad when the morning comes."

On our third day, we stopped to hike up to Ben Morris's old cabin near the mouth of Firewater Canyon on the Ute Reservation. The boxy little shack, tucked under a rock overhang, looked like an Anglo cliff dwelling. All kinds of relics lay strewn about inside: bottles brown with age, a two-man saw, an old jacket with holes and tears in it hanging from a nail, a pair of rodent-chewed boots on the floor. Out back, the finest spring we would see during the trip came gushing through ferns out of the conglomerate bedrock.

During Prohibition, Morris had made whiskey out of corn and apricots in a copper still, selling his moonshine to ranchers in the canyon and Utes on the reservation. He must have been a rough fellow, for according to James Aton, he was charged with horse rustling and nearly died in a shootout with a Basque sheepherder.

A popular misconception, passed on by some of the river guides (though not ours), has it that Firewater Canyon was named for Morris's hooch. Waldo Wilcox knew better. "That ain't right," he had said to Greg and me. "An old man in a nursing home told me it was named for a Ute Indian chief called Cunepah. Translates as 'firewater.'"

"Old Ben was quite a character," Waldo went on. "I knew him when I was just a little kid. He left Oklahoma for his health. They would've hanged him if he stayed."

"Why?" I asked.

"Killed somebody."

That third afternoon, a sudden rainstorm swept over the canyon, while lightning split the dark sky. In minutes the temperature dropped from seventy degrees Fahrenheit to forty-five. We pulled into the beach near the mouth of Flat Canyon and decided to call it a day. Huddling in the willows, wearing everything we owned, we waited out the tempest, then set up our tents.

The mouth of Flat Canyon boasts one of the finest rock art panels in all of Desolation Canyon. It's so accessible that all the commercial outfits make it an obligatory stop, and even the most jaded clients take the short hike to stare at it. Across fifty feet of dark-patinated cliff stretches a congeries of intertangled and overlapping petroglyphs. Spangler counts from 150 to 200 separate images here, nearly all Fremont, though two bighorn sheep etched in Glen Canyon Linear style testify to the craft of much earlier artists. A big chunk of the wall in the center of the panel has fallen away—not the work of vandals, but of erosion—cutting off the feet of a major anthropomorph and hinting at some forty or fifty other figures that are gone for good.

Already, in three days, we had seen so much rock art that our minds reeled as we tried to recall it. The glory of Deso, as of Nine Mile Canyon, shines from those petroglyph panels. But the mystery of the Fremont presence here lies in the scarcity of living sites. So far we had seen only one—the circle of dry-laid walls on the promontory the day before—but even that could have been a watchtower rather than a home.

Despite their low spirits in the canyon, Powell and his men hiked far up the surrounding slopes and buttresses to survey the Tavaputs Plateau, which Powell named, possibly for a chief of the Uintah Utes. (Other derivations gloss it as the Ute word for "small game" or "land of the sun.") On one such foray, he survived a truly close call. Despite having lost his right arm in the Civil War, Powell was a bold climber. The year before running the Colorado, he had co-led the first non-Indian ascent of Longs Peak in Colorado, a mountain that requires agile scrambling and canny route-finding. Now, at least six hundred feet above the Green River, faced with a "sheer precipice," Powell leapt upward, jammed his foot in a crack, and grabbed a hold above with his left hand. It was a mistake. As he later wrote, "I find I can get up no farther and cannot step back, for I dare not let go with my hand and cannot reach foothold below without." Clinging desperately to his stance, with a vertical drop of sixty to eighty feet below him, he called for help from his partner, George Bradley.

That man performed the plucky feat of finding a way up to the ledge some four or five feet above the trembling major. But he could not reach down to grab Powell's hand. Bradley looked around him for a stick, but could find none. In an inspired moment, he took off his trousers and dangled them over the edge. According to Powell, "I hug close to the rock, let go with my hand, seize the dangling legs, and with his assistance am enabled to gain the top."

To a modern climber, this rescue almost defies belief. But a woodcut in Powell's narrative of the journey, *The Exploration of the Colorado River and Its Canyons*, vividly depicts the near disaster.

The party also had all they could handle on the river. They were not, of course, floating in rubber rafts, but rather in heavy wooden dories rowed by a pair of men with a third in the back using a sweep oar to steer. On July 11, as they ran a rapid (probably Steer Ridge), the rowers in the *Emma Dean* managed to break both oars. Seeing no driftwood on shore from which to fashion replacements, Powell decided to bash through the next rapid without oars. The boat whirled backward and filled with water, dumping Powell and William Dunn, who barely managed to swim to shore, dragging the crippled dory with them. On the bank the men built a fire and tried to dry out themselves and their sodden blankets, but they had lost two vital guns and their barometer. Finally, however, the men found driftwood logs from which crude oars could be fashioned.

As Aton points out, by the time the team entered Desolation Canyon, morale was at a low ebb. One dory had long since been wrecked in the Canyon of Lodore, and now the tensions that would ultimately cause three men to desert the expedition at Separation Rapid, near the end of the Grand Canyon, were festering. (O. G. Howland, Seneca Howland, and William Dunn succeeded in hiking out the side canyon, but they were killed somewhere on the Kanab Plateau to the north. Investigating later, Powell was told that the men had been murdered by Shivwits Paiutes in retribution for the men's alleged killing of a Shivwits woman, but more recent evidence points to xenophobic Mormons as the executioners.)

Indeed, so battered and demoralized was the team by the time the men entered Desolation Canyon that Powell thought seriously about aborting the expedition. Had he done so, the first descent of the Colorado River would have had to await a later and luckier party.

On May 7, we got another sudden rainstorm, this time with winds gusting (upriver, naturally) as high as 40 mph. We'd been aiming for Rock Creek as our campsite, but the guides knew that the only drift-wood in the vicinity (with which they supplemented the store-bought firewood) was on the left bank. In pelting rain, we loaded up our boats with sticks and limbs, then jumped back aboard. But the wind was too strong to row against. All three rafts got blown back to the eastern shore, even as we careened on downstream.

The temperature had dropped dramatically, and all of us felt the first edge of hypothermia, since our clothes were soaked even under our spray gear. Finally, for fear we might miss the Rock Creek beach altogether, we frantically roped the rafts together as Marshall fired up the outboard motor. With that gas-powered boost, we barely made it across the river to land on the southern end of the long delta formed by Rock Creek, one of the three biggest western tributaries in Deso.

This time the storm persisted into the evening. We huddled by the campfire, joking about how it felt like winter in early May. But the next morning, we woke to a steady rain with the thermometer just above freezing point. All the high ridges were enveloped in dark mist, and new snow coated the slopes down to about five thousand feet (the camp lying at forty-six hundred feet above sea level).

Fortunately, we had planned a layover day here, for it would have been a grim business to load up and head downriver again. Rock Creek offered much to explore, including the Rock Creek Ranch, which really ought to be designated a National Historic Site.

There's a certain irony in the fact that no one lives in Desolation Canyon today, even though it was the headquarters for two major ranching outfits from the late 1880s through the mid-1960s (and in all likelihood the locus of small Ute settlements long before that). We spent the frigid morning of May 8 touring the half-ruined buildings of the classic Western homestead that is Rock Creek Ranch, treating it with all the care we would an archaeological site. (The family that still owns the ranch—Waldo Wilcox's in-laws—allows river runners to walk through their property, even while they've seen minor vandalism over the years diminish the museum-like perfection of the place.)

Rusted plows lay marooned in the tall grasses. Twisted hulks of wrought-iron chairs, old horseshoes, saws and axes, along with cattle skulls, dangled from nails on the outer wall of one building. An American flag flapped in the breeze atop the flagpole in the front pasture. The truly astonishing feature of the ranch, however, lay in the stonework of the buildings—even that of a humble chicken coop. And for that, we had Frenchy to thank.

The stonemason who crafted the buildings out of precisely shaped red sandstone blocks, both here and at the Cradle M Ranch fourteen miles downstream, remains a mysterious figure today. The man was a obviously a master, for the heavy blocks fit so seamlessly together they reminded me of the Inca stonework at Sacsaywaman in Peru. No one even knows Frenchy's true name, though he has been erroneously identified as one Eugene Eyraud, a refugee from France sent to California to avoid getting drafted in the First World War. But according to Waldo, "Grandad hired Frenchy up in Provo. You look at the front side of the house [at the Cradle M Ranch], it's real crude down low. Gets better higher up. That was Frenchy's work. But he was gettin' too expensive. Grandad said, 'You finish up in so many days, or you're out of here.' So Frenchy went up the river and built Rock Creek."

"Grandad" was Jim McPherson, who started the Cradle M in 1887. Two days after we toured the Rock Creek Ranch, we strolled through the equally haunting ruins of the Cradle M. Here Waldo had spent the first eleven years of his life, and he had many a story to tell about the place and its environs. One of them had to do with a visit to the ranch in his old age, which happened to coincide with a river guide giving a lecture about the place to her clients.

"She said," Waldo recalled, " 'There used to be a piano in there.' "

" 'No, ma'am, an organ.' "

"She went on to tell how many kids had grown up there. I said, 'Wrong. You got one too many.' "

"She looked at me like I didn't know what the hell I was talkin' about, so I said, 'By God, I oughta know how many aunts and uncles I had!' I had to take out my driver's license to show her who I was."

Both ranches evoke a certain sadness, for the vanished glory of those homesteads speaks in every homely rusted tool lying around the yards. But ranching in Deso had always been a hard way of life. Every summer the families moved their hundreds of cattle from one high Tavaputs pasture to another. And late each fall, they drove their herds downriver to the grasslands near the town of Green River. According to Aton, after a blizzard in 1925 or 1926 killed off nearly their whole herd, the Seamounts of Rock Creek had to sell their ranch. And Waldo's father, Budge, who had married into the McPherson family, was forced off the Cradle M in 1941 by the federal government.

Waldo had told Greg and me that the ranchers in Deso feared and even hated the river, for it posed a perpetual barrier to getting to the opposite shore. Both his great-uncles—Jim McPherson's brothers—had drowned trying to cross the Green. "It was at Jack's Rock," recalled Waldo. "They were on a ferry boat. They tried to go too straight, got flipped off. Only their dog came home."

Jack's Rock, a huge boulder moored in the middle of the river, is named after Trapper Jack, who lived in a cabin three miles up Florence Creek. According to Aton, Jack would cache his traps on the rock so that thieves couldn't get to them. He too drowned trying to cross the river, when his dugout canoe swamped. Waldo: "I can show you where he hewed his boat out of a cottonwood tree, near Three Fords. He ran three or four rapids before the next one got him. Grandad dug a hole and buried him."

On our seventh day, we pulled onto shore to hike to a low cliff where a Ute burial had been discovered. Brenda gave a little speech before we got there, about how she didn't take just any clients to the sensitive site and how reverently we should treat it. The small pile of stacked rocks failed to cover completely the bleached skull, which looked broken. Other bones were scattered beneath the skull. A hush fell over us, as we imagined the violent act that might have been committed here so long ago. According to Spangler, the site had been looted considerably since it was first recorded in 1976: "once human remains become known to river vistors," he wrote in the CPAA survey report, "visitation becomes substantial and human remains disappear with alarming regularity." It was hard for me to imagine a deed so crass as stealing a femur or fibula from this burial site for your Deso souvenir, but I didn't doubt that it had happened. (We refrained even from touching the bones.)

Waldo, however, had a more cynical take on the site. "I camped in that cave back in the forties," he told Greg and me. "There wasn't no skeleton there then. I think the boaters put it there. Show folks a dead Indian. I think it's a white person, probably a woman."

It was hard to know what to make of Waldo's thesis. But sure enough, just around the corner, we found, faintly scratched into the rock, the Flying X that was Waldo's cattle brand. He had confessed, "I told you I never put my name anywhere on the cliffs, but I put my brand in a couple of places."

Although it was I who had designed the day-by-day itinerary, Greg and Erica rivaled me in the energetic quest for obscure Fremont sites. Erica's crowning deed was discovering the faint traces of three pit-houses far up one side canyon, on terrain the rest of us had walked over twice. These were the only definite dwelling sites we found in nine days. Greg used his world-class climbing skills to reach a couple of structures that none of the rest of us could get to, and that no human had visited since the last Fremont had left perhaps eight hundred years ago. As climbers, four of us—Matt, Erica, and I, as well as Greg—managed to clamber up to granaries that Spangler's teams had had to admire from the ground. We also found obscure structures and rock art that those CPAA teams had missed. To our surprise, however, every granary was empty.

Yes, we rafted Deso to have fun. But the true reward for me lay in what the journey taught me about the enigmatic Fremont. By the end of our nine days, we had seen scores of rock art panels—I guessed that the total number of figures among the petroglyphs we beheld was six or seven hundred. The most striking rock art panel, however, far up a side canyon, was an assemblage of three huge shield-like pictographs, painted in red, orange, white, and creamy tan. Eerily suggestive of ghostlike faces, they bore no resemblance to any other rock art we found in Deso. But what were they about?

In his excellent 2013 book, *Nine Mile Canyon: The Archaeological History of an American Treasure*, Jerry Spangler grapples with the eternal problem of interpreting rock art. Unfortunately, it's a field that tends to attract wacko dilettantes with theories based on New Age revelations or the misguided effort to read the petroglyphs and pictographs as an undeciphered language. Archaeologists, in turn, tend to shy away from the phenomenon. As Spangler writes, "In many respects, rock art is commonly viewed as background noise, a distraction to scholars who grapple with broader behavioral questions like human responses to changing climates."

Yet in recent years, Spangler and several of his colleagues have built interpretations of the rock art in Nine Mile—justly called "the world's longest art gallery"—by carefully counting the numbers and types of figures found on all the panels, not just the "sexy" spectacular ones. Ray Matheny, a professor emeritus at Brigham Young University, sees the predominance of hunting scenes in Nine Mile as "suggest[ing] a socioeconomic system that extended far beyond the canyon and that may indicate that Fremont peoples exploited Nine Mile Canyon primarily for animal products that they exported." The proliferation of petroglyphs depicting men with bows and arrows, dogs, nets, ambush tactics, and "burden bearers" (prehistoric backpackers) buttresses his hypothesis.

No comparable analysis of the rock art in Deso has yet been attempted, though Spangler's survey teams may have collected the data on which to base their own theory.

During our nine days, we found about two dozen granaries, including ones on high ledges that we floated past and could only stare at with our binoculars, for it would have taken half a day to park the boats and figure out scrambling routes to get to each of them. But we found only one true habitation site—Erica's three pithouses—along with three or four dry-laid structures built on promontories or boulders that could have been either temporary shelters or lookout posts.

Most baffling of all was the fact that in our nine days, we found only a single potsherd—a nondescript piece of Emery gray that Greg picked up in Florence Creek. (On the Navajo Reservation, Ancestral Puebloan sites that I had hiked to contained as many as hundreds of potsherds each.)

So there's the conundrum of Desolation Canyon in a nutshell. So much rock art. So many granaries, most of them hidden away in nooks and crannies to thwart discovery by the "bad guys." Granaries imply food being stored—corn above all, but also beans and squash and wild grasses and piñon nuts. Why, then, almost no pottery? What are you going to carry your food in, if not pots? How do you cook the food, without pots? And finally, why so little evidence of habitation, and what there was of it, so fugitive and temporary?

In his *Nine Mile Canyon* book, Spangler speculates about Desolation. In all their months of survey work, his teams found only six possible habitation sites, and none had even a minimal midden, the associated rubbish heap that indicates long-term occupation. His tentative conclusion:

> In fact, the rarity of evidence that any of these farmers invested time or energy in the construction of residences would seem to support the idea that small groups of farmers came into the canyon in the spring to plant their maize [corn], moving frequently up and down the river corridor to tend their crops but never staying in any one place long enough for significant household trash to accumulate around them. Instead of formal residences, they likely used small rockshelters as temporary domiciles. In the fall, maize was harvested and stored in nearby granaries for retrieval

as needed, and the farming families abandoned the Green River in favor of a winter residence elsewhere.

Those winter dwelling places could have been, Spangler argues, as far away as twenty or thirty miles. Wherever they were—perhaps in Range Creek—that's where we might find the pots. However, in an earlier paper with the clever title "One-Pot Pithouses and Fremont Paradoxes," Spangler noted, "No substantial winter occupations have been demonstrated anywhere on the East or West Tavaputs plateaus."

Throughout our journey, even as I reveled in the beauty of Deso, I pondered the idea that something about the place might have been "bad juju" for the Fremont. If they needed its fields to grow their corn, was there an aura here that breathed, *Not where we ought to live*? Did that sublime river corridor seem to the ancients as spooky and threatening as it did to Powell's party in 1869? Was "Desolation" the proper epithet, after all?

By the last days of our trip, the temperatures had risen as high as eighty degrees again. Birds flitted along with our rafts, and the cottonwood leaves trembled in the light breezes over our camps. I didn't want the journey to end, and on the last morning, I felt the heavy thud of our imminent return to normal life.

Slouched in my raft, or lying on my back in camp, for hour after hour I had scanned the high ridges and cliffs that towered as much as two thousand feet above us. How I longed to get up there and poke around! In nine days, I guessed, we might have seen one-tenth of the sites that Spangler's teams had recorded, and maybe only one-fiftieth of what the Fremont had left behind.

In all likelihood, I will never go back to the canyon. As I lay in camp lost in dreamy thought, I told myself, it would take many lifetimes to explore this wilderness. But in May 2013, I was happy to spend a small part of the only lifetime I'll have scratching the surface of Desolation Canyon.

RETURN TO THE BASKET

The most astonishing artifact I ever found in the backcountry, I
didn't find. Instead, I walked right past it.

It was my wife, Sharon, trailing me by a few paces, who suddenly exclaimed, "Oh, my God, David, look at this!"

We were in the middle of an eight-day backpack in 1994. Five days
and many miles from the trailhead, we were exploring an obscure

stretch of canyon. Several hours away from our camp, we checked out a shallow alcove, searching, as always, for anything the Ancestral Puebloans might have left behind. It was an unpromising site, for the floor was strewn with breakdown boulders, and there was almost no surface level enough to support even a granary. I found a few red chert flakes lying in the dirt, but no rock art and not the faintest hint of an ancient structure or storage cist. Hiking from one end of the alcove to the other, we were about to exit the overhang and continue our prowl upcanyon. A jumble of jagged, scattered slabs made progress difficult, so I hugged the back wall as I stepped past the debris, barely glancing at it. Sharon, however, chanced to look down and to her left. It was then that she uttered her cry of astonishment.

I turned to see her bent over, hands on knees, staring into the dim recess formed by a pair of slabs that leaned against each other, forming a tent-like nook. I got down on my knees and crawled close to the accidental cavity. There, beneath the leaning stones, lying face down, was a perfectly intact basket made of either yucca or willow fiber. The weaving was so exquisite and tight that the basket almost certainly would have held water. I knew from similar objects I had seen in museums that this one must date from the Basketmaker II era, so at a minimum it was fifteen hundred years old.

The bottom of the basket was formed by a spiral of woven loops making thirteen revolutions. (It was that spiral that had caught Sharon's eye, though at first she thought it was a pattern in the dirt.) The sides of the basket were built around a framework of twigs bent to make perfect loops, around each of which the yucca or willow strands, all of the same exact breadth, had been woven in an unfathomably large number of tiny stitches. There were thirty-two bands in all from rim to bottom.

Next to the basket lay a pair of thin, shaped sticks, one with a cuphole bored in its side, into which the rounded end of the other fit snugly. I guessed that it was a fire-starting kit, but I couldn't be sure. We handled the sticks and photographed them before putting them back where we had found them, but refrained from touching the basket—except once, when I tapped very lightly on the upturned bottom, as we heard the hollow reverberation of empty space beneath. To try to take the basket out of its hiding place to look at it more thoroughly would in all likelihood have damaged it. And it would have seemed a profanation. If ever there was a case to be made for Fred Blackburn's Outdoor Museum, this was it.

We spent at least an hour and a half in the alcove, as I propped my camera on the ground to take long-exposure photos of the basket. It was only when we got home and saw the developed slides that Sharon and I realized we had missed a stunning design that graced the side of the basket away from the opening—an interlocked pattern of painted triangles, ten of them, shading from white to light blue to dark blue. The light in the nook had been too dim for us to see the pattern with the naked eye, or perhaps because we were so stunned by the object itself, we never thought to examine it for a painted design.

I closed *In Search of the Old Ones* with a rhapsodic account of our discovery. When we finally left the alcove, we had to wrench ourselves away from it, as I tried to convey in the book's final sentence: "Darts of sweet pain swam through my last image of the basket, for I knew that in the rest of my life, I would never see anything quite like it again."

Twenty-one years later, that verdict still holds. In all my backcountry sleuthing since 1994, I've never found anything like that basket, never found an artifact to match it for beauty or for the perfection of the craft its maker expended on it. It was, no doubt, naïve of me not to anticipate that readers would turn *In Search of the Old Ones* into a treasure map. As recounted in the prologue, it didn't take long for perspicacious seekers to rediscover the intact corrugated pot I had found in another canyon on Cedar Mesa, and by now a beaten path apparently leads to it.

The basket, however, lies in as obscure and inaccessible a place as Cedar Mesa offers, and my description of its whereabouts in the book was—or so I retroactively hoped—considerably vaguer than the clues I inadvertently dropped about the pot. Year after year went by without a single soul reporting to the Kane Gulch rangers that he or she had found the basket. That didn't mean that no one had independently stumbled across that priceless relic, admired it in turn, and chosen not to report the discovery. It would have been all right with me if this had happened. The point of the Outdoor Museum is not to "own" a wondrous ancient thing that one is lucky enough to find in the wilderness—not even to "own" it in the sense of being the only person who ever sees it—but to leave the object undisturbed so that later visitors can earn the thrill of their own discovery.

Yet every year Sharon, even more than I, agonized over the possibility that someone else had found the basket and taken it away. I hoped that the treasure map my book had become was not one that avaricious looters would consult, but of course, I had no control over that possibility. Even if the basket someday ended up in a museum, rather than in some collector's trophy case, that would seem to us the wrong place for it to be.

In September 2012, Sharon and I decided to return to the basket. We would take some of our close friends with us, to share in their joy at making their own discovery, albeit one guided by us. (In just that fashion, during my first years of hiking the canyons, more experienced friends such as Fred Blackburn, Vaughn Hadenfeldt, and Winston Hurst had guided me to their own best finds.) Studying the maps over the years, as well as hiking for hundreds of days on Cedar Mesa, had given me a blueprint for an entirely different approach to the obscure alcove from the route we had followed so leisurely in 1994. It would require a rugged three-day backpack, with water at our overnight camp an uncertain proposition, but it also promised a journey replete with canyon scenery as fine as Cedar Mesa had to offer.

Hanging over the trip in the weeks before we set out, of course, was the nagging worry, *What if the basket is gone?*

It was a foregone conclusion that Matt Hale and Greg Child would join us on our 2012 outing, for they were the two friends with whom I had done the most backcountry searching during the last decade. Shannon O'Donoghue, Greg's partner—now wife—was the former director of the Banff Mountain Film and Book Festival. In the last few years, she had become a devotee of the Southwest, and our trip was a must for her. I invited Stephanie Scott, my photographer friend, who had shown such enthusiasm when I hiked with her to ruins and rock art in the canyons of the Paria and elsewhere on Cedar Mesa. Stephanie's congenial boyfriend (now husband), Kelly Adair, would come along. The sleeper in our gang—pound for pound, the best hiker in our group—was Ariann, Greg's eight-year-old daughter.

I'd known Ariann since she was a baby, born in August 2004. On the twelfth afternoon of our traverse of the 125-mile-long Comb Ridge, where we crossed US 163, Greg and Vaughn Hadenfeldt had rendezvoused with their loved ones, as we camped inside a graffiti-trashed alcove not far from the highway. Barely a month old, Ariann whimpered and tossed and turned most of the night, allowing Greg no sleep whatsoever. Ever since, I've reminded Ariann that I shared her first campout ever, but when I say so, she looks at me as though I'm telling her a fairy tale.

By the age of five, Ariann was hiking with us in the canyons near Moab. She could stop in her tracks to study a flower that caught her fancy, or even an odd-shaped rock that she found noteworthy, and it took some coaxing to get her on the move again. Sometimes she took off running, skipping from one stone to another without losing her balance. Sometimes she'd hop or skip, just for variety. But then she'd tire and ask her daddy to carry her.

At age seven, Ariann came into her own. No more pleas for a free ride from Greg. She could hike for hours without a rest, and by now she had discovered her own passion for the Ancestral Puebloans. "Indian stuffing," she called it. During their first few visits to obscure ruins, Greg had sometimes discovered a pretty potsherd or chert flake that somehow made its way into Ariann's jeans pocket, but it

wasn't too hard for him to instill in her the ethic of leaving everything in place.

Just weeks before our trip to the basket, Ariann had accompanied
Greg, Shannon, Stephanie, and me on a grueling trailless descent into
a canyon, a long hike in the valley bottom to a ruin Greg had spotted
with binoculars from above, then a blind climb eight hundred feet up
a slope booby-trapped with loose boulders to get out of the canyon.
Just below the rim, a forty-foot cliff blocked our escape. Greg soloed
it, then dropped a rope so the rest of us could second the climb. I tied
an old-fashioned bowline-on-a-coil around Ariann's tiny waist, then
watched as she flashed the route, shrieking with delight. (Using a rope
to secure one's partner, as opposed to gaining access to a prehistoric
site, is legal throughout the Southwest.) Ariann, it was clear, had absolutely no fear of heights. And she was a natural-born climber.

After that long, hot, eight-hour hike, we were all tired, but Ariann
hadn't uttered a cross word all day. By September 2012, I knew she
would be up to a tough three-day backpack to look for the basket.

The temperature was well over eighty degrees on the morning we
set out from our vehicles. A mostly level plateau, intersected by a pair
of shallow, dry canyons, lay between us and the rim where we hoped
to camp. Besides three liters apiece, we carried an extra five or six
gallons of water, in case the bedrock hollows near the rim were as
dry as the nearly treeless terrain we crossed. In the heat, with our
heavy loads, we'd hike for half an hour, then take a five-minute break,
if possible in the shade of the odd hoodoo or outcrop. During one
such lull, Ariann speared a dead yucca with Greg's ski pole, then stood
behind me like a palace guard, ensuring her monarch's safety with her
upraised scepter.

After another stop, I propped my sixty-five-pound backpack in
front of Ariann and said, "Ari, why don't we trade packs now? I'll
carry yours, and you carry mine." "No!" she screamed, fiercely clutch-
ing the shoulder straps of her little purple daypack.

Five hours in, I was the first one to reach the rim. "Water!" I yelled.

"Tons of it!" The rains a week before had filled the "tanks" (as cowboys call the natural depressions in the slickrock) with enough H_2O to last us for weeks. Greg and I had camped here a few years before, and we had explored the boulder-choked gash of a side canyon that led steeply eight hundred feet down to the main canyon. We could always have pushed that descent with our backpacks, but it would have made for treacherous scrambling—and a very weary return on the third day. Instead, the rim offered one of the finest places to camp on all of Cedar Mesa.

With the setting sun, the thermometer dropped to a comfortable temperature. After dinner, Ariann made a project out of brushing and braiding Sharon's, Shannon's, and Stephanie's hair. When she was done with them, she chose me as her next victim, even though my graying locks were far too short to braid. The whole time, Ariann critically surveyed her handiwork until she got it right.

We happened to have chosen the night of a full moon. It rose in the east as the sky was still fading blue in the west. Matt and Stephanie set up their tripods and composed photographic homages to our perfect campsite. We stayed up late, even though we'd planned a predawn start for the morrow. We were all wired, I think, in anticipation of what we hoped to find miles from our camp the next day. Yet I sat on the slickrock, staring at the constellations dimmed by the moon, listening not to the chatter of my friends but to the whisper of the breeze in the piñons behind our camp.

At last our small fire flickered out. My drowsy companions, one by one, went off to their tents. I stayed up, immersed in a reverie. Why, I wondered for the umpteenth time, did the search for the ruins and rock art of the Old Ones preoccupy me year after year? Why did I save every spring and fall to head out to the canyon country, and why did those weeks in the Southwest unfailingly supply some of the most memorable experiences of my life?

In my twenties and early thirties, it was not the Southwest that sang me its siren song, but Alaska. For thirteen straight years, from 1963 to 1975, I went off on expeditions to unclimbed peaks and faces that few others had ever seen, much less attempted. Alaska seemed a limitless realm for mountaineering ambition. The whole rest of my year—in college first, then graduate school, then teaching at Hampshire College—served as a penance to be endured as I schemed up the next summer's project. I stared at maps for hours, planned approach routes as I drifted off to sleep, and debated logistics by mail and telephone and over beers in favorite taverns with a changing succession of partners, only one or two of whom was as obsessed with Alaskan mountains as I was.

Yet after 1975, that obsession faded, increasingly diluted with ambivalence. The sheer misery of waiting out five-day storms in a sagging tent on a remote glacier had taken its toll, as had the too many close calls I survived. Not to mention having been involved in three fatal accidents costing four lives by the time I was twenty-two. Along with those partners who died before my eyes, I lost more than a dozen friends in climbing disasters stretching from the Tetons to the Himalaya.

Still, all serious mountaineers know that death and close calls are an inevitable part of the game, and many of us keep climbing despite those scares and losses. As I look back on those years, I recognize that I have never in my life been seized with a purer ecstasy than I felt on the summits of Mount Huntington, Shot Tower, and Mount Dickey.

I had made two backpack trips into the canyon country during my climbing years, one solo on the Navajo Reservation in Arizona in 1973, and the other, lasting twenty-one days, with Hampshire students in the Maze district of Canyonlands during the snowy January of 1978. Both trips were intense, but neither set the hook that I finally swallowed in 1987. With a single companion that May, I made a three-day backpack into Bullet Canyon on Cedar Mesa. We camped by a spring not far from two magnificent though well-known Ancestral Puebloan ruins, called Perfect Kiva and Jailhouse. As beguiling as those cliff villages were, it was the smaller things that captured my imagination—the potsherds and chert flakes and corncobs scattered in the dirt (it had never occurred to me that such fugitive artifacts might have lain undisturbed for seven hundred years), the realization that the spring from which we drank was the same one that had sustained the ancients. And the rock art—in particular, the two baleful painted shields or moons or "hex symbols" (Polly Schaafsma's conjecture) that proclaimed some lost malediction from the upper level of Jailhouse ruin.

At first, it was Cedar Mesa that brought me back each spring and fall. In 1993 and 1994, Sharon and I covered the fifty-six-mile length of Grand Gulch in a pair of eight-day llama treks. In later years, during return trips, I realized that on our first two forays we had missed at least half the ruins and rock art in that matchless canyon, simply because we hadn't yet trained our eyes to spot the half-hidden granary on a high ledge or the petroglyph panel tucked behind a bend in the sandstone.

As the years went by, I branched out—to the Escalante and its side canyons, to the weird cavate dwellings of Bandelier National Monument and its neighboring canyons, to the Tsegi, Canyon de Chelly, and Rainbow Plateau on the Navajo Reservation, deep into Mogollon territory in the Sierra Madre of Mexico, and to dozens of other seldom-trod outbacks, including, after 2004, the Fremont domain of Range Creek and Desolation Canyon in central Utah.

Having turned seventy in 2013, I now hike the canyons with a presentiment, at once gloomy and optimistic, that murmurs in my ear: *How many more seasons like this will I have? Another ten springs and ten autumns, if I'm careful and lucky?*

The most ambitious backpack trip into the most remote wilderness in the Southwest, even solo, is far safer than mountaineering in Alaska. And far more comfortable. On those thirteen climbing expeditions in the far north, pitching a camp in which it was pleasant to hang out was a rare godsend. In the Southwest, I've come to expect it as the norm.

Yet it was only after I was about five years into my preoccupation with the Old Ones that I recognized the fundamental difference between the two exploratory passions of my life. Whether or not climbing is ultimately selfish (a proposition I've tussled with for decades), there's no denying that it's ultimately about oneself and one's partners. No one outside the arcane discipline of mountaineering cares whether you've made the first ascent of the north face of Peak X in the YZ Range. Your deed adds nothing to our geographical knowledge of the planet. The great French climber Lionel Terray titled his autobiography (the best, in my opinion, ever written by a mountaineer) *Les Conquérants de l'Inutile,* translated into English rather awkwardly as *Conquistadors of the Useless.*

It's not a coincidence that climbing is also fiercely competitive. If the feat of a first ascent is "useless," then it's all the more important that it be deemed "bold," a "breakthrough," setting "a new standard." The burgeoning legions of young climbers who comb such hardcore websites as Supertopo.com or 8a.nu are exquisitely attuned to whether Adam Ondra's new route on some diminutive crag in southern Spain is rated 5.15b or 5.15c. An ongoing debate, even while derided by its principal contenders, tries to determine who is "the best climber in the world" at any given moment.

Hiking the canyon country, in contrast, is only mildly competitive. Vaughn, Greg, and I can get downright rivalrous about who first spots an arrowhead peeping out of the dirt, but there's no forum in which we can claim that a certain outing on Cedar Mesa is a landmark of Southwestern prowling. The very notion of a "best backcountry seeker of the Ancestral Puebloans" is ludicrous.

Herein lies the fundamental difference. Looking for ruins and rock art is not merely about oneself. It's about *them*—the enigmatic ancients who left behind the prodigies of a culture we still only dimly comprehend. That's why archaeology is such a vibrant and, in the long run, noble pursuit. Every time I find a new petroglyph panel, I struggle to understand what it means. Every time I find a dwelling or granary tucked under an overghanging wall, I try to divine why *they* built it there, and how. I'm not a ruin-bagging birdwatcher with a life list on which to chalk up my new discovery. Vaughn, Greg, and I don't even keep lists of what we've found.

Yes, the fact that the Ancestral Puebloans, as well as the Fremont and the Mogollon, were genius climbers enhances their appeal for me. What I'm in search of, season after season, is another clue to a great cultural mystery. What I gain as a reward for my search is that elusive but inexhaustible blessing: wonderment. If that's what drives me still in the canyon country past the age of seventy, it's also what captivated Ariann in September 2012, just a month after her eighth birthday.

The moon was setting in the west as we started out before dawn. We had reconnoitered the tricky entry to the side canyon the previous afternoon, and now, in the ghostly penumbra, we skirted the two big pouroffs that blocked access and found the zigzag descent from slab to slab that took us to the boulder-choked defile that Greg and I remembered from several years before.

By the time we came to the junction with the main canyon, the first rays of sunlight were washing the rim far above us. There was not a breath of wind. It was pleasantly chilly, and as we hiked upstream, each bend revealed new vistas. Greg and I had each been here on three or four previous trips, Sharon on one. For the others, the canyon was utterly new, and even while they anticipated the goal of our three-day excursion, still miles ahead of us, they marveled at the beauty of our surroundings. On one of our previous trips, Greg and I had spotted several truly defensive structures high on the wall that now soared to the south of us—spotted from an opposite rim, not from below. Now there was no hope of seeing them again, for intervening cliffs blocked them from view—just as the ancients had intended. And it was obvious that those sites could not be reached from below, for the cliffs were nearly vertical and featureless. (Greg and I filed away a possible devious traverse from the far rim to those inaccessible ruins for some future outing: one more Ancestral Puebloan condundrum to try to solve.)

Ariann paused beside the stream, entranced by a tangle of slimy green moss that floated in a pool. She seized a stick and snagged the moss, then played it like a deep-sea monster for five minutes, chortling with the joy of her fantasy. Stifling my impatience, I allowed myself to empathize with Ariann's play: why did it matter what the point of the trip was, when she could live so wholly in the present with a stick and a swirl of gooey moss? At last Greg said, "C'mon, Ari, we've still got a long way to go."

Stephanie had given Ariann a white plastic Polaroid camera. It had become her favorite new toy. Now, as we hiked on upcanyon, she paused to shoot her landscapes, holding the camera with her right hand while she looked through the viewfinder, covering her left eye with her left hand. Each picture generated a magical moment of high-speed gratification, as she watched the blank paper blossom into photographic life. That the horizon in her pictures was often skewed by as much as thirty degrees was simply a facet of her aesthetic vision. She put her masterpieces in a plastic bag and tucked them into her purple pack.

I had underestimated the scope of the day's hike. Hidden in an out-of-the-way bend of the canyon lay a magnificent ruin that Greg and I had explored on a previous trip. I had hoped we could visit that site as well as the basket alcove, but now I realized that the hours of daylight we had at our disposal would preclude both. We had to sacrifice the ruin to do justice to the alcove. (The lines from a George Herbert poem came unbidden into my head: "Sweet day, so cool, so calm, so bright, / The bridal of the earth and sky; / The dew shall weep thy fall tonight, / For thou must die.")

We saw no one else during the day's hike, which would end up spanning eleven and a half hours—nor did we expect to run into strangers in this seldom-visited outback. Ariann was a trouper: not even in the last stretch of the exhausting hike, as we trudged back to camp, covering the last half mile in pitch darkness with the aid of our headlamps, would she utter a word of complaint.

It was past noon by the time we reached the bend in the nameless valley where we had made our discovery in 1994. Eighteen years later, Sharon was not sure she would even recognize the alcove, but as it drew into view, her memory clicked. We scrambled across the fronting talus to the back wall of the alcove, where we threw down our packs and retrieved our water bottles. It was near here that I had found the flakes of red chert on our first visit, before almost giving up on the alcove as barren of ancient remains. About thirty yards away, we could see the jumble of leaning slabs, but from where we sat, there was no telling if the basket still lay hidden among them.

During the previous hour, Sharon and I—especially Sharon—had grown more and more nervous about the outcome of our rediscovery mission. The unspoken curse cycled through our heads: *What if it's not there?*

Matt, Sharon, and I arrived at the back of the alcove first. We had all agreed that Sharon, as the original discoverer, should get the privilege of checking the leaning slabs by herself. Now she started to cover those thirty yards. But then she stopped and called down, "Come on, Ariann, let's see if we can find the basket together."

The eight-year-old flew across the talus, joining Sharon, where they moved on hand in hand. When they were four yards away from the dim recess, Ariann suddenly thrust her right hand forward, forefinger pointed. A look of total glee spread across her face, as she beamed wordlessly up at Sharon. They advanced together, then Ariann squatted low, staring into the dim cubbyhole beneath the slabs. She knew not to touch anything.

The rest of us came along. To Sharon's and my joy, the basket lay exactly as we had last seen it in 1994. The pair of shaped sticks—the possible fire-starting kit—rested in the dirt next to the basket.

We spent two hours there, most of it simply staring. Matt, Stephanie, and Greg documented the artifact with a variety of lenses and exposures. Lying prone in the dirt, Ariann captured the moment with her plastic Polaroid. This time, we all saw the triangular design in white and blue that covered the far side of the basket. Each of the eight of us seemed to shape his or her own experience during those two hours, though none of us tried to explain it out loud, beyond the murmured "Wow!" or "Amazing!"

The longer I looked at the slabs surrounding the ancient object, the more astonished I was that it had survived the centuries intact. On one side, a small chunk of sandstone, standing on end, held up a huge slab at least ten times its weight. It was like a chockstone wedged in a crack, supporting a massive boulder above it. On the other side, another hefty slab leaned at a sixty-degree angle against the bigger slab opposite. The whole geologic structure depended on the flimsy "chockstone." If that rock moved, or even pivoted under the great weight of the slab it held in place, the assemblage would collapse like a pile of pick-up sticks, smashing the basket flat. The configuration that shaped the tentlike shelter looked so fragile that we stepped around it with infinite care, lest the thud of a single bootstep upset the whole thing.

I wondered again, as I had in 1994, whether the rocks had been frozen in their equipoise like this at the time, at least fifteen hundred years ago, when someone placed the basket in the niche. Or had the slabs come crashing down in the interim, perhaps spalled loose from the ceiling of the alcove, only to come to rest in a position that miraculously saved the basket?

And I wondered who had left the basket here, and why. The first guess, like the one that had immediately struck me in 1993 when I found the intact corrugated pot on the high ledge in another Cedar Mesa canyon, was that its owner had cached it here, intending to come back and reclaim it, perhaps only a few years or even months later— only to leave it for the ages. But now Greg and I discussed a second scenario. Could the basket mark a burial site? Was a human interred in the dirt beneath the slabs, the precious possession left behind as a grave offering? Elsewhere in the Southwest—especially in the Mimbres region of southern New Mexico during the eleventh and twelfth centuries A.D.—the dead were buried with the exquisite figurative pots they owned inverted over their heads, usually with a small chunk in the bottom of the vessel knocked out (a "kill hole," as archaeologists call it), presumably to render the object unusable for domestic life, thus "retiring" the pot for good. But the Mimbres people were Mogollon, not Ancestral Puebloan, their homeland three hundred miles from Cedar Mesa, and their advent and demise at least five centuries later than the makers of this basket.

No matter what, we were not about to dig or even scratch in the sand to find out.

I was acutely aware of the sun wheeling lower in the west. But it was one of the others who finally said, "I suppose we should be heading back."

This time, as we hiked away from the alcove, it was not "darts of sweet pain" that swam before my eyes, but rather the rich satisfaction of having found the basket again and shared it with friends. Yet our departure was still tinged with sorrow. The basket, after all, is doomed. It may yet end up in the vitrine of some rapacious looter's living room. Or in a museum, thanks to the well-meaning but soulless "rescue" effort of some BLM official. Or crushed beneath the slabs that ultimately destabilize and fall to earth.

The basket cannot last *in situ* forever. The earth itself, after all, is not expected to survive the sun's transmogrification into a red giant, a mere six and a half billion years from now. Long before that, if no one takes it away, the fibers of the basket will decompose and merge with the surrounding dirt—as the Hopi believe a vessel left on the ground should attain its end.

Hiking back along our outward path, we were tired but jubilant. We had another night's camp on the rim to look forward to, with the moon rising now an hour past sunset, a shade on the gibbous side of full.

I suspect that all eight of us will remember the basket for the rest of our lives—even Ariann. When I was about eight years old, with my brother Alan, a year younger, I undertook a bold thrust into the wilds of Gregory Canyon, just west of Boulder, Colorado, where our family lived. It was my first hike without parental supervision. A sign at the mouth of the canyon indicated that the prospector and explorer John H. Gregory had pioneered this route in 1859, to reach the impossibly remote destination of Black Hawk. Alan and I felt like pioneers ourselves, paying homage to the scout from yesteryear.

We made it about two miles up the defile before halting to eat our peanut butter and jelly sandwiches. Before heading back, I hid a gray zinc penny—minted in 1943, the year of my birth—under a clump of moss on a rock ledge beside the faint trail. I never found that penny again. I doubt that anyone else did, either—there were simply too many clumps of moss on too many ledges. For all I know, the penny is still there, sixty-three years after I cached it in my secret place.

I like to think that Ariann, maybe after she's become a grownup, will take friends of her own on a backpack trip to show them the basket that so infused her autumn day in 2012. But I doubt that Sharon and I will make the pilgrimage again. There isn't time enough left in our lives, and there is still too much else to look for—too many canyons in the limitless Southwest, too few remaining days of perfect camps and blissful hikes. And too much still to fathom about the Old Ones, for whom this wilderness was home and heartland, every corner of which they knew better than we late intruders ever will.

Acknowledgments

During the last twenty-five years, many of the happiest days of my life have come as I explored the canyons and mesas of the Southwest. The landscape itself speaks to me, but it is the eternal mystery of the Old Ones that turns mere wandering into a quest. During those years, I've been blessed to hike with many companions who shared my passion, and their company in the outback has unfailingly enriched the experience. My most frequent partners on those outings have been the four men to whom this book is dedicated—Fred Blackburn, Vaughn Hadenfeldt, Matt Hale, and Greg Child—as well as my wife, Sharon, who joins me in the canyon country as often as she can spare time from her real job as a psychoanalyst in private practice in Cambridge, Massachusetts.

I've written about yet other friends in the preceding pages, as I recounted adventures pursued with Mary Tobin, Stephanie Scott, Connie Massingale, Charley LeCompte, the Wineland-Thomson family of Rick, Judi, and Erica, Shannon O'Donoghue, Kelly Adair, Marcia Hadenfeldt, Wilson King, and the incomparable Ariann Child. Other companions who added joy to my Southwest prowlings include Deanna De Cou, Caty Enders, Karen Roos, Gavin Wilson, and John Burcham. Several of my cronies were professional photographers on assignment, but I knew that they would have just as eagerly joined me on my walkabouts had no magazine paid them to do so. I thus salute Dawn Kish, Bill Hatcher, Stephanie Scott, Terry Moore, Russell Kaye, and Ira Block. Likewise, though Macduff Everton rambled across Kaiparowits Plateau on a separate trip from mine, it felt as though we were together in spirit, as his splended photographs attest.

I count myself fortunate also to have persuaded some of the leading Southwest archaeologists not only to take hours out of their professional lives to explain their cutting-edge research to me but in some cases actually to go out in the field to demonstrate their work. Foremost among those scholars is Steve Lekson, who has become my go-to guy for unraveling the knotty paradoxes of Southwestern archaeology. The breadth and depth of Lekson's learning are virtually unmatched in his field. The eleven-day road trip Lekson and I took with Bill Hatcher in 2004, as we retraced the Chaco Meridian, was an intellectual and geographic pilgrimage that remains unique in my experience.

Matt Liebmann, the leading expert on Jemez Pueblo and the Pueblo Revolt of 1680, has recently become a good friend, as well as a second go-to guy whose brain I pick regularly over coffee in various Harvard cafés. In August 2013, I hung out for a few days with Matt, his wife, Maria, and their adorable daughter Stella (then eleven months old), both in the funky hamlet of Jemez Springs and on the basalt cliffs of Santa Fe Canyon, where we searched for petroglyphs that might have recorded the Spanish *entrada* into New Mexico.

Sev Fowles gave me a magical day in the canyon of the Rio Grande as he showed me the Comanche rock art his teams had recently discovered—a phenomenon so subtle that all previous investigators had overlooked it. Always generous with his time and insights, Eric Blinman came to Grants, New Mexico, in 2004 for an impromptu debate with Lekson that was dazzling to witness, and spent hours in 2013 explicating for me his theories of Tewa origins. His opponent in that debate, Scott Ortman, also generously and patiently elucidated his own views about that thorny but pivotal problem in the Ancestral Puebloan past. In 2005 and 2006, Renee Barlow eagerly joined Greg Child and me as we hiked, climbed, and rappelled into Fremont ruins that only Waldo Wilcox had known existed.

Other archaeologists also met with me to explain ideas I would otherwise have had trouble fathoming. They include Jody Patterson, Blaine and Pam Miller, Mark Meloy, Tom Windes, Peter McKenna, Victoria Atkins, Ron Maldonado, and Winston Hurst. From a distance, over the phone and via his publications, Jerry Spangler vastly deepened my grasp of the Fremont culture, as did Shannon Boomgarden with respect to Range Creek.

We have the staff of the USU Eastern Prehistoric Museum in Price, Utah, and in particular archaeologist Tim Riley, to thank for keeping the irreplaceable Pilling figurines from vanishing altogether. The first time I saw that magnificent assemblage under glass, it took my breath away—as it still does on every subsequent visit. The same can be said for the Telluride Historical Museum in Telluride, Colorado, which saved the Telluride blanket—the single most astounding artifact I've ever seen from the prehistoric Southwest—by preventing its disappearance into private hands or even some trash dump. Director Erica Kinias was especially helpful in arranging both my own private viewing of the blanket and a subsequent public display during the Mountainfilm Festival. Other crucial players in the preservation of the blanket were Fred Blackburn, Lauren Bloemsma, and Kent Erickson. Bill and Beth Sagstetter not only provided the key to rediscovering the provenience of the blanket, they also wrote the definitive—the only—account of the strange story of that matchless artifact.

I was grateful that Don Simonis, chief archaeologist for the BLM office in Monticello, was willing to meet with me for a long discussion about the Outdoor Museum and the possible impact of my writing, even though I knew that his views differed substantially from mine. And I'm grateful that Scott Edwards and Laura Lantz, who for more than twenty years have been the chief BLM rangers at the Kane Gulch headquarters on Cedar Mesa, have become friends, after a rocky start nineteen years ago when visitors brought *In Search of the Old Ones* into their office, demanding to be told the whereabouts of the goodies I had rhapsodized about in my book.

Several guides have aided and abetted my appreciation of Southwestern wonders. Judith Harvier gave me a spirited tour of Puyé, the lordly butte-top pueblo ancestral to the people of Santa Clara. Kalvin Watchman was a canny and thoughtful informant about the Navajo history of Canyon de Chelly as Dawn Kish and I spent two days being led by him through arcane passages in that sandstone labyrinth. On our raft trip in Desolation Canyon, our guides, Marshall Dvorscak, Brenda Milligan, and Stephanie Berg, not only rowed us safely through the worst of the Green River rapids but spoiled us with luxuries as they cooked and served us delicious food in camp. Arlo Tejada, marketing manager of Sheri Griffith Expeditions, enthusiastically put together the customized trip I had set my heart on.

Escalante old-timer DeLane Griffin, who knew more about Kaiparowits Plateau than anyone alive, not only shared his lore about the Fifty but let me borrow his precious scrapbook of memories of the place where he'd run his cattle for decades. The finest of all my guides was another old-timer, Waldo Wilcox, who heroically preserved Range Creek for half a century, leaving all the "Indian stuff" in place. I consider it a rare privilege to have become Waldo's friend, and to have sat at his knee for many an hour as he unspooled yarns that no one else could have told. We shall not look upon his like again.

The Edge of the Cedars Museum in Blanding, Utah, dazzled me once again with its collection of rare vessels that had been illegally excavated. Though the proveniences of those splendid pots and baskets have for the most part been irretrievably lost, the collection testifies to the genius of ancient potters and weavers whose identities we will never know.

As has been true for most of my books, the incomparable Harvard libraries proved research resources I could scarcely have found anywhere else. Widener Library is one of the great institutions of its kind in the world, but I owe my greatest debt to the Tozzer Library, specializing in anthropology and archaeology. The staffs of both repositories have been unstintingly helpful to me over the years.

Jon Krakauer, Greg Child, and Sharon Roberts read this book in manuscript and offered many useful criticisms and suggestions.

It's been a delight to get to know Starling Lawrence, my editor at W. W. Norton & Company and a legend in the publishing business. This is my second book with Star. I only hope we'll collaborate on many more together. His light touch and shrewd eye gave me just the editorial direction I needed. Star's assistant, Ryan Harrington, blithely performed the countless tasks that turn a manuscript into a book, and saved me from many a sin of omission. Bobby Starnes at Electrographics produced the excellent map that appears after after the table of contents, without which my book might be geographically incomprehensible. Allegra Huston deftly copyedited the text, the second time she's helped me put the finishing touches on what I wrote. Emily Burke provided invaluable assistance as she organized the collection of photographs I chose to illustrate the world of the Old Ones.

Finally, this is the thirteenth book I've published with Stuart Krichevsky as my agent. If there's a better agent anywhere in America, I'd be mightily surprised. Stuart's colleagues Shana Cohen and Ross Harris were there at every hand, reminding me of duties I had absent-mindedly forgotten and expressing a steady enthusiasm for my latest project. My hearty thanks to all three.

Although he had not represented *In Search of the Old Ones*, which came out in 1996, Stuart saw at once why there might be folks out there eager to read a sequel to the single book I had the most fun researching and writing. As always, he knew when to push me to more ambitious heights and when to rein in my more self-indulgent whimsies. By now, I've come to realize how constantly I count on Stuart's support and advice to keep going as a writer. Whether or not a clinician might diagnose my plight as addiction or dependency, it calls for the response I offer here—boundless gratitude.

Bibliography

Dates in brackets indicate date of original publication.

Abbey, Edward. *Desert Solitaire: A Season in the Wilderness.* New York: McGraw-Hill Book Company, 1968.

Adams, William Y., Dennis P. Van Gerven, and Richard S. Levy. "The Retreat from Migrationism." *Annual Review of Anthropology* 7 (1978).

Allen, Steve. *Utah's Canyon Country Place Names.* Two volumes. Durango, CO: Canyon Country Press, 2012.

Aton, James M. *The River Knows Everything: Desolation Canyon and the Green.* Logan, UT: Utah State University Press, 2009.

Barlow, K. Renee. "Farming, Foraging and Remote Storage in Range Creek." Unpublished.

Belknap, Buzz, and Loie Belknap Evans. *Belknap's Waterproof Desolation River Guide.* Evergreen, CO: Westwater Books, 2008.

Bernheimer, Charles L. *Rainbow Bridge: Circling Navajo Mountain and Explorations in The "Badlands" of Southern Utah and Northern Arizona.* Albuquerque: Center for Anthropological Studies, 1999 [1924].

Blackburn, Fred M. *The Wetherills: Friends of Mesa Verde.* Durango, CO: Durango Herald Small Press, 2006.

Blackburn, Fred M., and Ray A. Williamson. *Cowboys and Cave Dwellers: Basketmaker Archaeology in Utah's Grand Gulch.* Santa Fe: School of American Research Press, 1997.

Boomgarden, Shannon Arnold. "An Application of ArcGIS Viewshed Analysis in Range Creek Canyon, Utah." *Utah Archaeology* 22, no. 1 (2009).

Boyer, Jeffrey L., James L. Moore, Steven A. Lakatos, Nancy J. Atkins, C. Dean Wilson, and Eric Blinman. "Remodeling Immigration: A Northern Rio Grande Perspective on Depopulation, Migration, and Donation-Side Models." In Kohler et al., *Leaving Mesa Verde.*

Brew, J. O. *Archaeology of Alkali Ridge, Southeastern Utah.* Cambridge, MA: Papers of the Peabody Museum, 1946.

Cordell, Linda S. *Prehistory of the Southwest.* Orlando, FL: Academic Press, 1984.

Correll, J. Lee. "Navajo Frontiers in Utah and Troublous Times in Monument Valley." *Utah Historical Quarterly* 39, no. 2 (Spring 1971).

Cummings, Byron. *Indians I Have Known.* Tucson: Arizona Silhouettes, 1952.

Fowles, Severin M. *An Archaeology of Doings: Secularism and the Study of Pueblo Religion.* Santa Fe: School for Advanced Research Press, 2012.

———, and Jimmy Arterberry. "Gesture and Performance in Comanche Rock Art." *World Art* 3, no. 1 (2013).

———, Jimmy Arterberry, Heather Atherton, and Lindsay Montgomery. "Comanche New Mexico." Unpublished.

Gay, Robert. *The Marauders.* [n. p.]: Lulu Press, 2009.

Gillmor, Frances, and Louisa Wade Wetherill. *Traders to the Navajos: The Wetherills of Kayenta.* Albuquerque: University of New Mexico Press, 1953 [1934].

Grant, Campbell. *Canyon de Chelly: Its People and Its Rock Art.* Tucson: University of Arizona Press, 1978.

Grey, Zane. *Wild Horse Mesa.* New York: Grosset & Dunlap, 1928.

Griffin, DeLane. Scrapbook about Kaiparowits Plateau. Unpublished.

Gunnerson, James H. *The Fremont Culture: A Study in Culture Dynamics on the Northern Anasazi Frontier.* Salt Lake City: University of Utah Press, 2009 [1969].

Gwynne, S. C. *Empire of the Summer Moon: Quanah Parker and the Rise and Fall of the Comanches, the Most Powerful Indian Tribe in American History.* New York: Scribner, 2010.

Hämäläinen, Pekka. *The Comanche Empire.* New Haven, CT: Yale University Press, 2008.

Hurst, Winston. "The Mysterious Telluride Blanket." *Blue Mountain Shadows* 13 (Summer 1994).

———, and Christy G. Turner II. "Rediscovering the 'Great Discovery': Wetherill's First Cave 7 and Its Record of Basketmaker Violence." In *Anasazi Basketmaker: Papers from the 1990 Wetherill–Grand Gulch Symposium*, edited by Victoria M. Atkins. Salt Lake City: Bureau of Land Management, 1993.

Johnson, Broderick H., ed. *Navajo Stories of the Long Walk Period.* Tsaile, AZ: Navajo Community College Press, 1973.

Kelly, Charles. "Chief Hoskaninni." *Utah Historical Quarterly* 21 (July 1953).

Kent, Kate Peck. *Prehistoric Textiles of the Southwest.* Santa Fe: School of American Research Press, 1983.

———. Untitled ms. about the Telluride blanket. Unpublished.

Kidder, Alfred Vincent. *An Introduction to the Study of Southwestern Archaeology.* New Haven, CT: Yale University Press, 1924.

Kluckhohn, Clyde. *Beyond the Rainbow.* Boston: Christopher Publishing House, 1933.

Kohler, Timothy A., Mark D. Varien, and Aaron M. Wright, eds. *Leaving Mesa Verde: Peril and Change in the Thirteenth-Century Southwest.* Tucson: University of Arizona Press, 2010.

Leake, Harvey, compiler. *Wolfkiller: Wisdom from a Nineteenth-Century Navajo Shepherd.* Salt Lake City: Gibbs Smith, 2007.

Lekson, Stephen H. "Amending the Meridian." *Archaeology* 62, no. 1 (January/February 2009).

———. *The Chaco Meridian: Centers of Political Power in the Ancient Southwest.* Walnut Creek, CA: AltaMira Press, 1999.

———. *A History of the Ancient Southwest.* Santa Fe: School for Advanced Research Press, 2008.

———. "The Idea of the Kiva in Anasazi Archaeology." *Kiva* 53, no. 2 (1988).

———, Curtis P. Nepstad-Thornberry, Brian E. Yunker, Toni S. Laumbach, David P. Cain, and Karl W. Laumbach. "Migrations in the Southwest: Pinnacle Ruin, Southwestern New Mexico." *Kiva* 68, no. 2 (2002).

Liebmann, Matthew. *Revolt: An Archaeological History of Pueblo Resistance and Revitalization in 17th Century New Mexico.* Tucson: University of Arizona Press, 2012.

———. "Signs of Power and Resistance: The (Re)Creation of Christian Imagery and Identities in the Pueblo Revolt Era." In *Archaeologies of the Pueblo Revolt: Identity, Meaning, and Renewal in the Pueblo World,* edited by Robert W. Preucel. Albuquerque: University of New Mexico Press, 2002.

Lipe, William D., and R. G. Matson. "Human Settlement and Resources in the Cedar Mesa Area, SE Utah." In *The Distribution of Prehistoric Population Aggregates: Proceedings of the Southwestern Anthropological Group,* edited by George J. Gumerman. Prescott, AZ: Prescott College Press, 1971.

Lister, Florence C. *Kaiparowits Plateau and Glen Canyon Prehistory: An Interpretation Based on Ceramics.* Salt Lake City: University of Utah Press, 1964.

Madsen, David B. *Exploring the Fremont.* Salt Lake City: Utah Museum of Natural History, 1989.

———, and Steven R. Simms. "The Fremont Complex: A Behavioral Perspective." *Journal of World Prehistory* 12, no. 3 (1998).

Martin, Paul S., and Fred Plog. *The Archaeology of Arizona: A Study of the Southwest Region.* Garden City, NY: Natural History Press, 1973.

McNitt, Frank. *Richard Wetherill: Anasazi: Pioneer Explorer of Southwestern Ruins.* Albuquerque: University of New Mexico Press, 1966 [1957].

McPherson, Robert S. "Murder and Mapping in the 'Land of Death,' Part I: The Walcott–McNally Incident." *Utah Historical Quarterly* 81, no. 3 (Summer 2013).

———. *The Northern Navajo Frontier 1860–1900: Expansion through Adversity.* Albuquerque: University of New Mexico Press, 1988.

———. *Sacred Land, Sacred View: Navajo Perceptions of the Four Corners Region.* Provo, UT: Brigham Young University Press, 1992.

Meloy, Ellen. *Raven's Exile: A Season on the Green River.* Tucson: University of Arizona Press, 1994.

Moore, Lucy. *Into the Canyon: Seven Years in Navajo Country.* Albuquerque: University of New Mexico Press, 2004.

Morss, Noel. *The Ancient Culture of the Fremont River in Utah: Report on the Explorations under the Claflin–Emerson Fund, 1928–29.* Cambridge, MA: Papers of the Peabody Museum, 1931.

———. *Clay Figurines of the American Southwest.* Cambridge, MA: Papers of the Peabody Museum, 1954.

Ortiz, Alfonso. *The Tewa World: Space, Time, Being, and Becoming in a Pueblo Society.* Chicago: University of Chicago Press, 1969.

Ortman, Scott G. *Winds from the North: Tewa Origins and Historical Anthropology.* Salt Lake City: University of Utah Press, 2012.

Pitblado, Bonnie L., Molly Boeka Cannon, Megan Bloxham, Joel Janetski, J. M. Adovasio, Kathleen R. Anderson, and Stephen T. Nelson. "Archaeological Fingerprinting and Fremont Figurines." *Advances in Archaeological Practice* 1, no. 1 (August 2013).

Powell, John Wesley. *The Exploration of the Colorado River and Its Canyons.* Washington, D. C.: Adventure Classics/National Geographic, 2002 [1875].

Rampton, Thomas G. *Desolation and Gray Canyons River Guide.* Nathrop, CO: Blacktail Enterprises, 2003.

"Relics of a Past Age." *Telluride Daily Journal,* August 14, 1896.

Roberts, David. "The Cowboy's Indians." *National Geographic Adventure* 9, no. 2 (March 2007).

———. "Escape from Forbidding Canyon." *Sports Afield* 219, no. 5 (May 1998).

———. "Ghosts of the Wild Horse Mesa." *National Geographic Adventure* 5, no. 2 (March 2003).

———. *In Search of the Old Ones: Exploring the Anasazi World of the Southwest.* New York: Simon & Schuster, 1996.

———. "The Long Walk to Bosque Redondo." *Smithsonian* 28, no. 9 (December 1997).

———. *The Pueblo Revolt: The Secret Rebellion That Drove the Spaniards out of the Southwest.* New York: Simon & Schuster, 2004.

———. *Sandstone Spine: Seeking the Anasazi on the First Traverse of the Comb Ridge.* Seattle: The Mountaineers Books, 2006.

———. "Stephen Lekson Has a Theory . . . And He's Sticking with It." *National Geographic Adventure* 7, no. 2 (March 2005).

———. "To the Center of the World." *National Geographic Adventure* 11, no. 2 (March 2009).

Sagstetter, Beth, and Bill Sagstetter. *The Cliff Dwellings Speak.* Denver: BenchMark Publishing of Colorado, 2010.

———. *Unravelling the Mysteries of the Telluride Blanket.* Privately printed.

Sando, Joe S. *Nee Hemish: A History of Jemez Pueblo.* Albuquerque: University of New Mexico Press, 1982.

Schaafsma, Polly. *Indian Rock Art of the Southwest.* Santa Fe: School of American Research, 1980.

Simms, Steven R. *Traces of Fremont: Society and Rock Art in Ancient Utah.* Salt Lake City: University of Utah Press, 2010.

Spangler, Jerry D. *Nine Mile Canyon: The Archaeology of an American Treasure.* Salt Lake City: University of Utah Press, 2013.

———. "One-Pot Pithouses and Fremont Paradoxes: Formative Stage Adaptations in the Tavaputs Plateau Region of Northeastern Utah." In *Intermountain Archaeology*, edited by David B. Madsen and Michael D. Metcalf. Salt Lake City: University of Utah Anthropological Papers, 2000.

———. "Site Distribution and Settlement Patterns in Lower Nine Mile Canyon: The Brigham Young University Surveys of 1989–91." Master's thesis, Department of Anthropology, Brigham Young University, Provo, UT, 1993.

———, and Kevin T. Jones. *Land of Wildest Desolation: Final Report: The Desolation Canyon Intuitive Surveys and Baseline Site Condition Assessments of 2006 to 2008.* Redacted edition, digital, February 2009.

———, and Donna K. Spangler. *Horned Snakes and Axle Grease: A Roadside Guide to the Archaeology, History and Rock Art of Nine Mile Canyon.* Salt Lake City: Uinta Publishing, 2003.

Steward, Julian H. *Archaeological Problems of the Northern Periphery of the Southwest*. Flagstaff, AZ: Museum of Northern Arizona, 1933.

Windes, Thomas C., and Peter J. McKenna. "The Kivas of Tsama (LA 908)." In *Southwestern Interludes: Papers in Honor of Charlotte J. and Theodore R. Frisbie*, edited by R. M. Wiseman, T. C. O'Laughlin, and C. T. Snow. Albuquerque: Archaeological Society of New Mexico, 2006.

Wyman, Leland C. *Blessingway*. Tucson: University of Arizona Press, 1970.

Index

Abajo Mountains, 100
Abbey, Edward, 7, 274
Acoma, N.Mex., 188, 199, 207
Acoma people, 129
Adair, Kelly, 291
Adams, Melvin, 46
adobe, 22, 51, 134, 136
Africa, 239
   West, 20
Alaska, 268, 295
   glaciers in, 294
   ice climbing in, 117
Albuquerque, N.Mex., 124, 190, 191,
   216, 218, 220
Alexandria library, 59, 66
   burning of, 58
Algonquian language, 15
Alkali Ridge, 53, 68
Allen, Steve, 99, 100, 272
all-terrain vehicles (ATVs), 109, 112,
   238
Altamira cave, 264
Alvey, Edson, 258
"Amending the Meridian" (Lekson),
   148–49
American Museum of Natural
   History, 21, 67, 69
American Revolution, 189
Amerind Foundation, 211–12
Anasazi (Ancestral Puebloans), 3,
   12–17, 20–27, 53, 68, 71, 114–18,
   123–25, 146, 159, 187, 203, 244,
   262
   agriculture of, 29
   art, artifacts, and ruins of, 27–28,
      32, 67, 72–98, 101, 105, 120–22,
      166, 172, 220, 229, 239–40, 242,
      248, 262, 285, 288–302
   egalitarian and autonomous
      nature of, 129, 131
   Fremont compared with, 26–30,
      248
   granaries of, 27, 71–72, 87, 115,
      165, 257, 295
   homeland abandoned by, 23–24,
      29, 124, 154, 157, 162, 165, 188,
      205–6, 219, 223–27
   Hopi descendants of, 162, 165
   intermarriage of Navajos and,
      162–63
   Kayenta, 254
   "magical powers " of, 164–66
   migration of, 29, 223–26, 254
   modern Puebloans as descendants
      of, 29, 126
   multistory masonry dwellings of,
      11–12, 26, 81, 92–95, 116, 118,
      129, 141–42, 257
   Navajos on, 156, 159, 162–63,
      164–67
   oral traditions of, 214
   origins of, 206, 208
   prime territory of, 154
   as a term, 14–16, 26, 214
   villages of, 26, 29, 52, 118, 130
Anasazi Basketry (Morris), 16

Anasazi Heritage Center, 79–80
Ancestral Puebloans, *see* Anasazi
"Ancient Anasazis: What Really
    Happened at Mesa Verde?" (TV
    show), 206
"Ancient Culture of the Fremont
    River in Utah, The" (Morss), 27,
    64
ancient cultures of Southwest, 25–31
    Archaic era of, 26, 29, 55, 61, 114,
        154, 229, 263, 269, 274
    Basketmaker eras I, II, and III of,
        26, 27, 68, 87, 114, 119, 253, 254,
        288
    Pueblo eras I, II, and III of, 26, 27,
        53, 68, 78, 114, 119, 134, 212
    three main groups in, 123–24
    see also specific peoples
Andrews Sisters, 162
Animas-La Plata Project (ALP),
    148–49
Antelope House, 154
antibiotics, 164
Antiquities Act of 1906, 32, 53, 72,
    87, 126
Apache, 15
    Chihenne, 223
    Jicarilla, 229
"Application of ArcGIS Viewshed
    Analysis in Range Creek
    Canyon, Utah, An"
    (Boomgarden), 50
"Archaeological Fingerprinting and
    Fremont Figurines" (Pitblado),
    64, 66
Archaeological Resources
    Protection Act of 1979 (ARPA),
    106
Archaeologies of the Pueblo Revolt
    (Preucel, ed.), 192
archaeology, 112–13, 118, 128–29,
    194, 198, 200, 236, 267, 296
    field, 195
    New, 213–14
    Pan-Egyptian School of, 214

reverse, 67, 70
science of, 213
Archaeology, 148
Archaeology from the Earth
    (Wheeler), 57–58
*Archaeology of Alkali Ridge,
    Southeatern Utah, The* (Brew),
    53, 68
Archaeology of Arizona, The (Martin
    and Plog), 213
Archaeology of Doings, An (Fowles),
    228
Arches National Park, 156
Arizona, 7, 14, 135, 151, 166, 187, 216,
    238, 294
    northeastern, 29, 153, 154
    northern, 254, 257
    south-central, 124
    southern, 130, 181
Arizona, University of, 198
Arizona Highways, 14
Arizona Historical Society, 13
Arizona State University, 208
Ark of the Covenant, 58
Army, U.S., 2, 168–71, 172–74, 235
    Cavalry of, 163
arrowheads, 3, 11, 21, 31, 33, 37, 54,
    120, 296
    obsidian, 41–43
Arrow Point, 120, 122
arroyos, 29
Arterberry, Jimmy, 230–33, 236
artifacts, 54, 112, 120–22, 287–302
    collecting and hoarding of, 3–4,
        32–33, 40, 42–43, 57–90, 194
    damage and destruction of, 58, 60,
        95–96, 98, 220
    display of, 61–64, 66, 67, 74–75, 80,
        105
    excavation of, 30, 40, 128, 231
    left in place, 3–4, 32, 35, 60, 62,
        163, 194, 288–90, 292, 299–302
    looting and stealing of, 63, 67,
        69, 98, 102, 105–7, 113, 188, 197,
        290

photographing of, 288–89, 298, 300
repatriation of, 197
selling of, 62, 67, 73, 80, 120, 197
survival of, 60–61, 300
see also artifacts of specific peoples
Asa Clan, 162
Aspen, Colo., 10
Astialakwa pueblo, 196
Athapaskans, 157
Atkins, Victoria, 78–80
atlatl darts, 120
atlatls (spear-throwers), 29
Aton, James M., 267, 268, 277, 279, 282
Austin, Tex., 211
Australia:
    Aboriginal rock art of, 232
    Cape York peninsula, 232
Automobile Club of Southern California, 153
Autun cathedral, 263
awls, 73, 77
Aztec language, 136
Aztec Ruins National Monument, 145
Aztecs, 130–33, 137–38, 143, 145–47, 151–52, 207, 225–27
    collapse of, 226, 227

Bandelier, Adolf, 136, 188
Bandelier National Monument, 96, 155, 187, 193, 199, 295
Bandiagara escarpment, 20–21
Banff Mountain Film and Book Festival, 291
Banister Ruin, 102
Barboncito, 173
Barlow, Renee, 2, 4–6, 18–20, 24, 31–33, 38, 47–52, 55, 261
    college appointment of, 48–49
    Range Creek granary work of, 40–43, 47–49, 64, 119
    scholarly papers of, 48–49, 50–52
Barnard College, 228

Barrier Canyon, 30, 34
Barrier Canyon style art, 263–64, 269
Basketmaker people, 26, 27, 68, 87, 127
baskets, 42, 61, 106, 144, 220
    construction and design of, 288, 289, 300
    discovery and rediscovery of, 288–90, 292, 299–302
Basque language, 207
Bayfield, Colo., 101
beads, 73, 77, 144
beans, 26, 29, 127, 285
bears, 3, 44, 233, 274
    black, 45, 88–89
    polar, 13
Beef Basin, 110
Beehive ruin, 162
Belknap, Buzz, 274
Bennett, Lee, 71
Berg, Stephanie, 270
Bernheimer Expedition of 1922, 179
Best Forgotten Kiva, 104
Beyond the Rainbow (Kluckhohn), 243–46, 247–48, 250–51
Big Burro Mountains, 139
Bighorn, 46
Big Man Panel, 103
Billings, Harriette, 76–77
birds, 30, 270, 286
Bisbee, Ariz., 181
bison, 29, 35, 45
Blackburn, Fred, 69–70, 72–75, 77–81, 83–86, 89–90, 101–4, 119–20, 206
    Outdoor Museum concept of, 32, 43, 66–67, 101, 113, 289, 290
Black Rock Canyon, 168–69, 302
Blanding, Utah, 17, 21, 46, 67, 82–83, 96–97, 105–6, 113
blankets, 59
    Navajo, 78
    see also Telluride blanket

Blinman, Eric, 21–22, 140–41, 144, 149
  on Chaco Meridian theory, 128, 131, 134, 147, 208, 227
  physical appearance of, 217
  Tewa origin debate of, 211–13, 215–23
Block, Ira, 9
Bloemsma, Lauren, 78, 79–80
Blue Mountain Shadows, 81, 82, 86
Bluff, Utah, 8, 82, 94, 99–100, 109–10, 214, 267
Board of Geographic Names, U.S., 102
Book Cliffs, 110
Bookfinder.com, 246
Book of Mormon, 62
Boomgarden, Shannon, 50, 52
Bosque Redondo, 168, 172, 177, 181
Boston College, 195
Boulder, Colo., 127, 139, 215, 238, 239, 302
Boulder High School, 222
boulins (hardwood sticks), 21
bows and arrows, 21, 29, 230, 232, 264, 284
Boyle, Mike, 265
Bradley, Bruce, 119–21, 190, 226–27
Bradley, George, 278–79
Bremer, Mike, 195
Brew, J. O., 53, 68
Brigham Young University, 284
Brown Palace Hotel, 74
Brushy Flat, 100
Burning Hills, 252
Butler Wash, 21, 70

Caesar, Gaius Julius, 58
cairns, 179–80, 182, 238
California, 281
California, University of, at Berkeley, 147
Cambridge, Mass., 117, 188
Cameron, Catherine, 214
Canada, 234, 253

Alberta, 230, 252
  subarctic, 157
Cañada Alamosa, 223–24
Candelaria ruin, 139
Cannon, Ken, 65
Cannon, Molly, 65, 66
Canyon de Chelly National Monument, 154–56, 159–62, 164, 166–68, 171, 244, 295
  twin gorges of, 156, 160
  visitors to, 160–61
Canyon del Muerto, 160, 166–68
Canyonlands National Park, 116, 156, 264
  Maze district of, 294
Canyon of Lodore, 279
Capitol Reef National Park, 238
Carleton, James H., 168, 173
Carrizo, N.Mex., 188
Carson, Kit, 168–69, 173, 181
  Navajo Roundup of, 173, 180
Carter, Howard, 58
Casas Grandes, 135
Cassidy, Butch, 43–44
Castle Valley, Utah, 84–85
catechresis, 199–200
cattle, 39, 45, 46, 59, 70–71, 73, 80, 99–100, 109, 238, 240, 242–45, 255–57, 265, 270–71, 282
  longhorn, 99
Cave 11, 102
caves, 71–73, 88–90, 154, 171
Cave 7, 67–69, 102
  prehistoric massacre in, 67–68
Cedar Mesa, 7–11, 18, 32, 58, 69, 86, 91–122, 172, 239–41, 267
  abandonment of, 119
  access to, 93
  artifacts, ruins and rock art on, 92–105, 116–21, 289–302
  Bullet Canyon on, 99–100, 294
  buttes of, 119–22
  cultural and environmental threats to, 105, 108–11
  early populations of, 114

Government Trail to, 9
guarding and policing of, 105–7, 111
Jailhouse Ruin on, 102–3, 294–95
national monument status considered for, 107–9, 111, 113
old-growth forest in, 110–11
Perfect Kiva on, 103, 294–95
place names on, 99–103
ranching on, 99–101, 109
survey work on, 114
vandalism on, 95–96, 98, 113
visitors to, 93–95, 104–5, 111
see also Citadel; Grand Gulch: Kane Gulch; Moon House
Cedar Ridge, 100
Cedar Ridge Canyon, 274
Ceremonial Cave, 154
Cerro Moctezuma, 135–37
atalaya on, 136, 137, 152
massive wall on, 136–37
Chaco, 129–35, 138–52, 218–19, 227
collapse of, 130, 131, 145, 219, 226
Great Houses of, 29, 53, 107, 129–30, 131, 134, 138–39, 141–42, 143, 149, 151
road system of, 117, 130, 139, 142
Chaco Canyon, 117, 129–35, 142, 143, 149, 209, 210
Chaco Culture National Historical Park, 107
Chaco Meridian, The (Lekson), 125, 128–29, 131–32, 140, 144, 147–49, 227
Chaco Meridian theory, 125, 128–29, 131–34, 138–40, 144, 147–52, 203
debate on, 134, 140, 208, 227
revision of, 147–51
three great centers in, 131–33, 147, 152
Chaco Project, 143
Chaco Wash, 129
Chama River, 220
Chandler Creek, 35

Chapoose, Betsy, 114
cheat grass, 29
Cherokee, 154
chert flakes, 3, 8, 11, 33, 40, 54, 119, 120, 245, 288, 291–92, 295
Chetro Ketl, 53, 143
Chicago, Ill., 69, 120
chicken pox, 257
Chihenne Apache, 223
Chihuahua, Mexico, 14, 152
Child, Ariann, 85, 291–93, 297–99, 302
photographs by, 298, 300
Child, Greg, 4–7, 17, 25, 34, 36, 38–45, 47–48, 51, 85, 103, 115, 186, 266–68, 277, 285, 290–93, 296–301
hiking and climbing of, 2, 6–7, 18–23, 32, 38–39, 41–43, 54–55, 64, 172, 174–75, 179–80, 182–84, 283, 293
Chimney Rock, 142, 151
Chinle, Ariz., 160, 167
Chinle Wash, 155, 157–58, 160, 163, 167
Chipewyan tribe, 157
cholla, 96
Christensen, Norm, 258
Christianity, 124
conversion to, 210
see also specific sects
Church of Jesus Christ of Latter-day Saints (LDS), 62
Archives of, 13
see also Mormons
Chuska Mountains, 143, 160
Citadel, 92–95, 108, 113
Ciudad Juarez, Mexico, 148
Civil War, U.S., 278
battles of, 241
Clark, Sharon, 77
Clear Creek Canyon, 262
cliff dwellings, 26, 68, 73, 81, 82, 92–96, 101, 118–19, 166, 247–48, 262, 277

climate change, 110
Clinton, Bill, 107–8, 238, 251
Cluny cathedral, 263
coal, 251
Coats, Larry, 50
Cochise, 13
Cochiti, N.Mex., 188, 218
Cochiti people, 195–96
Cochiti Pueblo, 207
Cody, Wyo., 270
College of Eastern Utah (CEU)
    Prehistoric Museum, 48–49,
    63–64, 66
Collins Spring, 99, 104
Colorado, 7, 30, 270, 271, 278
    Alamosa area of, 210
    northern, 234
    northwestern, 28, 29, 124
    southern, 157, 210
    southwestern, 68, 118, 124, 208
Colorado, University of (CU), 27, 30,
    52–53, 127, 151, 215
Colorado Plateau, 7, 13, 15, 16, 26,
    28, 68, 115, 130, 188, 205–6, 218,
    224–25, 227
Colorado Plateau Archaeological
    Alliance (CPAA), 30, 268, 269,
    283
Colorado River, 10, 26, 28, 239, 244,
    249, 274
    first descent of, 241, 279
    rafting on, 79, 266, 278, 280
    Separation Rapid in, 279
    Steer Ridge Rapid in, 279
Colorado State Mental Hospital, 71
Columbus, Christopher, 195
Columbus, N.Mex., 133
Comanche, 14, 15
    guns of, 230
    horses of, 230, 234
    long-distance trade of, 234
    raids and battles of, 232–34, 235
    rock art of, 227–35
Comanche Empire, The
    (Hämäläinen), 234–35

Comanche Nation Tribal Historic
    Preservation Office, 230
"Comanche New Mexico" (Fowles et
    al, eds.), 235–36
Comb Ridge, 17, 109, 267, 291
Comb Wash, 97
Congress, U.S., 250
Conquérants de l'Inutile, Les
    (Conquistadors of the Useless)
    (Terray), 296
conservationists, 102
Copper Canyon, 147
Cordell, Linda, 7, 124, 125, 214, 224
corn (maize), 19, 23, 26, 28, 29, 34,
    47, 51, 127, 169, 172–73, 186, 199,
    277, 285
    cultivation of, 61, 143, 156, 263,
    285, 286
    dating of, 224
    grinding of, 3, 27, 32, 34, 37,
    41–42, 136, 247
    hiding of, 42, 115
    stealing of, 115
    storage of, see granaries
Cornell University, 128
Coronado, Francisco Vázquez de,
    124, 189
Cortez, Colo., 52, 74, 125, 164, 208,
    211, 214, 226
Cosmos (TV series), 128
cotton, 73, 76
cougars, 37, 44
Cove, Ariz., 164
Cowboy Cache, 272
Cowboys and Cave Dwellers
    (Blackburn and Williamson), 70
coyotes, 253
Cradle M Ranch, 265, 269, 281–82
crampons, 117
Crazy Horse, 182
creation myth, 126, 157, 174
Crow Canyon Archaeological Center,
    125, 208, 211–12, 215, 220
Cuerno Verde (Tabivo Naritgant),
    235

Culiacán, 147–48
Cummings Mesa, 183, 243
Cunepah, Chief, 277
Curry, Flatnose George, 44
Curtis, Edward, 158
Cushing, Frank, 188, 198

Dante Alighieri, 240
Dark Canyon, 110
Darwin, Charles, 223
Davis Gulch, 13, 239
Day, Sam, 162
Dean, Jeffrey, 198
deer, 44
deer mice, 19
Denver, Colo., 70, 74
Department of Resource Protection
    (DRP), 196
Depression, 251
Desert Solitaire (Abbey), 7, 274
Desolation Canyon, 264–86, 295
    aborted dam projects in, 271
    ruins and rock art in, 268, 269,
        273, 275, 283–86
    spring storms in, 275–77, 280
    survey work in, 267–68, 283, 285
Desolation River Guide (Belknap),
    274
Devil's Gate (Roberts), 13
Dickey, Mount, 294
Diggers (TV show), 231
Dilly, Tom, 43
Dilly Canyon, 38–39
Dilly's Spring, 43
Diné people, 15, 156–57, 159, 164–72,
    216, 249
    see also Navajos
Dinétah canyons, 188
Dink (dog), 36–37, 38–39
Dinosaur National Monument, 28,
    30
Di Peso, Charles, 135–36
Dittert Site, 138
Dixon, N.Mex., 228
DNA, 106

dogbane, 20
Dogrib tribe, 157
dogs, 36–37, 112–13, 158, 256, 257,
    282, 284
Dolores, Colo., 79
Douglas Creek, 29, 124
Dragoon, Ariz., 211
Draper, Teddy, Sr., 170
drought, 23, 29, 110, 115, 156, 162,
    209–10, 224–26
    Great, 225–26
Dry Rock Creek, 240
Duck Ruins, 158
Dunn, William, 279
Durango, Colo., 67, 101, 120, 148
Dvorscak, Marshall, 270–73, 275–76,
    280

Eastern New Mexico University, 191
"eccentrics," 120
Edge of Cedars Museum, 21, 82, 106
Edwards, Scott, 106–7
Egypt, 214
    pharaonic tombs in, 58
El Capitan Mountain, 6
elk, 44
Elk Ridge, 110
Ellis, Florence Hawley, 145, 220–21
El Malpais National Monument, 138
El Paso, Tex., 188
El Pueblito, 136, 137
Ely, Nev., 48
Emma Dean, 279
Empire of the Summer Moon
    (Gwynne), 234–35
encomienda, 199
"Encounters with the Unexplained"
    (TV series), 206
England, 209
Erickson, Kent, 80
Escalante, Utah, 238, 239, 242, 255,
    260
    population of, 251
Escalante canyons, 116, 238, 239, 241,
    249, 295

Escalante River, 107–8, 238
Eskimos, 15
Ethiopia, 265
European art, 263–64
    in caves, 264
    in churches, 263
    as frescoes, 263
    Gothic, 263
    Paleolithic, 264
    Romanesque, 263
Everest, Mount, 6
"Evidence of a Mesa Verde Homeland
    for the Tewa Pueblos" (Ortman),
    212
Exploring the Fremont (Madsen), 28
Exporation of the Colorado River and
    Its Canyons, The (Powell), 279
extraterrestrial aliens, 206
Eyraud, Eugene, 281

fabric, 61
famine, 23, 29, 115, 172–73
"Farming, Foraging and Remote
    Storage in Range Creek"
    (Barlow), 50–52
Farmington, N.Mex., 159, 216
Far Out Expeditions, 94
FBI Panel, 103
Federal Bureau of Investigation
    (FBI), 105
fertility rituals, 65
Fewkes, Jesse Walter, 162–63, 188,
    198
Field Museum, 69, 120
figurines:
    Basketmaker, 27
    clay, 27, 59–66
    female, 60–61, 66, 264
    male, 60, 63
    painted, 59, 63, 64
    Pilling, 59–66
    see also humanoid figures
Finnish language, 207–8
fire-starting kits, 288, 299
Firewater Canyon, 276

Fisher Valley, 46
Flagstaff, Ariz., 124, 157
Flaming Gorge Reservoir, 271
flash floods, 107, 184
Flat Canyon, 277–78
Florence Creek, 43, 45, 265, 282, 285
foods, 45
    dwindling supplies of, 118
    farmed, 26, 28, 29–30
    Mexican, 133
    storage of, 50, 285
    wild, 29, 50
Ford, Harrison, 58
Ford, John, 234
Ford, Walter, 100
forest fires, 240
Fortress, 31, 38, 43, 49
Four Against the Arctic (Roberts), 13
Fowles, Severin, 227–36
    academic career of, 228
    works of, 228, 231–32, 235–36
France, 281
    Ardèche region of, 264
    empire of, 234
Franciscan friars, 189, 192, 193, 199,
    200
Freeman, Katie, 152
"Fremont Complex, The: A
    Behavioral Perspective" (Madsen
    and Simms), 28
Fremont people, 3–6, 14, 25–31, 46,
    49–52, 60, 123, 124–25, 254,
    261–64, 295, 297
    agricultural crops of, 26, 28,
    29–30, 41–43, 286
    Anasazi compared with, 26–30, 248
    ancestors of, 28–29, 30
    art and artifacts of, 3, 26, 30, 35,
    54, 64–65, 248, 262–63, 269, 273,
    275, 277–78, 283–86
    burial and graves of, 3, 34, 35
    corn as staple of, 19, 23, 28, 29, 34
    granaries of, 3, 5–7, 18–24, 27, 31,
    37, 39, 41–42, 50–52, 261, 262,
    274, 283, 284–85

pithouses of, 3, 26, 283, 285
as a term, 27, 28
theories on the fate of, 29–30,
33–34, 38, 124, 262
vertical engineering of, 22–23, 37,
38, 41, 51–52
villages abandoned by, 3, 23–24,
29
villages of, 262
Fremont River, 26–27
Friends of Cedar Mesa, 111
Frost, Kent, 104
Frost, Robert, 93

galaxies, 175, 215
Galisteo Basin, 187
Gallinas Springs ruin, 224
Gallup, N.Mex., 14, 124
game animals, 29, 44, 176
extinction of, 23, 29, 115
Gamow, George, 215
Garden of Eden, 210
Gauthier, Rory, 193
Gay, Robert, 11–12
Georgetown, Colo., 82
Gerbett, David, 110
Germany, 62
Geronimo, 182
"Gesture and Performance in
Comanche Rock Art" (Fowles
and Arterberry), 231
Gibbon, Edward, 58
Gila Wilderness, 138
Glen Canyon, 251, 253, 274
Global Positioning System (GPS), 11,
32, 40, 50, 95, 97–98, 112, 202
Globe, Ariz., 181
Gobernador Canyon, 188
Google, 112, 228
Gore Range, 271
graffiti, 34, 35, 87, 88, 102, 170, 185,
229, 230, 233, 248–49, 254,
258–59, 264
Graham, Charles Cary, 101, 102, 120
granaries, 32, 47–52, 104, 121, 247

Anasazi, 27, 71–72, 87, 115, 165,
257, 295
Fremont, 3, 5–7, 11, 18–24, 27, 31,
37, 39, 41–42, 50–52, 261–62,
274, 283–85
front-loading vs. top-loading, 27,
87
hidden, 6–7, 18–24, 31–32, 41, 48,
50–51, 115, 118–19, 297
see also Waldo's Catwalk
Gran Chichimeca, 135
Grand Canyon, 40, 156, 241, 250, 251,
265, 266, 279
Grand Gulch, 9–10, 14, 32, 99–102,
103–4, 295
Grand Junction, Colo., 10, 70, 77
Grand Staircase-Escalante National
Monument, 107, 238, 251
Grants, N.Mex., 140, 208
Great Basin, The: People and Place
in Ancient Times (Fowler and
Fowler, eds.), 49
Great Gallery, 103
Great Hunt Panel, 262–63
Great North Road, 139, 142
Great Plains, 29
Green Mask Panel, 103
Green River, 2, 3, 31, 34, 35, 37,
44–45, 54, 70, 265, 267–73, 278,
282
Coal Creek Rapid on, 275
Jack's Rock in, 282
Joe Hutch Canyon Rapid on, 275
rafting on, 270–76
rapids in, 275, 282
sources of, 271
Three Fords in, 282
Green River, Utah, 265, 282
Greenwich, England, 130
Gregory, Herbert, 244, 254–55
Gregory, John H., 302
Gregory Canyon, 302
Grey, Zane, 241–42, 243, 257, 259–60
Griffin, DeLane, 255–57, 259–60
scrapbook of, 255–56

Griffin, Quinn, 255
Griffith, Sheri, 266, 267, 268
Grotte Chauvet, 264
Guadalupe Mesa, 202
Guadalupe River, 194
Gulch canyon, 238
guns, 230
Gwynne, S. C., 234–35

Hadenfeldt, Marcia, 98
Hadenfeldt, Vaughn, 9, 13, 16–17, 21,
    94, 96–98, 103, 109–11, 290–91,
    296–97
  on Anasazi, 16, 88, 96
hair, 20, 61, 293
Hale, Matt, 115, 267, 283, 290–91,
    293, 299–300
Hämäläinen, Pekka, 234–35
Hampshire College, 294
hand-and-toe trails, 116–18, 158, 164,
    167
Hanks, Jim, 244
hantavirus, 19
Hardscrabble Canyon, 103
Harris, Llewellyn, 257–59
Harris Wash, 238
Harvard University, 60, 128, 193–94,
    195, 243
  archaeological digs of, 26, 53
  Tozzer Library of, 117
  Widener Library of, 246
Harveys Fear Cliff, 240
Harvier, Judith, 209–10
Hatcher, Bill, 133, 135, 137–39, 151–
    52, 203
Hat Flat, 103
Hayden Survey Report, 82
Hell's Half Acre, 100
Henry Mountains, 241, 249
Herbert, George, 298
Hesperus Mountain, 157
Hewett, Edgar Lee, 53, 126, 209
hex symbols, 295
Higgs, Peter, 223
Higgs boson, 223

Himalaya Mountains, 294
Hisatsinom people, 15, 16
History of the Ancient Southwest, A
    (Lekson), 53, 150, 214, 225–26
hogans, 158, 175–76, 178, 182, 184,
    186, 243
  abandonment of, 159, 163
  destruction of, 168
Hohokam culture, 14, 26, 124–25,
    226
Hole-in-the-Rock expedition, 100
Hole-in-the-Rock Gang, 43
Hole-in-the-Rock Road, 237, 239, 244
Holy Grail, 58
Hoover, Herbert, 156
Hopi, 15, 29, 55, 126–27, 129, 206,
    207, 219, 257–58, 273, 301
  Anasazi as ancestors of, 162, 165,
    208
  creation myth of, 126
  kivas of, 126, 209
Hopi, Ariz., 188, 224
Hopi Reservation, 15
Horned Snakes and Axle Grease
    (Spangler and Spangler), 262–63
Horse Canyon, 238
horses, 239, 240, 243, 244, 257
  rustling of, 277
  Spanish introduction of, 200, 230
  wild, 230, 233, 241–42, 258,
    259–60
Hoskinini, 173–74, 176–78, 180–86,
    267
  death of, 181
  nicknames of, 177, 178, 182
Hoskinini-begay, 176–78, 181, 185
Hosteen Dogi ("Mister Moustache"),
    244–45
Hotel Hacienda, 133
Hotel Utah, 271
houseboats, 243
Hovenweep National Monument,
    155
Howland, O. G., 279
Howland, Seneca, 279

Hoyle, Fred, 215
Huerfano Butte, 142, 151–52
humanoid figures, 35, 64–65, 103,
    232, 269
  heads of, 263
  lizard-like, 30, 139, 201, 262
  trapezoidal, 27–28, 59, 262
  yei'bi'cheis, 158–59
hunter-gatherers, 3, 20, 29, 30, 114,
    234, 254
Huntington, Mount, 294
Hurst, Winston, 21, 67, 70, 81–84, 86,
    96–97, 108, 290

"Idea of the Kiva in Anasazi
    Archaeology, The" (Lekson),
    125–26, 127, 142
Inca, 195, 281
increase cults, 61, 65
Indian Creek, 116
indios bárbaros, 15, 124
indios pueblo, 15, 124
infections, 164
In Search of the Old Ones (Roberts),
    7–9, 11–15, 27, 66, 84, 93, 101,
    111–12, 120, 125, 132, 147–48,
    190, 206, 226, 289
  "Exploring the Anasazi World of
    the Southwest" subtitle of, 14
  "In Praise of Cedar Mesa" chapter
    in, 7, 91–92, 95
  "The Outdoor Museum" chapter
    of, 32
Instituto Nacional de Antropologica
    y Historia (INAH), 135
Interior Department, U.S., 10, 162
Internet, 11, 12, 93, 95, 103
  e-bay on, 105
  e-mail on, 97, 108–9, 190, 227–28
*Introduction to the Study of
    Southwestern Archaeology, An*
    (Kidder), 26
Inuit, 15
iPads, 202
Ireland, 209

Isleta Pueblo, 188, 207
Italy, 58

jacal construction, 92, 102, 103
Jackson, William H., 82
Japan, 2, 62
Jeançon, Jean, 208–9
Jeffords, Tom, 13
Jemez Cultural Committee, 190,
    191–92, 195, 196–97
Jemez Mountains, 207
Jemez people, 190–200, 208, 209
Jemez Pueblo, N.Mex., 190–91, 193,
    194–98, 199–200, 207
Jemez River, 190, 191, 194
Jemez Springs, N.Mex., 201
Jenkins, Leigh, *see* Kuwanwisiwma,
    Leigh
Jesus Christ, 193
  golden statue of, 258, 259, 260
Jicarilla Apache, 229
Jones, Kevin, 31, 48, 268
Judd, Neil, 26, 60

K2 Mountain, 6
kachina masks, 128, 162–63, 193, 199,
    201–4, 216, 227
Kachina Phenomenon, 202, 216,
    226–27
Kaiparowits Plateau, 237–60
  Blondie Knoll on, 249
  coal deposits on, 251
  Collett Top on, 253
  Cougar Knoll on, 260
  Croton Road on, 251–52
  Fifty Mile Bench on, 237
  as Fiftymile Mountain ("the
    Fifty"), 239, 242, 248, 251–52,
    255–56, 258
  Kayenta Anasazi settlement on,
    254
  Lake Trail on, 259
  Lower Trail on, 237–38, 240, 246,
    257
  Navajo Point on, 242–43, 244

Kaiparowits Plateau (*continued*)
  Straight Cliffs of, 244, 251, 257, 258
  surveys of, 253–55
  as Wild Horse Mesa, 241–42, 244–46, 249–50, 259
Kanab Plateau, 279
Kane Gulch, 9, 104, 107, 111, 290
Kansas, 228
kaolin, 92
Kayenta, Ariz., 17
Keet Seel, 26, 262
Kelly, Charles, 176
Kent, Kate Peck, 77–78
Keresan pueblos, 218, 219, 224
Keres language, 207
Kerr, Andrew, 106
Kettle Country, 179, 182, 185
Kewa Pueblo, 207
Khatibi, Mehrdad, 196–97
Kidder, Alfred V., 14, 26, 53, 68, 73, 198
King, Wilson, 164
Kingdom of the Crystal Skull, The (film), 58
Kinias, Erica, 75–76
Kin Ya'a, 139
Kiowa people, 207
Kiowa-Tanoan languages, 207, 221
Kish, Dawn, 155, 158, 160, 162, 171
Kiva, 125–26
kivas, 13, 103, 104, 125–27, 133, 142, 146–47, 149, 210, 248, 254
  Anasazi, 126–27
  Hopi, 126, 209
  "keyhole," 218
  Mesa Verde, 218
  purported religious function of, 126–27, 150, 209
  Rio Grande, 218
  standard features of, 126
"Kivas of the Tsama, The" (Windes and McKenna), 13, 220
Kluckhohn, Clyde, 243–48, 250–51, 259

"Filthy Five" friends of, 244–49, 254, 257
Knipmeyer, James, 99
Kutchin tribe, 157
Kutz Canyon herradura, 145
Kuwanwisiwma, Leigh, 206

La Bajada escarpment, 201, 216
La Bajada-Velarde surge, 218
Laboratory of Tree-Ring Research, 51
Labyrinth Canyon, 271
La Cienega, N.Mex., 201
ladders, 37, 38, 51–52, 101, 116, 121, 126, 169
Laguna Pueblo, 207
Lake Canyon, 256, 257
Lake of Copala, 221
Lake Trail, 259
Lakota people, 195
"Land of Wildest Desolation" (Spangler and Jones), 268
Lantz, Laura, 107
Laquey, Keith, 78–79
Largo Canyon, 188
Lascaux cave, 264
Last Crusade, The (film), 58
Las Vegas, Nev., 14
Las Vegas, N.Mex., 14
Latin America, 61–62
Laughing Lizard Inn, 201
Laumbach, Karl, 223–24
Lawton, Okla., 230
Leaving Mesa Verde: Peril and Change in the Thirteenth-Century Southwest (Kohler et al, eds.), 212
LeCompte, Charley, 267, 274
Lekson, Steve, 118–19, 125–32, 134–52, 203, 207, 214, 227–28
  academic career of, 27, 127, 151
  Anasazi migration theory of, 223–26, 227
  criticism of, 132, 150
  personality of, 139, 141
  physical appearance of, 140–41

works of, 53, 125–26, 128–29,
    131–32, 140, 142, 144, 147–50,
    209, 214, 225–26, 227
Liebmann, Maria, 201, 203
Liebmann, Matthew, 192–203, 209
    academic career of, 193–95
    works of, 192, 194, 198–99
Liebmann, Stella, 201–3
Lincoln, Nebr., 65
Lipe, Bill, 114, 118, 119
Lister, Florence, 254, 257
lithics, 119, 121–22
Little Colorado River, 199
Little Death Hollow, 238
"Little People," 33–34, 35, 46
Lizard Head Pass, 75
lizards, 165
llama treks, 9, 104, 267, 295
Llewellyn Canyon, 259
Llewellyn Gulch, 259
Lobo Canyon, 139
Locomotive Rock, 42
Logan, Utah, 65
Long Flat, 100
Longs Peak, 278
Loosle, Byron, 49
Los Alamos, N.Mex., 209
Los Angeles, Calif., 251
Los Ojos Saloon, 201
Lowry, Colo., 118
Lucero, Tom, 197
Lukachukai Mountains, 143, 164
Lyman, Albert R., 100

Madsen, David B., 26, 28, 30
Mahon, Carl, 103–4
Maine, 70
Mali, 20
Malville, Kim, 151
Mancos, Colo., 21, 67, 101, 157, 181
Mangas Coloradas, 223
Mangus Mountains, 139
manos, 3, 27, 136
Mansfield, John, 83
Mansfield, Susie, 83

Mantle's Cave, 30
Manuelito, 173
Marauders, The (Gay), 11–12, 14
Martin, Paul S., 213
Massingale, Connie, 84–86
Matheny, Ray, 284
May, Albert, 46–47
Maya, 195
McKee Springs Wash, 28, 30
McKenna, Peter, 145, 220
McKonkie Ranch, 28, 30, 262
McLoyd, Charles, 68, 101, 102, 120
McNitt, Frank, 16, 69
McPherson, Fern, 35
McPherson, Jim, 43, 281–82
McPherson, Robert S., 164–65
Meloy, Ellen, 267, 268, 276
Meloy, Mark, 267, 272
Mendel, Gregor Johann, 223
Mera, H. P., 223
Merrick, Charles, 180–81
Mesa Verde, 12, 18, 124, 145, 155,
    208–10, 214–15, 218–19, 221–25,
    244
    artifacts of, 68, 86, 96, 227
    cliff dwellings of, 93, 118
    Cliff Palace on, 7, 26, 118, 244,
        245, 250, 260
    Spruce Tree House on, 118, 244,
        250
Mesa Verde Museum, 73
Mesa Verde National Park, 7, 73–74,
    250
Metal detectors, 231
metates (corn grinders), 3, 32, 34, 37,
    136, 247
    Utah-style, 27, 41–42
Metcalfe, Duncan, 31–34, 39–40,
    47–49, 52, 60, 106
Mexican War of 1916, 133
Mexico, 14, 61, 133–37, 143, 207, 295
    central, 147–48
    Chihuahua state, 14, 124, 130, 133,
        135
    northern, 134, 234

Mexico (*continued*)
  ruins in, 134–37
  Sonora state, 124
  U.S. border with, 133, 134
Mexico City, 135
middens, 97
Middle Mesa (Peninsula), 167, 172
Middle Trail, 258
Milky Way, 175
Miller, Blaine, 62–63, 65
Milligan, Brenda, 270, 272, 275–76,
  282
Mimbres people, 138, 226
  architecture of, 224
  pottery of, 262, 301
Mineral Mountains, 43
Mississippi, 61
Missouri River, 207
Mitchell, Robert, 180–81
Moab, Utah, 10, 14, 124, 266, 267,
  269, 291
"Moab Treehouse, The" (Roberts),
  10
moccasins, 27, 41
Mogollon Mountains, 138
Mogollon people, 14, 26, 123–25, 131,
  187, 224, 295, 297, 301
Mongolia, 239, 243
Montezuma Creek, 214
Montezuma Valley, 118, 208
Monticello, Utah, 9, 111–12, 120
Montrose, Colo., 71
Monument Valley, 110, 173, 181
moon, 165, 184, 193, 297
  rising of, 151, 253, 301
Moon House, 11–12, 26, 92–95
  access to, 93, 108, 113
  jacal construction of, 92
  rooms of, 92, 102
  visitors to, 93–95, 111
moonshine whiskey, 277
Moore, Terry, 86
Moqui, *see* Anasazi
Moqui Canyon, 257
Moqui steps, 116, 117

Morgan, Bob, 31
Mormons, 13, 62, 100, 108, 239, 241,
  244, 245, 255, 262, 279
  graffiti of, 248–49
  missionary work of, 257–59
Mormon Trail, 13
Morris, Ben, 276–77
Morris, Earl, 16, 145–46, 179
Morss, Noel, 26–28, 60–61, 63–66
mortar and pestle, 136
Mountainfilm festival, 74
mountain lions, 3, 36–37, 44
Muddy River, 26
Muley Point, 100
mummies, 67, 101, 105
Mummy Cave, 154
Musée de l'Homme, 264
Museum of Archaeology, 66
Museum of New Mexico (MNM),
  211, 216
  Office of Archaeological Studies
  at, 208
Museum of the American Indian, 67
"Mysterious Telluride Blanket, The"
  (Hurst), 81–82, 86

Nahuatl, 136
Nambé Pueblo, 207
Napoleon I, Emperor of France, 95
Narbona panel, 154
National Forest Service (NFS), 107,
  110, 112
National Geographic, 4, 9–10, 14, 21,
  95
National Geographic Adventure, 4,
  133
National Geographic Channel, 231
National Outdoor Leadership School
  (NOLS), 111
National Parks, 7
National Park Service (NPS), 7, 11,
  12, 16, 18, 73
Native American Graves Protection
  and Repatriation Act
  (NAGPRA), 197

Native Americans, 3–5, 14–16, 233
  Arctic, 15
  kinship of ancient peoples and, 29, 113, 124–25
  oral tradition of, 162–63, 169–71, 173–74, 177, 190, 198, 209, 210, 227, 236, 248
  religion of, 227
  religious subjugation of, 15, 124, 189, 192–93, 202, 257
  sacred artifacts repatriated by, 197
  tribute demanded of, 199
  U.S. campaigns against, 163, 167–71, 235
  see also specific tribes
Navajo code talkers, 158
Navajo Fortress Rock (Tsélaa'), 167–71, 173
Navajo language, 14, 15, 160, 167, 175
Navajo Mountain (Naatsis'áán), 174–75, 177, 179, 182, 241, 243, 244, 249–50
Navajo Nation:
  headquarters of, 154
  visitor permits issued by, 154, 174
Navajo Reservation, 138, 139, 153–86, 294, 295
  Anasazi sites on, 285
  size and population of, 154
Navajos, 15, 46, 110, 153–86, 214, 243–45, 257–58
  agriculture of, 216
  on Anasazi, 156, 159, 162–63, 164–67
  animal-skin clothing of, 169
  blankets and jewelry of, 78, 161, 178
  homeland of, 216
  horses and mules of, 244
  illness and starvation of, 172–73
  Long Walk of, 168, 170, 172, 185
  Nightway healing ceremony of, 159
  oral history of, 162–63, 169–71, 173–74, 177, 248
  origins of, 157
  privacy rights of, 154
  religious beliefs of, 156, 157, 159, 163–65, 174, 176
  sheepherding of, 172, 173, 177, 185
  smoke signals of, 245
  southern migration of, 159
  U.S. campaign of 1863–64 against, 163, 168–71, 172–74
  see also Diné people
Navajo Stories of the Long Walk Period (Draper), 170
Navajo Trail, 258
Neboyia, Chauncey, 158
Nebraska, University of, 65
Nee Hemish (Sando), 191
Nefertiti Canyon, 34–35
Nepal, 58
Nevada, 4
New Age beliefs, 97, 131, 206, 284
New Guinea, 265
"New Light on the Thirteenth-Century Depopulation of the Northern Southwest" symposium, 211–12
New Mexico, 4, 7, 14, 58, 62, 124, 126, 157, 166, 168, 187–94, 203, 216, 228, 243
  northern, 53, 200
  northwestern, 154, 216
  southern, 224
  Spanish conquest of, 199, 234
  Spanish driven out of, 189–92, 199
  western, 129, 157
New Mexico, University of, 53, 191, 220
New Year's Canyon, 34–35
New York, 62, 270
New York, N. Y., 228, 239, 246, 251
Niaux cave, 264
Nielson, DeReese, 99, 100
Nightway healing ceremony, 159
Nine Mile Canyon, 30, 31, 262–63, 270, 278, 284

Nine Mile Canyon: The Archaeological History of an American Treasure (Spangler), 284, 285–86

nomads, 29, 30, 55, 114, 124, 207, 228

North America, 231, 234
  arrival of Europeans in, 17, 30
  Great Basin area of, 28, 43
  Great Plains of, 29
  western, 28

Northwest Passage, 179

Northwest Territory, 157

Nova (TV series), 222

Nuevo Casas Grandes, Mexico, 133

Numic peoples, 29

Nusbaum, Jesse, 73–74

Nutter, Preston, 270–71

Nutter, Virginia, 271

Nutters Hole, 270

obsidian flakes, 119

O'Donoghue, Shannon, 291–93

Ohkay Owingeh Pueblo, 189, 207, 227

oil and gas deposits, 238, 263

Ojo Caliente spring, 223

Oklahoma, 228, 277

Old Kotyiti, 195, 196

"Old Ones of the Southwest, The" (Roberts), 9–10

Oliver, Geneve Howard, 60, 61

Oljato, Utah, 181

olla (water jar), 73, 80

Omar, Caliph, 58

Oñate, Don Juan de, 189, 199, 201, 210, 216

Ondra, Adam, 296

"One Pot-Pithouses and Fremont Paradoxes" (Spangler), 13, 286

Ophir, Colo., 75

Oraibi, 126

Orchard, Frederick, 60

Ortiz, Alfonso, 206

Ortman, Scott, 208, 209, 212–13, 215, 216–23

  Tewa thesis of, 220–23
  works of, 212, 217, 218, 228

Ouray, Colo., 269

Outdoor Museum, 32, 43, 66–67, 101, 113, 289, 290

Outlook of Desolation arch, 274

Outward Bound, 111

Owl Canyon, 100

Ozymandias statue, 96

Pachak, Joe, 83

Page, Ariz., 8, 12, 251

Pagosa Springs, Colo., 12, 151

Paiute language, 241

Paiutes, 29
  Shivwits, 279

Panguitch, Utah, 12, 242, 260

papyrus scrolls, 58, 59, 66

Paquimé, 130–37, 141, 143, 149–50, 152, 227
  architecture of, 133–34
  demise of, 147
  Mound of the Cross at, 134, 146
  Mound of the Heroes at, 146
  Mound of the Serpent at, 134, 137, 146

Paradox, Colo., 71

Paria canyons, 291

Paris, 264

Park View Motel, 61

Patokwa, 194

Peabody Museum, 60–61, 194

peaches, 155, 162, 169

Peche Merle cave, 264

Pecos Classification, 68

Pecos Conference:
  of 1927, 26
  of 2013, 112, 220

Pecos River, 172–73

Peekaboo canyon, 238

Peg House, 103

Pekkarine, Eino, 76–77

Peninsula House, *see* Citadel

Pennsylvania, University of, 192, 193–94, 195

Perfect Kivas, 103
Pershing, John J., 133
Peru, 58, 281
petroglyphs, 7, 11, 28, 30, 33–35, 42,
    54–55, 64–65, 86, 104, 119, 166–
    67, 199, 201–5, 249, 296
  Anasazi, 229, 295
  cowboy, 100
  cryptic, 210
  desecration of, 95–96
  erosion of, 278
  Fremont, 262, 269, 273, 277–78,
    284
  Glen Canyon linear style, 278
Phoenix, Ariz., 251
physics, 215
Pictograph Cave, 247–49
pictographs, 7, 13, 27, 30, 34, 41, 59,
    64–65, 103, 104, 158, 166
  Anasazi, 248
  desecration of, 95–96
  Fremont, 269, 284
Picuris Pueblo, 207
Piedra River, 151
Pierre's Ruin, 145
pigs, 200
Pilar Yacht Club, 228
Pilling, Clarence, 59–66
Piman language, 135
Pine Canyon, 100
Pine Ridge Reservation, 195
Pinnacle Ruin, 223–24
Pitblado, Bonnie L., 64, 66
pithouses, 3, 26, 37, 127, 148, 149, 283,
    285
pitons, wooden, 5, 22, 23
Plains Biographic Tradition, 230,
    231
Plains Indians, 228
  rock art of, 229–30
Plains of San Augustin, 138
Plog, Fred, 213
Point Lookout, 100
poison ivy, 182
Pojoaque Pueblo, 207

Polly's Pasture, 99
Popé, 192–93, 200
potsherds, see pottery, sherds of
Potter, Jim, 148
pottery, 20, 26, 28, 29, 31, 68, 86, 105,
    141, 212, 216, 264
  breaking of, 96
  ceramic, 8, 9, 96
  corrugated, 8, 9, 32, 58, 96, 113–
    14, 289, 300
  cryptic, 138
  Emery gray, 285
  Galisteo black-on-white, 219, 224
  Glaze A, 223
  grayware, 96
  Jemez black-on-white, 200
  "kill-holes" in, 301
  Magdalena black-on-white, 223,
    224
  Mesa Verde black-on-white, 219,
    223, 224
  Mimbres, 262, 301
  Reserve Indented Corrugated,
    223
  sherds of, 3, 8, 11, 32–33, 40–41,
    54, 96–98, 119, 138, 193–94,
    200, 247, 253–54, 285, 291–92,
    295
  Tusayan polychrome, 86, 96, 262
  unpainted, 27
Pottery Shrine, 96–98
Pottery Steps, 98, 102
Powell, John Wesley, 241, 254–55,
    265, 267, 274, 276
  exploration etc., 276, 278–79, 286
  first descent of the Colorado River
    by, 241, 279
Powell, Lake, 240, 243, 251, 252, 253,
    259, 274
Prehistoric Textiles of the Southwest
    (Kent), 78
Prehistory of the Southwest (Cordell),
    7, 124, 214
Preucel, Robert W., 192, 193,
    195–96

Price, Utah, 4, 33, 48, 60–63, 66, 262, 269
prickly pear, 146
Princeton University, 243
Prohibition, 277
Prospector Inn, 255
Proto-Tanoan languages, 221, 222
Pueblo Alto, 131, 142
Puebloans (modern), 29, 68, 126, 129, 144–45, 147, 188–89, 198
    ancestors of, 206
Pueblo Bonito, 29, 129, 130, 138, 142–44, 149, 262
Pueblo Cultural Center, 191–92
Pueblo Revolt of 1680, 188–94, 196, 199, 200, 216, 230
pueblos, 15, 96, 118, 128, 129, 130, 139, 145, 157, 188–90, 226, 244
    language diversity in, 206–7
Puyé Pueblo, 209–10

Quakers, 67

rabbits, 20
radiocarbon testing, 24, 51, 75, 264
Raiders of the Lost Ark (film), 58
Rainbow Bridge, 243, 249–50
Rainbow Bridge Trail, 179, 243
Rainbow Plateau, 249–50, 295
Rams Pasture herradura, 139
Range Creek, 1–5, 31, 261–62
    valley of, 4–5, 17–25, 30–56, 60, 64, 66, 115, 264–68, 271, 286, 295
Raven's Exile (Meloy), 267, 276
Red Breaks canyon, 238
Redd, James D., 105
Red Tail Aviation, 269
Reed, Ellick, 46–47
Reid, Arlene, 77–78
REI stores, 22
repartimiento, 199
Revolt: An Archaeological History of Pueblo Resistance and Revitalization in 17th-Century

New Mexico (Liebmann), 194, 198–99
Richard Wetherill: Anasazi (McNitt), 16, 69
Rio Grande canyon, 229, 235–36
Rio Grande Railroad, 70
Rio Grande River, 124, 130, 189, 192, 207–8, 210, 223, 224, 226, 229, 230
Rio Grande Valley, 206, 208, 212–14, 217–21, 227–28
River Knows Everything, The: Desolation and the Green (Aton), 267, 268
Roberts, Alan, 302
Roberts, Sharon, 266–67, 275, 287–90, 293, 295, 297, 299–300, 302
Rock Creek, 280–82
Rock Creek Ranch, 280–82
Rock House Bottom, 272
Rock House Canyon, 273
Rogers Canyon, 253, 254
Roman Catholic Church, 195
    baptism in, 15
    iconography of, 193, 199
    missionaries of, 189, 192, 193, 199, 200, 232
Roosevelt, Theodore, 44
rope, prehistoric, 18–23, 31, 115–16
Route US 163, 291
Ruess, Everett, 13, 239–40, 251, 255, 258
rugs, 79
    Navajo, 77
Russian language, 207–8

Sacred Land, Sacred View: Navajo Perceptions of the Four Corners Region (McPherson), 164–65
Sacred Ridge, 148–49
Sacsaywaman, Peru, 281
Sagan, Carl, 128
sage, 146, 240
Sage Creek, 270
Sagstetter, Beth, 72, 78–79, 82–84, 86

Sagstetter, Bill, 71, 72, 78–80, 82–86, 89
Salado culture, 14, 123
Salmon Ruins, 145
Salt Lake City, Utah, 13, 31, 33, 40, 271
Salvation Knoll, 100
Sammy (dog), 257
sandals, yucca, 27, 32
Sandia Pueblo, 207
San Diego, Calif., 251
Sando, Joe, 191
sandstone, 30, 119, 120, 142, 155, 166, 174, 176, 185, 239, 240, 243, 252, 262, 273, 275, 295
    Cutler Formation, 116
    Windgate, 116
Sandstone Spine (Roberts), 17
Sand Wash, 268–69, 274
San Felipe Pueblo, 207
San Francisco Peaks, 157
Sangre de Cristo Mountains, 124
San Ildefonso Pueblo, 157, 207
San Juan Advertiser, 81
San Juan Pueblo, 189, 206, 207
San Juan River, 100, 104, 142, 145, 160, 173, 176, 244, 249
San Miguel valley, 75
San Rafael Swell, 30, 110
Santa Ana Pueblo, 207
Santa Clara Pueblo, 157, 207–9, 213, 227
Santa Fe, N.Mex., 10, 21–22, 128, 140, 189, 201, 203, 205–8, 211, 215
Santa Fe Canyon, 201
Santa Fe Institute, 208, 216
Santa Fe River, 203
Santo Domingo Pueblo, 207
Sawtooth Mountains, 138
Schaafsma, Polly, 263, 295
Scott, Stephanie, 84–90, 291–93, 298–300
Seamount family, 282
Searchers, The (film), 234

Sedona, Ariz., 131
Sego Canyon, 34, 262
Severance, Owen, 70
Shabik'eschee Village, 149
shamans, 55, 96
Shardy (dog), 36–37
Sharp, Lauri, 247, 248
sheep, 46, 99, 172, 173, 176–77, 183, 185, 202, 238
    bighorn, 4, 27, 30, 45, 54, 269–71, 275, 278
Shelley, Percy Bysshe, 96
Sheri Griffith Expeditions, 266, 268
shibop, 199
Shield, 31, 41–42
shields, 27, 262, 295
Shiloh, Battle of, 241
Shivwits Paiutes, 279
Shoshone people, 29, 207
Shot Tower, 294
Shumway, Earl, 106
Siberia, 199
Sierra Blanca, 157
Sierra Madre Mountains, 147, 295
"Signs of Power and Resistance: The (Re) Creation of Christian Imagery and Identities in the Pueblo Revolt Era" (Liebmann), 192
silver, 177, 178, 180–81, 183
Silver City, N.Mex., 133
Simms, Steven R., 26, 28, 30
Simonelli, Jeanne M., 161
Simonis, Don, 112–14
Sinagua culture, 14, 123
Sinaloa, 147
    drug cartel of, 148
sipapu, 126, 127, 210
skeletons, 67–68, 101, 105, 144, 164
Slickhorn Canyon, 99
Sliding Rock Ruins, 157–58
Smith, Joseph, 62
Smithsonian, 14
Smithsonian Institution, 60, 188

snakes, 30, 263
  red racer, 203–4
Snake Society, 188
Sobek rafting company, 265
Society of American Archaeology
  (SAA), 211, 212
Socorro, N.Mex., 223
South America, 43
South Dakota, 195
  Black Hills of, 207
Southern Utah Wilderness Alliance,
  110
Southwest:
  canyons and mesas of, 1–13,
    17–18, 30, 33, 38–40, 45, 52–53,
    58–59, 69, 81, 91–122, 187–88,
    238–41, 244
  desecration of ancient sites in,
    95–96, 97–98, 113
  desert landscape of, 132
  Dinétah region of, 159, 188, 216
  excavation and discovery in, 26, 30,
    52–53, 57–90, 128, 148–49, 228
  Four Corners area of, 23, 29,
    67, 81, 105, 130, 150, 206, 209,
    224–26
  mapping of, 28, 123–24, 153, 224
  migrationism vs. diffusionism in,
    214
  Northern Periphery area of, 26, 27,
    123, 262
  ruins and rock art of, 2–12, 16,
    26–28, 30–35, 41–42, 46, 54–98,
    125, 142–47, 154, 155, 166–67,
    188, 216, 227–35, 262–63, 265,
    277–78, 283–84
  Spanish conquest of, 124, 130, 135,
    147, 157, 159, 186, 188–89, 190,
    195–96, 199–200, 210, 216
  Spanish driven out of, 189–92, 199
  see also ancient cultures of the
    Southwest; specific places
Southwest Symposium, 214
Spain, 264
  Catalonia, 263

empire of, 234
southern, 296
Spangler, Donna, 262–63
Spangler, Jerry, 30, 262–63, 268,
  277–78, 283–86
Spanish conquistadors, 124, 130, 135,
  147, 157, 159, 169, 186, 188–89,
  199–201, 210, 216, 228, 234
  horses and guns introduced by,
    200, 230
Spanish language, 15, 157, 160
Sphinx, 95
Spider Woman (deity), 156
spiritualism, 131
Split Level Ruin, 102
Spooky canyon, 238
squash, 26, 29, 127, 169, 285
Steele, Pete, 99, 103–4
Stein, John, 145
Step Canyon, 100
Stevenson, Matilda Coxe, 188
"stopper walls," 116, 247
Straight Cliffs, 239
suicide, 172
Supertopo.com, 296
sweat lodges, 46
syphilis, 172

Tabyago Canyon, 272
tamarisk, 29, 70, 155, 182, 271, 276
Tanoan language, 207
Taos, N.Mex., 15, 29, 188, 189, 207,
  228
Taos people, 129
Tavaputs Adaptation, 30
Tavaputs Plateau, 2, 3, 31, 45, 110,
  265, 269, 278, 282, 286
Taylor, Mount, 157
Tejada, Arlo, 266
Tellem, 20–21
Telluride, Colo., 72–81, 86
Telluride blanket, 59, 66, 70, 72–86
  discovery and rediscovery of,
    72–73, 80–81, 84, 90
  display of, 74–75, 78, 80, 84

Telluride *Daily Journal*, 72
Telluride Historical Museum, 72, 74–75, 77–80, 84
Telluride Ski Resort, 80
Terray, Lionel, 296
Tesuque Pueblo, 207
Tetons, 294
Tewa Basin, 218, 222
Tewa Indians, 157
    debate on origins of, 208–13, 215–23
    oral tradition of, 221–22
Tewa language, 15, 157, 207, 218, 221
Tewa Pueblo, 213
Tewa World, The: Space, Time, Being, and Becoming in a Pueblo Society (Ortiz), 206
Texas, 228
Thompson, Almon Harris, 254–55
Thompson, Mae, 166
Thompson Springs, Utah, 70
Thomson, Rick, 267
Tice, Susan, 83
Tice, Terry, 83
tipi rings, 230
tipis, 230
Tiwa language, 207, 221
toads, horned, 165
Tobin, Mary, 238, 242–43, 244–49, 251, 253, 257
Tombstone, Ariz., 181
tools, 119, 125, 127, 176, 229
Towa language, 190, 192, 196, 207, 221
Towner, Ron, 51
Toya, Vince, 196
Trail Hollow, 240
Transfer of Public Lands Act (TPLA), 110
Trapper Jack, 282
trees, 129, 143
    aspen, 256
    baobab, 21
    cherry, 192
    cottonwood, 46, 282, 286
    deforestation of, 23, 29, 115
    Douglas fir, 5, 20, 51, 102
    juniper, 4, 91, 97, 100, 121, 176, 184, 231, 238, 240, 242, 245, 251
    "marker," 230–31
    old-growth, 110–11
    peach, 155, 162, 192, 200
    piñon pine, 4, 6, 86, 91, 97, 121, 184, 238, 242, 245, 251, 293
    ponderosa pine, 102, 138
    ring dating of, 11, 26, 29, 51, 64, 159, 198, 253
    scrub oak, 18
    willow, 155, 182, 277
trophy heads, 27–28, 30, 103, 248, 262
trout, 4
Truth or Consequences, N.Mex., 223
Tsaile Creek, 160, 166, 169–70
Tsama ruin, 220
Tsegi canyon, 115–17, 295
Tua River, 265
Tuba City, Ariz., 182
Tucson, Ariz., 51, 216
Tucson Basin, 26
Tularosa, N.Mex., 224
tump lines, 20
Turkey, 58
Turkey Pen Ruin, 102
Turner, Ed, 70–73, 75–76, 80–81, 83–85, 87–89
Turner, Maggie Dresser, 72
Turner, Mel, 70–73, 75–76, 80–81, 83–85, 87–89
turquoise, 144
Tutankhamen, tomb of, 58
Twin Angels Pueblo, 145
Twist, The, 100

Uintah and Ouray Reservation, 45, 114, 265
Uintah Utes, 278
Uintas Mountains, 110
UNESCO World Heritage Sites, 134
United States:
    antiwar activism in, 214

United States (*continued*)
federal land in, 263
mapping of, 268
Mexican border with, 133, 134,
138
private land in, 62
public land in, 250–51, 263
universe, big bang vs. steady-state
expansion of, 215, 222
University of Arizona Press, 211
University of New Mexico Press,
191
University of Utah Press, 212
"Unraveling the Mysteries of the
Telluride Blanket" (Sagstetter
and Sagstetter), 78–79, 86
uranium boom of 1950s, 10, 269
USGS maps, 85, 102, 258, 268
Utah, 2–12, 29–31, 62–63, 82, 92, 182,
187, 243, 246, 259, 262, 270
archaeological digs in, 26
Bureau of Land Management
(BLM) of, 7, 9, 10, 18, 32, 34–35,
48, 49, 62, 93–94, 105–7, 109–14,
120, 263, 266, 268, 301
Carbon County, 31, 44
central and northern, 14, 27, 221,
295
Division of Natural Resources of,
31
Division of Wildlife Resources
(DWR) of, 4, 17–18, 48
northern, 271
San Juan County, 80, 93, 113
southeastern, 21, 28, 68, 70, 84, 97,
106, 154, 175, 264
southern, 237
southwestern, 124
Trust for Public Lands of, 4
Utah, University of, 50, 106
Utah Light and Power Company, 271
Utah Museum of Natural History
(UMNH), 3, 4–5, 47–50, 261
archaeologists of, 18, 24, 31, 32,
40, 48–50, 52–53, 55–56, 106

Range Creek exhibition at, 47–48
summer field school of, 49
Utah's Canyon Country Place Names
(Allen), 99, 272
Utah State University (USU), 66
Archaeological Services af, 65
Museum of Anthropology at, 65
Ute language, 278
Ute Reservation, 45, 70, 114, 272, 276
Utes, 15, 29, 33, 34, 38, 45, 70, 114,
177, 181–82, 207, 233, 257, 267,
277
graves of, 98, 282–83
rock art of, 229
settlements of, 280
Uto-Aztecan language, 207

Vanderbilt University, 191
Vargas, Don Diego de, 195–96
Venn diagrams, 124, 125, 224
Vernal, Utah, 28, 65
Victorio, 223
Vietnam War, 214
viewshed analysis, 50
Villa, Pancho, 133
Virgin Mary, 193, 199
Virgin River, 124

Waldo's Catwalk (double granary),
6–7, 18–24, 31–32, 41, 48, 50–51,
115, 119
Wales, England, 208
Walpi, 126
Wasatch Mountains, 110
Washington, D.C., 60, 188
Washington state, 22
Watchman, Kalvin, 155–63, 165–72
Water Canyon, 100
Watertown, Mass., 267
"Water Under the Rocks" canyon,
175, 178–80, 183–84
Watts, Harvey, 240
Wetherill, Ben, 244, 254
Wetherill, John, 179, 181, 183, 186,
244, 250, 254

Wetherill, Louisa, 181–82, 244
Wetherill, Richard, 67–70, 101–2, 144
Wetherill brothers, 21, 67, 73, 101–2
Wetherill-Grand Gulch Research
    Project, 67, 69–70, 81, 120
Whatley, Bill, 190, 196
wheat, 192
Wheat, Joe Ben, 52–53
Wheeler, Antoinette, 74, 76
Wheeler, R. E. Mortimer, 57–58
Wheeler, W. E., 73–74, 80–81
White House ruin, 145, 154, 161
White Sands Trail, 155, 157, 166
Wijiji ruin, 107
Wilcox, Don, 2–3, 47
Wilcox, Julie, 3
Wilcox, Ray "Budge," 2–4, 34, 44–47,
    59, 265, 271, 282
Wilcox, Waldo, 2–5, 17–18, 33–40,
    43–49, 52, 54–56, 59, 62, 264–65,
    268–69, 271, 277, 280–83
    cowboy skills of, 31, 36–37, 39,
    44–45, 265
    hidden granaries discovered by,
    6–7, 18–24, 31–32, 41, 48, 50–51,
    115, 119
    physical appearance of, 36
Wildcat Drilling, 109–10
Wilderness Areas, 111
Wilderness Study Areas, 109, 111
Wild Horse Mesa (Grey), 241–42
Williamson, Ray, 70
Willow Bend, 35, 54
Wilson, Dave, 170, 171
Wilson, George, 259
Windes, Tom, 220
Window arch, 159, 161–62
Window Rock, Ariz., 154
Window Wind Arch, 258–59
Wind River Range, 271

Winds from the North: Tewa Origins
    and Historical Anthropology
    (Ortman), 212, 217, 221–22, 228
    "Population History of the Tewa
    Basin" chapter in, 218
Wineland, Judi, 267
Wineland-Thomson, Erica, 267, 274,
    283, 285
Wolverine canyon, 238
Woodside, Utah, 47
Worcester, Mass., 239
World War II, 158
Wyman, Leland C., 176
Wyoming, 13, 239, 271
    northern, 234
    southwestern, 28

Yampa River, 271
Yapashi Pueblo, 96
Yazzie, Fred, 165–66
Yazzie, Ned, 157
Yellow Jacket ruin, 52–53, 118
Yellowstone River, 271
Young, Brigham, 257
Ysleta del Sur Pueblo, 188, 207
yucca, 20, 21–22, 27, 32, 192, 288,
    292
Yucca House National Monument,
    118, 208–9
Yukon Territory, 157

Zia people, 188
Zia Pueblo, 188, 191, 207
Zion National Park, 253
zoos, 36–37, 44
Zuni, N.Mex., 15, 188
Zuni language, 207
Zuni Mountains, 138
Zunis, 158, 207, 208
Zuni Trail, 158